Legal Innovations in Asia

STUDIES IN COMPARATIVE LAW AND LEGAL CULTURE

Series Editor: Vernon Valentine Palmer, *Tulane University, USA*

In today's shrinking world it's important to extend our horizons and increase our knowledge of other people's laws. This series publishes in-depth volumes covering various aspects of private and public law in diverse legal traditions. Additionally, it seeks to encourage improved techniques and methods of comparative legal research, including the use of interdisciplinary studies. Individual volumes may deal with the law and culture not merely of well-known and frequently studied countries, but also with lesser-known, mixed, religious, and plural systems of the world. The focus ranges from important aspects of legal history, culture, and institutions to local experience and evolving legal trends.

Titles in the series include:

Order from Transfer
Comparative Constitutional Design and Legal Culture
Edited by Günter Frankenberg

Corruption and Conflicts of Interest
A Comparative Law Approach
Edited by Jean-Bernard Auby, Emmanuel Breen and Thomas Perroud

Legal Innovations in Asia
Judicial Lawmaking and the Influence of Comparative Law
Edited by John O. Haley and Toshiko Takenaka

Legal Innovations in Asia

Judicial Lawmaking and the Influence of Comparative Law

Edited by

John O. Haley

Affiliate Professor of Law, University of Washington, Professor of Law, Vanderbilt University and William R. Orthwein Distinguished Professor of Law Emeritus, Washington University in St. Louis, USA

Toshiko Takenaka

Washington Research Foundation/W. Hunter Simpson Professor of Technology Law, University of Washington School of Law, USA

STUDIES IN COMPARATIVE LAW AND LEGAL CULTURE

Edward Elgar

Cheltenham, UK • Northampton, MA, USA

Published by
Edward Elgar Publishing Limited
The Lypiatts
15 Lansdown Road
Cheltenham
Glos GL50 2JA
UK

Edward Elgar Publishing, Inc.
William Pratt House
9 Dewey Court
Northampton
Massachusetts 01060
USA

A catalogue record for this book
is available from the British Library

Library of Congress Control Number: 2014938803

This book is available electronically in the ElgarOnline.com Law Subject Collection, E-ISBN 978 1 78347 279 6

FSC
www.fsc.org
MIX
Paper from responsible sources
FSC® C013056

ISBN 978 1 78347 278 9

Typeset by Columns Design XML Ltd, Reading
Printed and bound in Great Britain by T.J. International Ltd, Padstow

Contents

Contributors

Harald Baum is Senior Research Fellow and Head of the Japanese Department at the Max Planck Institute for Comparative and International Private Law, in Hamburg, Germany. He is also Professor at the University of Hamburg, Germany and Research Associate, European Corporate Governance Institute, Brussels.

Donald Clarke is Professor of Law at the George Washington University Law School, USA and was a faculty member of the Asian Law Center at the University of Washington School of Law, USA.

Jon Eddy is Professor of Law and was Director of the Asian Law Center (2010–2013) at the University of Washington School of Law, USA.

Daniel H. Foote is Professor of Law at the University of Tokyo, Japan. He was a faculty member of the Asian Law Center at the University of Washington School of Law (1988–2000) and is rejoining the faculty of the Asian Law Center from 2014, on a joint appointment with the University of Tokyo.

John O. Haley is Professor of Law at Vanderbilt University Law School, USA and was Director of the Asian Law Center (1988–2000) at the University of Washington School of Law, USA. He was awarded the Order of the Rising Sun from the Emperor of Japan for his contribution to the discipline of Japanese law and the education of Japanese legal professionals and academics.

Kyoko Ishida is Associate Professor of Law at Waseda Law School, Japan.

Kon Sik Kim is Professor of Law at Seoul National University (SNU), South Korea. He served as Dean of the SNU College of Law and was in charge of setting up a new US-style law school at SNU.

Vai Io Lo is Professor of Law and Director of the Tim Fischer Center for Global Trade and Finance at Bond University, Australia.

Clark B. Lombardi is Professor of Law and Director of Islamic Legal Studies at the Asian Law Center at the University of Washington School of Law, USA.

Shigenori Matsui is Professor of Law at the University of British Columbia Faculty of Law, Canada and was a Visiting Professor at the University of Washington School of Law, USA. Before joining UBC, he was Professor of Law at Osaka University, Japan.

Hyung Doo Nam is Professor of Law at Yonsei Law School and was in private practice as a partner at the law firm of Lee & Ko, South Korea, prior to entering academia. He is currently President of the Korean Entertainment Law Society and is Director of the Korean Copyright Law Association.

Orakanoke Phanraksa is Intellectual Property Policy Researcher at the National Science and Technology Development Agency (NSTDA), Technology Licensing Office, Bangkok, Thailand, where she leads the Intellectual Property Policy group. She is a member of the Global Young Academy (GYA) where she works with top young scientists to promote science and technology development.

Toshiko Takenaka is Professor of Law and holds the title of WRF/W. Hunter Simpson Professor of Technology Law at the University of Washington School of Law, USA. She is Director of the Center for Advanced Study and Research on Intellectual Property and served as Director of Japanese Legal Studies in 2012–2014 at the Asian Law Center.

Veronica L. Taylor is Professor of Law and Dean of the College of Asia and the Pacific at Australian National University (ANU). She was Director of the Asian Law Center (2000–2010) at the University of Washington School of Law, USA.

Kurnia Toha is Associate Professor of Law at the Faculty of Law at the University of Indonesia. He teaches courses on competition law, secured transactions, and bankruptcy law. He is also the Head of the Legal and Public Relations Department of the National Land Agency Republic of Indonesia.

Tomi Suryo Utomo is Professor at the Faculty of Law at the University of Gadjah Mada and the University of Janabadra, Yogyakarta, Indonesia. He is currently working with the Asia Foundation in Jakarta, Indonesia, as a clinical legal education expert on the Educating and Equipping Tomorrow's Justice Reformers (E2J) Project funded by USAID.

Tay-Sheng Wang is Professor at the National Taiwan University College of Law, Taiwan and holds the title of Distinguished Professor. He served as Associate Dean of NTU College of Law.

Ryuichi Yamakawa is Professor of Law at the University of Tokyo, Japan and was Professor of Law at Keio University Law School, Japan. In addition, he is a member of the Central Labor Commission and the Labor Policy Council in Japan.

Dongsheng Zang is Associate Professor of Law and Director of the Asian Law Center at the University of Washington School of Law, USA.

Foreword

Dongsheng Zang

In May 2013, the Asian Law Center (ALC) celebrated its fiftieth anniversary. That makes the Center one of the oldest and most fruitful programs in Asian legal studies in the United States, as Professor John O. Haley indicated in his chapter, "The First Decades, 1961–2000." Between 2012 and 2013, we held a series of events, not only to commemorate the past, but, more importantly, to envision the future of the field. Distinguished alumni, former faculty colleagues, and former students who are now law professors were invited back to Seattle for conferences, presentations, and workshops. In Tokyo, our events coincided with Professor John O. Haley's award of the prestigious decoration the Order of the Rising Sun conferred by His Majesty the Emperor of Japan. The chapters in this volume were originally papers presented in these events or are further reflections as a result of these events, and have been masterfully put together by Professors John Haley and Toshiko Takenaka.

Confucius says, at age thirty, a person establishes himself; at forty, he gains wisdom; at fifty, a person knows his destiny. At the Asian Law Center, we are experiencing all of the above at the same time. The Center is reinvigorated. At the same time as this volume is being published John Haley is coming back to the ALC; Daniel Foote is going to split his time between the University of Tokyo and ALC; Michael Young, the distinguished Japanese law specialist, has become the President of the University of Washington; Thomas Schoenbaum, who has extensive experience in both Europe and Japan, is joining us from George Washington University. Thanks to the past leadership of Veronica Taylor, we also have expanded our horizon: Professor Clark Lombardi, an Islamic law specialist, joined our faculty in 2004 and contributed his chapter in this volume. Between 2006 and 2012, Professor Jonathan Kang contributed to our understanding of Korean law as an ALC faculty member. I came to the ALC in 2006 to fill in the vacuum left by Don Clarke, one of the most distinguished Chinese law specialists of his generation.

Fifty years is a long time: Asia has changed enormously, so has the United States. While it is always a risky business to predict the future, one thing is quite certain – the need for the Asian Law Center to continue its objective of promoting mutual understanding will not go away. In 1985, nearly thirty years ago, at a conference hosted by ALC under Professor Dan Henderson, William P. Alford, then a young scholar on Chinese law, called for an "obligation to be vigilant" against unwarranted assumptions. To fulfill that obligation is the long-term mission of the ALC. This book is another effort in that direction.

Introduction

John O. Haley and Toshiko Takenaka

Celebration is both the aim and underlying theme of this volume. With its publication we commemorate the 50th anniversary of the founding of the Asian Law Center of the University of Washington School of Law. The volume comprises representative chapters by distinguished graduates that reflect their subsequent work as legal scholars in their respective countries and fields. Combined with those by present and former faculty and colleagues, their contributions exemplify the achievements of the Center – formerly Program – as its second half-century begins.

We commence with three chapters by three of the Center's past directors – all of whom were students at different times in what was then the Asian Law Program. They detail the history, achievements, and challenges of the Asian Law Center during its first half-century. The first chapter is by John Haley, who entered the Program as a student in 1969, joined the faculty in 1974, and served as director upon Dan Henderson's retirement in 1991 until 2000. Haley's recollections of the first decades are followed by those of Veronica Taylor, who received her master of laws degree in 1992 and served as director from 2000 to 2012. Upon her departure for a position at Australian National University, Jon Eddy assumed the directorship. Eddy, a 1969 J.D. graduate, served for one year when Professor Dongsheng Zang was appointed to fill the position.

These introductory chapters on the history of the Center are followed by a series of chapters by a remarkable group of scholars from four continents. They include eight of the Center's most distinguished graduates currently teaching in East Asia and the Pacific today – Vai Io (Farfalla) Lo, Tay-Sheng Wang, Kon Sik Kim, Kurnia Toha, Kyoko Ishida, Orakanoke Phanraska, Tomi Suryo Utomo, and Ryuichi Yamakawa – as well as six current or former members of the Center's faculty. This latter group is comprised of Dongsheng Zang, the current Center director, Clark Lombardi, a prominent Islamic law scholar, Donald Clarke, a former member of the Center's faculty who has long played a leading role in Chinese legal studies in the United States, and Dan Foote, a former member of the Center faculty who, it is hoped, will soon rejoin it as co-director. They are joined by two colleagues and close friends of the Center: Harald Baum, the Head of the Japan Law Department at the Max Planck Institute for Comparative and International Private Law in Hamburg, Germany, and Shigenori Matsui of the University of British Columbia. Completing the list of contributors are the editors – John Haley and Toshiko Takenaka, both of whom are also Asian Law Center graduates.

Harald Baum provides an overview of the Roman origins of Western law and the processes of its transplantation in Japan, with appropriate emphasis on the influence of modern German law in Japan. His contribution is a telling reminder of the universality of western law today, which is in no small measure a result of the Japanese experience – a theme that is taken up in a cluster of chapters on the influence of Japanese law.

Following Baum is a series of chapters on the role of courts in East Asia, commencing with a "dialogue" between John Haley and Dan Foote on law-making and norm creation by Japanese courts. Drawing on a January 2013 decision allowing online sales of over-the-counter drugs, Shigenori Matsui adds to the dialogue a "View from the East." Together they put to rest any notion that Japan's judiciary has been passive or merely the agent of political principals.

Dongsheng Zang and Vai Io (Farfalla) Lo continue the discussion with their companion studies of judicial law-making in China, followed by Clark Lombardi with a parallel examination of the role of courts in making law in Indonesia and other parts of Islamic Asia. Concluding the section are two further chapters. The first is Ryuichi Yamakawa's discussion of Japanese labor law. The second, by Kyoko Ishida, focuses on *pro se* litigation.

The discussion continues in a section on legal transplants and the influence Japanese law has had in Asia. Tay-Sheng Wang begins by detailing its influence in Taiwan. Three chapters continue the theme with discussions on the influence of Japanese as well as U.S. law in other legal systems in East Asia – Kon Sik Kim on Korean law, Donald Clarke on Chinese Law, and Kurnia Toha on Indonesian law.

The volume concludes with four chapters on legal innovations by judicial law-making in intellectual property. All are authored by Center Ph.D. graduates, one of whom – Toshiko Takenaka – has long served as Director of the University of Washington Law School Center for Advanced Study and Research on Intellectual Property (CASRIP). She begins the section with her chapter on Japan and is followed by Hyung

Doo Nam on Korea, Orakanoke Phanraska on Thailand, and Tomi Suryo Utomo on health law and intellectual property in Indonesia.

These chapters individually and collectively exemplify the quality of the scholars and the scholarship that has been the hallmark of the Asian Law Center for the past half-century.

PART I

Asian Law Center: The first half century

1.1 The first decades, 1961–2000

John O. Haley

The Asian Law Center commenced as the Asian Law Program in 1961 with receipt of the first of two foundational grants from the Ford Foundation. A year later, in 1962, the appointment of Dan Fenno Henderson as director fully launched the Program as the first center established outside of East Asia for research and teaching on East Asian Law and the only one ever to be established with a primary focus on Japanese law.

Henderson, a 1944 Phi Beta Kappa graduate of Whitman College, had studied Japanese at the U.S. Army Japanese Language School at the University of Michigan. After brief service in Occupied Japan, he enrolled in the Harvard Law School, graduating in 1949 with his first degree in law. He practiced law briefly in Seattle but decided to continue his study of Japan and Japanese law, earning a Ph.D. in Political Science from the University of California, Berkeley in 1955. He was licensed that year to practice law in Japan (and subsequently South Korea) and became a partner of Graham & James in its Tokyo Office. He left active practice in 1962 to become first a consultant to and then director of the Asian Law Program.

As an academic lawyer Henderson envisioned a program to equip "liaison" lawyers to deal professionally with trans-Pacific transactions, which at the time meant a primary focus on Japanese law. Language, he believed was critical. Hence from the start each student affiliated with the Program as either a J.D. or LL.M. (M.C.L.) candidate had to have demonstrable proficiency in English and Japanese or another East Asian language.

In 1966 Henderson began to teach the first regularly taught course on Japanese law offered outside of Japan. Among the first projects had been thus to develop of a set of teaching materials on Japanese law in English. The materials initially entitled *Cases and Materials for an Introduction to Japanese Law* (1966) comprised essays authored by Henderson as well as translations by research assistants as well as U.S. students. These materials were revised and made generally available in bound print editions as the *Law and Legal Process of Japan* (1978, 1988, and 1994). As of 2014 they will be fully updated and republished as a digital fifth edition.

At that time the only significant collection of articles and essays in English on basic features of Japanese law was a seminal volume edited by Harvard Law School Professor Arthur T. von Mehren (with the assistance of Rex Coleman) entitled *Law in Japan: The Legal Order in a Changing Society*, published by Harvard University Press in 1963. The collection comprised papers presented in a September 1961 conference held at Harvard and sponsored by the Japanese–American Program for Cooperation in Legal Studies, in which Harvard, Michigan, and Stanford had participated. The conference was the first and arguably the most significant academic meeting devoted to Japanese law ever held outside of Japan.

Growing out of the Harvard conference was the Japanese-American Society for Legal Studies (JASLS) a cooperative association of legal academics from both sides of the Pacific that sponsored the publication of two journals. The first, published by the Japan branch as *Amerika Hō*, a Japanese language journal devoted to U.S. law. The second, by the American Branch, was *Law in Japan: An Annual*, under the editorial chairmanship of Rex Coleman. In 1964 the Harvard Law School shifted focus from Japan to China with the establishment of the East Asian Legal Studies Center, the second U.S. center for research and teaching on East Asia, under the direction of Jerome A. Cohen. Subsequently *Law in Japan: An Annual* along with the American Branch of JASLS were relocated to the University of Washington under the auspices of the Asian Law Program. Henderson assumed Coleman's role as Chair of the Editorial Committee for the next three volumes (1968–1970) with one volume (1971) under the joint chairmanship of two Program-affiliated UW graduates, Lawrence W. Beer (Ph.D. '66) and Eugene H. Lee (J.D. '66, LL.M. '68). In 1973, I assumed this role for the next fifteen years (1973–1987), to be succeeded first by Malcolm Smith, then teaching at the University of British Columbia (1978–1982), next by Amy Porges (1988), and after her by Daniel H. Foote, who had joined the faculty the year before, and who served as Chair for seven years (1989–1995). Translations of articles by leading Japanese scholars for inclusion in *Law in Japan* became the most common means for non-Japanese students in the Program both to demonstrate and enhance their Japanese language proficiency.

The Program's research emphasis was apparent from the start. The *Washington Law Review* had between 1949 and 1951 published a series of articles and essays on the legal reforms undertaken during the Allied

Occupation (all of which were assembled and republished in 1977 as a special reprint volume). Between 1963 and 1967 the WLR published a symposium issue on Philippine law and three subsequent symposia volumes related to U.S.–Japanese business, trade, and investment problems. In 1968 a fourth symposium on the Japanese Constitution was published, which was later republished as the first volume in the newly established Asian Law Series of the University of Washington Press. The second book in the series was Henderson's seminal two-volume study, *Conciliation and Japanese Law; Tokugawa and Modern*.

As a research center, expansion of the law library's Asian law collection was critical. The library had a small collection of books on Japanese law before World War II. In 1947 Thomas Blakemore donated additional volumes from his own collection. With the establishment of the Asian Law Program and the enthusiastic support of Marian G. Gallagher, the law library began an acquisition effort that gave it preeminence in the field. With respect to Japanese law, no collection in the U.S. is more complete and accessible. Suzanne Lee was the first librarian to oversee its growth. She was later assisted by Robert Britt and, pursuant to a Program decision to build the Chinese and Korean collections, upon her retirement, William B. McCloy, a trilingual (Chinese, Korean, and English) comparative law librarian filled her position. Today, as a result of the efforts of Britt and McCoy, four superlative legal research guides for Chinese, Japanese, Korean, and Taiwan law are available on the library website.

In 1967 the Program embarked on its most ambitious effort to date. Under Program auspices the Law School established the first, and to our knowledge only, LL.M. program ever designed for the comparative study of U.S. law with that of a single national legal system. Its hallmark was the creation of a community of scholars and students with competence in both English and Japanese who would together engage in a collective effort of research and study of the two legal systems. Separate introductory courses for each of the two groups of students were offered. Henderson's Introduction to Japanese Law course served non-Japanese students, and Marjorie Rombauer, who had already initiated a seminal course for entering J.D. students on Legal Research and Analysis, undertook to offer a parallel course for Japanese and other non-U.S. students in the LL.M. program. Upon Rombauer's retirement, Linda Hume taught the course. The course a couple of years later ceased to be offered by a faculty member.

To achieve the ultimate comparative purpose, separate U.S.–Japanese law teaching materials also had to be created for each field of law to be covered. Thus the Program initiated a series of courses with corresponding teaching materials on various fields of law in addition to the introductory *Law and Legal Process in Japan* and sets of problems that Rombauer designed for her Legal Research and Analysis for students from East Asia. For purposes of both U.S. and Japanese materials, scholars who would work together as collaborative instructors and compilers had to be recruited. Henderson, working with a recent graduate, Yasuhiro Fujita, developed the first course and set of materials. Entitled *Justiciability under the Common and Civil Law*, the materials provided students with an introduction to the basic issues that arise in litigation between parties from the U.S. and Japan. Working with Misao Tatsuta as visiting professor from Kyoto University, Henderson began a second set on *U.S.–Japan Corporate Relations*. The materials were later revised and the course taught by Richard Kummert, also with the assistance of Professor Tatsuta. By 1970 a third set of materials on *U.S.–Japanese Contract and Sales Problems* had been completed for a course jointly taught by Professors Warren Shattuck and Zentarō Kitagawa, a visiting professor from Kyoto University who was returning to Japan from several years of study in Germany. Finally, John Huston was recruited along with another LL.M. graduate, Toshio Miyatake, to develop materials on *U.S.–Japanese Tax Problems* for a comparative tax course, taught for many years thereafter by Huston.

The emphasis on the comparative study of U.S.-Japanese law continued for another three decades. Upon Warren Shattuck's early retirement (and appointment to the Hastings Law School faculty), I returned to the Program as the second Japanese law specialist in the U.S. ever to fill a tenured faculty position. In addition to assisting Rombauer, I continued the comparative U.S.-Japan contracts and sales course and took over the Introduction to Japanese Law course. I subsequently began to compile materials for courses I was to teach on Japanese administrative law (*The Public Law System of Japan*) and, in collaboration with Mitsuo Matsushita, Japanese antitrust law (*Government Regulation of Business in Japan*). Upon joining the faculty in the late 1980s, Dan Foote similarly taught and compiled materials for courses on Japanese labor law and criminal law. The Marian G. Gallagher Law Library maintains a complete collection of each edition of these materials, which hopefully will soon be made available in digital form.

By 1989 the Program offered nine courses on Japanese law, two on Chinese law – the basic course taught by Don Clarke and one on the Chinese Legal Tradition by Paul Liu – and one on Korean law taught by Stan Wagner, J.D. '86. Also offered was a cross-listed course on Islamic law in the Department of Near East Languages and Literature, originally taught by Farhat Ziadeh, and which had been taken over upon his retirement by Aaron Zysow. Hugh Spitzer taught a foundational course on Roman law relevant for all of the civil law systems of East Asia. Also included in the Asian and comparative law curriculum was a supplemental course on Soviet law taught by Margaret Niles. In addition the Asian and comparative law curriculum included the required LL.M. seminar and open-ended opportunities for tutorials on any subject of interest to students and faculty.

The Program had also established what was to become one of its most distinguished features – the first Ph.D. in Law program of any U.S. law school. As noted, Henderson himself had received a doctorate in Political Science from Berkeley in the early 1950s and thus considered the addition appropriate. He also had the experience of advising two promising young scholars, Lawrence Beer and Hiroshi Itoh, who were working under the supervision of Political Science Professor John M. Maki in the UW Far East and Russian Institute (later to become the Henry M. Jackson School of International Studies). They received the first interdisciplinary doctorate degrees ever awarded by the UW in Asian law and political science. Maki's primary interest was Japanese constitutional law. He and his two students were to become the leading scholars in the field. Maki published the first collection of Japanese constitutional law decisions in English, a project that Beer and Itoh were to continue into the 1990s. In 2002 Maki and Beer authored one of the most thoughtful books on Japanese constitutional history, *From Imperial Myth to Democracy: Japan's Two Constitutions, 1889–2002* (University of Colorado Press), and in 2010 Ashgate published *The Supreme Court and Benign Elite Democracy in Japan*, Itoh's seminal study of the Japanese Supreme Court. Beer and Itoh were thus the precursors of many of the contributors to this volume who in subsequent years also received a Ph.D. in Asian Law and joined this "benign elite" of Asian law scholars throughout Asia and the Pacific. Those who received a Ph.D. in Asian Law between 1972 and 1997 include Paul Chang Bin Liu, Ph.D. '83, who, as noted, taught a course on the Chinese Legal Tradition in the Program for several years and is currently Professor of Technology and Innovation Management at the Graduate Institute of Technology and Innovation Management at Chengchi University in Taipei, Taiwan; Dae Kyu Yoon, Ph.D. '87, Professor of Law at Kyungnam University in Seoul, Korea, in 2001 Visiting Professor of Law at the Harvard Law School; Erman Rajagukguk, Ph.D. '88, Professor of Law at the University of Indonesia, who also served as Director General for Law and Legislation (Dirjen KUMDANG) within the Ministry of Justice and more recently as Indonesia's Deputy Cabinet

Secretary (WASEKAB); Toshiko Takenaka, Ph.D. '92, as noted below, Professor of Law and Director of the UW Center for Advanced Study and Research on Intellectual Property (CASRIP); Tay-Sheng Wang, Ph.D. '92, Professor of Law and former Associate Dean of the National Taiwan University Law Faculty; Kon Sik Kim. Ph.D. '95, Professor of Law and former Dean of Seoul National University's faculty of law; Sakda Thanitcul, Ph.D. '97, Professor of Law at Chulalongkorn University and also former Dean of the Law Faculty; and Vai Io (Farfalla) Lo, Ph.D. '97, Professor of Law at Bond University in Queensland, Australia. Contributing to this volume are also three subsequent Ph.D. in law graduates who are currently teaching as full-time faculty: Kurnia Toha at the University of Indonesia; Kyoko Ishida at the Waseda Law School in Tokyo, Japan; and Hyung Doo Nam of the Yonsei University Law School in Seoul Korea.

The Program's Ph.D. graduates have not been the only ones to pursue careers in teaching. No law school except perhaps Harvard has produced as many Asian law scholars. As noted above, for a number of years Stan Wagner taught the basic course Law in East Asia: Korea. Two J.D. classmates – the late Stephen Salzberg, J.D. '85, and Pittman Potter, J.D. '85 – joined the University of British Columbia law faculty. Mark Levin, LL.M. '90, teaches Japanese law at the University of Hawai'i Law School. He also taught in Japan at the University of Hokkaido for several years. Keith Hand, J.D. '00, teaches Chinese law at the U.C. Hastings College of Law. Those teaching in Japan include Larry Repeta, J.D. '79, at the Meiji University Law School, and Ryuichi Yamakawa, LL.M. '91, at the University of Tokyo. Leon Wolf, '96, taught Japanese law at the University of Sydney and more recently at Bond University in Australia. Two former directors, both LL.M. graduates, continue to teach. Veronica Taylor, LL.M. '92, is currently teaching at the Australian National University. I taught courses on Japan or including Japan (Reading on Japanese Law, Comparative Law, and Transnational Litigation) at Washington University in St. Louis from 2000 until my retirement in 2010. I am currently Professor of Law at Vanderbilt University.

The Asian Law Program had from inception hosted visiting scholars as an integral aspect of both its research and teaching missions. Some lectured; others taught; most pursued their own research. The first from Japan included Ichiro Kato, Takeyoshi Kawashima, Keishin Sunakawa, and Kyoto University professor and future justice, Itsuo Sonobe, in addition to Teruo Doi and, as previously mentioned, Misao Tatsuta and Zentarō Kitagawa. Later lecturers and visiting scholars included Justices Shigemitsu Dando and Takaaki Hattori, as well as Professors

Kōichirō Fujikura from Japan, Sang Hyun Song from Korea, Professor and Grand Justice Yueh-sheng Weng from Taiwan, as well as a group of senior distinguished professors from Peking University who gave a series of lectures on Chinese law as participants in an exchange program funded with the encouragement and support of University Provost George Beckmann. By the end of the fourth decade, the Program had hosted over 160 visiting scholars, judges, prosecutors, government officials, and lawyers from China, Germany, Indonesia, Japan, Korea, Kyrgyzstan, Taiwan, and Thailand for periods ranging from a few weeks to over a year.

In 1977 in cooperation with the Supreme Court of Washington, the Program hosted Judge Shintarō Kato, currently Presiding Judge of the Tokyo High Court, as the first in a series of visiting judges that continues today. Every year thereafter, the Supreme Court of Japan selected a judge at mid-career to participate, and thus far nearly three dozen Japanese judges have participated in this program. Within a few years it was expanded to include judges from China, Korea, and Taiwan. In 1999–2000 the Program similarly hosted two judges serving as judicial research judges on the Argentine Supreme Court.

Japan was never the Program's exclusive focus. The faculty responsible for obtaining the initial Ford Foundation Funding – Ralph Johnson, Neil Peck, and Arval Morris – envisioned a broad East Asian law emphasis as exemplified by the first WLR symposium on Philippine law. A course on Chinese law along with an effort to compile a Chinese legal dictionary was contemplated with the appointment of Philip Bilancia in 1966. (Bilancia's dictionary was published under the title *A Dictionary of Chinese Law and Government: Chinese–English* by Stanford University Press in 1981.) A relationship with David Buxbaum also commenced for studies on Chinese family law, an endeavor that culminated in the publication of *Chinese Family Law and Social Change* in the Asian Law Series in 1978. As the Program progressed under Henderson's direction until the late 1960s, hardly any attention was paid to Southeast Asia or even Korea.

During the 1960s faculty from at least three U.S. law schools had begun to offer courses and engage in research on Chinese law. In 1964 Harvard had, as noted, established the East Asian Legal Studies Center at Harvard under Jerry Cohen, who had begun his teaching career at Berkeley and was succeeded there by Stanley Lubman. Berkeley and Harvard were both preceded, however, with respect to faculty by Washington University in St. Louis. There Grey Dorsey had continued the interest in Republican Chinese law that he had acquired in the early 1950s as the first U.S. law professor to teach in Taiwan in the postwar period. Bill Jones, Henderson's Harvard classmate, continued Dorsey's interest at Washington University. Jones joined the Washington University law faculty in 1955. His primary research interest was the history of medieval European commercial law. With Dorsey's encouragement in the 1960s, he began his study of Chinese in Taiwan and began a 35-year career as a leading Chinese legal scholar.

Nor was China forgotten within the Asian Law Program. Assigned by the dean of National Taiwan University's law faculty to assist Grey Dorsey in 1951 was a young but very promising recent graduate, Herbert Han Pao Ma, who would two decades later join the UW faculty as a visiting professor. At the UW Ma taught a course on Law and Social Change in China and collaborated with UW Professors Richard Cosway and Warren Shattuck on one of the first studies of Taiwan law in English published in the U.S. – *Trade and Investment in Taiwan: The Legal and Economic Environment in the Republic of China* (1973). Simultaneously another visiting professor, Tung-pi Chen, taught a course on law in the People's Republic of China.

By 1968 both James B. Palais and Daniel Lev had joined the UW faculty. Palais was an historian concentrating on Korea; Lev, a political scientist with expertise on Indonesia and law. Their addition to the UW faculty signaled a growing interest in East Asia beyond Japan that was soon replicated within the Law School. The arrival of Palais is credited as making the UW's Korean Studies Program the largest in the United States, and possibly outside of Korea. His legacy remains. Lev ensured a connection with Indonesia and Southeast Asia as well as law and political science. Promoting this expansion was another addition to the UW faculty, George M. Beckmann, who as historian had initially concentrated on the Meiji Constitution. As Dean of Arts and Sciences at the University of Kansas, Beckmann had advised Eugene Lee, a Kansas undergraduate with an interest in law and Japan, to consider applying to the UW with its newly established Asian Law Program. By the time Gene Lee had become one of the first LL.M. graduates in 1968, Beckmann had reorganized the Far East and Russian Institute into the School of Comparative and Area Studies as its newly appointed director. He would later serve as Provost and in that post become an even more influential supporter of the Program, particularly its expansion into other areas of East Asia while maintaining its original emphasis on Japan. The inclusion of all faculty in East Asian studies throughout the university as active participants in the East Asian Studies Program, centered in what was to become the Jackson School of International Studies, enabled close ties to develop between the Program and its faculty and others in East Asian Studies. Both Henderson and I were active members of the Japan Program faculty. We were both to become editors of the *Journal of Japanese Studies* that had been formed the spring before I joined the faculty in November 1974 by a group of Japanese studies faculty. I was to become Director of the Jackson School for a brief period in the 1980s.

In 1969, the Program admitted Chan Jin Kim, its first Korean student. After completing his M.C.L. in 1970, he received his doctorate in 1972, the Program's first Ph.D. in Asian law. He was followed in the LL.M. program by David Huang, its first graduate from Taiwan. (Prior to the LL.M. program one student from Taiwan, Y.C. Chen, had joined the Program as a visiting scholar.)

By 1970, Japan had experienced its economic "miracle" as it completed a decade of high levels of economic growth. As the economy boomed and controls over foreign investment eased in the mid- to late 1960s, the inflow of capital, mostly from the U.S., began to increase significantly. During the 1970s the outflow of capital from Japan into the U.S. and elsewhere had increased even more dramatically. Japan was becoming a major international investor. The handful of law firms established by U.S. lawyers who remained in Japan after the Occupation and, like Henderson, had been licensed between 1949 and 1955 as quasi-members (*jun kai'in*) of a Japanese bar association thrived. The demand for U.S. lawyers knowledgeable about Japan and Japanese lawyers with similar U.S. law expertise grew concomitantly. The Program thrived. The number of Japanese students grew from an all-time low of only one graduating student from Japan in 1971 to six in 1975 and eight (including one in the Law and Marine Affairs Program) in 1979. As scholarship funding from the Ford Foundation lapsed, the number of graduating U.S. and non-Japanese J.D. and LL.M. students in the Program remained almost constant, with three J.D. graduates and only one LL.M. graduate in 1971, to two J.D. but no LL.M. graduates in 1979. In the 1980s, with new scholarship funding from the U.S.–Japan Friendship Commission (to an American Bar Association Japanese Law fellowship program) and the Dana Foundation, the number of U.S students began to increase. Moreover, the focus of the Program had also expanded. Chan Jin Kim and David Huang would be followed by an increasing number of students from both Korea and Taiwan in the LL.M. and Ph.D. degree programs, two of whom – Tay-Sheng Wang and Kim Kon Sik, mentioned previously and both contributors to this volume – have had extraordinarily distinguished academic careers. With Dan Lev's enthusiastic support, an increasing number of students from Indonesia were also admitted to the LL.M. and Ph.D. programs, two of whom – Kurnia Toha and Tomi

Suryo Utomo – are also prominent scholars and contributors to this volume.

Japan in the 1970s attracted other U.S. comparative law scholars. In Japan for extended periods of time in the early 1970s were Jerome Cohen from Harvard, Whitmore Grey from the University of Michigan, and a promising new entrant to the legal academy, Frank Upham, who would later join the law faculty first at Ohio State, then Boston College, with an affiliation with Harvard. In the 1990s he and Jerome Cohen had both accepted appointments on the New York Law University School faculty.

Columbia Law School led the pack. Timothy Williams, one of the U.S. students to study in Japan in the late 1950s under the auspices of the Japanese–American Program for Cooperation in Legal Studies, had begun to teach a course at Columbia in the mid-1960s using materials that Henderson had assisted in developing. By the early 1970s Charles Stevens, a Coudert Brothers partner, had continued with materials that he and Kazunobu Takahashi had compiled (a copy of which is also available in the Gallagher Law Library). By end of decade the current president of the UW, Michael K. Young, was appointed to a newly created chair in Japanese law at Columbia. Under the direction of Curtis Milhaupt, Columbia remains today one of the three U.S. centers for Japanese (as well as Korean) legal studies.

The Program reached a peak during the 1980s. In 1982 the first two students from the PRC graduated. One, Jerry J.H. Zhu, had entered the Law and Marine Affairs LL.M. Program the year before. With the remaining funds from a donation by the Dana Foundation, the Program provided Zhu with a full scholarship. In return, Zhu agreed to continue a project begun earlier with the assistance of Rosser Brockman (a Yale Law School graduate who had previously received a Ph.D. in Chinese history at Harvard and was then associated with the Law Office of Griffith Way in Seattle as well as Blakemore & Mitsuki in Tokyo) to develop new materials and teach a regularly offered course on the law in the People's Republic of China. The other, Guoyuan Liu, a legal officer in the China Ocean Shipping Company (COSCO), entered the Program as its first student from the PRC. Both were to have distinguished professional careers.

By the end of the decade, both Dan Foote and Donald C. Clarke had joined the faculty. George Beckmann as university provost had enabled Foote's appointment by allowing the Law School to replace Henderson four years before his mandatory retirement at age 70. As a result of Beckmann's support, the Program had three Japanese law specialists on the faculty for almost half a decade. Clarke's appointment similarly ensured that Chinese law would be a central concern of the Program.

At the end of the decade, the Program's curriculum included over ten courses on East Asian law being offered each year by six tenured or tenure-track faculty. In addition to three separate courses on the legal systems of Japan, China, and Korea, the courses on East Asian law included four comparative courses (contracts, transnational litigation, tax, and corporation law) on U.S. and Japanese law that enabled extraordinarily productive interactions among the non-Japanese and Japanese students. Three additional courses covered specialized fields of Japanese law (administrative, antitrust, labor, and criminal law). Law in East Asia: Korea, which I initially taught, was the first course on Korean law to be offered annually outside of Korea.

With the encouragement and support of Dan Lev, the Program began to admit an increasing number of LL.M. candidates from Indonesia. The first Indonesian student to receive a master of laws degree from the Law School was Abdul Rasjid, who had graduated with an LL.M. in Law and Marine Affairs in 1980. He was followed in the Asian Law Program by Timbul Lubis in 1981 and by two more in 1984 – Bambang Setijoprodjo and Arief Surowidjojo. The first Ph.D. in Asian Law graduate from Indonesia was Erman Rajagukguk in 1988. He had completed his LL.M. in the Law and Marine Affairs Program, the Law School's second LL.M. program, which was established in the late 1960s under the direction of William T. Burke.

In the late 1980s, the first student from Thailand – Jumpot Saisunthorn '88 – was accepted, and by 1993, a second – Sakda Thanitcul – had received both the LL.M. and Ph.D. in Asian Law.

By the 1990s the Program had more than fully achieved Henderson's primary aim to train "liaison" lawyers capable of dealing with the legal issues that arise in U.S.–Japan and other transpacific commercial transactions: Tasuku Matsuo, Toshio Miyatake, Yasuhirō Fujita, Nobuyuki Tomotsune, Griffith Way, and Eugene Lee in consulting then in business as CEO of a Siemens subsidiary in Japan. Lee is still active as a member of the board of directors of several Japanese firms and successor to Griffith Way as president of the Blakemore Foundation. Five more recent J.D. graduates also stand out. Sally Harpole, J.D. '78, helped to establish the office of one of the first U.S. law firms in Beijing in the early 1980s and remains in practice today in Hong Kong. Larry Repeta, J.D. '79, has had an extraordinary career involved with Japan, including bringing and arguing a case before the Japanese Supreme Court. John Pierce, J.D. '94 was among the first U.S. lawyers to become involved professionally throughout Southeast Asia, assisting in establishing law offices in Myanmar, Thailand, Vietnam, and Singapore. Two U.S. LL.M. graduates – Paul Clark, LL.M. '77 and

James Kittelson, LL.M. '85 – have spent their careers since graduation with law firms in Tokyo and Seoul, respectively. By 2000 more UW Law School alumni resided in Tokyo than any city or even country in the world outside of metropolitan Seattle, Olympia, and Tacoma.

Pursuant to the 1986 Foreign Lawyers Law (Law No. 66, 1987) led by Davis Polk & Wardwell, Shearman & Sterling, Sullivan & Cromwell, and White & Case of New York and Morrison & Foerster of San Francisco over a dozen U.S. law firms had established offices in Tokyo. They were followed in China by an equal if not greater number of firms, including offices of Seattle's Davis, Wright, Todd & Tremaine in Shanghai formed by Jerry Zhu. At the same time well-established Japanese firms began to expand by merger and recruitment of the increasing number of Japanese lawyers who had studied in the U.S. and had been admitted to the bar in New York and California as a result of new rules allowing foreign lawyers with LL.M. degrees from accredited U.S. law schools to take their bar examinations. Indeed the first Japanese to have been admitted to the New York bar under the new rules was a UW graduate, Michiko Ito Crampe, LL.M. '74. As of the mid-1990s, to my knowledge, no LL.M. graduate of the Asian Law Program had ever failed the New York bar.

The number of law schools with faculty expertise in Japanese or Chinese law had also increased. In addition to Harvard, Columbia, and Washington University in St. Louis; Hawaii, Michigan, New York University, and Pennsylvania had highly productive tenured faculty in both fields. Other law schools – Arkansas, Berkeley, Creighton, Georgetown, Hastings, Illinois, Minnesota, Syracuse, Wisconsin – had at least one Chinese or Japanese specialist among their tenured faculty. Schools such as Duke, Stanford, and UCLA, which had lost both Mark Ramseyer and Bill Alford to Harvard, were inviting visiting faculty on a regular basis. (Taimie Bryant, the leading U.S. legal scholar writing and teaching on Japanese family law in the 1990s, remains on the UCLA faculty but regrettably has shifted her primary scholarly interest to another field.) The number would grow even higher at the turn of the century.

As more law schools began to appoint faculty with expertise and teaching and research interest in East Asian law, the number of law reviews with an international and comparative focus also began to proliferate. In the mid-1990s the Law School too added a new student-edited journal with an Asian law emphasis – the *Pacific Rim Law & Policy Journal*. In addition, law reviews generally had begun on a routine basis to include articles on East Asian law. As a result, the need for a journal specializing on Japan, such as *Law in Japan: An*

Annual, or indeed the law of any single country in East Asia rapidly diminished.

Also during the 1990s an ever-increasing number of law schools were establishing LL.M. programs designed to attract international students seeking to develop expertise in U.S. law (and to qualify for the New York or other state bar examination). Hundreds of students from East Asia, especially China, had begun to enroll in these purposefully revenue-generating programs.

Within the Law School the decade also brought further expansion and new challenges. As noted, a second LL.M. program in Law and Marine Affairs was in full operation by the 1970s. Two decades later, the Law School was also offering master degrees in International Environmental Law and Law and Sustainable Development. Soon to be added were LL.M. programs in Taxation and Intellectual Property. As a result LL.M. applicants from East Asia were directed to the appropriate program based on their particular subject of interest. The Asian Law Program remained a comparative program without any field of special concern. Ironically, Jerry Zhu, who, as noted above, would later open the first office in China of a Seattle-based law firm, Davis Wright & Tremaine, had graduated from the Marine Affairs Program while Guoyuan Liu, the Asian Law Program graduate, returned to China and COSCO to head its Law and Policy Research Department. He is currently the CCO of the COSCO Group.

The ties between the Program and new field-of-law centers were closest in the case of the Center for the Advanced Study and Research on Intellectual Property (CASRIP). Originally formed by Donald Chisum and Harold C. Wegner at the George Washington University Law School as an independent non-governmental organization (NGO) in order to participate in discussions in Geneva for the formation of the World Intellectual Property Organization (WIPO), CASRIP was integrated in 1992 under Chisum's direction into the Law School as a field-of-law center. A year later the Program admitted Toshiko Takenaka. Takenaka, a law graduate of Seikei University was a licensed patent agent in Japan whose primary field of interest was comparative study of U.S.-Japanese patent law. She completed her LL.M. in 1990 and in 1992 upon receiving her Ph.D. in Asian Law with Chisum as the chair of her dissertation committee, she was asked to remain as assistant director of CASRIP. In 1993 she became the first Japanese woman to join a U.S. law faculty in a tenure-track position. With Chisum's departure in 1996, she became director. In 2002 Takenaka helped to recruit Robert Gomulkiewicz as the director of the new Intellectual Property Law and Policy LL.M. program. A year later she was promoted to professor of law.

Similar ties with other centers proved to be more elusive. Although the sustainable development program had originated in work by Roy Prosterman on land reform in Vietnam and the Program offered the only regularly comparative tax course in the U.S., otherwise, little if any attention was paid to East Asia. The expansion of subject-matter centers and addition of new LL.M. programs also produced new demands on funding and space.

Until the 2000s no school or department at the university directly received funds derived from student tuition. For the first four decades of the Program, all tuition paid by students went directly to the state to be reappropriated for the university in regular biennial budgets. The only exceptions were a few specialized self-sustaining programs originating in the Business School but allowed by the university for the Law School's LL.M. program in Taxation. As a result tuition was not a consideration. The number of faculty and staff positions as well as other state-supported activities depended on the Law School's budget as determined by the legislature and the university administration. A major consequence of new centers for the Law School and the Program was a severe shortage of staff. Without additional funding, the Program had to manage with fewer and fewer staff resources. In 1965, for example, June Votaw was hired as an administrative assistant for the Program. By 1980 the School's entire LL.M. program shared a single administrative assistant who also provided secretarial help for faculty. Space too had become a problem. Condon Hall could hardly accommodate a single program. Moreover, retirements forced recognition that the Program had failed to recruit new, younger faculty to teach and co-teach courses in their particular fields of interest and expertise with an East Asian comparative emphasis.

These were among the challenges that the Program faced at the end of its fourth decade at the turn of the century. In 2000 both Dan Foote and I left the Program. He departed for the University of Tokyo to fill a chair in the sociology of law that had never been occupied by a non-Japanese scholar. I joined the law faculty of Washington University in St. Louis to replace Curtis Milhaupt, who had just replaced Michael Young, who had been appointed Dean of the George Washington Law School. I am happy to say that with Young's subsequent appointment as President of the UW, that particular circle is now closed.

Our replacement as Japanese law specialist as well as director of the Program was Veronica Taylor, a native of Melbourne, Australia, who had received her LL.M. in Asian law in 1992. Taylor describes below how as the Program's third director she met the challenges of a rapidly changing environment within the Law School, the University, and the world.

As a postscript I should add that Dan Foote is planning to return to the Program as co-director next year with joint appointments. I have also returned, if only for a short period of time. I write this in the wake of a visit in the Fall Quarter of 2013, also in the late autumn of a 40-year career. During my return I taught the basic introductory course of Japanese while revising the fifth edition of materials Henderson had first compiled for the course. It was the first course on Japanese law that I had taken as an entering LL.M. candidate in the Fall Quarter of 1969 and the first course I taught after joining the faculty in the Fall Quarter of 1974. I also taught another course – Transnational Litigation – which I had taken as a student and was the last course I taught in the Program in 2000. The materials, now a published casebook that includes Canadian and European Union law, originated in the Program. It is one that I have taught and developed further every year since 2000 at Washington University in St. Louis until 2010 and now at Vanderbilt.

My experience teaching these two courses along with first-year contracts in law schools with large LL.M. programs for international students, which like most attract the vast majority of their students from China – the plurality – Japan, South Korea, and Taiwan – had made me reflect on what remains an unaccomplished mission of the Program. The community of scholars and students that I remember from my time as a student and member of the Program faculty does not exist elsewhere and may be dissipating even in the Law School. The challenge, in my view, is to integrate international students from whatever countries into the full life of the Law School, drawing upon the knowledge and expertise they have in their own legal systems and thereby enabling them to interact and develop what can be life-long relationships with U.S. students with whom they share comparative interests. Moreover, those teachers who enable such sharing also learn. Whether teaching contracts or transnational litigation, I have learned as much if not more from the international students in my classes than I have taught them. For me the Center has the opportunity to build on its achievements of the past half-century in encouraging and creating comparative courses and materials for every possible field of law, including international law. In so doing, we return to a mission that the founders had at its inception – to reduce the Eurocentric tendencies and pervasive parochialism of U.S. legal education.

1.2 Navigating law's "Asian Century"

Veronica L. Taylor

INTRODUCTION

The challenge of "the Asian Century"[1] for a law school such as the University of Washington (UW) is how to pursue its public service mission, "Leadership for the Global Common Good," while also achieving more pragmatic institutional aims,[2] in an increasingly complex world. International and comparative law scholars of 50 years ago imagined a simpler legal geography: sovereign domestic legal systems at different stages of development, overlaid with a light blanket of international law. Those were largely fictional taxonomies of how legal systems are constituted, but they remain remarkably robust.[3] In this century, the legal

[1] *Security and Development Assistance: Hearings before the Committee on Foreign Relations*, United States Senate, Ninety-ninth Congress, First Session, on S. 559 ... S. 560 ... S. 660 ... S. 656 ... March 15, 20, 21, 22, and 26, 1985, Volume 4, *available at* http://books.google.com.au/books?id=Dko1AAAAIAAJ&focus=searchwithinvolume&q=%22asian+century%22 (last visited Mar. 1, 2014); *See also*, *Australia in the Asian Century*, White Paper 2013, http://pandora.nla.gov.au/pan/133850/20130914-0122/asiancentury.dpmc.gov.au/white-paper.html (last visited Mar. 1, 2014).

[2] As scholars, of course, we recognize that invoking the redistributive power of law – and positioning ourselves as agents of justice in the service of the public interest – also builds professional profile, prestige and social capital. As Dezalay and Garth note, this elision of the possible contradiction between skillful support of business and economic growth and advocacy of the marginalized is a defining characteristic of the legal mind-set: Yves Dezalay and Bryant G. Garth, *Corporate Law Firms, NGOs, and Issues of Legitimacy for a Global Legal Order*, 80 FORDHAM L. REV. 2309, 2314–15 (2012), *available at* http://ir.lawnet.fordham.edu/flr/vol80/iss6/2 (last visited Mar. 1, 2014).

[3] Discussed in Veronica L. Taylor, *Beyond Legal Orientalism, in* ASIAN LAWS THROUGH AUSTRALIAN EYES 47 (Veronica Taylor ed., 1997) (identifying deep-rooted problems within the discipline of comparative law that propelled the rise of "Asian law" scholarship, but also recognising that: "The burden of proof lies with 'Asian law' academics to show that this new professional boundary

world looks more kaleidoscopic. The imperatives of legal education are framed by individuals, corporations, governments or NGOs, and also by whether the activity is taking place in the Pacific Northwest, or more widely on national or international stages. What remains in focus, however, is that this century's world population centers and engines for economic growth are located in "Asia," however we define it.[4]

So the question is: how do legal educational institutions such as UW navigate law's Asian century? Where can a law school do well, by doing good? What principles would we use to make those choices? As a publically located and increasingly privately funded law school, UW earns the right to make strategic choices through a "social license"[5] – that is, the legitimacy that different kinds of stakeholders confer on the enterprise. Law Schools and their constituent Centers and Programs are accountable to many stakeholders: the host university, contributing taxpayers, students, alumni, donors, and external partners. Many of these stakeholders care about one or more of the following:

- Professionally relevant legal education and training;
- Intellectual Advancement – Research that questions received wisdom, develops and debates new ideas, and tests these vigorously using scholarly conventions; and
- Institutional Sustainability – Securing the creative talent necessary to teach and research, and the financial support for doing this, in ways that enhance the prestige and reputation of the institution, making it a compelling choice for all stakeholders.

None of these interests aligns perfectly, and even the short list of legitimacy criteria above hints at the perennial tensions of embedding legal education and training as a higher degree within the university.[6]

---

marker is not simply comparative law in a different guise, nor an attempt to construct an exclusive, mythical body of knowledge which we seek to interpret and control", at 47).

4 See, for example the very wide definition of "East Asia and the Pacific" employed by the U.S. Department of States' Bureau of East Asia and the Pacific: http://www.state.gov/p/eap/ci/index.htm.

5 Neil Gunningham, Robert A. Kagan, and Dorothy Thornton, *Social License and Environmental Protection: Why Businesses Go beyond Compliance*, 29 LAW & SOC. INQUIRY 307 (2004) (advancing the concept of a corporation's "social license" as something distinct from the "legal license" to operate), *available at* http://scholarship.law.berkeley.edu/facpubs/675Gunningham (last visited Mar. 1, 2014).

6 There is now a vast literature on the "crisis" of American legal education's

Nor are strategic choices free: they come with political, social and financial constraints, with endowments, and with a degree of institutional path dependency.

Choosing Asia

Part of UW's endowment was the decision of 50 years ago to make a preferential choice for Asian legal systems – as a teaching focus, as a (then nascent) field of legal scholarship, as a source of students, as a destination for graduates, and as an institutional orientation. Then – as now – the choice was not clear-cut and its long-term consequences were not apparent to those involved at the time.

Professor Dan Fenno Henderson is justifiably venerated at the University of Washington Law School for his vision in establishing and sustaining an Asian Law program. But his choices were not unanimously supported by his contemporaries. Sorting through his administrative papers after he passed away unexpectedly in 2010, I found sheaves of law school correspondence from the 1960s and 1970s: wafer-thin sheets and carbon copies of letters in single-spaced typescript, often with handwritten corrections. They included bitter complaints to the Dean, demanding that the Asian Law program be shut down. As the authors said – at length and with considerable force on the typewriter keys – it was a frolic; it was one person's vision; it was a waste of resources; and it was draining energy from the law school's core activities. Professor Henderson seems to have ignored these objections.

---

institutional design, funding and results. Particularly useful and stimulating contributions include: Margaret Martin Barry et al., LEGAL EDUCATION 'BEST PRACTICES' REPORT, UNITED STATES (2010); Richard W Bourne, *The Coming Crash in Legal Education: How We Got Here and Where We Go Now*, 45 CREIGHTON L. REV. 651 (2012); Bryant G. Garth, *Crises, Crisis Rhetoric and Competition in Legal Education: A Sociological Perspective on the (Latest) Crisis of the Legal Profession and Legal Education* (2012), *available at* http://ssrn.com/abstract=2166441_ (last visited Mar. 1, 2014); Brent E. Newton, *The Ninety-Five Theses: Systemic Reforms of American Legal Education and Licensure*, 64 (55) S.C. L. REV. 5 (2012) *available at* http://ssrn.com/abstract=1994189_ (last visited Mar. 1, 2014); Judith Welch Wegner, *Symposium 2009: A Legal Education Prospectus: Law School and Emerging Frontiers: Reframing Legal Education's "Wicked Problems,"* 61 (4) RUTGERS L. REV. 867 (2009), *available at* http://ssrn.com/absract=1533778.

Even visionaries have their blind spots, and so in 2001, Professor Cornelius (Neil) Peck also took me aside and confided, "You know Henderson was never really that interested in China … I challenged him on this and he said – 'Well, they don't really have *law*.' And I said 'Well they have something, and we better find out what it is.'" What propelled Peck's desire to broaden the inquiry beyond Japan was a visit to Singapore, and perhaps a sense that "Asia" was unfolding more quickly, and in more interesting ways, than Henderson's personal experience of Occupied Japan in World War II might have suggested.

Henderson and his colleagues were motivated by a desire to prepare Americans to practice law in a world of postwar reconstruction, where bilateral US–Japan trade was becoming visibly important, and it was possible to predict that Korea and Taiwan would take a similar developmental path.[7] Thus the program's core faculty for the first decades of its life – Henderson and Haley, and later Foote and Clarke – placed a strong emphasis on commercial and transactional law and on deep understanding of the legal anatomies of Japan, and later Korea, Taiwan and China. In an "Asian Century" those remain critically important domains of legal knowledge.

Although very different in their intellectual style, both Henderson and his successor, Professor John Haley, used comparative methodology and formidable linguistic skills to rigorously interrogate the formal and informal operation of law in East Asia: work that set the international benchmark for comparative legal scholarship in English.[8] What elevates their scholarship from this period, and distinguishes it from simple doctrinal comparison of Japan and the United States, is a critical appreciation of historical and social context. These are nuanced analyses of how political, economic and social institutions shape a state's legal and regulatory responses. Both scholars write with astute awareness of how national legal choices are shaped by, and in turn affect, transnational encounters and legal developments in proximate systems within Asia.[9]

---

[7] On the systemic similarities of North East Asian legal systems a vehicles for industrial policy and national development, see John K.M. Ohnesorge, *Law and Development Orthodoxies and the Northeast Asian Experience, in* LAW AND DEVELOPMENT IN ASIA (Jerry McAlinn ed., 2012).

[8] DAN FENNO HENDERSON, VILLAGE "CONTRACTS" IN TOKUGAWA JAPAN: FIFTY SPECIMENS WITH ENGLISH TRANSLATIONS AND COMMENTS (1975); JOHN O. HALEY, AUTHORITY WITHOUT POWER (1995); JOHN O. HALEY, ANTITRUST IN GERMANY AND JAPAN: THE FIRST 50 YEARS (1947–1998)(2001).

[9] For an illustration of the liminality of Japan within Asia, see: TESSA MORRIS-SUZUKI, BORDERLINE JAPAN: FOREIGNERS AND FRONTIER CONTROLS IN THE POSTWAR ERA (2010), 147.

In this way, Henderson's studies of pre-modern Japanese contracts, and Haley's history of competition policy and enforcement in Japan, for example, became compelling accounts of how legal and political elites understood and sought to govern their worlds – with direct resonance for how we might ask and answer those questions today with regard to our own, as well as other, legal systems.

Less remarked upon is the public interest impulse that underpinned the UW Asian Law enterprise. The original grant from the Ford Foundation to the Program was to enable lawyers from developing countries to study in the United States in order to contribute to the rebuilding of their own legal systems. We readily forget that Japan at that time was a postwar reconstruction economy.[10] Henderson was unequivocal about this – "Remember when you are making decisions about students, that there is a rice bowl involved." By this he meant the economic future of an extended family often hinged on a student's ability to graduate, and that as privileged teachers and gatekeepers of credentials we have a responsibility for social, as well as academic, outcomes. That pragmatic expression of moral obligation and altruistic service, expressed in the relational ties between teacher and student – and through them to extended networks – shaped the ethos of the Asian Law Center and anticipated the law school's current mission statement by some decades.

So the Asian law endowment at UW has been not simply a geographic orientation, but also a tradition of serious and consequential scholarship, a commitment to national purpose and the public good, an ethical sensibility, and a deep awareness of how personal relationships and networks support and sustain institutions. Within Asia, and even within American universities, relationships, devolved responsibility and discretion shape institutions as much, or more than, corporate strategic planning. "Who we are", and who we might aspire to become, is the sum of cumulative decisions about prevailing political and economic conditions; how we resolve conflicting beliefs about legal education; the preferences and inducements of external stakeholders; the personal capacities of individual students and faculty; and the scope and flexibility of our resources.

This chapter, then, is a reflection on the individual and collective choices that shaped the Asian Law Center during the period 2000–2010, when I had the privilege of serving as its Director.

---

[10] John W. Dower, Embracing Defeat: Japan in the Wake of World War II (1999).

I. A RECONFIGURED WORLD

The 2000s were a time of convulsive change for both lawyers and for law schools in the United States.[11] The decade's geopolitical shifts were felt acutely in Seattle – Washington being at the time the most Asia-oriented, trade-dependent State in the country.[12]

September 11, 2001 was a watershed moment: it put the United States on a war footing and propelled it into conflict in Afghanistan. The subsequent invasion of Iraq interrupted the state-building focus of the Afghan campaign, something that continues to haunt the aftermath of both engagements. These civil-military state-building interventions and "the war on terror" that followed reshaped our imagined legal world dramatically. One consequence was that the Middle East, South Asia and South-East Asia became more visible and policy salient. Another was the rise in popular awareness of the breadth and complexity of the world's Islamic political and legal systems.[13] The "securitization" of the United States was felt immediately. It stalled visas for international students; it made travel to the United States profoundly unpleasant for non-citizens; and it sparked enormous debate about the role of the United States in both making and complying with international law. At the same time, security concerns propelled further investments by the United States and its allies in "rule of law promotion" worldwide, particularly in new fragile and conflict-affected places.[14]

This was the time when foreign direct investment (FDI) became as significant as trade as a driver for economic growth, particularly in the global South, and the difficulty of governing globalized trade and investment became more evident.[15] Although the World Trade

---

[11] Asian Law alumna and former Associate Dean at UW Law School, Paula Littlewood (JD '97), is a prominent and original thinker on these issues. She writes from her vantage point as Executive Director of the Washington State Bar Association: http://www.wsba.org/About-WSBA/Governance/Paula-Littlewood (last visited Mar. 1, 2014).

[12] *Not by Aircraft Alone*, 25 June 2009, THE ECONOMIST, http://www.economist.com/node/13906661 (last visited Mar. 1, 2014).

[13] For an accessible scholarly survey, see SHARIA INCORPORATED (Jan Michiel Otto ed., 2010).

[14] Central and Eastern Europe being the testing ground for the "rule of law revival" that followed the 1989 fall of the Berlin Wall: *see generally* THOMAS CAROTHERS, PROMOTING THE RULE OF LAW ABROAD: IN SEARCH OF KNOWLEDGE (2006).

[15] UNITED NATIONS, WORLD INVESTMENT REPORT 2013, http://unctad.org/en/publicationslibrary/wir2013_en.pdf (last visited Mar. 1, 2014).

Organization architecture was complete, the Doha round of trade negotiations that commenced in 2001 quickly stalled. The OECD-sponsored Multilateral Agreement on Investment had failed in 1998.[16] Both events contributed to the proliferation of regional and bilateral trade agreements and bilateral investment treaties (BITS) and the profusion of new laws and soft law instruments to govern investment and trade that characterized this decade.

The global growth in FDI matters for lawyers because of its potential for reshaping legal rules and norms on the ground in the host country. In the 2000s, however, it was unclear whether, how, or how quickly these would converge to American or European rules and norms. Lawyers accustomed to servicing American multinationals with close ties to Washington State, such as Boeing, Microsoft, Amazon, Starbucks and Costco and their suppliers, could assume convergence, because their clients operated on a scale that allowed them to dictate governing law and contract terms within their supply chains and sales channels. By contrast, the World Bank's "Doing Business" indicators were launched in 2002 as a form of policy pressure on developing states to reform their domestic legal and regulatory systems – precisely because they remained so diverse and resistant to globalized influences.[17]

The explosive growth in information technologies and their business applications created demand for legal, as well as technical services. Law students at UW in the 2000s aspired to be intellectual property licensing lawyers for Japanese electronic games maker Nintendo, rather than trade or maritime lawyers.[18] Those same technologies profoundly disrupted legal knowledge and services. No one needed a law degree or a legal advisor in order to Google legal information and procedural forms, or to consult wikis and on-line forums for advice, with the consequence that lawyers now needed to demonstrate, rather than simply claim, expertise. By the end of the decade "big law" would become "new law": portable and outsourced.[19]

Meanwhile, the East Asian economies were being recalibrated. China was clearly poised to overtake Japan as the world's second-

---

[16] *See* http://www.wto.org/english/tratop_e/dda_e/dda_e.htm (last visited Mar. 1, 2014).

[17] *See* http://www.doingbusiness.org/about-us (last visited Mar. 1, 2014).

[18] Indeed, the Law School's LLM program in Maritime Law was disestablished early in the decade for this reason.

[19] For a prescient analysis of the demise of the big law firm (now often abbreviated to "big law"), see William Henderson and Marc Galanter, *The Elastic Tournament: A Second Transformation of the Big Law Firm*, 60 STAN. L. REV. 1867 (2008).

largest economy. It was the new growth opportunity for US business,[20] including legal services. Japan was still important, but its prestige was waning as its economy weathered "lost decades" of deflation spanning the early 1990s to 2014. After a brief de-regulatory rally under the Koizumi Cabinet (2001–2006) politicians and bureaucrats seemed to lose their appetite for thoroughgoing regulatory reforms. In reality, the domestic legal reform proceeding in the background was intense and significant,[21] but the most commented-upon reform – the launch of an American-style graduate "law school" model in 2003 – proved to be self-defeating. Originally conceived as a pro-growth expansion of national legal capacity, as well as a progressive vehicle for remedying Japan's widening social inequality, the new institution was soon captured by protectionists and so produced a marginal increase in lawyers at extraordinarily high cost.[22] In its early years it also diverted significant human resources and intellectual energy away from substantive research. One early casualty was Japanese student interest in international and transnational legal topics and the opportunity to expand international institutional partnerships.[23] Nonetheless, it is a source of pride for us that two of the Asian Law Center's Japanese PhD graduates during this period were immediately hired by leading Japanese law schools.[24]

---

[20] See, for example, the single country focus on China in Washington State trade services support: http://choosewashingtonstate.com/i-need-help-with/international-trade/china-business-development/ (last visited Mar. 1, 2014).

[21] *See, e.g.,* Veronica L. Taylor, *Dollars to Donuts: Japanese Courts and Corporate Accountability, in* NEW COURTS IN ASIA (Andrew Harding and Penelope Nicholson eds., 2009); Veronica L. Taylor, *From Manners to Rules: The Reregulation of Japan, in* PUSHING BACK AGAINST GLOBALIZATION: REGULATION IN ASIA (John Gillespie and Randy Peerenboom eds., 2009).

[22] See generally the helpful bibliography assembled by Levin and Mackie: Mark Levin and Adam Mackie, *Truth or Consequences of the Justice System Reform Council: An English Language Bibliography from Japan's Millennial Legal Reforms* (March 21, 2013), 14 (3) ASIAN-PAC. L. & POL'Y J. (2013), *available at* SSRN: http://ssrn.com/abstract=2237663 (last visited Mar. 1, 2014).

[23] This observation is anecdotal and reflects the difficulties that foreign faculty members had in attracting students to "international" courses or courses taught in English at leading law schools in Japan after it became apparent that the Bar pass rate would drop, and that these curricular offerings would be of no immediate benefit in passing the Japanese Bar.

[24] Toshitaka Kudo (LLM '02, PhD '09) is an Assistant Professor at Keio University Law School and Kyoko Ishida (LLM '03, PhD '06) is a faculty member at Waseda University Law School.

For lawyers in Seattle, Japan-related practice opportunities at home had constricted as Japanese inbound investment and trade narrowed. This was hard: being the epicenter of Japanese legal knowledge and skills in the United States is no consolation if the opportunities to use them have fled. Local lawyers did what lawyers do everywhere; they re-tooled to develop new practice areas. Local law firm Davis Wright Tremaine, for example, announced its ambition to become the nation's leading China law practice.[25] But as American elites began to focus on emerging markets and, in particular, on China as a new competitive economy and military power, Japanese elites became increasingly anxious about their place in the world.[26] For 50 years, Japan's primary political, security, legal and intellectual ties had been with the United States, and the prospect of the US symbolically or actually stepping away from Japan in order to accommodate Japan's greatest threat, China, was traumatic for individuals and for institutions.[27]

By contrast, South Korea's democratization and economic growth during the same period resulted in historic shifts in legal and political design and process. From being a largely closed economy Korea gradually opened to services, and opportunities for intellectual and professional exchange with the United States blossomed rapidly. Who could have imagined that by 2015, among the many Asian Law Center alumni teaching at top-ranked Korean law schools, one would be the first female faculty member at one of that country's top private law schools?[28]

---

25 Personal communication to the author. It was not coincidental that this was also the law firm of former State Governor Gary Locke (1997–2005), later US Secretary of Commerce (2009–2011) and US Ambassador to China (2011–present): *See* http://www.dwt.com/practices/china/?op=overview_ (last visited Mar. 1, 2014).

26 My vantage point for observing this was as a member (2005–2012 and later Chair, 2008–2012) of the Japan Foundation's American Advisory Committee, the peak funding body for US–Japan academic and policy research and collaboration.

27 We can understand this volume as both symbolizing that very real anxiety and demonstrating that it is probably overblown. The intellectual and practical importance of Japan as a model and reference point for other Asian legal systems is undeniably great. On the other hand, Japan will be a necessary but insufficient lens through which to view increasingly hybrid and pluralist Asian legal systems in the coming decades, if simply because Japan as regional power, donor, or exemplar of constitutional democracy, will be only one point in a multi-polar region.

28 Dr. Patricia Goedde (LLM '03, PhD '08) is an Assistant Professor at Sungkyunkwan University Law School, Seoul.

South East Asian economies remained less prominent for many Americans during this decade, even while Thailand grew and Vietnam entered the WTO in 2006. By the end of the decade Indonesia had both democratized and staked a claim to secure middle-income status. ASEAN, which had been a loose grouping of developing states in South East Asia, had gradually become more consequential, both politically and legally.[29]

Many of the leaders in Washington State businesses and legal practices that had grown through trade with Asia became philanthrocapitalists, embracing both the university and the Law School in new patterns of support and investment. The Gates Foundation rapidly became the global paradigm: simultaneously, a large-scale donor, influential designer of education and health interventions worldwide, and a key stakeholder in the Department of Global Health, the Law School and a range of UW-linked research enterprises. For the Law School, the institutional turning point was the gift by William (Bill) Gates III in honor of his father that allowed the construction of a new Law School building – Gates Hall – on the main UW campus. Opened in 2003, it is hard to overstate the buoying effect that the building had on staff and student morale and the way in which it helped the institution imagine itself as having global potential.[30]

And then came the 2007–08 financial crisis, the 2009 election of President Obama, and his foreign policy "pivot to Asia". By 2010 unemployment in Washington State was heading toward 10% and it was clear that legal education would need to be rethought as declining demand for elite legal services in the United States morphed into more permanent restructuring of the sector. Significant local firms in Seattle had either merged, been acquired as part of national consolidations, and/or had established branch offices in Asia. Meanwhile, Chinese law firms were setting up local representatives in Seattle. One measure of the

---

[29] *See, e.g.,* Imelda Deinla, *Rule of Law Key to Building an ASEAN Community by 2015*, East Asia Forum, 8 March 2013 http://www.eastasiaforum.org/2013/03/08/rule-of-law-key-to-building-an-asean-community-by-2015/ (last visited Mar. 1, 2014).

[30] Other local lawyers who also sought to convert their business acumen into philanthropic investment included former Microsoft legal counsel Bill Neukom, later ABA President and founder of the World Justice Project and Stan Barer (JD '63), businessman and name partner of Garvey, Schubert and Barer, who also became a significant donor to the Law School in this period. The significant support to the Law School from Stan and Alta Barer is described at: http://www.law.washington.edu/ghs/.

anxiety that these changes elicited was ongoing opposition to allowing foreign-educated lawyers to sit for the Washington State Bar.[31]

Against this shifting background of political and economic change, law schools anxiously debated what kind of educational experience would yield "professional relevance" for their future graduates. Our task was to answer this in relation to the Asian law teaching program.

II. RETHINKING THE PROFESSIONAL RELEVANCE OF ASIAN LAW

By the time I accepted the invitation in 2000 to return to the Law School to lead the Asian Law program (as it then was), many of these trends had already begun to impact the much smaller and more trade-dependent Australian economy. As a proud Asian Law alumna, I had great affection for Dan Henderson and John Haley, who had been kind and inspirational figures early in my career. I benefitted from their wise counsel and from Haley's strategic advice. I needed to maintain the intellectual ambitions of Asian law, nurture its people, but also sharpen its professional relevance for the future. That seemed to require three programmatic adjustments:

(i) Broadening Our Legal Geography

"East Asia" had been defined at UW Law School as Japan, then China, and then in much smaller proportions, Taiwan and Korea. Enlarging our definition of Asia seemed both desirable and necessary: we needed to diversify and increase our LLM student enrolment and we needed to expand professional pathways for our graduating JD and LLM

---

[31] During this decade international students could take an LLM at UW, take a New York Bar preparation course in Seattle and then fly to New York to acquire the practice credential that would enable them to be employed in Seattle before returning to their home country to recoup the long-term benefits of their investment in an American law degree. Meanwhile, employers such as Microsoft were seeking to hire foreign attorneys as paralegals to support the expansion of their business. On the impact of the American LLM degree as a credential for non-US lawyers, see Carole Silver, *States Side Story: Career Paths of International LL.M. Students, or 'I Like to Be in America'*, 80 (6) FORDHAM L. REV. (2012) (arguing that the claimed increase in competition for law firm placements in the US is negligible and of short duration, since the majority of LLM students return to the country of origin).

students. Dean Ron Hjorth kindly cautioned me that I would "never" get American lawyers interested in South East Asia. But within months came 9/11 and the national political gaze swung to Islam and to Islamic Asia, particularly Indonesia. The Jackson School of International Studies at UW was home to distinguished scholar Professor Daniel S. Lev, who was a world authority on the Indonesian legal system. Lev welcomed the opportunity to join the Asian Law Center network and in doing so, enriched us intellectually and exponentially expanded our prestige and reach within Indonesia. Later, leveraging years of practical experience in Indonesia by Professor Jon Eddy and myself, we were able to recommence enrolling high-performing Indonesian LLM and PhD students,[32] after a hiatus of 20 years. Those graduates took up leadership positions in government and legal education, opening the door for serious research and externally funded opportunities in Indonesia.

The reinvigoration of our ties to our Thai alumni and partner institutions, and the recruitment of a new cohort of Thai PhD students and our first PhD student from Vietnam were also important milestones, and translated into a flow of talented students who would become influential voices in key South East Asian institutions. We hypothesized that our institutional knowledge of, and networks in, Japan, Korea and Taiwan could be directly relevant for colleagues facing legal and regulatory challenges in Thailand, Indonesia and Vietnam, and this indeed proved to be the case.

Asia was becoming more globally integrated, politically, economically and legally. Suddenly it was accessible and its issues relevant: legal and social issues of universal concern such as environmental sustainability, asylum seeker and refugee flows, or the impact of Islam within complex systems of legal pluralism. In a real sense we had the opportunity to give full expression to "Asian and comparative law" as the denominator for our JD, LLM and PhD teaching programs: Asia as a broad focus and comparative law as a capacious methodology. We redesigned the curriculum to become both deeper and broader. At a specialist level we piloted a course in South East Asian Law[33] and established new courses in Korean Law and Islamic law. Korean law

---

32 Support for this came from a multi-year USAID funded program, ELIPS II.

33 We benefitted greatly from the goodwill of the small group of South East Asian legal specialists in the United States, particularly Professors Mark Cammack, David Linnan, and Andrew Harding, who were generous in visiting, teaching and supporting the PhD and LLM programs at the Asian Law Center.

was ripe for expansion within the United States as ties between Korean, Korean–American, and other professors in American and Korean law schools expanded and the Korea Foundation stepped up its institutional support. In parallel, the community of Islamic law specialists within the United States was also broadening to embrace considerable disciplinary and geographic diversity. In time my hope was to realize a further important step, which would have been the build-out of serious legal expertise on South Asia.[34]

An important question became how to support the interest of non-specialists: the JD students, for example, who were curious about the world and were writing for the *Pacific Rim Law and Policy Journal*, but who would encounter Asia exclusively through English language sources and the narrow prism of a substantive interest such as gender equality or bioethical regulation. The American student s who aimed for a specialist JD/LLM credential in Asian and Comparative Law lacked the high-level fluency in an Asian language that had been a hallmark of the program in past decades. Asia was now "popular" in the true sense of the word and so we amended some of the more restrictive enrollment rules, contributed to a new first-year survey course in international and comparative law, and established a "Law through Global Eyes" seminar series that presented law school visitors and comparative law perspectives in accessible ways.

Asia was also a primary location for sustainable development, both as a policy imperative and as a growing area of legal professional practice. So at the suggestion of Professor Anita Ramasastry, we collaborated in developing a professionally oriented course, *Law Reform in Transition Economies*, which connected JD and LLM students across Asian Law, European Law, and Sustainable International Development clusters.

As we embraced "more" Asia, however, some colleagues and alumni inevitably perceived this as "less" focus on countries that they cared about. Partly this reflected Japanese sensitivities about a slightly diminished role in the world; but it was also informed by the Cold War legacy of seeing US foreign relations in strongly bilateral terms, so that focus on a new partner country must have an hydraulic effect on a

---

[34] There is now a sizeable and energetic group of South Asian legal scholars in the United States, many with diaspora or personal ties to the countries of that sub-region, contributing work of lively intellectual and practical benefit to the academy. *See, e.g.,* the American Association of Law Schools' Law and South Asian Studies Section: https://memberaccess.aals.org/eWeb/dynamicpage.aspx?webcode=ChpDetail&chp_cst_key=ac97380c-f0f7-461c-bc33-2901d751af17 (last visited Mar. 1, 2014).

pre-existing partnership.[35] In one sense this is true: if you are dividing a finite number of professors, time and cash across an expanding number of jurisdictions, you are diluting pre-existing "shareholdings" in the short term. But while every choice has an opportunity cost, the strategic choices themselves are not immutable. So, for example, a recovering Japanese economy in 2014 where the legal and policy ramifications of the catastrophic Tohoku earthquake are now clearer, is more obviously a salient subject of study than it might have been ten years earlier. The prospect of constitutional reform and political transition in Burma/Myanmar by 2015, coupled with its complex legal pluralism, make it more interesting and more accessible for comparative study now than it was in 2000. To the extent that you are thoughtfully expanding the educational resources, intellectual opportunities, and professional networks for current and future students in Asia, more really *is* more.

(ii) Understanding Asia as an Integrated Legal and Regulatory Domain

It is easy to overlook the importance of intra-regional economic and intellectual ties within Asia. By 2000, business lawyers servicing clients in Asia needed not only professional competence in their own law and that of another jurisdiction, but also familiarity with a third or fourth Asian market as well. The larger Japanese law firms (and later their Korean counterparts) began to establish offices in China and South East Asia. Their young practitioners came to Seattle for training in "American law", but they also sought exposure to technical legal areas such comparative corporate governance, or intellectual property law, as well as an overview of Chinese commercial law. Our response to this was to broaden the LLM program to include a stream in "global business law" that allowed students more flexibility about mixing and matching courses to customize a course of study that would support their individual career paths. We knew that UW alumni from all the Law Schools' programs were mobile, meeting each other all over Asia, and asking their alma mater to help them network more effectively. We invested heavily in meeting more regularly, formally and informally, with UW alumni, and in more locations in Asia, than ever before.[36]

---

35 On clientalism in American foreign policy and the role of development aid in maintaining a network of allies, see STEPHEN MAJESKI AND DAVID SYLVAN, *US FOREIGN POLICY IN PERSPECTIVE: CLIENTS, ENEMIES AND EMPIRE* (2009).

36 The talent of our law school colleague and Asian Law alumna, Professor

We could predict that the comparative advantage that UW had enjoyed as a "knowledge portal" for doctrinal law in East Asia would eventually dissipate. Top-tier American law schools, with their prestigious faculty and their luxurious facilities, still exercised a magnetic pull on lawyers from Asia. But legal education within Asia was itself developing rapidly and its law schools were forging intra-regional links and international alliances that would reshape flows of knowledge and students.[37] The centers of expertise and prestige in the field of Asian law in the future would not be limited to UW, or Harvard, or Cornell,[38] but would include institutions such as the National University of Singapore, Seoul National University, Korea University, Yonsei University, Tsinghua University, Shanghai Jiao Tong University, the University of Indonesia and Gadjah Mada University, Nagoya University, Leiden University, the University of Melbourne and Australian National University. We could choose to join and invest in those strategic alliances or stand apart – and we chose to participate and try to strengthen our UW brand at the same time.[39]

By 2010, a JD student wanting to specialize in Chinese law could now spend a semester abroad studying in English at a law school in China. At home in Seattle, the JD curriculum was increasingly crowded with courses in emergent fields such as intellectual property and health law. China or Vietnam could be referenced within any course without requiring arduous historical or contextual study of that whole foreign legal system. This kind of student and faculty "sampling" of Asia was not "Asian law" in the scholarly sense, but it was a logical outgrowth of a technologically more accessible Asia, and

---

Toshiko Takenaka, Director of the Center for Advanced Study and Research in Intellectual Property, in building alumni networks, particularly in Japan, was a significant asset during this period.

[37] *See generally*, Veronica L. Taylor, *Legal Education as Development, in* LEGAL EDUCATION IN ASIA (Stacey Steele and Kathryn Taylor eds., 2010).

[38] See in particular the innovative strategy advanced by Professor Annelise Riles at Cornell that uses a moderated discussion list, Meridian 180, to connect thinkers and alumni from a range of legal domains and Asian countries: http://meridian-180.org/_ (last visited Mar. 1, 2014).

[39] Examples of our strategy here included becoming the first US law school to join the Asian Law Institute (ASLI) – a collective of law schools in Asia – and a commitment to participate in ASLI annual conferences to mentor younger scholars. Another was the considerable effort by Professor Jonathan Kang to formalize collaborative agreements and joint academic credit arrangements between UW and leading Korean law schools. See for example: https://www.law.washington.edu/AsianLaw/Countries/SouthKorea.aspx (last visited Mar. 1, 2014).

a diverse student and faculty body with a heightened awareness of global legal and economic integration.

(iii) Building Portable, Generic Professional Skills

How to better prepare students for that mobile, trans-Asia future? Student interest in Japanese law was diminishing gradually, but not completely. One way of sustaining the claim that Japan could be useful professionally was to use it as a vehicle for building legal skills. Earlier iterations of the curriculum had included negotiating skills and simulations taught by Professor Haley, but former UW professor Daniel Foote used his move to the University of Tokyo in 2000–2001 to propose undertaking this in real time between the two law schools, using video-conferencing and instant messaging. The practical barriers to doing this were surprisingly steep, but heroic efforts by Foote and Asian Law alumnus and adjunct John ("Jody") Chaffee made the experiment a great pedagogical success. Chaffee was later joined by Rick Guinee, and their combination of deep knowledge of Japanese corporate law, transactional expertise and practice experience in Tokyo enabled us to offer two well-subscribed JD/LLM simulation courses – one with Tokyo and one with Waseda University.

As the legal job market became more competitive within and outside the United States, we also moved to institutionalize job search support for JD students seeking placements in Asia and for LLM students seeking post-graduation professional training placements in the US. To better prepare students for the job market, we incorporated more oral skills practice opportunities in coursework and more mentored resume writing and career advising opportunities. We redesigned our PhD program to include structured coursework, including research design planning and dissertation writing, oral presentation skills and socio-legal research methods. Being able to draw on the methodological expertise of adjunct Professor Susan Whiting (UW Political Science) and recruit Dr Elin Cohen (LLM '03) enabled us to offer a PhD environment that could compete effectively with other socio-legal programs similar to ours such as those at UC Berkeley, Stanford and Wisconsin.

III. ADVANCING KNOWLEDGE

An inevitable consequence of a more "global" outlook at the Law School was a reframing of what constitutes the field of "Asian law". In a world where any faculty member and student can travel to Asia and collaborate with Asia colleagues, the potential for developing and debating new ideas is necessarily more democratically distributed.

In some of my early work, I pointed out that "Asian law" was an institutional and political fiction that was every bit as contestable as the geopolitical labeling of Asia and its sub-regions.[40] Within the Law School, "Asian law" had functioned as a shorthand for a cluster of faculty and educational and research activities and the budget to support them, and so making distinctions between who or what Asian law was, or was not, did matter for practical purposes. Intellectually, however, I continue to see the domain of Asian law as inclusive and geographically expansive: for me, legally speaking, Azerbaijan is systemically closer to Indonesia than it is to Austria. This vision of Asian law also admits to wide variation in scholarly styles; whether a dense description of doctrine or procedure, a new applied theoretical insight, or an empirically grounded argument about legal and social change.

Where our deeper normative preferences do tend to surface, however, is when we adjudicate on the people and projects that will populate the field in future. While welcoming the diffusion of interest in Asia among faculty and students, it also seemed important to recommit to sustained research that genuinely advanced the boundaries of our knowledge. For that reason, a conscious strategic choice during 2000–2010, and perhaps the one in which I was most deeply invested, was the revitalization of the PhD in Asian and Comparative Law.

UW Law School was unique in having preserved its PhD qualification in law, at a time when almost every other law school in the United States created an SJD/JSD program. The point of difference for UW was that, outside the United States, the PhD remained the most prestigious terminal degree and the threshold academic appointment credential in all disciplines, including law. Beyond nomenclature and structure, what distinguished the UW credential from the SJD was its commitment to interdisciplinary inquiry. For many candidates this became their first

---

[40] Veronica L. Taylor, *Rule-of-Law Assistance Discourse and Practice: Japanese inflections, in* LAW IN THE PURSUIT OF DEVELOPMENT: PRINCIPLES INTO PRACTICE? (Amanda Perry-Kessaris ed. 2012); Veronica L Taylor and Michael Pryles, *The Cultures of Dispute Resolution in Asia, in* DISPUTE RESOLUTION IN ASIA 1–33 (Michael Pryles, ed. 3rd ed 2006).

immersion in theoretical and empirical insights from disciplines beyond the narrow domain of law. The rationale for demanding this additional work was that, in the professional future of educators and policy makers, more would be required than the fairly simply analytic toolkit of legal formalism.

We began the decade with two students enrolled in the PhD in Asian and Comparative Law and we finished with a cohort of 16 that included outstanding American scholars and a class distributed across about 12 countries.[41] The commencing student and their research topics in the 2000s represent a snapshot of the complex social issues that national policy makers and legal activists were grappling with throughout Asia. The successive dissertations by Taiwanese scholars Dr Awi Mona, Dr Ariel Cheng and Dr Hsin-yang Wu is a striking body of work on indigenous minority self-determination, human rights, and minority linguistic rights in Taiwan during a period of intense political change. The original contributions of Indonesian scholars Professors Melda Kamil, Kurnia Toha and Dr Hendrianto covered sustainable and internationally compliant fishing, the challenges of land law reform responsive to indigenous rights, and the first term of a new Constitutional Court in a rapidly democratizing Indonesia. Some projects, such as those by Dr Kyoko Ishida on the ethical regulation of the Japanese legal profession and Dr David Merrell on legal pluralism in Kyrgyzstan, broke completely new academic ground. Others, such as Professor Patricia Goedde's study of lawyer advocacy in South Korea, and Dr Kanaphon Chanhom's study of the history of Thai criminal justice, combined sophisticated applications of socio-legal theory and fresh empirical data to illuminate hitherto unknown aspects of those systems' legal institutions. These dissertations, as well as those scheduled for submission in the coming years, have the potential to radically reshape our understanding of legal and political systems in

---

41 We used the pedagogical premise that an annual intake of between five and seven high-caliber students would provide the best peer-learning environment and that the total number would give us sufficient personal time with students but also a scale that would allow systematic, course-based instruction in research design and methods. The only drawback was that a PhD program under our then budget system was a loss-leader: absent a generous scholarship or a subsidy, the real costs of a 3–4 year academic program at UW were beyond the means of most debt-laden American graduates and the talented young academics and policy makers that we might want to recruit from Asia. Accordingly we relied heavily on students talented enough to bring scholarships, and our ability to advocate for, and squeeze value from, a small number of State-funded tuition waivers.

Asia. The success of those PhD projects is largely attributable to the innumerable voluntary hours spent in supervision and on dissertation committees by generous faculty from the Law School, from other departments throughout the university, and from peer programs in the US and Asia.

We fell a little short of our programmatic goal of "50 by 50" – 50 Asian and Comparative PhD graduates by 2013 – but we created a value proposition that resonated beyond the Asian Law Center. That the PhD program is now Law School-wide and no longer geographically specific is an indication of its success. Our numerical target was really a proxy for the power of this program to reshape legal institutions in developing economies, as well as contributing to American educational and policy capacities. Some of our first-generation LLM and PhD alumni were honored at the 50th anniversary celebration of the Center;[42] later graduates populate the ranks of Japanese law professors around the world;[43] and at one point during the decade we were able to count seven serving Deans and Deputy Deans of leading law schools in Asia who were Asian Law Center alumni. If your mission is the formation of "leaders for the global common good", a PhD program is a natural incubator – these are people with the intellectual and personal qualities of determination and self-sacrifice who are postponing short-term benefits in order to pursue larger goals. As I explained when honoring Professor Dr Erman Rajagukguk (LLM '84, PhD '88),[44] fulfilling a public service mission in Asia means, in many cases, carrying out prominent university and government roles while being a beacon of integrity, and it is often the PhD credential that makes this possible.

My own research as a socio-legal scholar has frequently returned to questions of how legal knowledge is constituted, and by what kinds of people, operating in what kinds of formal and informal networks, with what effects. These questions matter in very practical ways for how rule of law interventions affect both ordinary people and legal elites. In partnership with Professors Susan Whiting (UW Political Science)

---

42 This group was Tasuku Matsuo M.C.L. '69; C.J. Kim PhD '72; Liu Guoyuan LLM '82; Erman Rajagukguk LLM '84, PhD '88; and Tay-sheng Wang LLM '90, PhD '92.

43 A partial list would include Professors John Haley (LLM '71), Lawrence Repeta (JD '79), Mark Levin (LLM '90), Tay-sheng Wang (LLM '90, PhD. '92), Veronica Taylor (LLM '92), Toshiko Takenaka (LLM '90, PhD '92), Jody Chafee (JD '91), Leon Wolf (LLM '96), Kyoko Ishida (LLM '06, PhD 2006), Toshitaka Kudo (LLM '02, PhD '09); and Vicki L. Beyer (JD '90).

44 http://www.youtube.com/watch?v=qyrqDr7bIG0&feature=youtu.be (last visited Mar. 1, 2014).

and Hualing Fu (University of Hong Kong), I was able to test some of these ideas by designing a State Department-funded rule of law project, *Empowering Rural Communities: Legal Aid and the Rule of Law in Rural China (2006–08).*[45] For the Law School, this marked the first interdisciplinary, federally-funded project in excess of $1 million. For our Chinese partners and the participants it was much-needed support, as rural people struggled with everyday legal problems that often resulted in personal and family calamity. In research terms, the significance of the project was to pioneer the experimentalist empirical design using a form of randomized control trial, to both test the outcomes of the intervention and evaluate the intervention itself. This was path-breaking for the field of rule of law and the comprehensive data from the project will continue to inform significant work on both legal empowerment and Chinese law for years to come.[46]

Sometimes advancing also involves strategic retreat or regrouping. A conventional boundary marker for a scholarly discipline or field is its publications. During the 2000s the *Pacific Rim Law and Policy Journal* and the journal that I had co-founded, the *Australian Journal of Asian Law*, developed strongly, while the Foote-edited volume *Law in Japan: A Turning Point* made a significant scholarly contribution to the field.[47] Individual faculty continued to publish and edit, but the venerable journal *Law in Japan* (with which UW faculty had been closely involved in prior decades) stalled, and in a difficult economic climate, the University of Washington Press declared its Asian Law Series of monographs financially unviable. However, loss is opportunity, and launching the SSRN electronic journal, *Asian Law*, enabled us to have a wider global reach and a capacious vehicle for legal research relating to Asia.

IV. SUSTAINING INSTITUTIONS

Universities endure, but neo-gothic architecture is an unreliable guide to the longevity of academic programs. So it is quite remarkable for an Asian Law Center to celebrate 50 years, even more so with the kind of leadership succession that is the envy of peer institutions.

---

45 Asian Law colleague Dongsheng Zang was also a generous practical and intellectual contributor to this project.

46 *See, e.g.,* RESOLVING LAND DISPUTES IN EAST ASIA: EXPLORING THE LIMITS OF LAW (Hualing Fu and John Gillespie eds., 2014).

47 DANIEL H. FOOTE, LAW IN JAPAN: A TURNING POINT (2008).

By the end of the decade, the Asian Law Program had fully transformed into an Asian Law Center. Our goal was unchanged: high-quality teaching anchored in East Asia, but attentive to the other parts of the region, coupled with world-class scholarship in Asian law. The significance of "center" was that it suggested a flexible and responsive resource and knowledge hub; something more than elements in a curriculum. It signaled an outward-looking stance and a willingness to deliver value to stakeholders including, but extending beyond, our students and alumni. Internally, a new name for a "new" enterprise also helped tactically in responding to the many financial and political challenges that unfolded as the decade wore on. That the Center emerged on the other side larger and financially stronger than at any time in the previous 50 years was due to the talent and efforts of many colleagues, as well as a large measure of good fortune.

On the face of it, leading Asian law at the University of Washington should have been an easy, as well as a pleasurable, responsibility. UW had an impressive institutional history and the prestige of distinguished and well-positioned alumni throughout Asia. Its East Asian law collection in the Gallagher library, developed and overseen by talented librarians Bill McCloy and Rob Britt, is unique in the world; so much so that many visiting scholars came to UW specifically to work in the library.[48] A cohort of senior faculty was talented and committed comparative law teachers, including former Dean Ron Hjorth, the late Associate Dean Dick Kummert and Professor (now Emeritus) Linda Hume. Each had a long association with the Asian Law Program and the ability to integrate international and US students' experiences in ways that really enriched the learning opportunities for both.[49] Assistant Dean Paula Littlewood was an Asian Law alumna and strong strategic thinker. The wider faculty was, on the whole, well disposed toward a moderate internationalization of the student body. Most importantly, the JD students were bright, motivated, curious about the world, and often able to mobilize knowledge and experience from prior degrees and/or professional experience in Asia.

The decade began, however, with some severe damage to scholarly capacity. The law school community had suffered a shock in 2000 by

---

[48] *See also*, The East Asian Law Department at the Univ. of Washington School of Law, Marian Gould Gallagher Law Library, FCIL NEWSLETTER 26(2), at 3, 7 (Feb. 2012), *available at* http://www.aallnet.org/sections/fcil/newsletters/vol26/Feb2012.pdf (last visited Mar. 1, 2014).

[49] Their former colleague, Professor Marjorie Rombauer, was by this time retired.

losing Asian Law Program Director Professor John Haley and Japan specialist Professor Daniel Foote simultaneously. In 2002, academic star in climate and environment Dan Bodansky was headhunted away, and the premature death of international law scholar Joan M. Fitzpatrick in 2003 marked the loss of a major force for research excellence. When Professor Donald Clarke told me in 2004–2005 that he would accept an offer from rival George Washington University, it really did feel as if the Asian Law program might not recover a second time. Clarke is a phenomenally talented teacher and a scholar of great originality. His wry humor and loyal collegiality had made it possible to reimagine the Asian Law program as a Center. He was instrumental in helping the Law School hire Professor Jane Winn – who had done important early work on Taiwan – as well as two talented early career Islamic law specialists, Kristen Stilt and Clark Lombardi – the latter with an impressive potential for original research on Asia.[50]

Losing Don Clarke threw into sharp relief the vulnerable resource base of the Center. For a few faculty, it represented the perfect moment to close the store: after all, I was the only tenured faculty member left. To be sure, we enjoyed much friendship and support in kind from the Center's "affiliated" faculty, but they had other primary responsibilities within the Law School. Our adjunct faculty, Chaffee and Guinee, were a stellar teaching team, but their token honoraria meant that they were effectively volunteers. We had an accomplished administrator in Alice Krauss Stokke, and a talented academic program coordinator in Mie Murazumi (JD '01). I had redesigned the Law School's Visitor Program to produce a healthy revenue stream, which allowed us to recruit the immensely talented Dr Dana Raigrodski, later Director of the general LLM stream. We now had sizeable JD, LLM and PhD cohorts. But how to reconfigure the faculty profile was a major challenge.

The watershed came in 2006 when we confirmed the appointment of Dongsheng (Don) Zang, the first Chinese-born Asian law scholar to occupy an intellectual leadership position at a US law school. In a very real way Zang embodies serious, critical intellectual engagement with Asia that is both deep in its China-specific expertise and wide in its comparative and theoretical ambitions. We are truly fortunate to have Zang as our Asian Law Center Director in 2014. With the happy coincidence of the Law School recruiting Jonathan (Yong-sung) Kang as a contracts scholar, we also had for the first time, the capacity to anchor intellectual and institutional ties with Korea. Jon Eddy (JD '69)

---

50 Regrettably, Professor Stilt was subsequently headhunted by Northwestern University Law School in 2007.

had decided to "retire" from top-tier legal practice in order to consult on legal reform in Indonesia. A conversation about how he might combine his interests in South East Asia and law and development persuaded him that the Asian Law Center might be a supportive environment for his extraordinary energy and talent. Neither of us knew that he would be instrumental in securing the future of the Center and would succeed me very ably as Director in 2010.

We could not have made successful strategic hires without the support of the then Dean, Professor W.H. ("Joe") Knight (2001–2007). His predecessor Ron Hjorth (1995–2001) was held in the highest regard, with his crowning accomplishment being securing the (then) largest private gift to the university for a new Law School building. Knight's challenge was to build the building and then to reinvigorate a law school community that seemed to be somewhat paralyzed by the new intellectual, political and economic pressures of the moment. As one alumnus remarked dryly, the Law School was "perpetually teetering on the brink of excellence, but could never quite summon up the courage to jump".

The material reality of a new law school building magnified the expectations of the law school's stakeholders, old and new, without delivering the infusion of uncommitted funds that would have made it easier to respond to these. Having come from Iowa, which had a vibrant program of international and comparative law, and with personal experience of rule of law reform, Knight had a strong appreciation of international stakeholders and saw the need to innovate, understanding that not every experiment would succeed. Although many will remember this as being, in many ways, a turbulent and financially difficult period for the School, Knight's support of the Asian Law Center was unwavering. By 2007 we had the capacity for the scholarly research and the resources to provide the teaching quality we had longed for. Then the financial crisis hit, just as competition in the American law school market was intensifying. Though we had enjoyed a first-mover advantage in Asian and comparative law for decades, we were now in a maturing LLM market where all the top-tier schools were recruiting in Asia and where the *US News and World Report* rankings were dictating applicant choice. This was not a good situation for an underfunded State law school that was bouncing around the rankings in the mid-20s and 30s. Knight's successor, Acting Dean Greg Hicks, filled the position with great integrity and moderation, and the eventual recruitment of an experienced and professional leader in Dean Kellye Testy was a breakthrough moment. Nonetheless four administrations in ten years, while not unusual for law schools, did not help sustain forward momentum.

Dick Kummert used to describe UW as a "plain brown pipe stem" law school. This was also code for a university budget system in which our tuition income passed directly to the university; we received an annual operating grant and oversaw an independent but negligible endowment, and thus of necessity practiced a culture of frugality. At the program or Center level we had absolutely no funds for student recruitment, no student scholarships, and no cash to advertise our LLM program. I had inherited a five-figure Asian Law "rainy day" fund from John Haley, and Kummert was both understanding and creative in helping me to invest that in ways that would grow the Center. Loyal alumni had contributed steadily, in small increments, to our Dan Fenno Henderson professorship fund and to the Law School Foundation but it was clear that, absent a major shift (or a major gift), in the medium term we would struggle to pay our adjuncts, contribute to the mounting costs of the library's East Asian collection, or cover the travel costs to meet with alumni in Asia. It seemed premature to ask alumni for significant funding before we had reestablished regular contact with them, and before we had any significant institutional achievements to showcase.

I worried about how to retain our talented pre-tenure colleagues when there were no tangible rewards for the extra work involved in researching in foreign languages, undertaking fieldwork in Asia, mentoring international students, or supervising our (now well-established) PhD cohort. Faculty salaries at private and East Coast law schools had ballooned, but at UW we had long relied on "the Rainier factor" to attract new faculty – people who because of family ties to the region or enthusiasm for a Pacific Northwest lifestyle would overlook the low starting salaries and prohibitive housing prices. There was a yawning gap between our institutional vision and the financial means for achieving it.

Against this background I took the bold and still-controversial step of submitting a tender to the US Department of State to partner with Kabul University Faculty of Politics and Law in the delivery of an LLM program for Afghan faculty. I fully expected that we would lose out to a more prestigious school, possibly Harvard or George Washington (not least of all because our collective experience of carrying out law reform projects in Asia led us to critique the design that the State Department was proposing). But the process itself offered an opportunity to craft a narrative about our capacities as scholar-practitioners of law and development in Asia. It allowed us to learn the university's and the State Department's procurement processes – initially costly and complex work, but something that Alice Krauss Stokke quickly became an unparalleled expert in. It allowed us to think about what we might accomplish if we had more scale and reach – and if we could transcend the perceived distance between Washington DC and Seattle, Washington.

It helped enormously that UW Law colleague Professor Anita Ramasastry had earlier introduced me to her contacts at USAID and had recommended me for some smaller project work in Eurasia that eventually blossomed into some mid-range research and consulting work in Indonesia and Vietnam carried out through the Asian Law Center. Success in those small projects paved the way for a credible claim to expertise in Islamic law and complex plural legal systems, practical experience in delivering programs in-country, and decades of refining LLM education for lawyers from developing Asia. To our surprise – and to the shock of our law school colleagues – we were successful. We had secured the first in what would become a series of competitively multi-million dollar federal grants for research, teaching and technical assistance. As well as giving us an entrée to new intellectual fields and opportunities for applied research and innovative teaching, those grants directly and indirectly funded salaries, research travel and administrative costs for a significant number of faculty and staff within the Law School, including the Asian Law Center. This in turn made possible post-2010 institutional expansion – of opportunities for the Center's professional staff, of LLM programs, and of the PhD program.

For me the measure of an institution's value is never its absolute size, but whether it delivers on its self-identified goals: whether it satisfies – for the most part – the social license demands of its many stakeholders (and by doing so fulfills a value proposition for them). The critical question is whether it has the human capacity and the dynamic capabilities to respond nimbly and imaginatively to new circumstances. To do this requires regular infusions of energy and fresh analysis. Henderson and Haley had long and distinguished tenures directing Asian law at the Law School, but in my career building and directing self-sustaining university centers, I had observed leaders who occupied their positions for too long and became impediments to necessary adjustment and change. One way to avoid this is to recruit well – surround yourself with people of extraordinary talent and make yourself dispensable. After declining many approaches, I unexpectedly received the one invitation that I could not refuse – to take up a leadership position at the Australian National University.

My affection for the students, faculty, staff and alumni of the Asian Law Center and for my UW colleagues is undiminished. My ambition, however, is that they will revisit, critique, strengthen – and also dismantle – my strategic choices of the last decade. They cannot do otherwise, because if we can predict anything it is that energy and nimble innovation will be key to navigating the next 50 years.

1.3 The Asian Law Center: An evolution

Jon Eddy[1]

What role can or should a center for the comparative study of Asian legal systems play in the present day? More than 50 years ago, the University of Washington School of Law became a leader in establishing such studies. An initial Japanese law program quickly expanded to include other corners of Northeast Asia and in time areas well beyond.[2] In this short chapter, I wish to examine the evolution of the Asian Law Center as it may shed light upon the contributions such a center can make to legal scholarship as the world becomes increasingly globalized.

In January 2010, I was asked to step in as Director of the Asian Law Center. It was a period of great stress, for American higher education, the University of Washington, the School of Law, and particularly for the Asian Law Center. On the positive side, the Center was nearing its 50th anniversary, an accomplishment in a world when centers often come and go in a single budget cycle. The Center's founding Director, Dan Fenno Henderson, and his illustrious successor, John O. Haley, played seminal roles in defining the study of the Japanese legal system.[3]

1 Professor of Law, Director, ALC (January 2010–June 2013).

2 As early as 1967, work was underway on a Chinese-English legal dictionary under the guidance of Prof. Philip Bilancia. The addition of Prof. Donald C. Clarke as a specialist in China gave further impetus. By 1974, the program included a PhD degree track, with the first PhD being awarded in that year to Chan Jin Kim of South Korea, who went on to play a key role in that country's phenomenal economic transformation.

3 The mention of these two figures should not obscure another very important fact that contributed to the early vitality of the program: the deep involvement of many 'non-Asian law' faculty in the program. Notably, these included Professors Warren Shattuck, Marjorie Rombauer, Linda Hume, Richard Kummert, and Ron Hjorth. As a young JD student, I enrolled in a number of the comparative courses taught by faculty associated with the program.

My immediate predecessor, Veronica Taylor,[4] had added promising young faculty members, and continued to widen the geographic scope of the Center beyond Northeast Asia.[5] Notably, in a time of very constrained resources, she had successfully brought significant federal grant funds to the Center, a development which has continued to grow in strength.[6] The Center stood upon a solid foundation of scholarship and had graduates who had become leading academics, government officials and business leaders throughout East Asia.

But the Center unquestionably faced challenges. The Center's very success had led it to acquire numerous responsibilities. By 2010, it was responsible for no fewer than four LLM programs, a PhD program, and oversight and/or implementation of multiple grants and gifts.[7] This growth, and the concomitant proliferation of interests and goals, resulted in a two-pronged line of critique, which I immediately encountered as the new representative of the Center. According to one analysis, the Center had 'lost its focus'. Originally conceived as a program for comparative study of the Japanese legal system and US–Japan legal relations, its reach now extended as far afield as Southeast and Central Asia. Shouldn't the Center return to its original base: Japanese legal studies, or at least, the study of legal systems of Northeast Asia alone?

At the same time, from the 1990s onward, 'globalization' was a word upon everyone's lips. So a counter-narrative ran as follows: why study Asian law? Don't we live in a globalized (or at least globalizing) world?

---

4 Taylor was Professor Haley's immediate successor.

5 At the time of Taylor's inauguration, the Center already had ties and graduates in both Indonesia and Thailand; Taylor considerably deepened these relationships and also extended activities for the first time to Central and Western Asia.

6 To date, the ALC has secured federal grants in excess of $20 million, funding activities through 2017. The Center also has had administrative responsibility for executing activities funded by gifts from various private sources.

7 LLM tracks included the traditional Asian and Comparative Law track, a track in Global Business Law, the previously independent track in Sustainable International Development created by Professor Roy Prosterman, and a General (personally customizable) track. Grants included State Department projects in China and Afghanistan, and a USAID-funded project in Indonesia; gift-funded activities included fostering academic relations in China and India in the field of Intellectual Property, and the Cape Town Convention Academic Project (studying many aspects of the 2001 Cape Town Convention on International Interests in Mobile Equipment).

Asia is passé; a contemporary center ought by definition to be a Center for Global Legal Studies.

Answering these critiques was not a purely conceptual or academic matter. The ability to articulate a strong case for the continued relevance of an Asian Law Center and chart a course forward would dictate whether the Center did indeed continue forward. The Center faced challenges from within key constituencies: the University, the Law School and its broader faculty, graduates – who often held strong opinions in this area – based on both their experiences as students and their subsequent professional careers; and not least, students and potential students, who would (or would not) enroll in the programs and share their views with others.

I. WHY NOT JUST A CENTER FOR JAPANESE LEGAL STUDIES?

The Asian Law Center owed its strong foundation to a visionary group, who saw the looming importance of the US–Japan relationship, and moved early to respond to its implications. Looking backwards from 1965, one sees a world in which the United States gave primacy to North Atlantic matters, whether in investment, trade or security policy. But if one looked forward, Japan was emerging as a power in Asia and beyond. Japan was leading a growth in trans-Pacific trade that would soon diminish the traditional primacy of Europe in American thinking and orientation. Although these trends would only become clear in the popular consciousness some years later, the Japanese Law Program (to become the Asian Law Center) was premised upon them.

Excluding Japan, in 1965 per capita income levels across Asia were extremely low. Countries that are now high and high-middle income countries were impoverished (e.g. Korea and Thailand). This was a world in which US–Japanese economic relations were of rapidly growing importance, but also one in which Japan stood out as the sole rising economy in East Asia. A program focused on developing a generation of scholars, practitioners and officials who had a deep comparative understanding of the US and Japanese legal systems, and the ability to compare existing institutions and create new institutions and transaction forms, made eminent good sense.

From an early date, the uniqueness of the University of Washington's Japanese Law Program and the strength of its faculty[8] enabled the

---

8 *See* notes 2 and 3 *supra*.

program to draw promising Asian students from beyond Japan. In short order, the program had strong candidates enrolled from (and returning to take meaningful roles in) Korea, Taiwan, China and beyond into Southeast Asia. In time, as the economies of the Asian Tigers advanced, Japan no longer stood alone pre-eminent in Asia. Throughout this period, the Asian Law Center evolved in tandem with economic and political developments in Asia. Usually, it moved somewhat in advance of events, due both to expertise within the Center, and its growing reputation in East Asia.

By 2010, the continued growth of the Asian Tigers led to conditions that stood in sharp contrast to the years when the center was founded. As suggested, the importance of trans-Pacific trade and investment had continued, accelerated and become the major engine of world economic growth. But beyond this important trans-Pacific trade, a further telling trend emerged: the growth of intra-Asian trade and investment.[9]

In recent times, Japan and South Korea have been major investors in Indonesia, Thailand and Central Asia; more lately, China has joined in this trend. A quick review of practice brochures from major law firms in Seoul and Tokyo would confirm this pattern. The same considerations that in 1960 led to the creation of a center focused on Japan alone would have a different application 50 years later. A widening of the ambit of the Asian Law Center's areas of interest and expertise to include Southeast and Central Asia does no more than reflect the altered economic and political geography of East Asia.

To 'focus on Japan' thus has a different meaning in 2010 than in 1960, because Japan itself has a different outward orientation, as does Northeast Asia generally. Additionally, just as trade and investment patterns have shifted, so too have patterns of development aid. South Korea offers a clear example: in 1960 it was a poor, agricultural country and a major aid recipient; at present, Korea is one of the world's wealthiest and most dynamic economies, and exports technical legal expertise to Southeast and Central Asia.[10]

This line of argument should not be stretched too far. In particular, the spectacular rise of China in the past 25 years has led some to adopt

---

[9] In 2008, intra-Asian trade topped 50% of total Asian trade, versus trade with NAFTA countries (20.7%) and the EU (14.2%); *see* Paul Gruenwald & Masahiro Hori, "Intra-regional Trade Key to Asia's Export Boom", *available at* http://www.imf.org/external/pubs/ft/survey/so/2008/car02608a.htm (last visited Aug. 31, 2013).

[10] Korea's Korean Legislative Research Institute provides a clear example; *see* the organization's website at http://www.klri.re.kr/eng/category/main.do (last visited Aug. 31, 2013).

a dismissive attitude toward Japan. This overlooks the fact that Japan remains a wealthy country, with enormous stocks of capital (financial, managerial and technological), and that most prognostications place Japan (in the worst case analysis) as no less than the world's fourth-largest economy through 2050. A great deal of uncertainty remains about the economic, strategic and political configuration of East Asia over the next 50 years, and in no wise would it make sense to neglect the major role that Japan is likely to continue to play.[11] Most particularly, the Asian Law Center at the University of Washington has its own enormous stock of intellectual capital in this area; while it has made sense to extend the Asian Law Center's interest beyond Japan (as Japan has itself re-prioritized its focus), it also makes sense to capitalize on prior attainments – which sensibly means maintaining a priority for Northeast Asian concerns (which, as just noted, may include Northeast Asian concerns in Southeast or Central Asia). *Inter alia*, supporting a focus which is broader than that of 1960 is a matter of retaining relevance to Northeast Asia.

II. WHY NOT BECOME A CENTER FOR GLOBAL LEGAL STUDIES?

An entirely different line of analysis questions the utility of an Asian Law Center in an age of globalization. Why restrict to a single region the study of systems, of problems, or of institutional responses to problems? Major problems today such as climate change and related environmental issues pose significant concerns both for international law and for most municipal legal systems. Are they not sufficiently global in nature that they must inevitably be studied from a 'global' perspective? No doubt there is some validity to such thinking, but it risks obscuring a deeper truth.

In the aftermath of World War II, the United States led a coalition of powers to establish the basic structures for a post-war international order. Notably these included the United Nations, the International Monetary Fund and World Bank, and the (long-delayed) World Trade

---

[11] *See* ROBERT KAGAN, THE RETURN OF HISTORY AND THE END OF DREAMS 37 (New York, 2008): "It is easy to forget, as everyone focuses on China's rise as a great power, that Japan is a great power, too. Its economy remains the second largest in the world [2008], a remarkable fact given its relatively small population, smaller territory, and lack of natural resources. … Japan is not only a great power, but increasingly displays great power ambitions."

Organization. Notwithstanding Cold War rivalries, the Soviet Union never competed effectively with the West in establishing the institutions that shaped developments from 1945 onward. However, from 1990 on, a series of events began to challenge those institutions and the American agenda: the collapse of the Soviet Union, the Iraq wars, the acceleration of the rise of China, the events of 9/11, and finally the Western financial crisis of 2008. Although at first these events seemed to foreshadow a unipolar world with a single hyperpower,[12] by 2010 a different picture was emerging.

In the post-2008 new world order, the single most evident fact is the reassertion of Asia's role in the world. From both East and West, a new spirit, self-confidence and independence of thought has been recognized.[13] Along with this confidence has come a willingness to forge ways forward without reliance on Western models or values;[14] this in turn, has promoted an extremely dynamic debate and interchange of ideas internal to Asia. What does this mean for a North American-based Asian Law Center?

III. ENVISIONING THE ASIAN LAW CENTER

With its rich history of scholarship regarding the legal systems of Northeast Asia, the Asian Law Center is superbly positioned to capitalize on its past as it charts a future that reflects the remarkable changes which have transpired in Asia since the Center's early years. There are three 'layers' of scholarly inquiry that call out for the deployment of the Center's resources. The first of these builds on the Center's core competency: searching inquiry and analysis of Northeastern Asian legal systems from both a historic and social perspective; at the present time, this capacity has been built out,

---

[12] Most famously, see FRANCIS FUKUYAMA, THE END OF HISTORY AND THE LAST MAN (New York, 1992).

[13] *See, e.g.*, KISHORE MAHBUBANI, THE NEW ASIAN HEMISPHERE (New York, 2008); PATRICK SMITH, SOMEONE ELSE'S CENTURY: EAST AND WEST IN A POST-WESTERN WORLD (New York, 2010).

[14] KLRI, the Korean Legislative Research Institute, again provides a good example. KLRI quite self-consciously promotes 'the Korean way' to development. Other examples would include CALE, Nagoya University's Center for Asian Legal Exchanges, or the Center for Asian Legal Studies at the National University of Singapore. Indeed, the proliferation of exchanges, centers, and other mechanisms for networking and sharing ideas and initiatives has been so pronounced in recent years that only time and space prevent a very long catalog.

particularly through the Center's many alumni, into corresponding abilities in parts of Southeast Asia, particularly Indonesia and Thailand. A second 'layer' of inquiry recognizes the inflection in the orientation of Northeast Asia, and thus focuses on intra-Asian issues, particularly the dynamic between Northeast and Southeast Asia. As already noted, these relationships are multi-faceted: they comprise trade and investment, but also issues of economic and legal development, and such challenging issues as labor, social safety nets, and environment. Increasingly, it is Northeast Asian experiences and institutions that are examined for models. A final 'layer' of inquiry develops 'Asian' perspectives on 'global' issues.

First and foremost, the Asian Law Center must remain a major North American center for scholarship on the legal systems of East Asia. Importantly, this would comprise both Northeast and Southeast Asia, and success in this endeavor maintains the foundation for any wider aspirations of the Center. This strategy is also quite consistent with the analysis at the outset of this chapter. The dynamic economies of China and South Korea already have significant trade, investment and strategic interests beyond Southeast Asia in South, Central and even Western Asia. To give attention to developments in these regions does not represent in any sense an abandonment of Northeast Asia or a diminution of interest in that region; rather, it accurately reflects the dynamic changes which have occurred in Asia, not least in the nature of the role played by Northeast Asia in the larger terrain. As underlying trends in economic activity indicate, Northeast Asia had undergone its own profound reorientation: in this new world, to focus bilaterally on US–Northeast Asian relations, rather than place Northeast Asia within its broader Asian context, would be retrospective.

To adequately perform its role, the Center will need to pursue aggressively additional partnerships with major academic and government institutions in East Asia and seek to participate where possible as a North American member of Asian networks. There is reason to believe that many Asian networks would be open to this role for the Center: the Center enjoys not only a historic legacy, but is valued as a 'clearinghouse' for exchange of variant Asian viewpoints. Unless a serious and sustained effort is made to become a part of this intra-Asian debate (for instance, by joining or co-sponsoring activities with these new Asian networks), there is a risk that a North American center will become increasingly marginalized.

This observation also speaks to the 'third layer' of potential Center interests: special expertise regarding 'Asian' perspectives on 'global' issues, and it rebuts directly the critique that the Asian Law Center should be 'nothing but global'. During the past 50 years, American interests and values predominated in setting the international agenda and the terms of dialogue. In what likely will strike many Americans as a stark contrast, the international agenda for the next 50 years will per force be strongly influenced by Asian views. *Thus, if one wishes to be regarded as an informed and useful participant in a global dialogue, it will increasingly be necessary to be comfortable and conversant with the Asian aspects of that dialogue.* Those who speak to 'the global' solely from a North American perspective will simply be viewed as parochial. And increasingly, Asians and others will enjoy the prerogative of ignoring such uninformed, parochial views. Globalization, occurring in the context of a renascent Asia, makes the case *for*, rather than the case *against*, an Asian Law Center.

IV. A BRIGHT FUTURE

Legal education across North America (and to a significant extent globally) is strongly influenced at present by three major trends: 1) the increasingly transnational (and therefore also comparative) nature of legal issues; 2) the increasingly inter-disciplinary nature of much legal problem-solving; and 3) the increasing pressure for skills-trained lawyers, who can analyze and solve problems, mediate disputes and manage negotiations and projects, not just recite legal doctrine. The Asian Law Center, through its activities and interests, is supportive of each of these trends and should benefit from them.

As noted at the outset, in its early years, the Asian Center and its personnel not only substantially defined the field of Asian Law studies, but in doing so also altered significantly the focus and methods of American comparative law research. Again, in the early years of the Center, this strong tradition placed the University of Washington well ahead of its peers in recognizing this important aspect of legal education. While a variety of factors make it challenging to sustain the Center's 'early mover' advantage,[15] it is nevertheless highly

---

[15] As already noted, one of the major strengths of the early years of the Center was the extent to which it integrated participation by a broad group of general faculty; this has more recently proven a challenge. No doubt this is in part due to the increased career pressures on faculty. As the trend of both the profession and the academy favors transnational insights, it may be hoped that this situation will improve. Other factors acting upon legal education generally also complicate matters: for instance, rising tuition rates and stagnating domestic

desirable that the comparative law resources of the Asian Law Center be maintained and strengthened, and serve the entire law school community, particularly those within the JD program.[16]

The Asian Law Center also stands well positioned to benefit from increased attention to interdisciplinary studies. This is due not only to the presence of a number of other LLM programs that allow shared resources and varied perspectives, but even more to the extremely high standing of the University as a whole, and the strength of the University and the regional community in a number of fields such as medicine, science and technology.[17]

---

job markets, which place great pressures on students to be satisfied with the 'least necessary amount' of education, rather than the best education. The 'curricular bloat' of the modern law school, where coverage has been substituted for analysis, forces intense intramural competition between different 'subject matter' segments of any given faculty.

[16] In recognition of this needed component of JD education, the faculty in 2009 introduced a required first-year course in Comparative and International Law (an innovation that had earlier been made at the Harvard Law School). Many feel that a better solution might be to introduce a comparative and/or international aspect into most courses. Although discussion on the best means of execution continues, there seems to be agreement throughout the community of legal educators that such perspectives are now fundamental for a well-rounded legal education. Needless to say, the Asian Law Center and its programs and associated faculty provide the nearest-at-hand resource base for these efforts, however executed.

[17] The tradition of the Asian Law Center has never been narrowly doctrinal; it already builds upon a strong view of law in context, and law as a product of variant forces. This fits easily into blending law, technology, economics and historical/cultural forces in a manner that allows students to see law in a holistic way, and prepares them to utilize legal knowledge and skills most effectively in practical settings. During the past two years, the Center has spun off various activities (for instance, the Sustainable International Development track). But in doing so, the Center has not lost relevance to those activities. On the contrary, the various LLM tracks at the School of Law might be viewed in a Venn diagram of partially overlapping circles. A single course offering (dealing with patent rights in new medicines) might support, and draw students from, the Asian and Comparative Law track, the JD program, Intellectual Property, Global Health Law, and Sustainable International Development. To give different LLM tracks independence to shape curriculum does not mean, and does not likely result in, a series of disconnected courses. On the contrary, the success of all the Law School's programs depends heavily in the future on the ability to make courses 'work across' curricular platforms. In this Venn diagram conception of the Law School's programs, different programs interact with each other in different areas. The restructurings that have occurred in the Law School's graduate programs

Finally, the Asian Law Center has pioneered in the introduction of experiential learning into graduate programs and the development of innovative courses and teaching methodologies. Much of this has been made possible by grant funding that was used to spur the development of new approaches and new materials. Although this only affects a minority of LLM students at present (and invariably, and desirably, in mixed classes with JD students), every effort should be made to broaden this exposure to include most LLM students.

The Asian Law Center enters its second 50 years poised for great accomplishments. It has been blessed with a solid half-century of accomplishments. It has largely completed a process of restructuring that will allow it to exploit its strengths in the coming years. It has a new, young Director in the Center's best traditions of scholarship, whose research interests also fit well with further development of inter-disciplinary work. Visits by former Director John Haley and the return to the faculty of Professor Dan Foote will add to the intellectual ferment of the Center as it presses its new agenda forward. There are many reasons to believe that, indeed, the best is yet to come.

---

thus should offer the opportunity to strengthen considerably inter-disciplinary approaches.

PART II

The role of comparative law in legal innovations

2.1 Comparison of law, transfer of legal concepts, and creation of a legal design: The case of Japan

Harald Baum

I. THE LONG JOURNEY

Some may find it surprising to realize that the modern civil laws of Japan – and in turn, those of Korea and Taiwan – are to a significant degree shaped by rules, to cite a provocative phrase by William Ewald, "… that were first struck upon by a leisured class of slave-holding Italian aristocrats – men who pursued law as a hobby, and who have been dead for nearly two thousand years."[1]

The enduring persistence of Roman legal concepts, their long journey through time, and their crossing of national borders and even continents are indeed remarkable. But then "… [Roman law] constitutes, in its ensemble, such a high level of cultural achievement that it will always retain its character as a model for the rational solution of legal conflicts."[2]

A society's reception of foreign laws can have different triggers. A foreign legal order may be forced upon a country as a consequence of military occupation and ensuing colonization. Or jurists may adapt a specific law simply because of its high prestige and superior quality that competing legal regimes lack at a given point in time. On the other hand, reception may be based on a comprehensive comparison of law that leads to the choice of selected legal rules, possibly in the form of a new bundling of varying rules of different origins into a new code. This latter case is different from the first two because comparative law

---

[1] William Ewald, *Comparative Jurisprudence (II): The Logic of Legal Transplants*, 43 AM. J. COMP. L. 489, 490 (1995).

[2] REINHARD ZIMMERMANN, THE LAW OF OBLIGATIONS. ROMAN FOUNDATIONS OF THE CIVILIAN TRADITION.

obviously plays a crucial role in shaping the legal innovation for the adopting state.

The voyage of Roman legal concepts through time came in all three forms depending on the historical situation. The classical period of Roman law, when its characteristic features developed, was roughly the time shortly prior to the end of BC and the first two centuries AD.[3] It spread as the conqueror's law along with the military power of the Roman Empire over much of Europe (and around the Mediterranean), but when the Romans retreated the old chthonic laws revived.[4]

In the sixth century AD, the Byzantine emperor Justinian had the *Corpus Juris Civilis* assembled, a massive piece of legislation that is regarded as the "most influential document for European legal culture."[5] This work was part of Justinian's comprehensive program to restore the lost might of the former Roman (now Christian) Empire. The main part of the Corpus Juris is the Digest. Completed in AD 530–533, it is an enormous compilation of excerpts from writings about classical Roman law covering some 700 years of legal development.[6] However, with its fortunes tied to the waning might of the Byzantine Empire, Roman law was again all but forgotten during the "dark ages" in Western Europe.

Its renaissance started in the Italian town of Bologna in the late eleventh century when Roman law, as preserved in the Digest, was rediscovered and again became the subject of academic education at the city's university. From there it spread quickly to other Italian universities, later to France and Spain, and then gradually to other parts of Europe in a complex historical process of reception spanning centuries.[7] This so-called *ius commune* (common law) "permeated the relevant European legal systems via the universities."[8] It competed with particular local

---

[3] For a concise overview, see Reinhard Zimmermann, *Roman Law*, in THE MAX PLANCK ENCYCLOPEDIA OF COMPARATIVE LAW (Jürgen Basedow, Klaus J. Hopt, & Reinhard Zimmermann with Andreas Stier ed., 2012) 1487–91.

[4] H. PATRICK GLENN, LEGAL TRADITIONS OF THE WORLD 139 (4th ed. 2010).

[5] Reinhard Zimmermann, *Corpus Juris Civilis*, in THE MAX PLANCK ENCYCLOPEDIA OF COMPARATIVE LAW, *supra* note 3, at 415.

[6] For a brief authoritative analysis, see Zimmermann, *supra* note 5, at 415-18; for a comprehensive analysis, see Zimmerman, supra note 2.

[7] The widespread reception of Roman law is the subject of the famous treatise by ALAN WATSON, LEGAL TRANSPLANTS. AN APPROACH TO COMPARATIVE LAW (2nd ed., 1993); see also Glenn, *supra* note 4, at 140–42.

[8] Gebhard Rehm, *Reception*, in THE MAX PLANCK ENCYCLOPEDIA OF COMPARATIVE LAW, *supra* note 3, at 1415, 1417; for an overview of these developments, see Nils Jansen, *Ius Commune*, in THE MAX PLANCK ENCLOPEDIA OF COMPARATIVE LAW, *supra* note 3, at 1006–10.

(written or customary) laws but often proved superior because of its high level of abstraction, its logical order, and its loftier prestige.[9] In the course of its reception, Roman law naturally adapted and evolved into what was called its "modern use" (*usus modernus*).[10] Though in widely varying ways and intensities, Roman law was applied in principle in most of Europe to a significant degree.

This "second life" of Roman law ended in the nineteenth century with the rise of national codifications in continental Europe.[11] The two codifications that would become most internationally influential, especially in Japan, were the French *Code civil* of 1804 and later on the German Civil Code, the *Bürgerliches Gesetzbuch* (*BGB*) of 1900. Though the *ius commune* was no longer applied directly, the concepts of Roman law were clearly instrumental in conceiving these (and other) codices and can easily be traced back.[12] And as will be shown later in greater detail, it was from there that the legal rules originating in Roman law started their travel as "legal transplants" to Japan and elsewhere in Asia (see *infra* at III.) – an intermediate stop on a journey that had started almost two millennia before.

II. LEGAL RECEPTION, LEGAL CULTURE, AND LEGAL "TRANSPLANTS" OR "IRRITANTS"

The phenomenon of "legal transplants," a phrase more or less simultaneously brought into use by the legal historian Alan Watson[13] and the comparatist Otto Kahn-Freund[14] is, of course, by no means restricted to the (archetypical) comprehensive reception of Roman law. A modern example is the widespread reception in industrial countries of selected legal concepts in company law and securities regulation originating

---

9 Also, the Roman rules might have possibly been the only ones the jurists of that time really knew; *see* Rodolfo Sacco, *Legal Formats: A Dynamic Approach to Comparative Law*, 39 AM. J. COMP. L. 1, 2 (1991).

10 See Klaus Luig, *Usus Modernus*, in THE MAX PLANCK ENCYCLOPEDIA OF COMPARATIVE LAW, *supra* note 3, at 1755–58.

11 Zimmermann, *supra* note 3, at 1490.

12 See Zimmermann, *supra* note 3, at 1490; for a comprehensive analysis, see ZIMMERMAN, *supra* note 2; Zimmerman, *Europa und das römische Recht* [Europe and the Roman Law], 202 ARCHIV FÜR DIE CIVILISTISCHE PRAXIS 243–316 (2002).

13 WATSON, note 7 (1st ed. 1974).

14 See Otto Kahn-Freund, *On Uses and Misuses of Comparative Law*, 37 MOD. L. REV. 1–27 (1974).

from the US since the 1980/90s. The ubiquitous terms "corporate governance," "business judgment rule," and "insider trading" – to name but three – have gained an almost universal acceptance and usage and can as easily be found as *termini technici* in standard Japanese legal texts of 2013 as in Dutch or German ones.[15]

These – at least at first sight – presumably successful legal transfers of old and new notwithstanding, it is still a hotly disputed subject whether a reception of foreign legal institutions is actually feasible in a sensible way.[16] Some analysts, such as Alan Watson, regard "borrowing ... [as] the most fruitful source of legal change,"[17] and some see legal borrowing as a movement toward efficiency in the context of legal competition.[18] Others are more skeptical, Pierre Legrand, for example, flatly denies the possibility of any meaningful legal transfer.[19] In the view of cultural comparatists, law can only be understood within the culture it belongs to; any interpretation within a different cultural

---

[15] For the reception in Japan, see Hideki Kanda & Curtis Milhaupt, *Re-examining Legal Transplants: The Director's Fiduciary Duty in Japanese Corporate Law*, 51 AM. J. COMP. L. 887 (2003); Kenjirō Egashira, *The Influence of American Law in the Field of Commercial Law in the Post-World War II Era*, 26 LAW IN JAPAN 50 (2000); for Germany see JAN VON HEIN, DIE REZEPTION US-AMERIKANISCHEN GESELLSCHAFTSRECHTS IN DEUTSCHLAND [Reception of US Company Law in Germany] (2008).

[16] For an authoritative overview on the discussion, see Gebhard Rehm, *Rechtstransplantate als Instrument der Rechtsreform und transformation* [Legal Transplants as an Instrument of Legal Reform and Transformation], 72 THE RABEL J. COMP. & INT'L L. (2008); see also Gunter Teubner, *Legal Irritants: Good Faith in British Law or How Unifying Law Ends Up in New Divergences*, 61 MOD. L. REV. 11, 14–17 (1998); Michele Graziadei, *Comparative Law as the Study of Transplants and Receptions*, in THE OXFORD HANDBOOK OF COMPARATIVE LAW 441–75 (Matthias Reimann & Reinhard Zimmermann eds., 2006); Roger Cotterrell, *Comparative Law and Legal Culture*, in THE OXFORD HANDBOOK OF COMPARATIVE LAW, *supra*, at 709–37.

[17] Alan Watson, *Aspects of Reception of Law*, 44 AM. J. COMP. L. 335 (1996); *see also* WATSON *supra* note 7, at 95; similar already ROSCOE POUND, THE FORMATIVE AREA OF AMERICAN LAW 94 (1938): "History of a system of Law is largely a history of borrowings of legal materials from other legal systems"; for a nuanced discussion of Watson's views, see Ewald, *supra* note 1; *see* also Roger Cotterrell, *Is There a Logic of Legal Transplants?*, in ADAPTING LEGAL CULTURES 71–92 (David Nelken & Johannes Feest eds., 2001).

[18] See Ugo Mattei, *Efficiency in Legal Transplants: An Essay in Comparative Law and Economics*, 14 INT'L REV. L. & ECON. 3 (1994).

[19] *Cf.* Pierre Legrand, *What "Legal Transplants"?*, in ADAPTING LEGAL CULTURES, *supra* note 17, at 55, 57: see also Pierre Legrand, *European Legal Systems Are Not Converging*, 45 INT'L & COMP. L.Q. 52, 57 (1996).

context leads automatically to a different meaning.[20] According to this viewpoint, a legal transplant is necessarily read in a different cultural environment, so it amounts to no more than a "meaningless form of words" because the actual meaning of the rules does not survive the journey to a different legal culture.[21]

This kind of principled skepticism against the possibility of legal transfers can be traced back more than 200 years to the first comparative lawyer, Charles de Secondat Montesquieu, who saw any given law as defined by a mix of highly individualistic factors – such as climate, geography, culture, religion, politics, and economics – that prevail in the pertinent country.[22] Thus, in his view it would be "*un grand hazard*" to try to implement foreign legal rules elsewhere.[23] But as Otto Kahn-Freund has already pointed out, external environmental and cultural factors have lost most of their relevance as obstacles against the migration of legal ideas in today's modern urbanized and globalized societies, whereas political factors have gained importance.[24] Different areas of law show a varying adaptability to legal transplants. For example, fewer obstacles will exist in contract law and economic law in general than in family law.[25] Japan's experience in drafting her Civil Code is a telling example.[26] However, in any case, using comparison of law with the purpose of transferring a legal rule requires not only the knowledge of that foreign law but also a careful investigation and understanding of its social and political context.[27]

The primary question – whether a meaningful transfer is prohibited by the embeddedness of legal rules mirroring their legal culture and the perceived dominance of external factors on shaping these rules –

---

20 See the analysis by Cotterrell, *supra* note 16, at 712.

21 Pierre Legrand, *The Impossibility of Legal Transplants*, 4 Maastricht J. Eur. Comp. L. 111, 120 (1997).

22 Charles de Secondat Montesquieu, *Livre I, Chap. 3: Des lois positive*, in De l'Esprit des lois (Edition Galimard 1951) (1748).

23 *Id.*, at 237.

24 Kahn-Freund, *supra* note 14, at 8–9; see also Cotterrell, supra note 16, at 721–26.

25 Kahn-Freund, *supra* note 14, at 27; but see Graziadei, *supra* note 16, at 472, who regards this search for consistency and rationality as a potential distortion of reality.

26 See *infra* at Part III ii.

27 Kahn-Freund, *supra* note 14, at 27; Rehm, *supra* note 16, at 31; accord Vivian Grosswald Curran, *Cultural Immersion, Differences and Categories in U.S. Comparative Law*, 46 Am. J. Comp. L. 43, 85; Bernhard Grossfeld, Dreaming Law: Comparative Legal Semiotics 254–56 (2010).

loses some of its pointedness when one acknowledges that legal rules and their interpretation are changing in the course of time even *within* a given legal order. Legal institutions are basically responsive to a changing environment without necessarily losing their characteristics. In most cases, transferring a legal rule will, of course, lead to adaptations in the recipient legal system with its different institutional features. But that does not mean that a legislator (or judge) should not look to foreign legal solutions for inspiration.[28] Perhaps the metaphor "legal transplant" is misleading for a transfer of legal rules because it suggests a strict alternative between repulsion or integration. Rather, to use a famous metaphor coined by Gunther Teubner, the foreign rule may act as a "legal irritant" in the recipient legal system which "triggers a whole series of new and unexpected events. …"[29]

III. THE JAPANESE EXPERIENCE

(i) Three Different Forms of Law Reception

Historically, Japan has experienced three major receptions of law in the course of the last 1500 years that came in the different forms mentioned at the beginning.

The first was the reception of the Chinese institutions of governance and administration that included concepts of public law in the seventh century AD. By and large, this reception was arguably undertaken by Japan for the same reasons the *ius commune* became successful in Europe from the late eleventh century onward: the perceived superior quality and the high prestige of the foreign law that competing domestic legal institutions lacked.[30] Comparison of law in the actual sense of the term, as opposed to the simple knowledge of a foreign law, most probably played no role in this process.

The second reception in the late nineteenth century was initiated by external pressure but was based on one of history's most thorough comparisons of law (cf. *infra* (ii)). Here, the role of comparative law in legal innovations was most prominent. The civil laws of continental Europe were of specific comparative interest for the Japanese

28 Rehm, *supra* note 8, at 1419.

29 Teubner, *supra* note 16, at 12.

30 *Cf.* John O. Haley, Authority without Power; Law and the Japanese Paradox 19–23, 29–32 (1991).

reformers, and in this way the Roman legal concepts enshrined in these codifications became part of modern Japanese law.

The third reception came after the end of World War II when the allied forces under the leadership of the United States started what was dubbed the "democratization" of Japan. An important goal of that program was the drafting of a new constitution for Japan and a fundamental revision of the country's major laws and legal institutions along the lines of the US model. In contrast to the second reception, this reception strongly resembled an imposed one in the form of a victor's law: the Japanese legislators had no real alternative, even though formally the desired legal reforms were implemented in a legalistically "correct" way. It should be noted, however, that especially the Constitution of 1946 met with overwhelming approval among the populace from the very beginning, and it has enjoyed consistently high approval rates ever since. If anything, the Constitution seems to be an example of a highly successful legal transplant or, given the far-reaching implications it had for the rest of Japan's legal order, rather a successful "legal irritant." Yet comparison of law played no – or at best a very minor – role, with the US legal system acting as a mandatory role model.

The result is a fascinating mix of legal conceptions in modern Japanese law: the Confucian legal – or rather moral – concepts created an overlay over the chthonic law of Japan's beginnings. The modernization during Meiji Japan with the French and German legal concepts as role models in turn significantly altered the Confucian way of regulating society. After 1945, the adoption of American legal ideas replaced or reshaped many of these civil law institutions. Japan's present legal system is probably the most refined mixed legal order of all, dwarfing Louisiana, Scotland, or South Africa as the candidates usually cited.

(ii) The Comparative Basis of Japan's Modern Civil Law

After some 250 years of self-chosen isolation, Japan saw herself in the 1850s confronted with a sudden need to open up the country. Western powers, namely the US, demanded an opening of the country's harbors to foreign vessels and an integration of its economy into the international trade system. The Japanese government realized that it had no means to resist these claims and thus agreed on the opening of the country. As a consequence, it rapidly concluded a series of trade agreements with most Western industrial nations. These so-called 'unequal treaties' resulted in a severe loss of sovereignty for

Japan. Among other effects, foreign residents were granted legal extraterritoriality and were not subject to Japanese jurisdiction. Instead, a system of consular jurisdiction was introduced.[31]

One of the top priorities of the reformist Meiji government that came to power after the revolution of 1868 was to build up a modern law regime modeled on Western conceptions. Among other things, this was a prerequisite demanded by Western powers for a revision of the humiliating "unequal treaties." Under the motto *wakon yōsai* – "Japanese spirit, Western knowledge" – the reformers courageously undertook this task. It was a tall order because virtually all essential institutions of a functioning modern law-based society were missing in Japan at that time. Specifically, the separation of powers, an independent judiciary, and a legal profession with its tradition of representation of parties by attorneys in courts of law were non-existent. Also, no codified law to speak of nor collections of law based on precedents were known.[32]

To set up a modern legal system, the Meiji government sent young Japanese abroad to be educated as jurists and to gain practical experience. Again, we see a parallel to the way the *ius commune* was spread in twelfth-century Europe via the universities. Japan also invited various foreign legal advisors who were at least initially of critical importance for the drafting of laws and the setting up of judicial institutions. In this way, Japan successfully managed to create a fully functioning Western legal system within 30 years – a cultural achievement of the highest proportions.

The legal reforms in Japan were based on broad comparative foundations.[33] As very soon became clear, only the adoption of codified law was feasible for practical reasons. Thus the Japanese interests focused on the civil laws of continental Europe. Within these legal orders, first French and later German law was of primary though not exclusive interest. In the early Meiji years, mostly French jurists were

---

31 *See* RICHARD T. CHANG, THE JUSTICE OF THE WESTERN CONSULAR COURTS IN NINETEENTH CENTURY JAPAN (1984).

32 For a brief overview over the Tokugawa concept of law and the legal institutions of the pre-Meiji area see 1 DAN FENNO HENDERSON, CONCILIATION AND JAPANESE LAW; TOKUGAWA AND MODERN, 47–62 (1965); detailed materials can be found in LAW AND JUSTICE IN TOKUGAWA JAPAN (John Henry Wigmore ed., 1967–78).

33 For a comprehensive overview, see A HISTORY OF LAW IN JAPAN SINCE 1868 (Wilhelm Röhl ed., 2005); CHRISTOPH SOKOLOWSKI, DER SO GENANNTE KODIFIKATIONENSTREIT IN JAPAN [The So-called Battle for the Codification] (2010). For a classic Japanese treatise, see MASASUKE ISHIBE, HŌSEI-SHI [Legal History] (1964).

invited as advisors to Japan.[34] However, from the 1880s onward German jurists increasingly took their place.[35] The foreign advisors naturally brought their own laws with them, but most were competent enough to put the legislative work undertaken jointly with their Japanese colleagues in a broad comparative context. The latter were influenced by the legal order of the countries where they had studied – mostly in France, Germany, and the United Kingdom.

The work on a civil code had started as early as 1870 by attempting to simply translate the French *Code civil* into Japanese.[36] The Code was the most influential codification of its time and had gained international attention. The translation, however, met with many difficulties.[37] A first major problem was terminology because the Japanese language did not provide for the necessary expressions. A Japanese translation presented in 1875[38] was finally rejected as a draft for a civil code for Japan because of its exclusively French character.

The government started a new attempt to create a civil code in 1880 when it commissioned the French jurist Gustave Emile Boissonade de Fontarabie (1825–1910),[39] a former law professor at Grenoble, to draft the sections on property and contract law. The work on family law and the law of succession was entrusted to native jurists to make sure that the pertinent Japanese traditions were attended to. Although Boissonade looked at the *Code civil* for a basic orientation, his draft was nevertheless

---

[34] On the French influence, see Masao Ishimoto, *L'influence du Code civil français sur le droit civil japonais* [The Influence of the French Civil Code on Japanese Civil Law], 6 REVUE INTERNATIONALE DU DROIT COMPARÉ 744–52 (1954).

[35] PAUL-CHRISTIAN SCHENCK, DER DEUTSCHE ANTEIL AN DER GESTALTUNG DES MODERNEN JAPANISCHEN RECHTS- UND VERFASSUNGSWESENS [The German Contribution to the Making of the Modern Legal and Constitutional System of Japan] (1997); Anna Bartels-Ishikawa, *Deutsche Juristen in Japan in der Meiji-Zeit* [German Jurists in Meiji-Japan], in RECHTSTRANSFER IN JAPAN UND DEUTSCHLAND [Legal Transfer in Japan and Germany], at 3 (Harald Baum, Moritz Bälz & Karl Riesenhuber eds., 2013).

[36] For details see Ronald Frank, Hans-Peter Marutschke & Petra Schmidt, *Civil Code*, in A HISTORY OF LAW IN JAPAN SINCE 1868, *supra* note 33, at 166–329.

[37] Ken Mukai & Nobuyoshi Toshitani, *The Progress and Problems of Compiling the Civil Code in the Early Meiji Era*, 1 LAW IN JAPAN 25 (1975).

[38] FURANSU HŌRITSU-SHO: MINPŌ [French Laws: The Civil Code] (Rinshō Mitsukuri trans., 1875).

[39] *See* Yoshiyuki Noda, *Gustave Boissonade, comparatiste ignoré* [Gustave Boissonade, a Forgotten Comparatist], in 2 PROBLÈMES CONTEMPORAINS DE DROIT COMPARÉ, 235–56 (Institut Japonais de Droit Comparé Université Chuo ed., 1962).

a codification of its own.[40] Thereafter, Japanese jurists reworked and supplemented his translated proposals. The resulting legislative draft, the *Kyū-minpō* [Old Civil Code], was enacted in 1890 but never entered into force.

At more or less the same time that the Japanese government had asked Boissonade to start his work on the civil code, it commissioned the German jurist Carl Friedrich Hermann Roesler (1834–1894),[41] a former law professor at the northern German University of Rostock, to draft a commercial code.[42] Roesler had already been active in the preparatory works for the first Japanese constitution of 1889, the so-called Meiji Constitution. He presented a comprehensive draft in 1884 that included not only commercial law, but also company law, parts of insolvency law, and other areas. In order to create a truly modern codification, Roesler chose a comparative approach and combined elements of the French *Code de commerce* of 1870 with those of the German *Allgemeines Deutsches Handelsgesetzbuch* of 1861. Additionally, he took special note of the Egyptian *Code de commerce* and *Code de maritime* of 1874. On the other hand, he purposely excluded all the customary law of the Japanese merchants that he regarded as thoroughly outdated, a move that would later turn out to be politically disastrous. In form, the draft law reflected French influence; in substance, it predominantly made reference to German law. After a substantive revision by Japanese jurists, parts of the draft, later called the *Kyū-shōhō* [Old Commercial Code], went into force from 1893 until 1899.

However, like the Old Civil Code, the remaining parts of the draft fell victim to what was termed the "codification controversy" (*hōten ronsō*) that was ignited in 1889 with the publication of a fierce criticism of the drafts of the two codes.[43] Above all, its opponents criticized the neglect of Japanese customs. The dispute, which also reflected the interests of the different legal schools in Meiji Japan, became increasingly vicious

---

40 See Jean-Louis Sourioux, *L'influence de Boissonade sur le project de Code Civil Japonais à la fin du XIXème siècle* [The Influence of Boissonade on Drafting the Japanese Civil Code at the End of the 19th century], in HUNDERT JAHRE JAPANISCHES ZIVILGESETZBUCH [100 Years of Japan's Civil Code] 329–40 (Rolf Knütel & Shigeo Nishimura eds., 2004).

41 See HERMANN ROESLER: DOKUMENTE ZU SEINEM LEBEN UND WERK [Hermann Roesler: Documents Regarding His Life and Work] (Anna Bartels-Ishikawa ed., 2007).

42 For details, see Harald Baum & Eiji Takahashi, *Commercial and Corporate Law in Japan*, in A HISTORY OF LAW IN JAPAN SINCE 1868, *supra* note 33, at 330–81.

43 For a comprehensive analysis, see Sokolowski, *supra* note 33.

and emotional. A climax was the publication of a famous polemic by Yatsuka Hozumi, a well-known constitutional lawyer, in 1891.[44] The author denounced the introduction of individual rights based on the European model in the Old Civil Code as grossly contradictory to the traditional Confucian ethics and morals and called the law a "murder weapon" applied against the Japanese people. Given the general discontent with the Western influence that was increasingly regarded as foreign alienation, the government had no choice but to postpone the coming into force of both laws and to start yet another revision. To this end it set up two reform commissions in 1892 under the supervision of the prime minister and staffed exclusively with Japanese jurists.

Responsibility for the Civil Code rested with three law professors, Nobushige Hozumi, Masaaki Tomii, and Kenjirō Ume, who had studied at different European universities. The reformers orientated themselves predominantly, but by no means exclusively, on the legislative work for a German civil code, the BGB, undertaken simultaneously in Germany. Of special interest was the first draft of the BGB published in 1887, but also the second draft of 1895 was consulted. This heralded an end to the dominant French influence on Japanese civil law, though numerous French legal institutions are still embedded in the Japanese Civil Code today.

The shift toward German developments had different reasons.[45] Politically, Germany had gained in reputation in the wake of its military victory over France. In addition, the enactment of the Meiji Constitution in 1889 helped to shift the balance in favor of German law. Most importantly from a technical point of view, the nascent BGB was regarded as more modern and sophisticated than the *Code civil*, which had been created almost a century before. The complete revision of the Old Civil Code lasted from 1892 to 1898. Its aim was the creation of an original *Japanese* civil code that would be free of the deficits of the Boissonade draft without either denying its French roots or becoming a carbon copy of the German Code. In this the three reformers were successful. The amended law – and especially its sections on the law of property and the law of obligations – has been characterized as the fruit of an intense and thoughtful comparison of law, even though its formulation in fact represents more of a technical rather than a doctrinal comparative approach. Japanese traditions were taken into account as well.

---

[44] See Yatsuka Hozumi, *Minpō idete, chūkō horobu* [If the Civil Code Comes, Japanese Values Are Out], HŌGAKU SHINPŌ August 25, 1891.

[45] See Frank et al., *supra* note 36, at 182–86.

In contrast to the Old Civil Code, the new Civil Code (*Minpō)* follows the Pandectist system (thus also structurally reflecting Roman law concepts). As with the BGB, the *Minpō* is divided into five books, though the order differs slightly. It is less detailed than the BGB and contains only half as many provisions. The Civil Code is characterized by a mix of provisions; some of which are of German origin while others originate in French law. The general provisions, for example, are strongly influenced by German legal thinking, and the articles on juridical acts, expression of intention, and representation are of German origin. On the other hand, the rules on prescription follow the French model, and the law of property is to a larger extent shaped by French legal thinking. Thus, like the *Code civil*, the *Minpō* does not encompass the so-called *Abstraktionsprinzip*, which is the hallmark of German property law. Also, the preferential rights provided for in the second book of the *Minpō* originate from French law and are unknown in the BGB.

The third book on obligations has a particularly broad comparative foundation: the general provisions on obligations are influenced by the Swiss *Obligationenrecht* (which in turn was also influenced by Roman law concepts). The rules on sales contracts are influenced by Japanese customary law. The substitution of the creditor is modeled after the French *action oblique*. The sections on unjust enrichment and agency without specific authorization are similar to those of the BGB. The rules on torts and damages are shaped along the lines of English case law.

The first three books went into force in 1896. The revision of books four and five containing family law and the law of succession took another two years until 1898. Because these areas are especially interwoven with tradition, the drafters took into account the demands from conservative circles to respect Confucian ethics and morals to a much larger extent than was the case in the three other parts of the *Minpō*. In this context, the Pandectist system showed its functionality: the separate books of the Meiji Civil Code could partly adopt Western models and partly preserve the Japanese tradition. Throughout the *Minpō* but especially in the first three parts one finds a multitude of legal institutions that can easily be tracked back to their Roman origins.[46]

Simultaneously with the reform commission on civil law, a second commission on commercial law was set up in 1892 under the supervision

---

[46] For example, see the extensive analysis by Rolf Knütel, *Das Japanische Zivilgesetzbuch und das Römische Recht* [The Japanese Civil Code and the Roman Law] in HUNDERT JAHRE JAPANISCHES ZIVILGESETZBUCH, *supra* note 40, at 131–84.

of the prime minister; this was also staffed with three Japanese law professors. The revision of the Old Commercial Code was even more strongly modeled after the German *Allgemeines Deutsches Handelsgesetzbuch* of 1861 than the *Roesler* draft. The enactment of the revised Commercial Code, the *Shōhō*, in 1899 concluded the period of practical legislative receptions.

A period of significant adoption of legal theories and doctrines followed. This lasted until the 1920s and was almost entirely focused on German legal reasoning. Regardless of the institutional diversity found in the Civil Code, German legal doctrine was more or less exclusively used for the Code's systematic order and interpretation.[47] As the different origins of the individual provisions were mostly disregarded, frictions between their wording and their understanding were unavoidable. Furthermore, various legal concepts newly developed in Germany were imported into the Japanese civil law without much heed for the existing legislative framework.

From the mid-1920s onward, however, German legal influence started to wane, criticism against it grew, and the theoretical discussion became increasingly autonomous. In other words, the acculturation of the transferred civil law institutions had started in earnest.[48]

IV. SUMMARY

Seen from the perspective of legal transplants, Japanese modern civil law is but another intermediate stop on the long journey of Roman legal concepts that has spanned both time and continents. The reception of Roman law had already covered an era of nearly two millennia when it reached Japan in the Meiji period via the reception of European law. The French and German civil codes acted as role models, which were in turn shaped to a significant degree by Roman legal concepts. Roman law thus became part of the Japanese civil law of today. The fruits of Roman legal thinking can be found in various institutions throughout the Japanese Civil Code.

---

47 See ZENTARŌ KITAGAWA, REZEPTION UND FORTBILDUNG DES EUROPÄISCHEN ZIVILRECHTS IN JAPAN [Reception and Development of European Civil Law in Japan] (1970).

48 A seminal study about the acculturation can be found in GUNTRAM RAHN, RECHTSDENKEN UND RECHTSAUFFASSUNG IN JAPAN [Legal Thinking and Legal Consciousness in Japan] (1990).

PART III

Role of courts in Japan and legal innovations: Japan, China, and Islamic Asia

3.1 Judicial lawmaking and the creation of legal norms in Japan: A dialogue*

John O. Haley and Daniel H. Foote**

According to a widely accepted stereotype, Japan's judiciary plays a very limited role within the legal system. By this view: Japan is a civil law system, modeled during the Meiji era on the two primary legal systems of continental Europe – France and Germany. In keeping with the dominant perceptions, at least in the United States, of the ethos of

---

* Some readers might quibble over our use of the terms judicial "law-making" and the "creation" of legal norms. On one hand, some may define "law" narrowly, at least in civil law systems, to include only the rules or standards of a code or statute. If so, by definition (and in our view, by definition only) judges are not making or creating legal rules but are merely engaged in processes of statutory interpretation and gap-filling. On the other hand, those who define "law" broadly to include widely shared social or customary norms irrespective of judicial recognition might object to the notion that judges are "creating" rather than merely recognizing preexisting legal norms. We prefer a middle-ground definition: In our view, adjudication is a law-making or (legal) norm-creating process. Rules or norms, even though preexisting as custom, that are recognized, articulated, and applied by courts in the formal process of adjudication are by our definition legal rules or norms. Once thereby applied as a "rule of decision" and adhered to as precedent, the norm ceases to be customary. The critical distinction between a purely customary and a judge-created legal norm lies in the separate processes that determine continuity and change. Community consensus determines when and whether custom continues to be viable or changes. In a legal system in which norms are recognized and applied in an adjudicatory context, they remain viable now as law so long, and only so long, as judges continue to recognize the norm in subsequent cases. In other words, they are viable so long as they continue to be recognized by the courts as precedent. Adherence to precedent, not community consensus, thus becomes the linchpin of continuity and change.

** Daniel Foote wishes to express his appreciation for support by Japan Society for the Promotion of Science (JSPS), Grant-in-Aid for Scientific Research (A) #24243001; JSPS, Grant-in-Aid for Specially Promoted Research #23000001; and prior grants that supported his earlier work on this theme.

civil law systems generally, Japanese judges merely interpret presumably all-inclusive codes; they do not create law through precedent in the manner of common law judges. The courts' role is further circumscribed by the vaunted non-litigiousness of the Japanese people. Even when cases reach the courts, according to this stereotyped view, the Japanese judiciary is a paragon of judicial restraint. Judges hardly ever question the constitutionality of statutes and are loath to second-guess bureaucrats or the Diet. Furthermore, to the extent the courts play a role, they are conservative in nature and tend to support the establishment. Finally, on those rare occasions when the judiciary steps in, the Diet and the bureaucracy are quick to reestablish their dominance, through new legislation taking matters out of the courts' hands.

We take a different view. As we discuss below, for over a century Japan's judges have played a central role in the formation and development of law. To be sure, in the great majority of cases, Japanese judges straightforwardly apply standards embodied in statutes enacted by the legislature. Yet judge-made legal institutions and judicially recognized norms constitute an ever-growing corpus within law's domain. Adherence to judicial precedent is an ingrained feature of law and practice. No field of Japanese law today can be adequately described or understood without analysis of often formative judicial decisions. Nor is the story of judicial law-making solely one of restraint and deference. Rather, we believe, even a cursory review of the role of the judiciary in adjudicating civil and criminal cases reveals that Japan's judges have been active, highly creative and sensitive to underlying community concerns and needs. In a considerable number of instances they have led not followed legislative action. Our intention here is to explain and elaborate the role that judges have had and continue to play in articulating norms and making legal rules in the context of adjudication that respond to social needs and the judicial "sense of the community" (*shakai tsūnen*). In the process we address what we jointly and individually consider to be misconceptions about the judicial role in terms of both judicial restraint and subservience to the legislative and administrative branches. We begin with our commonly and individually held views on the issue of precedent as "law" (as defined above), and continue with a discussion of the two related themes of judicial "conservatism," and legislative and administrative dominance with a dialogue based on our particular areas of research.

I. PRECEDENT

Judicial adherence to precedent is a preeminent feature of Japan's legal system. Judicial law-making requires a consistent pattern of deference over time to prior decisions in like cases, at least by the highest court within a hierarchy of courts. In Japan, such observance of precedent is foundational. From the inception of West European codes at the end of the 19th century, the courts were instrumental in developing the case law that gave the codified words meaning and, most significant, transformed mixed borrowings into a comprehensive and more coherent transplantation of concepts drawn from German legal science. As early as 1922, only 15 years after the last of the modern codes was adopted,[1] the precedential effect of judicial decisions by the highest court was instrumentally recognized with the change in designation of the official compilation of *Daishin'in* (Great Court of Cassation) judgments. That compilation, previously entitled a "record of judgments" (*hanketsuroku*), was henceforth the official "collection of judicial precedents" (*hanreishū*).[2] Moreover, Japan is hardly exceptional, even as a civil law jurisdiction.

Courts in all legal systems, of course, take into account and generally follow prior rulings by the highest court in like cases. Within judicial hierarchies, as a matter of general practice if not law or theory, lower courts are expected to adhere to such decisions. Moreover, were the highest court not to follow its own prior decisions, any expectation of judicial consistency would be undermined, producing uncertain and unpredictable outcomes even in factually identical cases. If that were to occur, judicial decisions would inevitably reflect the arbitrary judgments of individual judges. The resulting lawlessness would subvert any notion of a "rule of law" and the very essence of a functioning legal order. Japan may be exceptional, but if so, only to the *extent* to which over the past century the judges on its highest courts have adhered to the rules and norms articulated in the prior decisions of their predecessors in subsequent like cases. To this we now turn.

Haley: To commence our dialogue, we might begin discussion of judicial precedent in Japanese law with a long exposition on its historical pedigree. Eschewing such exposition, however, let me

---

1 KEIHŌ [Criminal Code], Law No. 45, 1907.

2 *See, e.g.*, Takeyoshi Kawashima, *The Concept of Judicial Precedent in Japanese Law, in* Ernst von Caemmerer, Soia Mentschikoff & Konrad Zweigert, eds., IUS PRIVATUM GENTIUM: FESTSCHRIFT FÜR MAX RHEINSTEIN ZUM 70. GEBURTSTAG AM 5. JULI 1969 (1969), pp. 87–99.

simply point out here, first, as I argued in my Waseda lecture,[3] that the historical role of the courts in articulating and enforcing legal rules – especially what we would today label as private law rules, on the basis of precedent is as notable in Japan as in continental Europe. What Japan lacked was a Corpus Juris Civilis or any conception of law in which private law was primary.[4]

Second, more relevant to our discussion here is the experience with what the late Professor Zentarō Kitagawa referred to as "Theory Reception," that is, how rules and principles of the civil code were construed by the courts based on writings of scholars returning from study in Germany.[5] The best-known example of this "second" reception of Western law is the outright substitution of the foreseeable damages provision of Article 416 of the Civil Code as written, which incorporated the Hadley v. Baxendale[6] rule (which itself, some believe, was implicitly borrowed from the French Civil Code[7]), with the notion of "adequate causation" in German law. This example illustrates what I consider to be the prevailing pattern. As I believe our individual research reveals and thus anticipate that we both will show here, judges have not fully created the rules, principles, or norms that they have recognized and applied in their decisions. Rather judicial law-making has in all or nearly all cases commenced first with an introduction by scholars addressing the legal community of new principles or doctrines sourced primarily in European law – as illustrated by the "abuse of rights," "good faith," and "changed circumstances" doctrines – but today sourced occasionally in US law, as in the instance noted below of the "corporate disregard" doctrine (in typical US terminology, "piercing the corporate veil"). These doctrines were not already imbedded, we should emphasize, in any code or statute as positive law. If they had

---

[3] *See* John O. Haley, *The Role of Courts in "Making" Law in Japan: The Communitarian Conservatism of Japanese Judges*, 22 PAC. RIM L. & POL'Y J. 491 (2013).

[4] *See, e.g.*, JOHN OWEN HALEY, AUTHORITY WITHOUT POWER: LAW AND THE JAPANESE PARADOX (1991), pp. 10–11, and, more recently, John O. Haley, *Rivers and Rice: What Lawyers and Legal Historians Should Know about Medieval Japan*, 36 J. JAP. STUD. 313 (2010).

[5] *See* ZENTARŌ KITAGAWA, REZEPTION UND FORTBILDUNG DES EUROPÄISCHEN ZIVILRECHTS IN JAPAN (1970). For a brief English language account, see Zentarō Kitagawa, *Theory Reception: One Aspect of the Development of Japanese Civil Law Science*, in 4 L. JAPAN: AN ANN. 1 (tr. Ronald Lee, 1970).

[6] 156 ER 145, 9 ExCh 341 (1854).

[7] *See, e.g.*, Franco Ferrari, *Comparative Ruminations on the Foreseeability of Damages in Contract Law*, 53 LA. L. REV. 1257, 1265–66 (1993).

been, one could argue that the courts were merely engaged in a routine process of code or statutory "interpretation" in light of the accepted meanings of the provision in the legal system of origin. The law-making process has instead more often than not involved the selection, recognition, and application by judges in deciding a case of one out of many continental European or US legal doctrines or theories that scholars – or judges, even justices, as pointed out – who have studied abroad introduced upon their return, followed by subsequent recognition by the highest court as precedent. No one who has reviewed the precedents established by Japanese courts in a myriad of areas of law over the past century could reasonably conclude that they have been the "agents" of political masters.

Foote: I agree that judicial "law-making" has deep historical roots. As to historical antecedent, one discovers that judicial creation of norms through precedent is by no means a new phenomenon. To the contrary, up through the Edo-era private law norms were to a considerable degree the product of precedential development by judicial officials. In fact, when John Henry Wigmore published his monumental study of the world's legal systems in 1928, he concluded that in history there had been only two major legal systems in which law was developed through precedent by a class of professional judges: the Anglo-American common law system and the Tokugawa system in Japan.[8] That conclusion has been the object of some debate, but Wigmore's observations reflect the extent to which, in the field of private law, Japan had a longstanding tradition of judge-made law. As you also noted in your Waseda lecture, Wigmore was responsible for the most extensive collection of Tokugawa-era precedents now available in any language.[9]

I would add, however, that gap filling, used when there is a lacuna in the code or statute in question, is also a common yet still creative technique. Here too, however, judges often draw on newly introduced doctrines. This was arguably the case in the Supreme Court's adoption of the corporate disregard doctrine (discussed further below). No specific language of the Commercial Code was the basis for the new doctrine. Rather, the Court grounded the doctrine in the very concept of the corporate form, evidently deriving the doctrine from the penumbra

---

8 JOHN HENRY WIGMORE, 2 PANORAMA OF THE WORLD'S LEGAL SYSTEMS 504 (1928).

9 JOHN HENRY WIGMORE, LAW AND JUSTICE IN TOKUGAWA JAPAN: MATERIALS FOR THE HISTORY OF JAPANESE LAW AND JUSTICE UNDER THE TOKUGAWA SHOGUNATE 1603–1867, 9 parts in 26 vols. (1967–1986).

of various provisions in the Commercial Code but with US legal doctrine, however implicit, as the primary source. Second, I would add "fair dealing" to your list of essentially equitable standards, along with abuse of right and good faith. All are reflected in the courts' creation of extensive sets of protections for both workers and tenants. Interpretation of statutory language is, in form, undoubtedly the most frequently used technique. However, the "interpretation" in question at times is rather creative in nature as, for example, in the case of the authorization of wiretapping despite the absence of any specific reference to wiretapping in the Criminal Procedure Code.

I also agree that adherence to precedent has been critical in all of these instances. Former University of Tokyo professor and Supreme Court Justice Itō Masami affirmed the great weight accorded to precedent, in the following reflections based on his experiences as a justice:

> The level of respect for precedent by courts in Japan is extremely high. When I compare Japan to the so-called precedent-based Anglo-American nations, I often feel that the value of precedent is evaluated even more highly here in Japan. In this context, the judicial way of thinking is strongly at work. … It is strongly thought that the greatest weight is placed on legal stability, and that changes in precedent will harm legal stability and undermine faith in the law itself. … [L]ower court judgments that do not conform to Supreme Court precedent are reversed almost without exception. Accordingly, unless special circumstances exist, lower courts follow Supreme Court precedent even if they are dissatisfied with it.[10]

I would not go so far, however, as to fully endorse your statement that "judicial law-making has in all or nearly all cases commenced first with an introduction by scholars … of new principles or doctrines sourced primarily in [foreign] law." As you observe, such instances are common. Yet, as reflected in the traffic accident context discussed below, at times the "interpretation" in question serves as the basis for the creation of an elaborate set of new standards that may or may not have any doctrinal scholarly or "foreign" source. In the environmental pollution field, also discussed below, the Japanese judiciary established precedents that went well beyond standards found in other nations. I would offer the relief granted for victims of *karōshi* (death from overwork) as another example of creation of norms distinctly Japanese in origin; and I tend to think one could rather easily find numerous

---

[10] Itō Masami, Gakusha to saibankan no aida [Between Scholar and Justice] (1993).

other examples of such "homegrown" norms. I would further submit that it is often risky to infer that judicial precedents have arisen from the influence of scholarly commentary or foreign law. It is relatively rare for Japanese decisions to include express citations or references to such commentary or foreign standards. Even where they do, or where the decisions, without citation, have utilized concepts or language that closely parallel the scholars' views or foreign standards, one cannot necessarily infer influence. The judges may have included the citations or adopted the concepts or language in order to justify or provide a further imprimatur of authority for the decision. In this connection, I am reminded of Carl Steenstrup's observation, based on an analysis by Guntram Rahn, that "Japanese judges often make decisions in civil cases more acceptable to the parties by first finding in Japanese custom a solution both parties can live with, and afterward quoting a provision from a Western-inspired code that somehow justifies that solution."[11]

Here, let me introduce three patterns that illustrate both the law-making or norm-creating process, and the manner in which precedent is followed but the norms are creatively changed.

(i) Top-Down, Individual Initiative

The first pattern is top-down creation of norms, in which one can identify the individual initiative taken by one or more Supreme Court justices. Two of the most striking examples of this pattern I have found involve retrials in criminal cases and the corporate disregard doctrine in corporate law – which, as you pointed out, is commonly referred to in the US as "piercing the corporate veil".

Criminal Retrials: The Japanese Code of Criminal Procedure grants the right to a new trial "when clear evidence is newly discovered requiring the declaration of innocence of … one who has been found guilty."[12] For many years the various elements of this right were interpreted so strictly that it was regarded as "the door that never

---

[11] Carl Steenstrup, *New Knowledge Concerning Japan's Legal System before 1868, Acquired from Japanese Sources by Western Writers since 1963*, in Daniel H. Foote, ed., LAW IN JAPAN: A TURNING POINT (2007), 7, 8 (basing his observation on GUNTRAM RAHN, RECHTSDENKEN UND RECHTSAUFFASSUNG IN JAPAN: DARGESTELLT AN DER ENTWICKLUNG DER MODERNEN ZIVILRECHTSMETHODIK (1990)).

[12] KEIJI SOSHŌHŌ [Code of Criminal Procedure], Law No. 131, 1948, art. 435 item 6.

opens."[13] Beginning in 1959, the Japan Federation of Bar Associations began pushing for legislative reform to relax the conditions. The legislative efforts stalled, but in 1975, in the landmark *Shiratori* case,[14] the First Petty Bench of the Supreme Court announced a new interpretation of the relevant provision, which greatly relaxed the standards for obtaining new trials.

A close examination of the record suggests that two justices, Dandō Shigemitsu and Kishi Seiichi, played the key roles in this dramatic change in the standards. Nearly 40 years earlier, as young scholars, both had indicated their views that a nearly identical provision in the prewar Code should be interpreted liberally. By chance, both were appointed to the same Petty Bench of the Supreme Court (Dandō after a career as a scholar, Kishi after a career as a judge). Rather than referring the *Shiratori* case to the Grand Bench, as they arguably should have for a major change in precedent, they retained it at the Petty Bench and issued a path-breaking new interpretation.

That decision opened the door to retrials in four celebrated death penalty cases and to many other retrials. In the four death penalty cases, the wrongly convicted defendants spent virtually their entire adult lives on death row; collectively they spent over 130 years in confinement. In turn, the revelation of the miscarriages of justice in those four cases led to great debate over many aspects of the criminal justice system. While the resulting debate did not lead to immediate reforms, a strong case can be made that the soul-searching that accompanied those four cases helped lay the groundwork for the major set of criminal justice reforms that Japan has undertaken over the past decade, including the introduction of the *saiban'in* (lay juror) system.[15]

Corporate Disregard/Piercing the Corporate Veil: As with the retrial standards, in the case of the corporate disregard doctrine (under which the shareholders of a corporation may be deemed directly responsible

---

[13] For a detailed examination of the retrial standards and the process through which they were reinterpreted, see Daniel H. Foote, *"The Door That Never Opens"?: Capital Punishment and Post-Conviction Review of Death Sentences in the United States and Japan*, 19 BROOKLYN J. INT'L L. 367 (1993).

[14] Murakami v. Japan, 29 KEISHŪ 177 (Sup. Ct., 1st P.B., Ruling, May 20, 1975).

[15] For an examination of the soul-searching that accompanied the death penalty retrial cases and the early impact of the resulting debate, see Daniel H. Foote, *From Japan's Death Row to Freedom*, 1 PAC. RIM L. & POL'Y J. 11 (1993). For discussion of the recent reforms, see, e.g., Daniel H. Foote, *Policymaking by the Japanese Judiciary in the Criminal Justice Field*, 72 HŌSHAKAIGAKU 6 (2010).

for corporate liabilities) one can point to the central role played by two justices. In the mid-1960s a scholar, Ōsumi Ken'ichirō, and a career judge, Matsuda Jirō, were both appointed to the First Petty Bench. Both studied US corporation law and both had long voiced the need for a corporate disregard doctrine in Japan to counter abuse of the corporate form. Longstanding efforts to establish this doctrine legislatively had proven unsuccessful. Nonetheless, the two justices were able to persuade the First Petty Bench to issue a decision announcing a very broad statement of the corporate disregard doctrine, in the 1969 case of *Yamayoshi Shōkai v. Hoshihara*.[16] The only statutory basis cited for the new doctrine was the definition of a company as a juridical person. Although it took some time, the doctrine has taken root and has been utilized by Japanese courts in hundreds of cases.[17]

Notably, despite the passage of over 35 years since the *Shiratori* and *Yamayoshi Shōkai* decisions were announced, the Diet has not amended either the Code of Criminal Procedure or the Commercial Code to reflect the relaxation of the retrial standards or the adoption of the corporate disregard doctrine. Nonetheless, courts have continued to apply and develop both sets of standards.

(ii) Bottom-up Responses to Newly Emerging Concerns

A second pattern of policy making by the judiciary involves bottom-up responses to newly emerging, or newly recognized, issues. In his classic work *Law and Social Change in Postwar Japan*,[18] Frank Upham examined and analyzed two such examples in detail: environmental law and employment discrimination. Sexual harassment law is a third such field.

Mass Environmental Torts: The creation of new standards for fault in pollution cases in the late 1960s and early 1970s represents a classic example of judicial policy making. Although pollution in Minamata Bay, Niigata City, Toyama, Yokkaichi, and elsewhere had been building up for many years, it was not until the 1960s that the dimensions of the environmental disasters became apparent. Pollution victims and the teams of lawyers (*bengodan*) representing them began pursuing

---

16 23 Minshū 511 (Sup. Ct., 1st P.B., Feb. 27, 1969).

17 For a detailed examination of the corporate disregard doctrine and its adoption, see William B. Horton II, *Disregard of the Corporate Entity in Japanese Law* (LL.M. thesis, University of Washington School of Law, 1981).

18 Frank K. Upham, Law and Social Change in Postwar Japan (1987).

campaigns for recognition and redress, of which litigation was an important element. The judiciary responded quite dramatically in a series of cases, most notably what have come to be known as the Big Four pollution cases.[19]

In those decisions, issued over a two-year period by four separate district courts from across Japan, the Japanese judiciary created a path-breaking regime for handling pollution cases. The decisions were all based on the standard tort provision of the Civil Code, Article 709, which provided: "A person who has intentionally or negligently infringed a right of another shall be liable to compensate for damages resulting in consequence."[20] The decisions greatly expanded the reach of that provision, however. Among other steps, the courts imposed a high degree of care on defendants, relaxed the standards for proving foreseeability of harm, and created a presumption of causation in favor of the plaintiffs. As leading scholar Fujikura Kōichirō has explained, through these cases, "the courts in essence imposed strict liability on the polluters, while still using the terminology of negligence under Article 709."[21]

The standards established by these decisions regarding matters such as attribution of fault and causation go well beyond the stances of supposedly activist US courts, not only as of the time the decisions were issued over 40 years ago, but even today. And the decisions, together with the publicity surrounding the litigation, played an important role in shaping public opinion and subsequent environmental policy in Japan.

Employment Discrimination: The field of employment discrimination offers another example of bottom-up policy making by the judiciary, in response to newly recognized societal issues.[22] In the late 1950s and

---

[19] These are the so-called Kumamoto Minamata Case [Watanabe v. Chisso K.K., HANREI JIHŌ (No. 696) 15 (Kumamoto Dist. Ct., Mar. 20, 1973)]; Niigata Minamata Case [Ōno v. Shōwa Denkō K.K., HANREI JIHŌ (No. 642) 96 (Niigata Dist. Ct., Sept. 29, 1971)]; Toyama Cadmium Case (otherwise known as the Itai-itai Disease Case) [Komatsu v. Mitsui Kinzoku Kōgyō K.K., HANREI JIHŌ (No. 635) 17 (Toyama Dist. Ct., June 30, 1971)]; and the Yokkaichi Asthma Case [Shiono v. Shōwa Yokkaichi Sekiyū K.K., HANREI JIHŌ (No. 672) 30 (Tsu Dist. Ct., Yokkaichi Branch, July 24, 1972)].

[20] MINPŌ [Civil Code], Law No. 89, 1896, art. 709.

[21] *See* Kōichirō Fujikura, *Litigation, Administrative Relief and Political Settlement for Pollution Victim Compensation: Minamata Mercury Poisoning after Fifty Years*, in Daniel H. Foote, ed., LAW IN JAPAN: A TURNING POINT (2007), 384, 387.

[22] For overviews of the employment discrimination cases, see Catherine W. Brown, *Japanese Approaches to Equal Rights for Women: The Legal Framework*, 12 L. JAPAN: AN ANN. 29 (1979); UPHAM, *supra* note 18, at 124–65.

early 1960s, a number of women working in banks and other corporations, and the *bengodan* supporting them, began pursuing a litigation campaign challenging gender discrimination with regard to conditions of employment. Initially, however, they experienced difficulty establishing a foundation for their claims. The Labor Standards Act prohibits discrimination against women with respect to pay, but not hiring, discharge, or other conditions of employment. Article 14 of the Constitution sets forth the equal protection principle and states "there shall be no discrimination in … economic … relations because of … sex …." In keeping with the pattern in the United States and most other jurisdictions, however, Japanese courts took the position that constitutional claims could not be used to challenge actions of private employers, because of the absence of state action.

Then, in its 1966 decision in the *Sumitomo Cement* case,[23] the Tokyo District Court announced a new standard. That case involved the challenge to Sumitomo Cement's discharge of a woman who married but refused to resign, despite having signed an agreement required by the company as a condition for the hiring of all women, promising to retire upon marriage or upon reaching the age of 35. The lawsuit was premised primarily on the Constitution, including claims based on Article 14 and Article 24, which guarantees freedom of marriage. In its judgment, Tokyo District Court did not accept the arguments based directly on the Constitution. Instead, it adopted what at the time was a novel theory (also advanced, as a subsidiary theory, by the *bengodan*). The court ruled that the requirement for retirement upon marriage violated Article 90 of the Civil Code, which provides: "A juristic act with a purpose against public policy is void."[24] Pointing to the provisions of the Labor Standards Act relating to gender discrimination, as well as various articles of the Constitution, the court held that "the prohibition of discriminatory treatment on the basis of gender and the guarantee of freedom of marriage constitute matters of 'public policy,' and, unless a rational reason can be found to exist, employment agreements … providing for termination upon marriage are void as being in violation of public policy."

This new approach had far-reaching implications. As the court was well aware, differential retirement policies and other types of differential treatment of men and women in employment were very widespread at the time. By recognizing the availability of Article 90 of

---

[23] Suzuki v. Sumitomo Cement K.K., HANREI JIHŌ (No. 467) 26 (Tokyo Dist. Ct., Dec. 20, 1966).

[24] MINPŌ, art. 90.

the Civil Code as the medium, the court provided private parties with a vehicle for invoking equal protection, freedom of marriage, and other fundamental rights set forth in the Constitution with regard to employment matters between private parties, regardless of the absence of state action. Moreover, the reasoning of the opinion shows that the Tokyo District Court recognized that it was engaged in shaping policy. In addition to highlighting the spirit of the Labor Standards Act and various articles of the Constitution, the court emphasized the adverse impact on women from the employment practices in question.

Other courts quickly followed suit. In a long series of opinions, courts applied this approach in invalidating differential employment policies, including the termination of employment of women upon pregnancy and the setting of earlier retirement ages for women than men. In 1981, the Supreme Court formally endorsed the Article 90 approach, upholding a lower court ruling that Nissan Motors' differential retirement policy, in which the retirement age for men was set at 60 and that for women at 55, violated Article 90.[25]

In 1985, nearly two decades after *Sumitomo Cement*, the Diet finally enacted the Equal Employment Opportunity Act.[26] Notably, as originally enacted that law did little more than codify standards the courts had already developed.[27] For a time, moreover, the enactment of the EEOA seems to have slowed down further extension of the Article 90 line of cases by the courts, as Upham predicted.[28] A few years after the passage of the EEOA, the courts again extended the Article 90 line of cases, this time to the promotion context. Thereafter, the Diet acted much more quickly and extended some statutory protections beyond where the courts had reached. The 1997 amendments to the EEOA prohibited discrimination not only in assignments and promotions, but in recruitment and hiring, as well.[29]

---

[25] Nissan Jidōsha K.K. v. Nakamoto, 35 MINSHŪ 300 (Sup. Ct., 3rd P.B., Mar. 24, 1981).

[26] The official title of the Act is: Law concerning the Improvement of the Welfare of Women Workers, including the Guarantee of Equal Opportunity and Treatment between Men and Women in Employment (*Koyō no bun'ya ni okeru danjo no kintō na kikai oyobi taigū no kakuho ni kansuru hōritsu*), Law No. 113, 1972, as amended by Law No. 45, 1985.

[27] The Act prohibited discriminatory retirement ages and dismissal policies, *id.* Art. 11, but established only so-called endeavor obligations with respect to recruitment, hiring, assignments, and promotions, *id.* Arts. 7 (recruitment and hiring), 8 (assignment and promotion).

[28] *See* UPHAM, *supra* note 18, at 60–65.

[29] Equal Employment Opportunity Act, as revised in 1997, Arts. 5 and 6.

I do not mean to suggest that Japan has succeeded in eliminating gender discrimination; the glass ceiling remains thick, despite the judicial precedents and statutory developments.[30] Yet, as the above account reflects, in the field of employment discrimination, the courts took the lead in formulating a substantial body of protections for women workers. This was a classic case of bottom-up policy making, in which one judgment by the Tokyo District Court adopted a creative statutory interpretation, which other lower courts then developed and expanded to other settings, before it ultimately was endorsed by the Supreme Court and, in substance, incorporated into statutory form by the Diet.

Sexual Harassment: Without going into detail, the development of a sexual harassment doctrine has followed a similar pattern. A 1992 decision by the Fukuoka District Court first recognized a claim for sexual harassment, based on tort doctrine;[31] other lower courts quickly followed suit in applying that doctrine to other cases; and the Diet enacted related legislation (albeit initially quite limited in scope) a few years later.

(iii) Bottom-up Creation of Norms in the Service of Stability

In several extensive sets of cases, courts have strictly regulated parties' attempts to terminate such relationships as employment, leases, and marriage, notwithstanding statutes that on their face seem to provide the parties with considerable freedom to terminate those relationships. This is another type of bottom-up policy making. In contrast to the cases in the preceding pattern, which involved newly emerging or newly recognized societal issues, I view this pattern as resting on the underlying theme of maintenance of relationships, and thus reflecting a preference for a traditional view of society. Accordingly, I have chosen to label this pattern of precedential creation of norms as "bottom-up creation of norms in the service of stability."

Termination of Employment: The example of this type of law-making that I have examined in the greatest detail is the so-called abusive

---

30 According to the *Global Gender Gap Report 2013*, compiled by the World Economic Forum, with regard to gender equality Japan ranked 105th out of 136 nations surveyed. Report available at: http://www3.weforum.org/docs/WEF_GenderGap_Report_2013.pdf.

31 Kōno v. K.K. Otsuno, HANREI JIHŌ (No. 1426) 49 (Fukuoka Dist. Ct., April 16, 1992).

dismissal doctrine in labor law.[32] This is not a case where the courts have simply been filling a gap left by the Diet. Here, the courts have overridden what seems clear statutory language.

Under Article 20 of the Labor Standards Act, an employer who wishes to fire a regular employee must provide 30 days' notice or pay 30 days' wages in lieu of notice. But there is no need for notice at all if the discharge is "for reasons attributable to the worker."[33] So, by its terms, the statute appears to allow discharge with cause at any time and discharge without cause upon 30 days' notice. Nonetheless, beginning in the late 1940s, almost as soon as the Labor Standards Act took effect, the courts began building a large body of protections for workers.

The courts initially considered two major theories as the basis for these protections: just cause and abuse of right. I will not go into the debate here,[34] except to say that abuse of right won out in 1951, apparently because it was viewed as more flexible. Starting in 1950, Japanese courts began to develop a major body of protections against dismissal, initially in the context of regular employees. By the time the Supreme Court finally gave formal recognition to the so-called 'abusive dismissal' doctrine in the mid-1970s, lower courts had long since been scrutinizing discharges carefully to determine whether they "were based on reasons that can be objectively affirmed as sufficient to justify dismissal," in light of the common sense of society. Typically, what that meant was that mere incompetence was not enough; a much more serious reason would have to be shown.

Although most of Japan's large companies offered so-called lifetime employment for most regular employees, management was not happy about losing the right to dismiss unsatisfactory workers. Businesses adopted various techniques seeking to get around the abusive dismissal doctrine. In turn, the courts kept responding to these attempts by expanding the doctrine.

The upshot of all these decisions, spanning nearly half a century, is that Japan has some of the strictest protections against dismissal in the world, virtually all created by the courts, through a process of incremental development of precedent in which the judges of the specialized labor section of the Tokyo District Court played a leading role. The terminology of the opinions themselves – with references to

---

32 *See* Daniel H. Foote, *Judicial Creation of Norms in Japanese Labor Law: Activism in the Service of Stability?* 43 UCLA L. REV. 635 (1996).

33 RŌDŌ KIJUNHŌ [Labor Standards Act], Law No. 49, 1947, art. 20(1).

34 For those who are interested in a more detailed account, see Foote, *Judicial Creation of Norms in Japanese Labor Law*, *supra* note 32, at 639–51.

such factors as the employment market and the economic vulnerability of workers – reflects the policy orientation of the decisions. Contemporaneous books and articles written by the judges show they were well aware they were shaping policy through their decisions.

Notably, in formulating, extending, and refining the abusive dismissal doctrine, the courts were not just filling gaps in existing legislation. Rather, they were creating protections for workers in the face of a statute that seems in unambiguous terms to permit dismissal without cause, subject only to a notice requirement. It was only in 2003, over 50 years after the courts began erecting the protections under the abusive dismissal doctrine, that the Diet amended the Labor Standards Act to incorporate that doctrine. The newly added provision, Article 18-2, reads as follows: "In the event a dismissal lacks objectively reasonable grounds and is not deemed to be appropriate in light of the common sense of society, that dismissal shall be void as an abuse of the right of dismissal." In this case, the Diet acquiesced; the statutory language quite deliberately codifies the standard previously developed by the judiciary.

House Lease and Other Contexts: Perhaps the most prominent example of the pattern of bottom-up creation of norms in the service of stability, other than the employment cases, lies in the area of house leases. In this connection (as in so many others), I am deeply indebted to your research; the summary that follows is primarily derived from your work on lease law.[35] The judicial decisions in the house lease context stretch all the way back to near the turn of the 20th century; and the parallels to abusive dismissal are striking. Initially, the relevant statute, Civil Code Article 617, permitted termination upon three months' notice; but even where the parties had supplemented that provision with explicit contractual language saying exactly the same thing, courts in numerous cases prior to 1920 refused to allow landlords to terminate leases. The courts dismissed the contractual language as mere boilerplate and overrode the statutory notice provision by finding either a custom or an implied intent not to follow it. As you observed, "By 'interpretation' [Japan's judiciary] had imposed a legal regime in which neither the parties' stated intentions in their lease contracts nor the provisions of the Civil Code prevailed."[36]

---

35 John O. Haley, *Japan's New Land and House Lease Law*, in John O. Haley & Kozo Yamamura, eds., LAND ISSUES IN JAPAN: A POLICY FAILURE? 149 (1992).

36 *Id.* at 158.

In 1921, the Diet revisited this field. The House Lease Act[37] allowed fixed-term leases without specifying a minimum term, and did not require a landlord to show just cause to terminate. Nonetheless, through interpretation, the courts continued to require landlords to show just cause for terminating *and* for refusing to renew leases. In 1941 (in the midst of great inflation and housing shortages in major cities initially brought on by economic activity related to Japan's militarization), the Diet finally gave in and codified that approach, with amendments stipulating that a landlord could only terminate or refuse to renew a lease by showing a personal need to use the property or "other just cause."[38] That still did not end the courts' role. During the intense housing shortages and extreme inflation after World War II, courts interpreted the exception for "other just cause" so strictly that they in effect merged it with the first standard: the landlord typically had to show a personal need to use the property. Frequently, the courts went even further and required the landlord to show fault or bad faith on the part of the tenant.

The divorce context provides another example of the emphasis on maintaining existing relationships. In addition to specified causes such as adultery and desertion, the Civil Code authorizes divorce in the case of "grave cause that makes continuation of the marriage difficult."[39] Yet the courts have interpreted this provision so strictly that it is almost impossible to obtain a divorce on this basis unless one's spouse consents.[40] As the courts have interpreted the relevant provisions, a blameless spouse has virtual veto power.[41] A key reason given for these strict interpretations of the divorce provisions is protection of the perceived weaker party, especially when that party is blameless. Here again, however, a central theme is the maintenance of existing relationships.

---

[37] SHAKUYA HŌ [House Lease Act], Law No. 50, 1921.

[38] *See id.*, arts. 1–2.

[39] MINPŌ, art. 770(1), item 5.

[40] Over 90% of Japan's divorces are consensual, and if one adds in cases in which the parties have reached agreement through court-ordered conciliation, that figure goes up to 99%, Ninomiya Shūhei, *Bekkyo ni yoru rikon no kahi to kakoku jōkō* [The Pros and Cons of Divorce Based on Separation and the Hardship Clause], JURISUTO (1059) 63, 65 (1995). Obtaining a contested divorce is especially difficult if the spouse contesting the divorce has not engaged in "blameworthy" behavior.

[41] In the words of one commentator, "It is generally said that [the Civil Code] guarantees the right to divorce. Yet, viewed from the opposite perspective, [the courts' insistence upon a showing of 'cause' for the divorce] can be said to guarantee a right not to be divorced unreasonably ...," *id.* at 65.

As a final example, the theme of maintenance of existing relationships also affects judicial attitudes toward contracts between commercial entities, again through the essentially equitable vehicles of the good faith and trust, and abuse of right doctrines. In a case involving distributorship agreements between music record manufacturers and a retail shop, for example, the Tokyo District Court emphasized the ongoing nature of the relationship and the vulnerability of the retailer in holding that, despite seemingly broader language in the contracts: "the agreements could be terminated only for such a serious breach on the part of [the retailer] ... as to render it unreasonable for [the retailer] to expect the agreements to continue ...."[42]

In all of these cases, a statute or a contract, or frequently both, seem to give the "stronger" party the right to terminate a relationship. In each, however, the courts have said no, and instead have sharply circumscribed the right to terminate. Given the very great importance placed on maintenance of the marriage relationship in Japanese culture, the divorce cases may represent either the paradigm example or a special case. In any event, the parallels among the other instances are striking. In fact, during the early years of the abusive dismissal doctrine, one decision (albeit by a Labor Relations Commission) relied explicitly on the landlord-tenant cases.[43]

Haley: Your examples of both a "top-down" initiative of individual Supreme Court justices as well as the more diffuse "bottom-up" processes of collaboration and decision making among lower court judges provoke consideration of a number of questions. Some we should revisit. Let me first, however, add to your list of fields in which precedent mattered and was nominally maintained but which the court has followed more in form than substance. The Supreme Court has only rarely explicitly overruled prior decisions, including those of its prewar predecessor, the *Daishin'in*. Decades-old precedents are followed in nearly every field of law. I am especially familiar with the long line of cases involving secured transactions in which the courts through a long series of cases developed an extensive corpus of law enabling the creation of security interests by contract as effective rights

---

[42] K.K. Miyagi Family Club v. Nihon Columbia K.K., HANREI JIHŌ (No. 1110) 13 (Tokyo Dist. Ct., Mar. 29, 1984).

[43] Shin-Nihon Hikōki Koyasu [New Japan Air Koyasu] case, Kanagawa Local Lab. Rel's Comm'n, Order of April 12, 1954, cited in Liu Shiho, *Nihon rōdōhō ni okeru kaikoken ran'yō hōri no keisei – sengo kara Shōwa 25 nen made no saibanrei o chūshin to shite* [The Creation of the Abusive Dismissal Doctrine in Japanese Labor Law – Centered on Judicial Precedents through 1950], Masters Thesis, University of Tokyo Faculty of Law (1991), at 63.

in rem despite explicit prohibition of such recognition in the Civil Code.[44]

The 1975 Supreme Court's unanimous decision in *Sumiyoshi v. Governor of Hiroshima Prefecture*[45] illustrates the point best. In that case, the Court unanimously held unconstitutional a licensing standard restricting the location of pharmacies to avoid competition with nearby pharmacies. The Court applied a "least restrictive alternative" standard in finding that the desired regulatory goal of avoiding the sale of below-quality drugs, which, it was argued, could result from "excessive" competition of closely located drug stores, could be achieved more appropriately by direct administrative enforcement of existing drug standards without restricting completion and thereby running afoul of constitutionally protected rights. In so doing, the Court did not overrule the otherwise controlling precedent in *Shimizu v. Japan*[46] (better known as the *Fukuoka Bathhouse* case). The cases are nearly identical except for the businesses involved and the fact that the *Bathhouse* case was a criminal action. The justification for the location restrictions in both cases were nearly identical – to prevent any threat to public safety and health from the foul bath water and diluted drugs that might result from "excessive" competition. The Court simply ignored the earlier bathhouse case, which has continued to have precedential value within its narrow domain.

An equally significant instance has been the continued adherence to the reasoning, albeit not necessarily the ruling, of the Court in its 1964 judgment upholding the constitutionality of the allocation of members of the prefectural districts for election to the House of Councillors in the 1962 election.[47] A dozen years later the Court held unconstitutional a similar allocation of seats in districts for the 1972 Lower House

---

44 JOHN OWEN HALEY, NON-CODE SECURITY INTERESTS: A STUDY OF JAPANESE CASE LAW (1971), *available in* the Gallagher Law Library, University of Washington School of Law.

45 29 MINSHŪ 4 (Sup. Ct., G.B., April 30, 1975). For an English language translation, see LAWRENCE W. BEER & HIROSHI ITOH, THE CONSTITUTIONAL CASE LAW OF JAPAN, 1970 THROUGH 1990, 188–99 (1996). For my comment, see John O. Haley, *The Freedom to Choose an Occupation and the Constitutional Limit of Legislative Discretion – K.K. Sumiyoshi v. Governor of Hiroshima Prefecture*, 8 L. JAPAN: AN ANN. 178–204 (1976).

46 9 KEISHŪ 89 (Sup. Ct., G.B.) (1955), *translated by* Masaaki Ikeda *in* JOHN M. MAKI, COURT AND CONSTITUTION IN JAPAN: SELECTED SUPREME COURT DECISIONS, 1948–60, 293–97 (Univ. of Wash. Press, 1964).

47 Koshiyama v. Chairman, Tokyo Metropolitan Election Supervision Commission Commission, 18 MINSHŪ 270 (Sup. Ct., G.B., Feb. 5, 1964) (House of Councillors election of 1962).

election.[48] The latter decision affirmed the standard used in the earlier judgment to determine the issue. A disproportionate distribution had to be sufficiently egregious to be deemed unconstitutional. However, a majority of justices considered the distribution and degree of inequality in the relative value of individual votes to have reached the impermissible level. The basic test articulated in the 1964 judgment remains the litmus test for all subsequent decisions, including the two most recent Grand Bench decisions.[49]

I am familiar with only two major constitutional cases in which the Court explicitly overruled a precedent. The first was the Supreme Court's 1973 decision in *Aizawa v. Japan*.[50] In that decision, the Court declared unconstitutional on equal protection grounds the provisions of Article 200 of the Criminal Code that imposed a more severe penalty for murder of a lineal ascendant than for any other murders. The decision explicitly overturned a 1950 Grand Bench case that, although criticizing the greater severity of the punishment for murder of lineal ascendants under Article 200, nevertheless refused to hold it to be unconstitutional.[51] However, the 1973 decision left standing a 1949 decision in which the Court affirmed the constitutionality of a similar Criminal Code provision in Article 205 that imposed a greater penalty for the crime of causing death by physical injury to a lineal ascendant than to others.[52] The second was the Court's September 4, 2013, judgment holding unconstitutional the provision of Article 900(4) of the Civil Code limiting the compulsory share (*legitim*) of an acknowledged (registered) illegitimate child to half of that of a legitimate child.[53] The judgment explicitly overruled a 1995 judgment upholding the constitutionality of the provision.[54]

---

48 Kurokawa v. Chiba Prefecture Election Comm'n, 30 MINSHŪ 223 (Sup. Ct. G.B., April 14, 1976) (House of Representatives election of 1972).

49 Kanegami v. Tokyo Prefecture Election Commission, 66 MINSHŪ – (Sup. Ct. G.B., Oct. 17, 2012); X v. Y., 67 MINSHŪ – (Sup. Ct., G.B., Nov. 20, 2013).

50 27 KEISHŪ 265 (Sup. Ct., G.B.) (1973), *translated in* BEER & ITOH, *supra* note 45, *at* 143–70.

51 *See* Otōki v. Japan, 4 KEISHŪ 10 (Sup. Ct., G.B.) (1949).

52 Yamato v. Japan, 4 KEISHŪ 2037 (Sup. Ct.) (1950), *translated by* Kurt Steiner, in MAKI, *supra* note 46, at 129–55. The contested sections of Article 205 remained effective if not often enforced until fully removed, along with repeal of Article 200, by the Diet under Law No. 91, 1995, although previously modified by Law No. 156, 1989.

53 X v. Y., 67 MINSHŪ – (Sup. Ct., G.B., Sept. 4, 2013). [Case: Heisei 24 (ku) Nos. 984, 985.]

54 Kōno v. Otsuno, 49 MINSHŪ 1789 (Sup. Ct., G.B., July 5, 1995).

Viewed in terms of the patterns of law-making or norm creation within the judiciary, "top-down" or "bottom-up," your classifications make perfect sense. However, I would cluster the cases you cite along with others that are similar under a complementary but somewhat different set of categories.

I have previously characterized many of the cases and areas of law you mention as examples of the courts confirming community.[55] The most salient are the cases involving unilateral termination of employment. I view the judicial rejection of the language of Article 20 of the Labor Standards Act, a statute notably enacted in 1947 in the first full year of the Allied Occupation when legislation received at least some oversight by Occupation authorities, to represent a rejection in the end of any transplant of US "at will" employment. The context also deserves mention. Nearly all larger organizations (public and private from the Ministry of Finance and the judiciary itself to all manufacturing and commercial enterprises except small and medium businesses owned and controlled by a controlling individual or family) share an organizational feature that is at least rare in Europe and, to my knowledge, unknown in the US except for the military. They uniformly hire their core managerial employees only at the entry level and maintain a central personnel office (staffed by rotating career personnel) responsible for hiring and assignment of all core employees. Few if any lateral employment opportunities exist, and there is no mobility even among government agencies. Seconding of personnel from one agency to another, as in the case of judges seconded to the procuracy, is practiced but still not common. The consequence is that persons join government and private organizations in their early 20s with the full expectation that they will remain with the same organization until they retire 30 to 40 years later. The result is a cohesive community in which the interests of the community as a whole subsume those of each member. As your research also shows, the courts have deferred to employer decisions "to manage" their employees, including overtime, transfers, and even "seconding" or "farming out," as you phrase the practice.[56] In my view the career employees constitute the community and the "employer" is the community.

---

55 John Owen Haley, The Spirit of Japanese Law (1998), Chapter 6, pp. 123–55.

56 Foote, *Judicial Creation of Norms in Japanese Labor Law*, *supra* note 32, at 665–70.

We could go through your entire list of protected "relationships" and in each case discover a "community" whose stability or cohesion the courts seek to maintain, or to be more precise, to protect against legal rules that permit unilateral, nonconsensual dismissal, eviction, divorce, termination, or any other form of unilateral expulsion. In each area of law you describe, I would simply rephrase your description to say that the courts have acted to reject or at least to modify legal rules that enable community expulsion of objecting members.

Some might take issue with my generalized characterization, arguing in your favor by pointing to divorce and landlord-tenant disputes. These examples of the courts' creating rules that limit unilateral action to rupture the relationship appear to fit more perfectly into your schema than mine. These cases seem surely to involve prototypical relations between two parties in which one side seeking termination (the husband or the landlord) usually has the advantage of financial resources that make him the stronger of the two. My best retort is to say that community is at stake in these cases as well. In both instances, I would argue that a "community" was involved, which the courts, in order to preserve, fashioned rules and norms to prevent unilateral eviction or dissolution or eviction. The judges may have looked beyond the husbands and wives to consider the children, parents, and even grandparents of the extended family as a community. Similarly, the landlord tenancy disputes of the 1920s, the era in which these disputes and the judicial creativity flowered, as Ann Waswo points out in two superb studies,[57] generally involved landlords who had moved into the expanding urban areas, especially along the Inland Sea from Osaka to Hiroshima. In the process, many abandoned both their native villages and as absentee landlords their customary community obligations, especially those owed to their tenants. Even termination of urban leases accompanied by efforts to evict tenants may be similarly viewed as rupturing neighborhood, as well as commercial communities. In the end, we may each be partially accurate, a bit of both, as we inevitably look through lenses tainted by our own perspectives or proclivities; yours perhaps more individualistic, mine more communitarian.

Foote: Before turning to the next topic, allow me to mention one other prominent constitutional case in which the Supreme Court explicitly altered, and in effect reversed, its own precedent: the 1973 *Zennōrin Public Employees Case*, involving the right of public

---

[57] Ann Waswo, *The Origins of Tenant Unrest*, in B. S. Silberman & H.D. Harootunian, eds., JAPAN IN CRISIS 374 (1974) and ANN WASWO, JAPANESE LANDLORDS: THE DECLINE OF A RURAL ELITE (1977).

employees to engage in dispute activities.[58] In an 8–4 Grand Bench decision issued in 1966, the Court held that in order for restrictions on strikes and other dispute activities by public employees to survive challenge under Article 28 of the Constitution (which guarantees the "right of workers to organize and to bargain and act collectively"), those restrictions "must be confined to the necessary and reasonable minimum."[59] The Grand Bench reaffirmed the reasoning of that opinion in a 1969 decision, with eight of the 14 justices who participated supporting the strict scrutiny approach, and a ninth going even further to say the restrictions were unconstitutional pure and simple.[60]

Just four years later the Court reversed course. In the 1973 *Zennōrin* case, in a bitterly contested Grand Bench decision, the Court greatly relaxed the applicable standard, with eight justices supporting the relaxed standard while seven continued to advocate either strict scrutiny or outright unconstitutionality. While stating that the guarantees of fundamental rights of workers under Article 28 also apply to public employees, the Court held that those rights may be restricted as necessary in light of the common interest of people as a whole. The Court stressed that, in return for restrictions on their fundamental rights as workers, public employees enjoy measures to guarantee the right to a livelihood, and held that the prohibition on dispute activities "should be deemed inevitable for the public interest of the nation as a whole … and does not violate Article 28." The Court specifically stated that "no element of coercion, as under the pressure of a strike or other dispute activity, is admissible" for public workers. The Court also explicitly stated that the 1969 judgment "must be altered to the extent it is in conflict with the … present judgment."

This decision is especially noteworthy because a strong case has been made that the shift in the Court's position grew out of a deliberate decision in December 1968 by Prime Minister Satō Eisaku to promote Ishida Kazuto, who as Associate Justice had participated in a strong dissent in the 1966 decision (and would also participate in a strong dissent in the 1969 decision), to Chief Justice, rather than former

---

[58] Tsurusono v. Japan, 27 KEISHŪ 547 (Sup. Ct., G.B., April 25, 1973), translated at BEER & ITOH, *supra* note 45, at 244-86.

[59] Toyama v. Japan (The Tokyo Central Post Office Case), 20 KEISHŪ 8 at p. 901 (Sup. Ct., G.B., Oct. 26, 1966), translated at HIROSHI ITOH & LAWRENCE WARD BEER, eds., THE CONSTITUTIONAL CASE LAW OF JAPAN: SELECTED SUPREME COURT DECISIONS, 1961–70, at 83–103 (1978).

[60] Japan v. Sakane (The Court Worker Incitement Case), 23 KEISHŪ 5 at p. 685 (Sup. Ct., G.B., April 2, 1969), translated at ITOH & BEER, *supra* note 59, at 103–30.

academic Tanaka Jirō, who had been widely regarded as the front runner.[61] According to a detailed account by Yamamoto Yūji, a *Mainichi Shinbun* reporter who covered the Supreme Court for many years, the choice of Ishida was influenced by worries that the judiciary was becoming too liberal, with the Supreme Court's stance on strikes by public employees being one of the areas of greatest concern.[62] In turn, Yamamoto recounts in considerable detail, Ishida, in his role as Chief Justice, proceeded to influence subsequent appointments to the Court until the conservative bloc had attained a majority, at which point the *Zennōrin* case, which had been filed with the Court in 1969, finally was scheduled for oral argument.

If this account is accurate, it offers a concrete example of direct political intervention in the appointment process, based both on broad ideological concerns and concerns over a specific legal issue. Most American readers would undoubtedly say, "So what?" Given the fact that the Prime Minister heads the Cabinet, which in turn, under the Constitution, has authority for appointing the Associate Justices and designating the Chief Justice (who, as a matter of formality, is appointed by the Emperor), most American readers probably would wonder why it even merits comment for a Prime Minister to take into account ideology or positions on specific issues in deciding whom to choose. In the Japanese context, though, where it is often said that the politicians routinely defer to the judiciary in selecting candidates for judicial appointments, even at the Supreme Court level, accounts such as this do merit attention. And even though the events in question occurred over 40 years ago, if Yamamoto's account is accurate, the impact of the appointment, over a period of several years, of a cohort of reliably conservative justices would have extended well into the future.

---

[61] *See* YAMAMOTO YŪJI, SAIKŌSAI MONOGATARI [Supreme Court Stories], vol. 1, pp. 287–323 (1994); HIROSHI ITOH, THE SUPREME COURT AND BENIGN ELITE DEMOCRACY IN JAPAN 201 (2010). Since that time, the position of Chief Justice has been dominated by career judges; every Chief Justice since 1966 has been a career judge except one. As of the time of Ishida's appointment in January 1969, though, that pattern had not taken firm hold. Only one of the first four Chief Justices (Ishida's predecessor, Yokota Masatoshi, who served as Chief Justice for under two and a half years) had been a career judge; and former University of Tokyo professors Tanaka Kōtarō and Yokota Kisaburō together had occupied the position of Chief Justice for over 16 of the Court's 21 years of existence up until the time of Ishida's appointment.

[62] *See* YAMAMOTO, *supra* note 61, vol. 1, at 287–293.

Haley: I would only add that Prime Minister Satō may have helped to institute what has become an established pattern of appointments. Not only did he not appoint a more politically responsive outsider, but in selecting Ishida Kazuto, a former career judge, who was, as you note, already serving on the Court, he seems to have helped to affirm an enduring pattern. Appointed in 1969, Ishida was the second career justice to become Chief Justice. Since then the lawyer Ekizō Fujibayashi, who served as Chief Justice for only a year (from May 1976 to August 1977) was the only Chief Justice to date who was not a former career judge. Moreover, I would also note that the Court's ultimate decision in the case reflected current US law as well. Public employees do not have a constitutionally protected right to strike except in a few states with constitutional provisions that explicitly guarantee such a right.

II. POLICY MAKING WITHIN A CAREER JUDICIARY

Foote: Let me now return to our earlier discussion and, putting differences in classification aside, let me add a final pattern of judicial law-making of a kind that fits under a very different category. I find this to be especially fascinating, because there is little of the same sort in the United States. That category is what I characterize as the pattern of "top-down, institutional initiative," in which the judiciary as an institution encouraged and facilitated the creation of norms by its career judges, at times in a process much more akin to rule making by administrative agencies than traditional precedent-setting by courts.

Traffic Accidents: The most dramatic example of this pattern of which I am aware involves traffic accidents.[63] In the early 1960s, the Japanese courts began to experience a flood of traffic accident cases. The judiciary concluded that it needed some means of dealing with this flood of litigation. Evidently at the behest of the General Secretariat of the Supreme Court, Tokyo District Court established a new civil section, Section No. 27, and charged that section with handling traffic accident cases.

Shortly after its creation, Section 27 began to devise various ways of dealing with the cases more efficiently. These measures included efforts to streamline the fact-finding process and the creation of standard

---

[63] For an examination of the courts' role in developing standards for handling traffic accidents, see Daniel H. Foote, *Resolution of Traffic Accident Disputes and Judicial Activism in Japan*, 25 L. JAPAN: AN ANN. 19 (1995).

form litigation documents. Of far greater importance were Section 27's efforts to standardize resolution of traffic accident disputes. The judges in Section 27 undertook standardization efforts on two major fronts: first, with respect to the determination of comparative fault, and second, on the level of damages. They created an extensive set of diagrams of the typical accident scenarios and assigned percentages of fault for the parties involved. They also created standard formulae for damage awards, with separate standards for elements such as property damage, lost income, and pain and suffering.

In addition, Section 27 (along with the assistance of the General Secretariat and even the organized bar) undertook extensive efforts to disseminate and establish the standards. Within the judiciary, those steps included convening meetings among judges handling traffic accidents in various courts around Japan, designed to achieve consensus on the appropriate standards, and the transfer of Section 27 judges to other courts where they could directly disseminate the results of their efforts to other judges. Measures designed to disseminate the new standards externally began with informal communication with members of the bar and culminated with the publication of special journal issues, prepared and edited exclusively by the judges, setting forth both the causation standards and the damage standards.

The stated objective of these efforts was to establish a set of detailed, clear, and widely recognized standards, in order to facilitate simple and speedy resolution of cases by the courts and, ultimately, in order to avoid the need for litigation altogether by facilitating out-of-court settlement of traffic accident disputes. One may argue over whether the standards adopted were appropriate or even whether this standardization itself is appropriate. Nonetheless, the Section 27 judges were successful in achieving their goal. The standards took root and are maintained to this day, with the bar association itself now having taken over revision and publication of the standards. Coupled with the establishment of various traffic accident consultation centers, these standards have helped keep the vast majority of traffic accident cases out of court.

The efforts of Section 27 have had an even broader impact. The compensation standards the judges helped establish have also formed the basis for compensation awards in many personal injury cases outside the traffic accident context, thereby facilitating settlement of a much wider range of cases

Insolvency: A more recent example, which bears many similarities to the traffic accident context, may be found in the field of insolvency. After hovering at under 4000 cases per year nationwide through about 1980, the number of insolvency cases began to rise steadily thereafter. In

1992, the number of cases topped 45,000; and over the following decade nearly quadrupled again, reaching almost 170,000 cases in 2001.[64] Tokyo District Court had the single largest load of insolvency cases, accounting for about 8% of the nationwide total.

As in the traffic accident context, a specialized division of Tokyo District Court, Civil Section No. 20, had responsibility for the insolvency cases; and that Section set out to streamline procedures in order to meet the huge caseload. As discussed in an article by the head of Civil Section 20, Judge Sonoo Takashi, that Section introduced two new procedures for disposing of cases: same-day interviews with the claimant promptly after filing (*sokujitsu mensetsu*) and receivership procedures for small matters (*shōgaku kanzai tetsuzuki*).[65]

Without going into the details, the judges of Section 20 introduced the former procedure in 1999. After observing how it was functioning for several months thereafter, the judges of Section 20 concluded that it was working well and decided to maintain it. They also sought the understanding of creditors by undertaking efforts to explain the new system. These efforts paid off. By 2001, just two years after its introduction, over 50% of all insolvency cases in Tokyo District Court were being resolved through this procedure.

The latter procedure was also initially introduced on an experimental basis, limited to small individual insolvency cases. Further, at the onset the judges thought this procedure would help resolve only a small percentage of insolvency cases. After again holding consultations with bar associations, Section 20 decided to institutionalize this procedure, and rather quickly extended it to corporate insolvencies and to larger scale insolvencies. By early 2002, over 40% of all insolvency cases in Tokyo District Court were handled through this procedure; and the two procedures combined were accounting for the rapid resolution of some 95% of all cases.

As this brief summary reflects, the activities by the judges of Section 20 bear numerous similarities to those of Section 27 in the traffic accident context. The judges found themselves facing a wave of litigation that threatened to swamp the courts. They set out to deal with the caseload by introducing new procedures to streamline the review

---

64 *See* Sonoo Takashi, *Tōkyō chisai ni okeru hasan jiken no jitsujō to kadai – kako 10 nenkan no tōkei sūchi no bunseki to saikin no tetsuzuki no shinten jōkyō* [Actual circumstances of and issues for insolvency cases at Tokyo District Court – Analysis of statistical figures for the past ten years and the status of progress in procedures], KIN'YŪHŌMU JIJŌ (No. 1644) 6 (2002).

65 *Id.*

process. In doing so, they undertook discussions with the bar associations, representatives of creditors, and others; and there was a high level of cooperation between the judges and the bar associations. Section 20 also undertook broad efforts to publicize the new systems, including issuing numerous announcements regarding the procedures, some complete with Frequently Asked Questions sections. Also, Section 20 achieved all of this without any change in the legislative standards. A new Insolvency Act was enacted in 2004,[66] but at the time of the above activities the applicable law was still the old Insolvency Act, which dated all the way back to 1922. As a final observation, it seems clear that the Supreme Court highly evaluated the efforts of Section 20; immediately thereafter Judge Sonoo was promoted to the position of Head of the Civil Division of the Supreme Court General Secretariat.

Mass Environmental Tort Law Reconsidered: In an earlier section I introduced the mass environmental tort law field as a classic case of bottom-up policy making by lower courts, through the incremental development of precedent in a series of decisions by district courts in various regions of Japan. In another sense, however, the environmental field stands as yet another prominent example of policy making by the judiciary as an institution as a whole.

From virtually the very start, the pollution cases involved broad institutional involvement by the top ranks of the judiciary. In March 1970, the Supreme Court General Secretariat convened a meeting of 57 District Court and High Court judges from across Japan with expertise in civil cases to discuss the best means of responding to the pollution cases. This in effect amounted to a brainstorming session in which members of the judiciary could consider collectively the best approach to mass pollution cases. At the start of that meeting, Chief Justice Ishida Kazuto reportedly told the gathering that traditional legal interpretations were inadequate to meet the needs of society and encouraged the judges to devise new methods of interpretation.[67] The General Secretariat's Civil Division helped organize that meeting. In reflecting on the meeting, the head of the Civil Division at the time, Yaguchi Kōichi, who later served as Chief Justice, commented that it had produced "many important results."[68] As Yaguchi's account suggests, the discussions at that meeting presumably helped shape the decisions in the Big Four pollution cases. Thus, to some extent those decisions reflected not only

---

66 HASANHŌ [Insolvency Act], Act No. 75 of 2004.

67 See YAMAMOTO, *supra* note 61, vol. 2, p. 28.

68 YAGUCHI KŌICHI, SAIKŌ SAIBANSHO TO TOMO NI [Together with the Supreme Court] 65 (1993).

the views of the individual district courts, but a collective statement of policy by the judiciary as a whole on a very important matter of public concern.

III. THE MANAGERIAL ROLE AND "ACTIVISM" OF THE CAREER JUDICIARY

Haley: Your comments on policy making within the career judiciary raise issues that go well beyond judicial adherence to precedent and norm creation. They illustrate managerial features of the judicial system that in turn have had a major effect on litigation: the efficiency and the availability of judicial relief.

Your narrative fits comfortably within a series of studies published over the past two decades on the settlement of traffic accident claims. Three stand out. Your predecessor at the University of Tokyo, Kahei Rokumoto, led the pack with his 1978 study of settlement of traffic accident cases.[69] A decade later Mark Ramseyer and Minoru Nakazato followed with their complementary study of "rational" litigants.[70] Finally in 1990 Takao Tanase completed the trilogy with his article on the judicial management of such cases.[71] All three studies focus on an issue you do not raise but is dear to my heart: Japanese litigiousness. Although they all cited my first (and some might say final) significant published work on Japanese law,[72] none acknowledged the accuracy of my findings. Rokumoto and Ramseyer (with Nakazato) simply ignored the prefatory points that I raised. Tanase appears to have misread the piece (or relied, as many others, on an extracted version).

Hopefully without sounding overly defensive or self-congratulatory, in my view they confirmed my findings. First, noting that the Japanese appeared to be more litigious than some and less so than others, I explicitly rejected any attempt at an in-depth comparative analysis of

---

[69] Rokumoto Kahei, *Higaisha-gawa tōjisha no hōkōdō* [The legal process from the perspective of the victim as a party], in Kawashima Takeyoshi & Hirano Ryūichi, eds., JIDŌSHA JIKO O MEGURU FUNSŌ SHORI TO HŌ [Law and resolution of automobile accident disputes] 33–82 (1978).

[70] J. Mark Ramseyer and Minoru Nakazato, *The Rational Litigant: Settlement Amounts and Verdict Rates in Japan*, 18 J. LEGAL STUD. 262 (1989).

[71] Takao Tanase, *The Management of Disputes: Automobile Accident Compensation in Japan*, 24 LAW & SOC'Y REV. 651 (1990).

[72] John O. Haley, *The Myth of the Reluctant Litigant*, 4 J. JAP. STUD. 359 (1978).

litigation with other countries, especially the United States.[73] The variables are too numerous. Instead I looked at eight decades of litigation rates per capita only within Japan. I did, however, explain in some detail the process of negotiated settlement of disputes that might otherwise be litigated and how the certainty of litigated outcomes ordinarily leads to more settlements and fewer lawsuits.[74] I also expressly noted that culture did matter, pointing out that Japanese litigants, particularly in the pollution cases you cite, expressed a reluctance to litigate out of shame in instances of overt physical impairment.[75] Finally, based on a regression analysis, I then concluded that delay in the disposition of cases provided the only empirically viable explanation for the remarkable variance in litigation rates from 1890 through the 1930s and that no variable explained the variations of postwar litigation rates from 1950 through 1973.[76] At no point in the postwar period through 1973 did the volume of new cases filed for trial in district courts ever reach the level of cases filed between 1924 and 1934, when the number of lawyers also increased to similarly unparalleled levels. From these data I concluded that the lack of institutional capacity, particularly the paucity of judges relative to litigation rates with consequently greater delay and costs, could be reasonably understood as a significant factor in reducing litigation and producing the extreme variations of the prewar period.[77]

In a subsequent visit of the issue a quarter century later, I again reviewed both the literature and the data on litigation.[78] What I discovered confirmed the significance of your 1995 article and its conclusions, which you repeat here. First, a Justice System Reform Council survey of 591 prior litigants in 16 district courts (published in 2000[79]) found that their main reasons for any hesitation to file a lawsuit were delay (72%) and cost (67.2%). Rokumoto's study, on the other

---

[73] *Id.* at 362–64. For an inaccurate assertion to the contrary, see Christian Wollschläger, *Historical Trends of Civil Litigation in Japan, Arizona, Sweden, and Germany: Japanese Legal Culture in Light of Judicial Statistics*, in Harald Baum, ed., JAPAN: ECONOMIC SUCCESS AND LEGAL SYSTEM 89 (1997).

[74] Haley, *supra* note 72, at 365–66.

[75] *Id.* at 367.

[76] *Id.* at 368–71.

[77] *Id.* at 380–81.

[78] *See* John O. Haley, *Litigation in Japan: A New Look at Old Problems*, 10 WILLAMETTE J. OF INT'L L. & DISP. RESOL. 121–42 (2002).

[79] SHIHŌ SEIDO KAIKAKU SHINGIKAI [Justice System Reform Council], MINJI SOSHŌ RIYŌSHA CHŌSA: HŌKOKUSHO [Survey of users of civil litigation: Report], December 22, 2000.

hand, almost perfectly predicted Ramseyer and Nakazato. He classified the claims into four categories: injury resulting in death, serious injury (presumably primarily to property), personal injury resulting in lasting physical disfigurement or other disability, and minor injury. In two-thirds or more of the cases involving wrongful death, serious property injury, and minor injury, the responding claimants generally settled in cases where in effect they were offered at least as much as they thought they would receive if they pursued their claims in court. Most of those who did actually pursue their claims in court were apparently not offered as much to settle as they predicted a court would award. The majority also expressed the view that they had made the correct choice in the end. Those who suffered some personal injury were the only category of claims in which the respondents indicated in effect that they settled for less than what they calculated they would have received had they litigated. In other words, those who were physically disfigured to some extent were apparently the most likely to abandon their claims. This result is easily explained, as I suggested, by an acute sense of shame and fear of social humiliation from public exposure of physical disability.

Your study, on the other hand, helps to explain the causes of the remarkable change in institutional capacity and its effect on litigation since the mid-1970s. Since 1973 the number of new civil cases filed for trial as well as the number of lawyers have both steadily increased, exceeding the prewar peaks by the mid- to late 1980s. The number of new cases filed for trial in district courts more than doubled between 1990 and 2010 (106,871 to 222,594 new filings). By Japanese standards, the nation has become remarkably litigious. Not coincidentally, during the same period the number of lawyers more than doubled from 13,800 in 1990 to 28,789 in 2010. Yet these increases in the number of lawsuits and lawyers were unrelated to any increase in the number of judges. The number of judges per capita has almost steadily declined over the past century. In 1890, with 1531 judges and a total population of 40,968,835, Japan had one judge per 26,760 persons. Sixty years later in the early postwar period (1950), the population had grown to 83,199,637, but the number of judges had increased only to a total of 2621, resulting in a judicial system with one judge per 31,743 persons. The situation became progressively worse during the next six decades as increases in population outstripped annual increases in the number of judges. In 2010 Japan had 3588 judges for a population of 128,057,352. The result was now one judge per 35,650 persons. Yet, commencing around 1975, despite steady increases in population, bar membership, and caseloads, with a declining number of judges relative to all three, delay has been equally dramatically reduced.

In 1973 the disposition of 32,088 first instance civil cases had taken more than two years from filing. This delay was reduced to the extent that despite a two-fold increase in the number of new cases filed, by 2011 in only 7003 cases had the final disposition required more than two years. From a slightly different vantage point, in 1965, slightly more than 65,000 new civil cases were filed in a district court. On average during that year, from filing to judgment took a year and a half. As caseloads mounted, by 1975 nearly 75,000 new civil suits were filed, but on average a case required 16.2 months from start to finish. Yet in 1997, with twice as many newly filed district court cases (152,678), the cases were completed within less than a year (9.2 months).[80] In other words, the judges increased institutional capacity by effective management, not increasing numbers. And those judges who managed their caseloads best were, as one of Ramseyer's most recent articles shows,[81] rewarded.

I would hesitate to use the term "activism" to label the judges' managerial performance. To me what you have described reflects their competence or, as Ramseyer puts it, their talent. You are absolutely correct, however, in your assessment that in the process they also develop substantive norms that are then applied in cases and widely disseminated nationwide. The result is the certainty or predictability that enabled settlements and an overall reduction of litigation.

Foote: I should perhaps add to my comments by saying that we need to keep in mind that the norms the Japanese judiciary has created have important policy implications. I admit to having used the term "activism" in a number of works as a dramatic device for countering the dominant image of Japan's judiciary as a passive body, the model of judicial restraint. I would point out, however, that I typically either placed the word "activism" in quotation marks or followed it with a question mark, and I always included a careful explanation of the sense in which I was using that term. Even so, whenever I presented my research I inevitably was bogged down in a discussion of the meaning

---

80 Statistics compiled from various sources, including SAIKŌ SAIBANSHO [Supreme Court of Japan], SHIHŌ TŌKEI [Judicial statistics] (2013) [http://www.courts.go.jp/search/jtsp0010?] and JAPAN FEDERATION OF BAR ASSOCIATIONS, WHITE PAPER ON ATTORNEYS (2012), as well as sources cited in Haley, *supra* notes 72 and 78.

81 *See* J. Mark Ramseyer, *Talent Matters: Judicial Productivity and Speed in Japan*, 32 INT'L REV. L. & ECON. 32 (2012).

of the word "activism," and I have moved away from using that term to instead using phrases such as "creation of norms" or "policy making" by the judiciary.

That said, much as I approve of the role the Japanese judiciary has played in many of the contexts discussed above, I have no doubt that if the same types of activity occurred in the United States, one or more constituencies would brand virtually every one of these examples as a case of "judicial activism."

Unlike "judicial activism" in the United States in its narrow sense, none of the lines of decisions discussed above involves constitutional rights. Thus, none of the decisions directly infringes the legislature's ability to deal with the issues. As it has done in the pollution and employment discrimination contexts, the Diet is free to enact its own legislation governing the issues.

Nonetheless, the courts' role in creating law carries the potential for conflicts with the legislature. Indeed, the cases described above provide examples of implicit conflicts, and even some explicit conflicts, between the courts' vision of law and that of the legislature. In numerous situations, including the corporate disregard doctrine and the criminal retrial context, the courts acted to embody new standards even though the Diet directly considered the issues and failed to act. Moreover, as discussed above, in those cases in which they have utilized the abuse of right doctrine, including the abusive dismissal and land lease/house lease contexts, the courts have consciously overridden the standards enacted by the Diet.

In fact, the abuse of right doctrine carries much the same potential for thwarting the legislature's will as the constitutional invalidation technique that forms the heart of "judicial activism" in the United States. Just as with constitutional invalidation, when the courts utilize the abuse of right doctrine the legislature may find it difficult to overcome the standards announced by the courts. Thus, for example, after the Diet relaxed the standards for termination of leases in 1921, the courts applied the abuse of right doctrine to reach similar outcomes, as had been the case prior to the amendments.

One pattern of creation of norms by the Japanese judiciary, I would suggest, would appear especially activist to American eyes: the pattern I have labeled "top down, institutional initiative." The activities of the judges in Section 27 of the Tokyo District Court, in the traffic accident context, and Section 20 in the insolvency context, went far beyond simply developing law through the accretion of precedent. The judges undertook extensive efforts to promulgate new standards and disseminate them to the bar and the public. Those activities, I would submit, are more akin to administrative or legislative policy making than traditional judicial decision making.

In this connection, I will close by discussing a situation I view as highly analogous to the traffic accident context: asbestos. In Japan, the genesis for the standard setting by Section 27 lies in the flood of traffic accident litigation that began to hit the courts in the early 1960s. Fearing the courts would quickly be overwhelmed by these cases, the judiciary consciously sought to develop means to handle these cases expeditiously and to channel the cases out of litigation into a more efficient resolution process.

In the United States, asbestos litigation bears close parallels. Indeed, if ever there were a field that called for streamlining, standardization, and rationalization, it would be asbestos. In the late 1970s and early 1980s, trial courts in many areas of the United States began to experience a flood of asbestos litigation. By 2002, over a decade ago, the number of asbestos-related claims filed in US courts already reached 730,000.[82] As with traffic accidents, many of the asbestos cases involve highly similar fact patterns, with the same diseases and similar exposure history. In the 1980s groups of US district court judges sought to adopt an approach to asbestos similar to that undertaken for traffic accidents by the Japanese judiciary, using jury awards in representative cases to set compensation standards for similar cases. The organized bar strenuously fought these efforts, and appeals courts forcefully struck down the efforts, finding that the judges exceeded their authority, by in effect acting in a legislative or administrative capacity, and intruded on litigants' rights to trial.[83] In other words, the appeals courts themselves found this approach to be an impermissible case of "judicial activism." As this example reflects, in some respects the roles played by Japanese courts in creating law would be branded as unacceptable "judicial activism" even under US standards.

The United States still lacks an effective, rational means for handling asbestos claims and the costs continue to rise. According to a comprehensive study conducted by the RAND Corporation, as of 2002 insurers and defendants had paid a total of $70 *billion* on asbestos

---

[82] *See* STEPHEN J. CARROLL, DEBORAH HENSLER, JENNIFER GROSS, ELIZABETH M. SLOSS, MATTHIAS SCHONLAU, ALLAN ABRAHAMSE, J. SCOTT ASHWOOD, ASBESTOS LITIGATION 70–72 (Rand Inst. Civ. Just., 2005).

[83] *See, e.g.*, Linda S. Mullenix, *Problems in Complex Litigation*, 10 REV. LITIG. 213, 218–19 (1991); Linda S. Mullenix, *Beyond Consolidation: Postaggregative Procedure in Asbestos Mass Tort Litigation*, 32 WM. & MARY L. REV. 475, 504 (1991).

litigation. Of that amount, a total of $40 billion, 58%, had gone to legal fees and other litigation-related expenses; only $30 billion, 42%, had gone to compensation for victims.[84] While some aspects of the standard setting by the Japanese judiciary in the traffic accident context are open to criticism, whether or not one characterizes those efforts as "activism" should not obscure the great achievements of the standardization in providing prompt and effective relief, with low transaction costs.[85]

Haley: Perhaps you are correct that some in the US would label as "activism" any effort by US courts to engage in the types of caseload management you describe in Japan. The pejorative charge of "activism" would be made simply because, as you say, any such attempt would be so extraordinary. In large part, however, such an effort would not be as easily achieved even if possible within our judicial system. Unlike Japan's career judges, our judges have both individual and collective autonomy. Standardization of the applicable rules and norms, and much less cooperation among the judges even within a single federal or state district or circuit would be extremely difficult to realize. It would be akin to a frog trying to set hopping standards while herding other frogs. Consensus and cooperation are more imbedded features of the Japanese culture to begin with. Achieving both is made easier as well by the structure of the career judiciary. Senior judges who have known and worked together throughout the judicial system for decades are not only in charge of the central administrative controls but sit along with their junior colleagues on every trial and appellate bench.

However, your distinction between the "activism" of the courts in civil (as well as administrative and criminal cases), in contrast to those that involve constitutional law issues, is especially prescient. During the discussion of papers at a conference held at Washington University in St. Louis in 2010 on "Decision Making on the Japanese Supreme Court,"[86] a participant questioned former Justice Izumi Tokuji as to the apparent "conservatism" of the judiciary with respect to the constitutional protections of women's rights related precisely to the issues of law that you describe above. His response is worth noting. He defended the judiciary's record, distinguishing the decisions like those

---

84 *See* CARROLL ET AL., *supra* note 82, at 87–105.

85 While the topic lies beyond the scope of this chapter, Japan's performance with respect to asbestos also leaves much to be desired. For a discussion of this topic, in Japanese, see DANIEL H. FOOTE, SAIBAN TO SHAKAI: SHIHŌ NO "JŌSHIKI" SAIKŌ [The Courts and Society: Reconsidering "common knowledge" regarding justice] (Tamaruya Masayuki tr., 2006), at 82–85.

86 *See* 88 WASH. U. L. REV. (No. 6, 2011) for the published papers.

you point out in which the Civil Code provisions on gender equality and public policy (Article 90) have been applied with the dearth of similar constitutional decisions. Constitutional decision making, he emphasized, involves separate considerations. In a word, constitutional decisions are momentous. They cannot be altered by the legislature and apply to all state actions. The courts must thereby be more "cautious" (my words) in construing and applying constitutional rights in contrast to Civil Code protections. In stark contrast to other constitutional courts, the justices of the Japanese Supreme Court are both more mindful of the enduring impact of their precedents and less arrogant (also my term) in any assumption that they have the authority to impose their individually held values and normative judgments as constitutional norms. Justice Izumi reminded us that Supreme Court constitutional law precedents bind all state actors and thereby foreclose nationwide any political departure without the subsequent approval of a handful of judges, who change their minds or agree to overturn precedent. It is much easier and more responsible for the courts to make private law than constitutional law.

That said, another difference between the appropriate roles of the courts in adjudicating constitutional cases should be emphasized. Constitutionally mandated rights and norms in Japan can be protected nationwide without constitutional adjudication. As a unitary system with national codes, by interpreting and applying provisions of private and public law, for example, through the application of Article 90 of the Civil Code as you describe, the courts are able to protect individual rights throughout Japan. Constitutional principles can be applied and enforced and thereby realized throughout Japan in construing the Civil Code in a private law case without the necessity of a decision on the constitutionality of any state action. In a federal system like ours, without a federal constitutional mandate, the interpretation and enforcement of even the most fundamental rights can differ by state or region. Japanese judges do not need to address the question of whether those who live in California should enjoy the same protections that they would enjoy were they to live in New York.

Foote: Your point is well taken that the Japanese judiciary need not rely on constitutional adjudication to ensure conformity. As we have discussed, within Japan's unified national system, great weight is placed on legal stability and respect for precedent. At the same time, in Japan's overwhelmingly career judiciary,[87] numerous mechanisms exist

[87] In the 1990s there was a push for mid-career lawyers to enter the judiciary; and, since early in the 21st century, there has been a push to broaden and diversify the sources for and experiences of judges, both through a renewed

for socializing young assistant judges into the established norms and values of the judiciary and ensuring continued compliance with those norms and values.[88] Taken together, as you have observed, these features ensure widespread conformity within the judiciary for precedents in the civil, criminal, and administrative law fields, without the need for further buttressing by constitutional doctrine. In turn, as you highlighted earlier, the relative certainty provided by this system has facilitated settlements and private ordering by the parties, often without the need for resorting to the courts.

IV. "COMMUNITARIAN CONSERVATISM"?

Foote: Let me now turn to a somewhat different topic. In your Waseda lecture you proffered the ethos of "communitarian conservatism" as a unifying theme for creation of norms by the Japanese judiciary. That interpretation fits very closely to one of the categories of cases I have included in my typology: the Japanese judiciary's exposition and promotion of the norms of respect for and preservation of ongoing relationships, which I have labeled "creation of norms in the service of

---

effort to encourage mid-career lawyers to enter the judiciary and a program through which assistant judges spend a significant period of time (typically two years) working in law firms or other law-related positions. To date, the numbers resulting from these efforts have been low. *See, e.g.*, Daniel H. Foote, *Recent Reforms to the Japanese Judiciary: Real Change or Mere Appearance?* 66 HŌ SHAKAIGAKU 128 (2007). The judiciary continues to be dominated by the career pattern, as discussed by Haley above.

[88] For discussions of these mechanisms, see, e.g., Masaki Abe, *The Internal Control of a Bureaucratic Judiciary: The Case of Japan*, 23 INT'L J. SOCIOL. L. 303 (1995); Setsuo Miyazawa, *Administrative Control of Japanese Judges*, in Philip S.C. Lewis, ed., LAW AND TECHNOLOGY IN THE PACIFIC COMMUNITY 263 (1994); J. MARK RAMSEYER & ERIC B. RASMUSEN, MEASURING JUDICIAL INDEPENDENCE: THE POLITICAL ECONOMY OF JUDGING IN JAPAN 7–15 (2003); and John O. Haley, *The Japanese Judiciary: Maintaining Integrity, Autonomy, and the Public Trust*, in Daniel H. Foote, ed., LAW IN JAPAN: A TURNING POINT 99, 120–21 (2007). I have also discussed these mechanisms and other features of the judicial career system at length in a book in Japanese, NA MO NAI KAO MO NAI SHIHŌ: NIHON NO SAIBAN WA KAWARU NO KA [Nameless Faceless Justice: Will Japan's Courts Change?] (Tamaruya Masayuki tr., 2007). As reflected in the title of that book, I have characterized the Japanese judiciary as a system of "nameless faceless justice," with core values of uniformity and anonymity, based on the ethos that the identity of the judge should not matter, the handling and result should be the same regardless.

stability." Indeed, as examples of the communitarian conservative ethos, you point to several of the same examples I have cited for the "stability" thesis: the land lease/house lease situation, divorce, and the employment relationship.

In those instances, the courts may well have been capturing the common sense of society. It bears note, however, as you mention, that in each of the land lease/house lease, employment, and divorce contexts, the courts consciously interpreted around, or, to put it more bluntly, consciously overrode, seemingly explicit language in statutes passed by the Diet. In the employment context, for example, the courts effectively made meaningless the statutory provision permitting employers to terminate workers upon providing 30 days' notice or 30 days' wages in lieu of notice. And my own interpretation of the land lease/house lease context differs from yours. While you see the 1921 Land Lease and House Lease Acts as affirmation of the judicial precedents, my understanding is that those laws, while acquiescing in some aspects of the precedents, sought to limit their effect. As originally enacted, the House Lease Act, for example, permitted fixed-term leases of one year or more and did not require landlords to show just cause to terminate. Despite this seemingly clear expression of the Diet's intent to override the judicial precedents in those respects, the courts continued to interpret the Act very narrowly, requiring landlords to show just cause for terminating *and* for refusing to renew leases.

Moreover, in both the employment and real property contexts, the barriers to termination have come under pressure in recent decades, as societal attitudes have shifted a bit in the direction of favoring greater flexibility for restructuring relationships. While the Diet ultimately acquiesced with respect to the abusive dismissal doctrine (albeit over 50 years after the courts first began following that doctrine), in the land and house lease context the Diet again relaxed the standards for terminating leases in 1991,[89] in part in an effort to provide greater flexibility so as to enable real estate development.

Furthermore, other instances of policy making by the judiciary (or, if you prefer, creation or adjustment of norms by the judiciary) do not fit so easily under the rubric of "communitarian conservatism." This, I would suggest, is true for most of the other examples discussed above, including the environmental law field, employment discrimination, sexual harassment, traffic accidents, and insolvency, as well as criminal retrials and the corporate disregard doctrine. In many of these contexts, the judiciary was responding to newly recognized societal issues, which

---

[89] SHAKUCHI SHAKUYA HŌ [Land and House Lease Act], Act No. 90 of 1991.

the Diet had failed to address. One could make the argument that many of these instances of norm creation are communitarian and conservative in nature. By combating pollution, for example, the environmental cases help preserve communities and conserve the natural environment. And the employment discrimination and sexual harassment cases, by seeking to ensure respect for women, might be seen as promoting communitarian and conservative values. I have no doubt, however, at least in the US context, that protection of the rights of pollution victims, women, convicted criminals, and perhaps even traffic accident victims, as well as protection of employees and tenants, would be branded as "liberal" by many observers.

Haley: As you note and I explain above, I see an overriding "community" interest in nearly all of these cases. Although they might be viewed through a lens colored by an "individual rights"-oriented tint and thus may appear in the US context as more "liberal" or progressive, to me they are more affirming of community. Those cases in which the courts have by all accounts protected individual rights, particularly the equal rights of women, your view persuades even me. Yet I would at least offer the suggestion that the courts in such cases are not creating norms but rather implementing existing constitutional as well as private law rights through private law adjudication, as described above. Both the postwar constitution and the Civil Code as amended during the Occupation to conform to the new constitution are quite explicit in the guarantee of gender equality. Constitution Article 14 provides: "All of the people are equal under the law and there shall be no discrimination in political, economic or social relations because of race, creed, sex, social status or family origin." Article 24 reiterates this mandate with retrospect to marriage and divorce. These protections are supplemented in Article 2 of the Civil Code, which reads: "This Code *must be construed* in accordance with honoring the dignity of individuals and the essential equality of both sexes." [Emphasis added.] In the example of judicial denial of contested divorce, if you accept the possibility of an underpinning albeit unstated premise that wives who more often than not are not working but are maintaining house and home, paying the bills and caring for children and other family members, they generally would suffer particularly serious economic and social disadvantages were their husbands able to terminate the marriage unilaterally. Viewed in this light, the decisions to deny contested divorce take on an added dimension. They protect wives because of the advantages divorcing husbands enjoy and thus help to ensure the essential equality of women.

One can also view such decisions as confirming consensus if not community, in other words, curtailing arbitrary exercise of legal rights.

The first "abuse of rights" case serves as a prime example. As I noted in the Waseda lecture, the doctrine was apparently first applied in a late Meiji Period decision in *Sonoda v. Sonoda*,[90] limiting the "absolute" authority of registered household heads to determine the residence of house members. A similar case, also noted in the Waseda lecture, that also illustrates the prewar protection of women was the judicial recognition – creation, if you will – of a *naien* marriage. The recognition of a *naien* wife (albeit without the full rights of a legal spouse, especially in terms of succession) provided some legal protection to women between the time of a formal wedding ceremony and the newly required registration of the marriage, with the consent of the household head. The development began with a 1915 decision by the *Daishin'in*. Although, I might add, the rights of *naien* wives were recognized in subsequent special statutes, such as the 1923 Factory Act, no recognition is afforded by the Civil Code even as amended pursuant to postwar abolition of the *ie* system and other "democratization" reforms of the Occupation era. The Supreme Court has applied the notion once more in one of its most recent decisions recognizing the *naien* wife's claims to insurance proceeds upon the husband's death.[91]

V. LEGISLATIVE AFFIRMATION OF JUDICIAL PRECEDENT

Haley: Shifting to a related topic, I take it from your observations that we generally agree that few if any features of Japanese law have been more distinctive than the pattern of subsequent legislative action affirming judicial precedent, in many instances years later. Among the best-known examples were the inclusion of the "good faith" and "abuse of rights" principles in the postwar amendments to Article 1 of the Civil Code. Legislative recognition, albeit with modification of the prewar judicial precedents related to land and house leases described above, are early examples. The 1921 Land Lease Law[92] and House Lease Law,[93] not to mention the 1900 Law Concerning Superficies[94] and the 1909 Law Concerning the Protection of Buildings,[95] may be somewhat exceptional

---

[90] 7 MINROKU (No. 6), 47 (Gr. Ct. Cass., June 20, 1901).

[91] *Arai Akira v. Shakai Hokenchō Chōkan*, 61 MINSHŪ 518 (Sup. Ct., 1st P.B., Mar. 8, 2007).

[92] SHAKUCHI HŌ (Law No. 49, 1921).

[93] SHAKUYA HŌ (Law No. 50, 1921).

[94] *Chijōken ni kansuru hōritsu* (Law No. 72, 1900).

[95] *Tatemono hogo ni kansuru hōritsu* (Law No. 40, 1909).

in that they appear to reflect a common legislative concern to supplant judicial activity as soon as possible and thereby, arguably, reduce judicial innovation, or at least to avoid inconsistency and the tensions between codified and judge-made rules. Aside from our interpretations of the extent of legislative deference, I take it that we agree that ultimately the legislature did not fully overturn the judicial decisions, and that, at least as significant, the Diet either acquiesced (my emphasis) or gave up (your emphasis). In either event, the courts had the last word.

We both cite numerous examples of legislative acquiescence to judicial law-making. You provide a plethora: employment termination and gender discrimination, sexual harassment, environmental law, not to mention the house and land lease law cases. We both note the postwar codification of the prewar, judicially recognized abuse of right and good faith principles in Article 1 of the Civil Code. In my Waseda lecture I noted the 1971 amendment of the Civil Code that finally included the "base" or "maximal" hypothecs (*neteitōken*), a 50-year-old judicial creation, as a now codified right *in rem* (*bukken*). Similarly over eight decades after the 1906 judgment in which the Daishin'in (Great Court of Cassation) recognized contractual *jōtō tampo* arrangements as legitimate and effective secured transactions,[96] the Diet recognized them by statute.[97] By then they had long become the most commonly used convenient forms of secured transactions in registered collateral, particularly immovables. I would include as two recent examples the long line of cases on international adjudicatory jurisdiction and the landmark decision on foreign sovereign immunity. In both instances, the Diet ratified the prior cases, fully codifying, in the case of international adjudicatory jurisdiction, a half-century of judicial development. The 2011 amendments to the Code of Civil Procedure simply codified the preexisting case law with no appreciable alteration.[98] Similarly in 2009, the Diet affirmed the 2006, 2nd Petty Bench decision in *Tokyo Sanyō Bōeki K.K., et al. v. The Islamic Republic of Pakistan*,[99] in which the

[96] Shirono v. Higashi, 12 MINROKU 1172 (Gr. Ct., Cass., 1906).

[97] Law concerning Provisional Registration of Security Interest Contracts (*Kari-tōki tanpo keiyaku ni kansuru hōritsu*), Law No. 78, 1978.

[98] Law No. 36, 2011, adding Code of Civil Procedure article 3-2 through 3-12, enacted on April 28, 2011, and promulgated on May 2, 2011, effective in 2012.

[99] 60 MINSHŪ 2542 (Sup. Ct., 2nd P.B., July 21, 2006). The Japanese justices took the lead in this case, which was affirmed by subsequent legislation, in contrast to the US experience of judicial deference to the State Department's position until Congress acted, as well as the Canadian example of legislative action after the failure of the courts to adopt the restrictive approach. *See, e.g.*, *Gouvernement de la République Démocratique du Congo v. Venne* [1971] S.C.R. 997.

Court adopted the restrictive theory of foreign sovereign immunity, thereby allowing civil and commercial suits against foreign states and foreign state agencies arising from their commercial activities. The Diet by statute affirmed the decision in the 2009 Act on Civil Jurisdiction of Japan with Respect to a Foreign State.[100] Other examples include the codification of judicial precedents in the 2004 amended version of the Administrative Case Litigation Law,[101] Article 9(2) in particular.[102]

One of the most articulate and persuasive studies of the interrelationship of creative judicial law-making and legislative responses is a recently published article by University of British Columbia Law Professor Shigenori Matsui.[103] He focuses on Supreme Court decisions related to consumer loans. He begins with the prefatory example you give of judicial "activism" in protecting workers against unilateral dismissal without just cause. He then continues with his conclusions:

> Recently, the Supreme Court of Japan showed a similar kind of judicial creativity in establishing a pro-consumer jurisprudence against consumer loan companies. This jurisprudence is remarkable because it was accomplished by ignoring the legislature's contrary intent. Although the Diet enacted a statutory provision in order to overturn a previous pro-consumer judgment, the Supreme Court of Japan ignored this legislative intent and practically wiped out the new provision. The judgments of the Supreme Court of Japan had a tremendous impact on the consumer loan industry and consumer loan regulation. As a result of this pro-consumer jurisprudence, millions of consumers could now demand refunds from consumer loan companies. Consumer loan companies went into serious financial trouble, triggering massive reorganization of the industry. Moreover, these developments forced the Diet to amend the regulatory statute in order to introduce more demanding regulation against consumer loan companies.[104]

In other words, once again the Court was more the master, with the Diet and the ruling party its deferential agents.

---

[100] *Gaikoku tō ni taisuru wagakuni no minji saibanken ni kansuru hōritsu* (Law No. 24, 2009).

[101] GYŌSEI JIKEN SOSHŌ HŌ, Law No. 139, as amended by Law No. 84, 2004.

[102] *See* Narufumi Kadomatsu, *Judicial Governance through the Resolution of Legal Disputes? A Japanese Perspective*, 4 NAT'L TAIWAN U. L. REV. 141, 158 (2009).

[103] Shigenori Matsui, *Cloudy Weather, with Occasional Sunshine: Consumer Loans, the Legislature, and the Supreme Court of Japan,* 22 PAC. RIM L. & POL'Y J. 555 (2013).

[104] *Id.* at 556–57.

Even in the most politically sensitive constitutional cases of all, the continuously recurring malapportionment cases, the Diet has responded by amending the election law to accommodate at least to some extent the constitutional objections addressed by the Court. The Supreme Court has in nearly all instances with great anguish (as expressed in the opinions) upheld the constitutionality of the allocation of seats in elections for members of the lower house (pre-1994 under the single vote, multi-member system) and districts (post-1994 under a single member single vote system with some seats allocated by proportional representation), as well as for the upper house.[105] Even though the Court has upheld the constitutionality in nearly all the decisions, the Diet has responded time and again to concerns raised by the Court with some attempt at least at modest electoral reform. No decision has been

---

[105] *Koshiyama v. Chairman, Tokyo Metropolitan Election Supervision Commission Commission*, 18 MINSHŪ 270 (Sup. Ct., G.B., Feb. 5, 1964) (House of Councillors election of 1962); *Kurokawa v. Chiba Prefecture Election Comm'n*, 30 MINSHŪ 223 (Sup. Ct. G.B., April 14, 1976) (House of Representatives election of 1972); *Shimizu v. Osaka Prefecture Election Comm'n*, 37 MINSHŪ 345 (Sup. Ct.. G.B., Apr. 27, 1983) (House of Councillors election of 1977); *Kamuta v. Tokyo Prefecture Election Comm'n*, 37 MINSHŪ 1243 (Sup. Ct., G.B., Nov. 7, 1983) (House of Representatives election of 1980); *Kaneo v. Hiroshima Prefecture Election Comm'n*, 39 MINSHŪ 1100 (Sup. Ct., G.B., July 17, 1985) (House of Representatives election of 1983); *Kawano v. Tokyo Prefecture Election Comm'n*, 47 MINSHŪ 67 (Sup. Ct., G.B., Jan. 20, 1993) (House of Representatives election of 1990); *Osaka Prefecture Election Comm'n v. Kawazoe*, 50 MINSHŪ 2283 (Sup. Ct., G.B., Sept. 11, 1996) (House of Councillors election of 1992); *Yamaguchi v. Tokyo Prefecture Election Comm'n*, 52 MINSHŪ 1373 (Sup. Ct., G.B., Sept. 2, 1998) (House of Councillors election of 1995); *Nonoyama v. Tokyo Prefecture Election Comm'n*, 53 MINSHŪ 1704 (Sup. Ct., G.B., Nov. 10, 1999) (House of Councillors election of 1996); *Yamaguchi v. Tokyo Prefecture Election Comm'n*, 58 MINSHŪ 56 (Sup. Ct., G.B., Jan. 14, 2004) (House of Councillors election of 2001 – Open-List Proportional Representation System under Law No. 118 of 2000); *Yamaguchi v. Tokyo Prefecture Election Comm'n*, 60 MINSHŪ 2696 (Sup. Ct., G.B., Oct. 4, 2006) (House of Councillors election of 2004); *Takemura v. Tokyo Prefecture Election Comm'n*, 61 MINSHŪ 1617 (Sup. Ct., G.B., June 13, 2007) (House of Representatives election of 2005); *Yamaguchi v. Tokyo Prefecture Election Comm'n*, 63 MINSHŪ 1520 (Sup. Ct., G.B., Sept. 30, 2009) (House of Councillors election of 2007); *Tamaguchi v. Tokyo Prefecture Election Comm'n*, 65 MINSHŪ 765 (Sup. Ct., G.B., Mar. 23, 2011) (House of Representative election of 2009); *Kanegami v. Tokyo Prefecture Election Commission*, 66 MINSHŪ – (Sup. Ct., G.B., Oct. 17, 2012); X v. Y., 67 MINSHŪ – (Sup. Ct., G.B., Nov. 20, 2013).

simply ignored.[106] I will not attempt to explain the underlying problems in terms of the questionable validity of all statutes and regulations enacted by the Diet after each challenged election had the Court held the elections (which usually occurred more than two years before the decisions) unconstitutional, as the plaintiffs argued. Nor should it be necessary to go into any detail on the lack of judicial authority in most if not all civil law systems to retain jurisdiction over a case after a final judgment (none has jurisdiction over the parties in the common law sense). Suffice it to say that the remedial capacity of the courts was extremely limited, as compared with US or general common law standards, and little effective relief was available.

Few can argue that legislators in the ruling parties have effectively manipulated or even dominated the courts. What seems best to explain this remarkable deference to the judiciary and judicial law-making is the greater public trust in judges than politicians. The legitimacy of the courts seems hardly in doubt. This repeated pattern of legislative affirmation of judicial decisions may also be explained by an imbedded emphasis on consensus as a societal value as well as a product of structural political configurations. The need for consensus in the face of disagreement over the appropriate direction of the law arguably enhances the legitimacy of consensus-confirming decisions by the courts and likewise precludes any significant change in any status quo determined by the courts. The consequence is ultimate legislative acquiescence to judicial law-making.

Foote: I agree that there are many prominent examples of legislative (and, I would add, administrative) affirmation of norms and standards set forth in judicial decisions. To me, one of the most striking such examples was the Diet's enactment of a rather elaborate compensation scheme for pollution-related illnesses and deaths in 1973, based heavily on standards established by the courts.[107] As a much more recent example, promptly after the Supreme Court held in 2010 that it constitutes illegal double taxation to impose income tax as well as inheritance tax on the beneficiaries of life insurance money paid in pension form,[108] the National Tax Agency announced not only that it was changing the applicable rule prospectively but that it would grant

---

[106] The Diet amended the Election Law five times (1964, 1975, 1986, 1993, 1994) while cases were pending or had been decided. Yusaku Horiuchi & Jun Sato, *Reapportionment and Redistribution: Consequences of Electoral Reform in Japan*, 47 AM. J. POL. SCI. 669, 671 (2003).

[107] *See* Fujikura, *supra* note 21, at 387.

[108] Hamanaka v. Japan, 64 MINSHŪ 1277 (Sup. Ct., 3rd P.B., July 6, 2010).

retrospective rebates for the prior five years to all similarly situated persons who applied.[109] Moreover, while some readers may be surprised to see you treat it as legislative affirmation when the Diet enacts legislation that incorporates judicial precedents 20, 50, and even 80 years after the relevant decisions were rendered, I agree that in many such instances the legislature, through its non-action over the intervening years, effectively acquiesced in the decisions, even though it did not actively endorse those decisions until much later.

As I mentioned earlier, though, in my view it is a stretch to characterize the house lease field, in which the Diet tried on multiple occasions to relax the standards adopted by the courts, as an example of legislative affirmation. And while I agree that Professor Matsui's recent article on the consumer loan field is a wonderful, detailed study of judicial creation of norms and the interaction between the courts and the Diet, I read the central message of his article rather differently from you. You evidently focus on the last sentence of the excerpt quoted above, with the observation that "these [judicial] developments forced the Diet to amend the regulatory statute in order to introduce more demanding regulation against consumer loan companies," when you conclude that the Diet affirmed the judicial stance and hence "the Court was more the master with the Diet and the ruling party its deferential agents." I would highlight two earlier sentences in the same excerpt, in which Matsui observes, "This jurisprudence is remarkable because it was accomplished by ignoring the legislature's contrary intent. Although the Diet enacted a statutory provision in order to overturn a previous … judgment, the Supreme Court of Japan ignored this legislative intent and practically wiped out the new provision." It is true the Diet eventually gave in and adopted stricter regulation – notably, after lawyers all across Japan began bringing a massive wave of lawsuits on behalf of borrowers in reliance on Supreme Court precedent. Yet, given the Diet's original legislation and its prior effort to overturn the Supreme Court precedent, I would not go so far as to characterize the Diet as "deferential."

Finally, I will offer a few remarks regarding the malapportionment cases. As you observe, this is an extremely politically sensitive issue, since it directly affects the seats occupied by the Diet members

---

[109] *See* Kokuzeichō [National Tax Agency], *Sōzoku tō ni kakawaru seimei hoken keiyaku tō ni motozuku nenkin o jukyū sarete iru kata e* [To persons who are receiving pensions based on life insurance contracts, etc., in regard to inheritance, etc.], http://www.nta.go.jp/sonota/sonota/osirase/topics/data/h22/sozoku_zoyo/.

themselves. And as you also observe, if the Supreme Court, two or more years later, were to declare an election invalid, the practical ramifications for legislation adopted and other actions taken in the interim would be complicated and potentially severe. In part as a consequence of these features, the two sides have engaged in a very long and rather elaborate dance. It is true that the Supreme Court has upheld the constitutionality of the allocation of seats in most of the decisions it has rendered and has yet to declare an election invalid (although in 2013 two lower courts did issue decisions declaring elections invalid). In eight cases, though, including Grand Bench decisions in each of the past three years (2011–2013), the Supreme Court has declared the allocations unconstitutional (albeit, in several, including the most recent three, with the proviso that, while the allocation was unconstitutional, it could not be said that the Diet had failed to act within a reasonable time to remedy the malapportionment). Moreover, even in the cases in which it has upheld the constitutionality of the allocations, the Court typically has expressed grave reservations about vote inequality; and it has been sending increasingly strong warnings to the Diet about the need for prompt action. As you note, the Diet has not entirely ignored the warnings. With regard to the overall legislative response, however, I would stress the adjective you used, "modest." As another apt adjective I would offer "grudging." But, at least in this context, most assuredly not "deferential." And with that, I will turn back to you for the final word.

VI. SENSE OF SOCIETY

Haley: The legitimacy of the courts to make legal rules and create new legal norms as well as recurring affirmations by the Diet brings us back to that ubiquitous phrase "the sense of society" (*shakai tsūnen*). Does it have bearing on this question or, indeed, any substantive meaning or function or is it merely a rhetorical throwaway?

Writing in the early 1980s Osaka University Philosophy of Law Professor Yasaki Mitsukuni began to explore the repetitive insertion of the phrase "the sense of the society" in judicial decisions throughout the past century.[110] Based on review of published judgments in which the phrase appeared, he found that judges principally use the phrase to justify interpretation or "modifying" construction of applicable

---

[110] Mitsukuni Yasaki, *Law and Shakai-Tsūnen as a Legal Form of Consensus Idea*, 29 OSAKA U. L. REV. 1 (1981).

provisions of the relevant code, statute, or constitution. Noting the judges may believe that they are expressing the actual "sense" of the community or may simply be giving "lip service" to such notion, he unfortunately stopped short of a more ambitious effort to determine the meaning and function of its use. I am unsure that we have or can add much to Yasaki's findings; however, I suggest that, as Yasaki pointed out, the phrase has a justifying function and, as he speculated, judges in many instances believe "heartily" that their view of the sense of society is accurate. In other words, the phrase is not simply a rhetorical device inserted in opinions to obscure application of collective judicial value judgments.

To conclude, the examples of judicial law-making and norm creation we have described both here and in previously published research occur in a society in which the structures and values of consensus and community are deeply imbedded. The judiciary shares both, as we observe. Whether sincere or disingenuous, the pervasive resort to the phrase "the sense of society" signals at least to me the judiciary's realization that community trust and thus its legitimacy depends at least on justification of the judicial law-making in terms of community values. The history of legislative reaction indicates recognition of the legitimacy of the judicial role and the effectiveness of grounding judicial decisions in *shakai tsūnen*.

3.2 The Supreme Court of Japan and online pharmacies

Shigenori Matsui

I. INTRODUCTION

It is a well-known fact that the Supreme Court of Japan has developed a conservative and restrained constitutional jurisprudence.[1] The Supreme Court of Japan is often reluctant to strike down statutes passed by the Diet, or Japan's national legislature, on constitutional grounds. But this does not mean that the Supreme Court of Japan categorically avoids judgments that might have a significant impact on society. Indeed, the Supreme Court of Japan has handed down a number of judgments with far-reaching social implications. Its decisions on consumer lending are a classic example. In these decisions, the Supreme Court of Japan allowed millions of consumers to claim refunds for excessive interest payments, thereby causing the collapse and subsequent widespread reorganization of the consumer lending business.[2]

However, the Supreme Court of Japan has rendered other judgments with significant social implications. One such judgment, the focus of this chapter, overturned the ban on online sales of over-the-counter drugs, which radically liberalized the online sale of drugs.[3] This chapter describes the background for that decision and lays out the statutory and regulatory framework for the regulation of pharmacy and online sales of drugs. It then traces the history of litigation against a ban on online

---

[1] SHIGENORI MATSUI, THE CONSTITUTION OF JAPAN: A CONTEXTUAL ANALYSIS 145–47 (2011); Shigenori Matsui, *Why Is the Japanese Supreme Court So Conservative?*, 88 WASH. U. L. REV. 1375 (2011).

[2] Shigenori Matsui, *Cloudy Weather, with Occasional Sunshine: Consumer Loans, the Legislature, and the Supreme Court of Japan*, 22 PAC. RIM L. & POL'Y J. 555 (2013).

[3] Saikō Saibansho [Sup. Ct.], Jan. 11, 2013, 67 SAIKŌ SAIBANSHO MINJI HANREISHU [MINSHU] 1 (2nd petty bench).

sales of drugs and examines the basic reasoning of the judgment of the Supreme Court of Japan. Finally, this chapter explores the judgment's social and political implications, illustrating the Supreme Court of Japan's willingness, in some cases, to change the course of society and politics through its judgments.

II. PHARMACEUTICAL AFFAIRS ACT AND ONLINE PHARMACIES

(i) Regulation of Pharmacies and Drugstores

In Japan, production as well as distribution of medical drugs is regulated by the Pharmaceutical Affairs Act,[4] under the regulatory power of the Ministry of Health, Labor and Welfare (MHLW). Drugs registered on the drug list, the Japanese Pharmacopoeia,[5] are medical drugs, whereas marijuana, hallucinogens, and narcotics are not considered medical drugs and their distribution is strictly prohibited in Japan.[6] A "pharmacy" is defined as "a place where a pharmacist compounds a drug for a sale or for a provision (including an area necessary for business of sale if its operator intends to engage in business of sale of drugs)."[7] In order to open a pharmacy, one needs a permit from the prefectural governor;[8] only those who have a permit to open a pharmacy can use the term "pharmacy" to describe their establishment.[9] Furthermore, only those who open a pharmacy with a permit or those who have a business license to sell drugs are allowed to sell drugs as a business.[10] A business license for the sale of drugs is divided into the following three categories: a license to sell drugs at a store, a license to sell drugs by delivery, and a wholesale license.[11] When a pharmacist receives a permit to open a

---

4 Yakujihō [Pharmaceutical Affairs Act], Law No. 145 of 1960.

5 *Id.* art. 2, para. 1, no. 1.

6 Taima torishimarihō [Cannabis Control Act], Law No. 124 of 1948; Kakuseizai torishimarihō [Stimulants Control Act], Law No. 252 of 1951; Mayaku oyobi kouseishinyaku torishimarihō [Narcotics and Psychotropics Control Act], Law No. 14 of 1953.

7 Yakujihō [Pharmaceutical Affairs Act], Law No. 145 of 1960, art. 2, para. 11.

8 *Id.* art. 4, para. 1.

9 *Id.* art. 6.

10 *Id.* art. 24, para. 1.

11 *Id.* art. 25. A license to sell drugs by delivery permits traditional methods of selling drugs by permitting sales representatives to visit homes regularly,

pharmacy, he or she must manage the pharmacy, but when a person who receives a permit to open a pharmacy is not a pharmacist, a pharmacist must be designated as a manager of the pharmacy.[12] Additionally, only a licensed physician can prescribe drugs for a patient,[13] and only a licensed pharmacist can prepare drugs prescribed by a physician.[14]

In Japan, over-the-counter drugs, known as "drugs for general use," are defined as "drugs whose effect and impact upon the human body are not serious and that are left for the choice by those who need them based upon information provided by the pharmacists and other medical professions."[15] Consumers can buy such drugs without a prescription and can decide what medication, if any, to buy and what medication to take based on the principles of self-medication. Those with a business license to sell drugs at a store are only allowed to sell "drugs for general use."[16] Of course, all drugs produced and sold in Japan must be approved by the Health, Labour and Welfare Minister.[17]

For the purpose of drug sales regulation, the Pharmaceutical Affairs Act, as amended in 2006, divides all over-the-counter drugs into three different classes. Class 1 drugs are defined as "those that are capable of bringing health hazard to cause problems in ordinary life due to their side effects and are designated by the Health, Labour and Welfare Minister as requiring special care for their use."[18] Class 2 drugs are defined as "those that are capable of bringing health hazard to cause problems in ordinary life due to their side effects except for class 1 drugs and are designated by the Health, Labour and Welfare Minister."[19] Class 3 drugs comprise the rest of the approved drugs.[20]

Under the Pharmaceutical Affairs Act, individuals who open a pharmacy and are licensed to engage in the business of selling drugs at

---

leaving packages of drugs and charging the customer if the customer uses any of the drugs provided.

12 *Id.* art. 7.

13 Ishihō [Physicians Act], Law No. 201 of 1948, art. 20 & art. 22.

14 Yakuzaishihō [Pharmacists Act], Law No. 146 of 1960, art. 19 & art. 23.

15 Yakujihō [Pharmaceutical Affairs Act], Law No. 145 of 1960, art. 25, no. 1.

16 *Id.* art. 27.

17 *Id.* art. 14.

18 *Id.* art. 36-3, para. 1, no. 1.

19 *Id.* art 36-3, para. 1, no. 2.

20 *Id.* art. 36-3, para. 1, no. 3. According to the finding of the Tokyo High Court, class 1 drugs occupy 4%, class 2 drugs occupy 63%, and class 3 drugs occupy 33% of the total sales of drugs for general use. Tokyo Kōtō Saibansho [Tokyo High Ct.], Apr. 26, 2012, 1381 HANREI TAIMUZU 105.

stores, namely pharmacies or drugstores, must make sure that in accordance with the regulation adopted by the MHLW only pharmacists sell or provide class 1 drugs.[21] Furthermore, in accordance with the regulation adopted by the MHLW only pharmacists and "registered sales representatives," i.e., people who pass an examination administered by the prefectural governors necessary to sell or provide drugs for general use, can sell or provide class 2 or class 3 drugs.[22]

When selling or providing class 1 drugs, a pharmacy or drugstore must ensure in accordance with the regulation adopted by the MHLW that a pharmacist provides the necessary information with respect to each drug's proper use to customers, using documents describing all the items prescribed by the MHLW regulation.[23] However, this obligation is not applicable when a customer declines an explanation.[24] Similarly, when selling or providing class 2 drugs, a pharmacy or drugstore must strive in accordance with the regulation adopted by the MHLW to make a pharmacist or a registered sales representative provide a customer with the information necessary to explain a drug's proper use.[25] Provision of information is not mandatory with respect to class 2 drugs and is merely a matter of the duty to try to provide it. There is no corresponding obligation with respect to class 3 drugs. However, when a customer or consumer of a drug provided by a pharmacy or drugstore asks for a consultation, the pharmacy or drugstore must make sure in accordance with the regulation adopted by the MHLW that a pharmacist or a registered sales representative provides the customer or consumer with the necessary information regarding the drug's proper use.[26]

Therefore, the MHLW was authorized to specify the requirements for sale, provision of information as well as for consultation for sale of drugs by regulation. In addition, the MHLW is authorized to specify the other matters to be observed by the operator of the pharmacy and drugstore for their business by regulation.[27] In other words, the legislature delegated the power to the MHLW to specify the requirements for sale, provision of information and consultation as well as matter to be observed for operators of pharmacies and drugstores all by regulation.

---

[21] Yakujihō [Pharmaceutical Affairs Act], Law No. 145 of 1960, art. 36–5.

[22] *Id.*

[23] *Id.* art. 36-6, para. 1.

[24] *Id.* art. 36-6, para. 4.

[25] *Id.* art. 36-6, para. 2.

[26] *Id.* art. 36-6, para. 3.

[27] *Id.* art. 9, para. 1 & art. 29-2, para. 1.

(ii) Convenience Stores and Online Sales

In the past, it was mostly small pharmacies that filled prescriptions and sold drugs for general use. Gradually, much larger drugstore chains came to fill prescriptions, sell drugs for general use, and sell other kinds of household goods. Both traditional pharmacies and new drugstores could sell all kinds of drugs for general use. The traditional pharmacy and drugstore monopoly is being challenged, however, by changes in lifestyle and new developments in technology. Of particular importance are the growing popularity of convenience stores, with their desire to carry some over-the-counter drugs, and the possibility of online pharmacies.

Convenience stores are very popular in Japan and can be found on practically every corner in urban areas. With Japan's population totaling 120 million people, there are 48,057 convenience stores in Japan, with the total number of customers reaching 1.3 billion and the total amount of sales reaching 785 billion yen ($7.8 billion USD).[28] Convenience stores have indicated that they would like to carry some types of drugs on their shelves. Indeed, it would be tremendously convenient for customers if they could buy common drugs such as painkillers or cold medications in convenience stores, given that convenience stores are located in close proximity to places of residence and work and are open 24/7.

Moreover, with the development of the Internet, more than 96 million people now have access to it, which amounts to almost 72.6% of Japan's population.[29] The Ministry of Economy, Trade and Industry (METI) estimated that the market for online shopping was 8.5 trillion yen ($85 billion USD) in 2011[30] and has currently grown to more than 9 trillion yen ($90 billion USD).[31] Understandably, pharmacies, drugstores, and online shopping malls all want to sell drugs online. Such pharmacies accept offers through the Internet and deliver the drugs by

---

[28] Japan Franchise Association, Convenience Store Monthly Statistics (June 2013), http://www.jfa-fc.or.jp/folder/1/img/20130722142434.pdf.

[29] Ministry of Internal Affairs and Communications, Information and Communications Statistics Database, Total Number of People who Have Access to the Internet, http://www.soumu.go.jp/johotsusintokei/field/tsuushin01.html.

[30] Ministry of Economy, Trade and Industry, News Release (Aug. 28, 2012), http://www.meti.go.jp/policy/it_policy/statistics/outlook/H23ECnews%20release.pdf.

[31] Toyōkeizai, *Shijōkibo 9 chouen! Shirarezaru netto tsūhanno jittai [9 Trillion Yen Market: Reality of Internet Shopping Not Well Appreciated]* (July 1, 2013), http://toyokeizai.net/articles/-/14530.

mail or personal delivery, thus making online sales quite convenient. Furthermore, online sales are tremendously helpful for patients who have difficulty physically visiting pharmacies or drugstores because they have physical disabilities or are living in a rural or remote area. With the Internet, such patients can order the drugs online and have them conveniently delivered.

The MHLW originally recommended face-to-face sales for pharmacies and drugstores to sell drugs and was thus reluctant to allow this new avenue of drug sales. In response to these new developments, the Welfare Science Council, an advisory group to the Health, Labour and Welfare Minister, established a study on drug sales reform and subsequently proposed to make face-to-face sales mandatory with one exception. The Welfare Science Council proposed dividing over-the-counter drugs into three different categories depending on the risk to customers and only allowing an exception from the face-to-face sales requirement for the least risky category of drugs.[32] This proposal led to a 2006 amendment to the Pharmaceutical Affairs Act, which was supposed to take effect in 2009. Basically, the MHLW decided to allow convenience stores and online pharmacies to sell only class 3 drugs. It is important to note, however, that, although the advisory council proposed mandating face-to-face sales, the official amended text did not mandate such sales.

The push to create new avenues for drug sales received a boost from the Regulatory Reform Council of the Cabinet Office, an advisory board for the prime minister on deregulation, which proposed the liberalization of drug sales outside of pharmacies and drugstores.[33] Anticipating the full implementation of the 2006 amendment to the Pharmaceutical Affairs Act, the Regulatory Reform Council pointed out that face-to-face sales were not widely observed and that no reported serious accidents were filed for online sales. It proposed prioritizing consumer welfare and allowing online drug sales.

However, the MHLW was still reluctant. After the 2006 amendment, the MHLW initiated another study[34] and subsequently in 2009 adopted a

---

[32] Kouseikagakushingikai, Iyakuhintō seidokaisei kentoubukai [Welfare Science Council, Study Group on Drug Sale Reform], Houkokusho [Report] (Dec. 15, 2005), http://www.mhlw.go.jp/shingi/2005/12/s1215-9a.html.

[33] Kiseikaikakukaigi [Regulatory Reform Council], Internet wohukumu tsūshinhanbainiyoru ippan-you iryouhinno hanbaikisei nikansuru kisei kaikakukaigino kenkai [Opinion of the Regulatory Reform Council on the Regulation of Sale of Drugs on the Internet] (Nov. 11, 2008), http://www8.cao.go.jp/kisei-kaikaku/publication/2008/1111/item081111_01.pdf.

[34] Kouseiroudoushou [MHLW], Iyakuhinno hanbaitō nikakawaru taisei

new regulation in response to the 2006 amendment[35] mandating face-to-face sales or provision for pharmacies and drugstores to sell or provide class 1 and class 2 drugs.[36] The regulation also required pharmacists to provide necessary information for selling class 1 drugs by face-to-face explanation[37] and similarly required pharmacists or registered sales representatives to strive to provide necessary information for selling class 2 drugs by face-to-face explanation.[38] Additionally, when asked for a consultation by the customer or consumer, the regulation required that pharmacists provide consumer information with respect to class 1 drugs by face-to-face consultation,[39] whereas it required that pharmacists or registered sales representatives provide consumer information with respect to class 2 and class 3 drugs also by face-to-face consultation.[40] Last, it explicitly prohibited online sales of drugs except for class 3 drugs.[41]

The Regulatory Reform Council was not impressed and, in response, called for the total deregulation of online drug sales.[42] Similarly, public comments against the proposed regulation amendment revealed that the overwhelming majority of public comments supported the liberalization of online drug sales.[43] This meant that the stance of the Regulatory

---

oyobi kankyouseibi nikansuru kentoukai [Study Group on Sale of Drugs and Its Regulation], Houkokusho [Report] (July 4, 2008), http://www.mhlw.go.jp/shingi/2008/07/dl/s0704-14a.pdf.

35 Yakujihō sekō kisoku [Ordinance for Enforcement of the Pharmaceutical Affairs Act], MHLW Regulation No. 10 of 2009.

36 *Id.* art. 159-14, para. 1 & para. 2. It must be noted that registered sales representatives and general sales clerks are allowed to sell class 1 drugs under the supervision and guidance of pharmacists and general sales clerks are allowed to sell class 2 and class 3 drugs under the supervision and guidance of pharmacists or registered sales representatives. *Id.*

37 *Id.* art. 159-15, para. 1, no. 1.

38 *Id.* art. 159-16, no. 1.

39 *Id.* art. 159-17, para. 1.

40 *Id.* art. 159-17, para. 2.

41 *Id.* art. 15-4, para. 1, no. 1.

42 Kiseikaikakukaigi [Regulatory Reform Council], Ippan-you iryouhinno hanbaitaisei nikakaru kiseikaikakukaigino kenkai [Opinion of the Regulatory Reform Council on the Regulation of Sale of Drugs] (Apr. 2, 2009), http://www8.cao.go.jp/kisei-kaikaku/publication/2009/0402/item090402_04.pdf.

43 2353 comments were sent to the MHLW on the ban on online drug sale and 2303 of them were against the ban. But the MHLW never revealed that 97% of all comments were against the proposed ban. IT Media News, *Iyakuhinno tsushinhanbai kisei, 97%ga hantai iken: Pabukome kekka [97% of the Comments toward Proposed Ban on Online Sale of Drugs Opposed to the Proposal: Outcomes of the Public Comments Revealed]* (Feb. 13, 2009), www.itmedia.

Reform Council was backed by many people. The ban on online sales of class 1 and class 2 drugs was quite unpopular.

(iii) Why Was Online Sale of Class 1 and Class 2 Drugs Prohibited?

Not surprisingly, pharmacists, physicians and victims of adverse drug side effects actively supported both the face-to-face sales requirement and the ban on online sales of class 1 and class 2 drugs. Specifically, the Japan Pharmaceutical Association believed that a face-to-face sales requirement was necessary to secure the safety of drugs and correspondingly opposed online sales of drugs.[44] Likewise, the Japan Medical Association insisted that a face-to-face sales requirement would ensure that a pharmacist would actually look at the condition of a patient and could recommend seeing a doctor.[45] The National Federation of Groups of Victims of Pharmaceutical Harms supported a total ban on online drug sales, as it insisted that all drugs were capable of causing serious health hazards and that a pharmacist should see a patient to make sure that a drug was safe for the patient.[46] Apparently, the MHLW basically accepted these objections when it adopted the 2009 regulation amendment.

However, the face-to-face sales requirement was neither strictly observed nor enforced in pharmacies or drugstores. For instance, even when a pharmacist took a break, a drugstore would sometimes continue selling drugs. Similarly, even when selling class 1 drugs, some pharmacists would simply provide the information orally without using the required document.[47] Moreover, the face-to-face sales requirement

co.jp/news/articles/0902/13/news013.html.

[44] Japan Pharmaceutical Association, Iyakuhinno Internet hanbai nikansuru gyoukai 9 dantaino kyoudou seimei [Joint Statement of Nine Associations on Online Sale of Drugs] (Nov. 28, 2008), http://www.nichiyaku.or.jp/action/wp-content/uploads/2011/04/kyoudou_seimei.pdf.

[45] Japan Medical Association, Gyouseisasshinkaigino kisei/seidokaikakuni taisuru nihon ishikaino kenkai [Opinion of the Japan Medical Association on Regulatory Reform by the Regulatory Reform Council](Aug. 3, 2011), http://dl.med.or.jp/dl-med/teireikaiken/20110803_1.pdf.

[46] Zenkoku yakugaihigaishadantai renrakukyougikai [National Federation of Groups of Victims of Pharmaceutical Harms], Ippan-you iyakuhinno Internet hanbaino kiseiwo motomeru youbousho [Request for Regulation of Online Sale of Drugs] (Nov. 17, 2008), http://homepage1.nifty.com/hkr/yakugai/iyakuhin-hanbai/naikakufu-youbou081117.pdf.

[47] Even the MHLW admits that only 60% of the pharmacists and drugstores provide necessary explanations to customers using the designated

proved mostly ineffective, given that most customers simply declined to receive information. Pharmacies and drugstores also allowed family members of a patient to buy drugs on behalf of the patient. The face-to-face sales requirement is meaningless in such cases. All of this cast doubt on the necessity of the face-to-face sales requirement for online sales of drugs and the ban on online sales of class 1 and class 2 drugs.

Furthermore, other countries facing similar online pharmacy issues are struggling to cope with both online sales of prescription drugs and illegal drugs.[48] However, in Japan, no legitimate online drugstore is willing to provide prescription drugs online and no physician is willing to fill a prescription after an online consultation. Moreover, there is no doubt that selling illegal drugs online is illegal. Online sales of approved over-the-counter drugs have therefore been the focus of the debate.

III. KENKO.COM CASE

(i) Kenko.com

Kenko.com (literally health.com) is a pioneer in the online pharmacy industry and started selling drugs online before the 2006 amendment. At that time, the MHLW advised the face-to-face sales for pharmacies and drugstores to sell drugs, but such advice was merely a recommendation and not a statutory obligation. However, the 2009 regulation made face-to-face sales a requirement and prohibited online sales of class 1 and class 2 drugs.

Kenko.com wanted to sell all three classes of drugs online. Kenko.com required its customers to provide their age, sign a consent form after reading an information document on the drug's side effects, and list any other medications the customer was taking to make sure that the ordered drug would not create any adverse drug combinations all through the Internet. It also established a call center where qualified

---

document for a sale of class 1 drugs. Kouseiroudousho [MHLW], Heisei 24 nendo ippan-you iyakuhin hanbaiseido teichaku joukyo chousakekka nitsuite (gaiyo) [On the Actual Implementation of Drug Sale Regulation for Drugs for General Use: Summary] (Aug. 7, 2013), http://www.mhlw.go.jp/stf/houdou/2r98520000037iru-att/2r98520000037itb.pdf.

48 *See* Phil Ayres, *Prescribing a Cure for Online Pharmacies*, 72 TENN. L. REV. 949 (2005); Jeff Karberg, *Progress in the Challenges to Regulate Online Pharmacies,* 23 J. LAW & HEALTH 29 (2010).

pharmacists would answer questions 24/7 via telephone, video phone or e-mail, and it also kept customer order records to make sure that a customer could not order an excessive amount of a drug. Kenko.com insisted that such measures would satisfy statutory requirements and it questioned the validity of the amended regulation that prohibited online sales of class 1 and class 2 drugs.

Kenko.com, together with another online pharmacy, Wellnet, thus filed a suit and sought a judicial revocation of the regulation, a declaration that the regulation was void and a declaration that the plaintiffs had a right to sell class 1 and class 2 drugs.

(ii) The Tokyo District Court

The Tokyo District Court[49] found the claims seeking a judicial revocation of the amended regulation and a declaration of its invalidity inadmissible because the enactment of the regulation was not an administrative action that could be challenged under the Administrative Case Litigation Act.[50] But it held the suit seeking a declaration that the plaintiffs had a right to sell class 1 and class 2 drugs online admissible.[51]

However, the Tokyo District Court upheld the face-to-face sales requirement of the amended regulation because it found that it was a reasonable exercise of discretion granted by the delegation of power to specify the permissible method or manner of sale under the 2006 amendment.[52] It emphasized the report of the advisory council and statements from the Health, Labour and Welfare Minister during the amendment process as presupposing the introduction of the face-to-face sales requirement after the 2006 amendment.[53] The Tokyo District Court thus rejected Kenko.com's challenge of the ban.

(iii) The Tokyo High Court

Upon appeal, the Tokyo High Court reversed the judgment of the Tokyo District Court and struck down the amended regulation.[54] In its

---

49 Tokyo Chihō Saibansho [Tokyo Dist. Ct.], Mar. 30, 2010, 2096 HANREI JIHŌ 9.

50 *Id.;* Gyouseijikensoshohō [Administrative Case Litigation Act], Law No. 139 of 1962, art. 3, para. 2.

51 Tokyo Chihō Saibansho [Tokyo Dist. Ct.], Mar. 30, 2010, *supra* note 49.

52 *Id.*

53 *Id.*

54 Tokyo Kōtō Saibansho [Tokyo High Ct.], Apr. 26, 2012, *supra* note 20.

reasoning, the Tokyo High Court emphasized, there was no statutory ban on online sales of class 1 drugs and class 2 drugs. Specifically, even though the advisory council's report and statements of the Health, Labour and Welfare Minister indicated that the MHLW would require face-to-face sales after the amendment, the text itself did not impose such a requirement.[55] Furthermore, the purpose of the 2006 amendment was to provide customers with sufficient information to make an informed decision on drug purchases and was not to totally prohibit online sales.[56] Moreover, although the regulation restricted the freedom to choose an occupation as protected by article 22 of the Constitution of Japan,[57] there were no discussions on the problems of selling drugs online or on whether alternative regulatory measures were unavailable to justify such a ban during the enactment of the 2006 amendment.[58]

The Tokyo High Court thus concluded that the 2006 amendment did not intend to require face-to-face sales, that the 2009 regulation was ultra vires, and that plaintiffs have a right to sell class 1 and class 2 drugs online.

(iv) The Supreme Court of Japan

Upon second appeal, the Supreme Court of Japan affirmed the Tokyo High Court's judgment on January 11, 2013.[59]

According to the Supreme Court of Japan, the regulation of the production and sale of drugs by the Pharmaceutical Affairs Act was designed to ensure the safety of drugs and to prevent injury from defective drugs.[60] Although the regulation of drugs depends on the Health, Labour and Welfare Minister's medical and pharmaceutical scientific expertise, there are other considerations to be considered.[61] Specifically, there was a particular need for online sales of drugs, and both consumers and some experts opposed the overly stringent

---

55 *Id.*

56 *Id.*

57 "Every person shall have freedom to choose and change his residence and to choose his occupation to the extent that it does not interfere with the public welfare." NIHONKOKU KENPŌ [CONSTITUTION OF JAPAN], art. 22, para. 1.

58 Tokyo Kōtō Saibansho [Tokyo High Ct.], Apr. 26, 2012, *supra* note 20.

59 Saikō Saibansho [Sup. Ct.], Jan. 11, 2013, *supra* note 3.

60 *Id.*

61 *Id.*

regulations on online drugs sales. Even among the government departments, there is also a consistently voiced skepticism of the necessity of the face-to-face sales requirement, given the lack of evidence showing the superiority of face-to-face sales over online sales and the fact that there was no reported case filed of an accident due to a pharmacist's absence. Moreover, the Supreme Court of Japan emphasized that the freedom to choose an occupation as protected by article 22, paragraph 1, included the freedom to engage in a chosen occupation. Accordingly, it found that the new regulation on online drug sales, which was not illegal prior to the amendment, significantly restricted the freedom to engage in a chosen occupation.[62] Considering these factors, the Supreme Court of Japan held that the authorization for the regulation of online drug sales, in other words a delegation of power to the agency, must be explicitly based on the statutory language of the Pharmaceutical Affairs Act.[63]

However, the Pharmaceutical Affairs Act neither requires face-to-face sales nor explicitly provides for the necessity of a ban on online sales. Other provisions of the Pharmaceutical Affairs Act similarly do not require face-to-face sales or explicitly require a ban on online sales. Thus, the authorization for a ban on online sales of class 1 and class 2 drugs is not explicit and it is difficult to argue that the Diet intended to prohibit online sales of class 1 and class 2 drugs. [64]

Accordingly, the Supreme Court of Japan concluded that a provision of the MHLW regulation requiring face-to-face sales of class 1 and class 2 drugs, provisions requiring a face-to-face provision of drug information for class 1 drugs and a face-to-face consultation upon request for class 1 and class 2 drugs, and a provision prohibiting online sales of class 1 and class 2 drugs were invalid as ultra vires, and affirmed the judgment of the court below holding that the plaintiffs had a right to sell class 1 and class 2 drugs online.[65]

---

[62] *Id.*
[63] *Id.*
[64] *Id.*
[65] *Id.*

IV. IMPLICATIONS OF THE SUPREME COURT OF JAPAN'S JUDGMENT

(i) Significance of the Judgment

The judgment was not an outright constitutional invalidation of the regulation as an infringement on the freedom to choose an occupation as protected by article 22 of the Constitution of Japan. The Diet could technically amend the Pharmaceutical Affairs Act and ban online sales of class 1 and class 2 drugs. Nonetheless, the holding, which denied the statutory authorization for a ban and struck down the regulation adopted to implement the Pharmaceutical Affairs Act, was a serious blow to the MHLW.

This is a remarkable holding especially since the courts in Japan are generally quite supportive of the broad authorization and delegation of power and are willing to grant very broad discretion to administrative agencies. While rejecting a claim seeking judicial revocation of the regulation and seeking declaration of its invalidity, this decision accepted a claim seeking a declaration that the plaintiffs have a legal right, struck down an administrative regulation and declared that the plaintiffs had a legal right. Moreover, its holding that the authorization or delegation of power to the administrative agency needs to be expressly provided when it comes to significant curtailment of freedom to choose an occupation to be protected by the Constitution is quite radical and could have far-reaching implications for the future of administrative law.

(ii) Online Sales of Drugs Liberalized

The social impact of the decision is also astonishing. As a result of the Supreme Court of Japan's judgment, the amended MHLW regulation on online sales of drugs was held invalid with respect to Kenko.com and Wellnet. Technically, the judgment was limited to the specific plaintiffs, but, in practice, the judgment extended to all those who wanted to sell drugs online.

The MHLW issued a notification to its local branches and local government to hold off enforcement of the invalidated provisions.[66]

---

[66] Kouseiroudoushou iyakushokuhinkyoku soumuka [MHLW, Pharmaceutical and Food Safety Bureau, General Office], Iyakuhinno Internet hanbaisosho (Saikousai hanketsu) wouketa taiou nitsuite [On Responses to the Online Drug Sales Litigation (judgment of the Supreme Court of Japan)] (Jan.

Consequently, online sales of drugs became considerably liberalized, but the MHLW did not have any intention of liberalizing online sales of drugs. It thus urged online pharmacies to wait for the adoption of new rules before initiating online sales of drugs.[67]

As a result of the judgment, on January 11, 2013, Kenko.com started selling drugs online again. For example, popular class 1 drugs such as Gaster 10 (heartburn drugs), Nicolette (smoking cessation drugs), RiUp (hair growth drugs), or Loxonin.S (painkillers), are now available from Kenko.com's website.[68] While Kenko.com's short-term goal is to reach its pre-shutdown sales of 0.5 billion yen [$5 million USD], the market for over-the-counter drugs in Japan is estimated in excess of 600 billion yen [$6 billion USD] and the possible market for online pharmacies is projected to significantly expand.[69]

Of course, other pharmacies and drugstores are paying close attention to the development of online drug sales. It would not be a surprise if other pharmacies and drugstores followed the lead of Kenko.com and start selling over-the-counter drugs online. Similarly, large online shopping mall sites, national supermarket stores and discount shops have a keen interest in the aftermath of the judgment. Indeed, Rakuten, Japan's largest online shopping mall site, became the majority stockholder of Kenko.com during the litigation and, as Kenko.com's parent company, Rakuten started selling drugs through its online site.[70] Other online shopping mall sites such as Yahoo! Shopping soon followed.[71] Furthermore, Aeon, Japan's second-largest supermarket store chain, already selling some over-the-counter drugs

17, 2013), http://www.mhlw.go.jp/seisakunitsuite/bunya/kenkou_iryou/iyakuhin/ippanyou/dl/130117-01.pdf.

[67] *Id.*

[68] Nihonkeizai Shimbun, *Taishuyaku netto hanbai: Mikainochi kaitaku nerau kakusha [Online Sales of the Over-the-Counter Drugs: Companies Are Eyeing for Uncultivated Land]* (Jan. 11, 2013), http://www.nikkei.com/article/DGXNASFK1104H_R10C13A1000000/.

[69] *Id.*

[70] *Id.*

[71] *Id.* Amazon also started selling class 2 drugs online. Nihonkeizai Shimbun, *Amazon, taishuyaku hanbaiwo kaishi: Ichouyakunado dai2rui [Amazon Starts Selling Over-the-Counter Drugs: Class 2 Drugs Including Stomachache Medication Available]* (Sept. 24, 2013), http://www.nikkei.com/article/DGXNASDD240PB_U3A920C1TJ1000/.

in their stores, started selling drugs online.[72] Other large discount stores, such as Bic Camera, one of Japan's largest electric products discount stores with 16 pharmacy stores called Bic Drugs, also started selling drugs online.[73] The judgment of the Supreme Court of Japan had a tremendous social impact.

V. THE FUTURE OF ONLINE PHARMACIES

(i) Bumpy Road to Liberalization

The road to the total liberalization of online pharmacies is still quite bumpy. As stated above, right after the judgment the MHLW indicted its willingness to reconsider the ban on online sales of class 1 and class 2 drugs, but it had no intention of liberalizing online sales of drugs.[74]

No one denies the need to regulate the online sales of drugs to some degree.[75] Indeed, Kenko.com initiated some safety measures to prevent adverse side effects and drug abuse by providing detailed explanations of drugs and allowing customers to ask pharmacists questions. It is expected that the same kind of safety measures would soon be required. Thus, the question was whether to uphold the ban on online sales of some drugs and whether to allow online sales of all over-the-counter drugs with appropriate safety regulations.

There are still many who oppose online sales of drugs. For instance, the Japan Association of Chain Drug Stores, the Japan Pharmaceutical Association and the National Federation of Groups of Victims of Pharmaceutical Harms issued a joint statement opposing the

---

72 Nihonkeizai Shimbun, *Kusuri netto tsūhan, Aeon sente: Kiseikanwa nirami hanbai [Aeon Took Advantage of Online Sales of Drugs: Started Selling Drugs in Anticipation of the Deregulation]* (Apr. 4, 2013), http://www.nikkei.com/article/DGXNASDD040OT_U3A400C1TJ0000/. Aeon started selling class 2 drugs.

73 *Id.* Bic Camera started selling class 3 drugs and plans to include class 2 drugs in the coming future. Askul, a leading online shopping mall for office equipment, already started selling class 3 drugs online and plans to start selling class 1 and class 2 drugs in the future; President Online, *Kusuri netto hanbai kaikin: Igyoushusannyude sengokujidai totsunyue [Liberalization of Online Sales of Drugs: Competition Stiffened because of the Entry of Other Business Corporations]* (July 15, 2013), http://president.jp/articles/-/9786.

74 *See supra* note 66.

75 Nihonkeizai Shimbun, *supra* note 68.

liberalization of class 1 drugs.[76] The Japan Medical Association also opposed lifting the face-to-face sales requirement for certain drugs.[77] Not surprisingly, these associations are all quite critical of the Supreme Court of Japan's judgment. Additionally, the MHLW was similarly committed to maintaining a ban on online sales of certain drugs and thus created a study of new rules regarding online sales of over-the-counter drugs.[78] Although its report published on May 31 was not a clear-cut endorsement of the ban, the report clearly indicated strong support for the ban.[79] Indeed, some members of the ruling Liberal Democratic Party (LDP) formed a coalition of members of the Diet concerning online sales of drugs and expressed a plan to propose an amendment to the Pharmaceutical Affairs Act that would ban online sales of class 1 drugs.[80]

However, concern for public safety might not be a convincing justification for the ban on online sales of approved over-the-counter drugs. In the past, the Pharmaceutical Affairs Act had a minimum distance requirement for new pharmacies or drugstores,[81] which prevented new pharmacies or drugstores from opening in close

---

[76] Zenkoku yakugai higaisha dantai renraku kyougikai [National Federation of Groups of Victims of Pharmaceutical Harms] et al., Ippan-you iyakuhinno Internet hanbai nitsuite (iken) [On Online Sales of Over-the-Counter Drugs] (June 4, 2013), http://www.nichiyaku.or.jp/action/wp-content/uploads/2013/06/130604_02.pdf.

[77] Japan Medical Association, Ippan-you iyakuhinno Internet hanbai nitsuiteno nihon ishikaino kenkai [Opinion of the Japan Medical Association on Online Sales of Over-the-Counter Drugs](June 5, 2013), http://dl.med.or.jp/dl-med/teireikaiken/20130605_1.pdf.

[78] Kouseiroudoshou [MHLW], Ippan-you iyakuhinno Internet hanbaito no aratana rule nikansuru kentoukai [Study Group on New Rules Regarding Online Sales of Over-the-Counter Drugs], http://www.mhlw.go.jp/stf/shingi/2r9852000000ax9a.html#shingi128770.

[79] Kouseiroudoshou [MHLW], Ippan-you iyakuhinno Internet hanbaito no aratana rule nikansuru kentoukai [Study Group on New Rules Regarding Online Sales of Over-the-Counter Drugs], Torimatome [Summary] (May 31, 2013), http://www.mhlw.go.jp/file.jsp?id=140920&name=2r98520000034awn_1.pdf. The report included arguments for and against online sales of drugs. The study group counted supporters of online sales of drugs among its members. This was a reason why the report could not make a clear endorsement of the ban.

[80] Business Journal, *Iyakuhin net hanbai, saikousai hanketsude kaikin demo giin renmeiga mattano wake [Why Politicians Want to Stop the Liberalization of Online Sales of Drugs Brought by the Judgment of the Supreme Court]* (Feb. 18, 2013), http//biz-journal.jp/2013/02/post_1529.html.

[81] Yakujihō [Pharmaceutical Affairs Act], art. 6, para. 2 (repealed 1975).

proximity to existing stores. This requirement was added to the statute not by a cabinet bill but by a private bill and was justified as a public safety measure. The rationale behind the requirement was that if a new store were allowed to open in close proximity to an existing store, both stores could be forced into fierce competition. Such competition could lead to sloppy and improperly supervised management or sale of drugs that subsequently could be harmful to consumers. The Supreme Court of Japan doubted, however, whether such a distance requirement would secure the safety of drug sales and whether it was necessary to achieve this safety, and accordingly struck it down[82] as an unconstitutional infringement on the freedom to choose an occupation as protected by article 22 of the Constitution of Japan. Although pharmacists and doctors relied upon public safety as a justification for the ban on online sales of drugs, many suspected that the ban was just another protectionist measure for existing pharmacies[83] and doctors.[84] Especially in light of the facts that the face-to-face sales requirement is not observed in a substantial number of pharmacies and drugstores and that the face-to-face sales requirement is practically ineffective and could be meaningless, the public safety justification becomes even more difficult to accept as a justification for the ban on online sales of drugs.

Apparently, the Regulatory Reform Council shared the same suspicion. The Regulatory Reform Council thus published a report on June 5, 2013, recommending the removal of any ban on online sales of over-the-counter drugs and the introduction of safety measures.[85]

---

[82] Saikō Saibansho [Sup. Ct.], Apr. 30, 1975, 29 SAIKŌ SAIBANSHO MINJI HANREISHU [MINSHU] 572 (grand bench).

[83] With the development of drugstore chains, traditional pharmacies have lost many customers and an increasing number of small pharmacies have been forced to close their businesses. Apparently, the small pharmacies fear that the liberalization of online sales of drugs will lead to a further loss in customers.

[84] The Japan Medical Association supports the ban on online sale of drugs hoping that a pharmacist through the face-to-face sales might encourage the customers to see the doctors. The protection of the health of patients is surely a legitimate concern. Apparently, however, doctors are also worried about losing patients by allowing online sales of drugs. Nihonkeizai Shimbun, *Iyakuhinhanbaiwa shoubaidewanai: Interview [Drug Sales Is Not a Business: Interview]* (Apr. 4, 2013), http://www.nikkei.com/article/ DGXNASGC02011_ S3A400C1000000/.

[85] Regulatory Reform Council, Kiseikaikaku nikansuru toushin: Keizaisaisei eno toppako [Report on Regulatory Reform: A Breakthrough into the Economic

The revitalization of the economy is one of the three main elements called three arrows of "Abenomics," the economic philosophy of Prime Minister Shinzo Abe. Deregulation and facilitation of competition are among the top priorities for Abe. Abe thus expressed his determination to remove the ban on online sales of drugs,[86] thereby creating considerable tension between Abe and the Cabinet and the MHLW and its supporters.[87] It was therefore unclear in which direction the government would go: to amend the Pharmaceutical Affairs Act to ban online sales of some drugs or liberalize online drug sales.

(ii) Cabinet Economic Development Strategy and Online Sales of Drugs

On June 14, 2013, as part of its economic stimulus strategy, the Abe Cabinet eventually approved the policy to liberalize online sales of drugs, excluding about two dozen class 1 drugs.[88] In sum, the Cabinet declared a liberalization policy for online sales of almost all drugs.[89] The judgment of the Supreme Court of Japan provided a very strong impetus for this liberalization movement.

Upon Cabinet approval of the liberalization policy, the Japan Association of Chain Drug Stores decided to abandon its previous policy of encouraging its members to refrain from online sales of drugs and instead, promoted the liberalization of online sales with

---

Revitalization] (June 5, 2013), http://www8.cao.go.jp/kisei-kaikaku/kaigi/meeting/2013/committee/130605/item3.pdf.

[86] Prime Minister Abe's Speech on Third Economic Stimulus Strategy (June 5, 2013), http://www.kantei.go.jp/jp/96_abe/statement/2013/0605speech.html.

[87] *See also* Huffington Post, *Ippan yakuhinno Internet hanbaiwa naze seichousenryakuni morikomaretanoka [Why Liberalization of Online Sales of Drugs Was Incorporated into the Development Strategies?]* (June 9, 2013), http://www.huffingtonpost.jp/2013/06/08/shopping_medicine_on_internet_n_3408446.html.

[88] Cabinet Decision, Kiseikaikaku jisshi keikaku [Regulatory Reform Implementation Plan] (June 14, 2013), http://www8.cao.go.jp/kisei-kaikaku/kaigi/publication/130614/item1.pdf.

[89] Japan Times, *Japan to Allow Online Sales of 99% of All OTC Drugs* (June 5, 2013), http://www.japantimes.co.jp/news/2013/06/05/national/japan-to-allow-online-sales-of-99-of-all-otc-drugs/. The MHLW was supposed to reach a decision on these exempted drugs by September 2013. *See infra* note 93.

its new self-restraint guidelines.[90] The MHLW immediately decided to set up a study on the treatment of the drugs exempted in Cabinet approval.[91] These drugs used to require a prescription but became over-the-counter drugs within four years. The MHLW insisted that the information regarding possible side effects, in the context of the liberalization, was insufficient[92] and it thus suggested that it might reclassify these drugs again to require a prescription.[93] Although Abe's policy was hailed as a total liberalization, it might not be a total liberalization after all.

Moreover, the MHLW had to come up with new safety rules regarding online sales of drugs. It thus established another study group to propose new rules for online sales of drugs. In the end, the MHLW might end up establishing overly stringent requirements for online pharmacies, which would effectively prohibit online drug sales.[94]

---

90 Japan Association of Chain Drug Stores, Gyoukai jishukijun "Iyakuhin netto hanbai guideline" [Industry Self-Restraint Standard on Online Sales of Drugs], http://www.jacds.gr.jp/netsales/guideline0702.pdf.

91 Kouseiroudoshou [MHLW], Ippan-you iryouhinno hanbai rule sakutei sagyou group [Working Group on New Rules on Online Sales of Drugs], http://www.mhlw.go.jp/stf/shingi/2r9852000000ax9a.html#shingi128770; J-cast News, *Shihanyakuno nettohanbai zenmenkaikin: Abe shushouno houshinni kourous-houga teikou? [Total Liberalization of Online Sales of Drugs: Is the MHLW Revolting against the Policy of the Prime Minister Abe?]* (Aug. 6, 2013), http://www.j-cast.com/2013/07/08178839.html.

92 Some of the popular drugs are included in this list. Mainichi Shimbun, *Shihanyaku, netto hanbai kaikin: Kou risk 25hin kenshou e, shihanyaku torikeshimo [Liberalization of Online Sales of Drugs: Reconsideration of 25 High Risk Drugs]*(June 6, 2013), http://mainichi.jp/select/news/20130606ddm008040032000chtml.

93 The study group published a draft report calling for different treatment for these exempted drugs and requiring careful interactive consultation between a pharmacist and a customer before selling exempted drugs but the report was ambiguous whether the MHLW would once again require prescriptions for them. Kouseiroudousho [MHLW], Switch chokugo hinmokutōno kentou kensho ni kansuru senmonkakaigou [Expert Study Group on Review for Exempted Drugs], Switch chokugo hinmokutōno tokusei oyobi hanbaijouno ryuiten nitsuite [On the Characteristics of the Drugs Switched to Over-the-Counter Drugs Recently and the Points for Concerns for Their Sale] (Oct. 8, 2013), http://www.mhlw.gp.jp/file/04-Houdouhappyou-11121000-Iyakushokuhinkyoku-Soumuka/0000025619.pdf.

94 Toyōkeizai, *Kusurino nettohanbai kaikin e: Soredemo kusuburu hidane [Liberalization of Online Sales of Drugs: Still Contentious Issues Left]* (June 15, 2013), http://toyokeizai.net/articles/-/14295.

Whether the MHLW is actually willing to liberalize the online sale of drugs,[95] to bring further liberalization,[96] or to halt liberalization depended upon the outcome of these studies.

(iii) The 2013 Amendment to the Pharmaceutical Affairs Act

On December 9, 2013, the Diet finally passed a bill to amend the Pharmaceutical Affairs Act to implement proposals on online sales of

---

[95] The working group proposed the following safety measures for online sale of drugs: The online pharmacy must ascertain via e-mail the age, sex, condition, history of side effects, other medical conditions, current medical treatment if any and also other information the user freely provides. Then the online pharmacy must provide information as to appropriate dosage, the number of times the customer should take the drugs, important points to observe, and possible side effects via e-mail and provide the customer an opportunity to ask questions. Then, the customer must acknowledge that he/she understood all the information and that he/she did not have any more questions. After following all these procedures, the online pharmacy could send drugs to the customer. (With respect to class 2 drugs the online pharmacy is mandated to strive to follow all these procedures.) The proposal also requires the presence of a pharmacist during all the business hours, display of the pharmacist's name, interactive consultation using telephone, transmission of a pharmacist's name to the customer, record of transaction, and establishment of a surveillance system using TV phones. Moreover, the proposal would require a restriction on the number of drugs to be sold if there is a possibility of abuse, a ban on auctioning of drugs, and a ban on comments or recommendations by the customers. Further, the proposal would require the registration of URL of the online pharmacy with the MHLW. Kouseiroudoushou [MHLW], Ipppan-you iryouhinno hanbai rule sakuteisagyou group [Working Group on Rules for Sale of Drugs for General Use], Torimatome [Summary], (Oct. 8, 2013), http://www.mhlw.go.jp/stf/shingi/0000025526.html.

[96] Right now, for instance, stores that sell drugs are allowed to offer drugs online. Thus, an online pharmacy must have a physical store even if no one is actually visiting the store. Such a requirement might be absurd. In order to promote further liberalization, an online pharmacy without an actual store must be allowed. So long as the safety measures are followed, there may be no need for a physical store to be in existence. However, the working group proposal requires the existence of an actual pharmacy or licensed drugstore, which is open 30 hours a week, a display of a picture of a store, the kind of license, and the name of a pharmacist as well as display of the contact line during off-business hours. *Id.* The proposal would thus ban a store without effective actual operation from opening an online store. Furthermore, an online store would be allowed to sell drugs only stored inside the store. *Id.* These additional requirements might deprive many of the advantages of the online pharmacy.

drugs as submitted by the government.[97] The amendment will take effect within six months after promulgation.[98] The amendment would require applicants who want to open a pharmacy and applicants who want to apply for a license to sell drugs at drugstores to submit very detailed information regarding the pharmacy or store, including the structure of the pharmacy or store together with a floor map, summary of the business plan and, if a pharmacy or store sells drugs for general use to customers who are not in the pharmacy or store, documents describing the telecommunication method and other matters designated by the MHWL.[99] It would create a new category of drugs named "drugs necessitating guidance," which require a pharmacist to provide information and guidance as to their proper use face-to-face and are so designated by the Health, Labour and Welfare Minister.[100] Included in the "drugs necessitating guidance" would be drugs switched from prescription drugs within a specified period[101] and drugs that are more powerful and could be poisonous. These drugs would be excluded from the definition of "drugs for general use." The amendment would impose the obligation on pharmacies and drugstores to ascertain the age of the consumer, the use of other drugs, and other matters designated by the MHWL from the customers who want to buy class 1 and class 2 drugs.[102] With respect to "drugs necessitating guidance," the amendment will require a pharmacist to provide them,[103] mandate the pharmacist to provide information and guidance face-to-face by using a document prescribed by the MHWL, and require the pharmacist to ascertain the age of the consumer, the use of other medications and other matters designated by the MHWL.[104]

Thus, online sales of drugs will be legal except for "drugs necessitating guidance" and the online pharmacy must follow the specific

---

[97] Yakujihō oyobi yakuzaishihōno ichibuwo kaiseisuru hōritsu [Act to Amend Parts of the Pharmaceutical Affairs Act and the Pharmacists Act], Law No. 103 of 2013.

[98] *Id.* addendum, art. 1.

[99] *Id.* art. 1, amending art. 4 and art. 26 of the Pharmaceutical Affairs Act.

[100] *Id.*, adding para. 5 to the art. 4 of the Pharmaceutical Affairs Act.

[101] Although initially the MHLW indicated that it would exempt drugs switched from prescription drugs within four years, the MHLW has now indicated that it will exempt drugs switched from prescription drugs within three years.

[102] *Id.*, adding new para. 2 and 4 to art. 36-6 of the Pharmaceutical Affairs Act and converting art. 36-6 to 35-10.

[103] *Id.*, adding new art. 36-5, para. 1 to the Pharmaceutical Affairs Act.

[104] *Id.*, adding new art. 36-6 to the Pharmaceutical Affairs Act.

requirement specified by the MHWL after the amendment takes effect. Online shops were deeply disappointed by the exclusion of drugs necessitating guidance and have prepared to challenge the exclusion's constitutionality before the court.[105] We must wait and see what specific requirements the MHWL will impose on online pharmacies and the outcome of the possible legal challenges in order to see to what extent online sales of drugs will be finally liberalized.

(iv) The Online Sale of Prescription Drugs

When online sales of over-the-counter drugs are liberalized, the next question is whether online sales of prescription drugs should be allowed.[106] For many patients who have difficulty in visiting a pharmacy, such as those who have physical disabilities or who are living in rural or remote areas, it would be tremendously useful if they could order prescription drugs online and have them delivered to their homes. However, prescription drugs are generally more powerful than over-the-counter drugs and can cause serious side effects. Accordingly, there may be a heightened need for a pharmacist to check with a customer when providing prescription drugs. Furthermore, many pharmacies rely on the preparation of prescription drugs for their livelihood and the liberalization of online sales of prescription drugs could drive many pharmacies out of business. Thus, many existing pharmacies may strongly oppose a liberalization of online sales of prescription drugs. It is therefore unlikely that the liberalization of online sales of prescription drugs will become an actual issue in Japan.

Indeed, the 2013 amendment would create a new category of drugs named "pharmacy drugs," defined as "drugs except for drugs necessitating guidance and drugs for general use," limiting the sale of pharmacy drugs to pharmacies, mandating a pharmacy to allow a pharmacist to sell pharmacy drugs, mandating a pharmacist to provide

---

[105] Nihonkeizai Shimbun, *Mikitanishi, seihuiinnjininwo kento: Kusuri netto hanbaiwomeguri [Mr. Mikitani Hinted to Resign from the Government Committee Membership: Over the Online Sale of Drugs]* (Nov. 6, 2013), http://www.nikkei.com/article/DGXNASDD06030_W3A101C1000000/. Mr. Mikitani is a chairperson/president of Rakuten and is a vocal critic of ban on online sales of drugs.

[106] Diamond Online, *Kusuri netto hanbai gironno sakiniaru shohousen-yakutoiu aratana hidane [Contentious Issue of Treatment of Prescription Drugs after the Liberalization of On-line Sale of Drugs]* (May 20, 2013), http://diamond.jp/articles/-/36131.

information and guidance face-to-face with customers as to its proper use, using the document designated by the MHWL, and requiring a pharmacist to ascertain the age of the consumer, the use of other drugs and other matters designated by the MHWL.[107] Prescription drugs are included in the "pharmacy drugs." Moreover, the 2013 amendment specifically imposed all these requirements to the provision of prescription drugs.[108] The government thus made it clear that it had no intention of liberalizing online sales of prescription drugs.

VI. CONCLUSION

Research shows that 58.7% of consumers support the liberalization of online sales of drugs while 10.7% oppose such liberalization.[109] No one doubts that strict safety rules must be in place regarding online sales of drugs. But the ban on online sales and the requirement that certain drugs must be sold to patients after a face-to-face consultation is meaningless. It is not surprising that the Japanese government is headed toward the liberalization of online sales of drugs.

It is noteworthy, however, that the judgment of the Supreme Court of Japan striking down the MHLW regulation played a very significant role in prompting the liberalization of online pharmacies. The Justices of the Supreme Court of Japan were certainly sensitive to the social and political implications of the judgment. But the Supreme Court of Japan did not hesitate to strike down the MHLW's regulation as ultra vires. It is true that, given that the judgment was not a constitutional invalidation, the Diet can amend the statute and reauthorize the regulation struck down. The fact remains, however, that the judgment of the Supreme Court of Japan has had tremendous social and political implications and the Justices were not reluctant to hand down a judgment that carried such social and political implications.

---

107 Yakujihō oyobi yakuzaishihōno ichibuwo kaiseisuru hōritsu [Act to Amend Parts of the Pharmaceutical Affairs Act and the Pharmacists Act], Law No. 103 of 2013, art. 1, amending art. 27 of the Pharmaceutical Affairs Act, adding new art. 36-3 and art. 36-4.

108 *Id.* art. 1, adding new art. 9-2, amending the previous art. 92-2 and converting it to art. 9-3 to the Pharmaceutical Affairs Act.

109 Dentsu, News Release (Mar. 27, 2013), http://www.dentsu.co.jp/news/release/2013/pdf/2013038-0327.pdf.

3.3 Civil procedure and anti-modern myths in the "Harmonious Society": China and pre-war Japan compared

Dongsheng Zang

INTRODUCTION

In some areas of law, such as patent, the judiciary in China plays important roles in filling in the gaps in statutory language, thus making necessary policy decisions just like its counterparts in Japan, Korea, and Taiwan. In many other areas of social life in China today, however, the judiciary's function is strikingly different. For example, in environmental pollution disputes, labor disputes, village governance, land taking and property disputes, etc., there emerges a movement to push for mediation under the slogan of "harmonious society." The real function of the mediation campaigns in China today, however, is to deprive citizens of their legal rights in formal law. "Harmony," often justified as a cultural preference, is in reality often forced upon citizens from above. In other words, cultural assertion of "harmony" is a discursive technique deployed by the ruling elites to suppress resistance and safeguard the status quo.

In the United States, early studies of China's mediation were conducted in the 1960s through interviews with refugees fleeing Mao's China, so no one was under any illusion in regard to China's mediation. Nor are contemporary observers impressed by the campaigns in the name of "harmonious society" in China today.[1] Indeed, Professor Vai Io

[1] Stanley B. Lubman, *Mao and Mediation: Politics and Dispute Resolution in Communist China*, 55 CAL. L. REV. 1284 (1967) [hereinafter, *Mao and Mediation*]; Jerome Alan Cohen, *Chinese Mediation on the Eve of Modernization*, 54 CAL. L. REV. 1201 (1966). More recent insightful comments on this issue include, Carl F. Minzner, *China's Turn against Law*, 59 AM. J. COMP. L. 935 (Fall 2011, No. 4); Benjamin L. Liebman, *A Return to Populist Legality? Historical Legacies and Legal Reform*, *in* MAO'S INVISIBLE HAND:

Lo's chapter in this edited volume is a good example of this growing body of literature that provides insightful critiques of mediation. Curiously, despite some limited efforts to introduce a comparative perspective, current literature tends to treat mediation campaigns as a Chinese phenomenon, thus isolating it from similar experiences in other societies. The most notable similar experience is conciliation in prewar Japan, which is well documented by Japan studies literature in the United States. The self-isolation tends to generate an unhistorical narrative about the mediation campaigns in China. More importantly, the unhistorical narratives offer little assistance in understanding the deeper meanings of the mediation campaigns as an anti-modern project in a country that appears to be fairly successful in achieving a certain level of modernization.

This chapter aims to make a modest step in overcoming the self-isolation by borrowing some key insights developed by US studies of Japanese conciliation before World War II. At the center of Japan studies is Professor John O. Haley, whose decisive influence has shaped the whole generation of Japan studies since the publication of his article in 1978. The chapter starts by discussing the notion of myth-making, and the particular insights developed in Japan studies (Section I). Then, it proceeds to apply the insights to China by looking into the mediation campaigns since 2006 (Section II). The chapter concludes with some general observations on the similarities and differences between China today and prewar Japan (Section III).

I. THE MODERN AND ANTI-MODERN MYTHS IN JAPAN

In 1978, Professor John O. Haley published an article titled "The Myth of the Reluctant Litigant" in the *Journal of Japanese Studies*,[2] where he challenged the widespread perception that the Japanese do not go to the court for dispute resolution because of their culture. The most significant discovery in this article was not only that the number

---

THE POLITICAL FOUNDATIONS OF ADAPTIVE GOVERNANCE IN CHINA 165–200 (Sebastian Heilmann & Elizabeth Perry eds. 2011). Discussion of mediation in China (*tiaojie*) and conciliation in prewar Japan (*chōtei*) in this Chapter is limited to mediation in the judicial process only.

[2] John O. Haley, *The Myth of the Reluctant Litigant*, 4 J. JAP. STUD. 359 (1978) [hereinafter, *Reluctant Litigant*].

of civil cases varied substantially in history,[3] but also that, in certain periods of history, e.g., 1931 (peak), 1915, and 1903, the number of cases was much higher than that of the postwar period. This was "even more startling,"[4] Haley noted, considering the population increase in postwar Japan: "It is apparent that these patterns are inconsistent with conventional ideas about the reluctance of Japanese to litigate; moreover, they contradict the widely held belief that there has been a greater willingness to sue in the postwar period."[5] In demystification of the "apparent," Haley pointed to the use of cultural claims and in the meantime, the aggressive deployment of institutional barriers to prevent citizens from pursuing justice by way of private litigation. Haley noted that this was exactly the case when "… a conservative reaction to the rising tide of lawsuits in the 1920s and early 1930s and a concern on the part of the ruling elite that litigation was destructive to a hierarchical social order based upon personal relationships."[6]

It may well be more than a historical coincidence that in the same year as Haley's above article, literary critic Edward Said published his landmark work *Orientalism* (1978), arguing that European perceptions of the Arab world in the eighteenth and nineteenth centuries were shaped by the Self–Other divide, which was itself driven by colonial policy. A few years later, British historians Eric Hobsbawm and Terence Ranger edited a collection of essays titled *The Invention of Tradition* (1983), discussing the use of tradition as a discourse technique in a widespread European historical context. In the Anglo-American context, Haley, Said, and Hobsbawm can be understood in the context of a broad intellectual movement led by anthropologist Clifford Geertz, who set the conceptual foundation in his *The Interpretation of Cultures* (1973).[7]

---

[3] *Id.*, Figure 1, at 363, and Table 3, at 369.

[4] *Id.*, at 368.

[5] *Id.*, at 370.

[6] *Id.*, at 373.

[7] EDWARD W. SAID, ORIENTALISM (1978); THE INVENTION OF TRADITION (Eric Hobsbawm & Terence Ranger eds. 1983); CLIFFORD GEERTZ, THE INTERPRETATION OF CULTURES: SELECTED ESSAYS (1973). On Geertz's influence in anthropology and sociology in general, *see*, CLIFFORD GEERTZ BY HIS COLLEAGUES (Richard A. Shweder & Byron Good eds. 2005); JEFFREY C. ALEXANDER, TWENTY LECTURES: SOCIOLOGICAL THEORY SINCE WORLD WAR II (1987), Chapter 17 ("Cultural Sociology: Clifford Geertz's Rebellion against Determinism"). Earlier works following this line of thinking includes PETER L. BERGER & THOMAS LUCKMANN, THE SOCIAL CONSTRUCTION OF REALITY: A TREATISE IN THE SOCIOLOGY OF KNOWLEDGE (1967). Of course, to the extent that this was not exclusively an Anglo-American invention, Geertz's conceptual

(i) Haley's Critique of Kawashima

However, Haley's 1978 article is often read and understood more narrowly as a critique of Takeyoshi Kawashima [川島武宜],[8] the renowned Japanese legal sociologist. This section questions this view. Clearly Kawashima was a target in Haley's 1978 article, as both his name and his works were referenced; also, Kawashima was identified as the one of the "most articulate exponents of this belief."[9] On the other hand, however, it seems Haley was citing Kawashima as the popular representation of the view. For example, when Haley stated, "[t]he most ubiquitous are the works of Kawashima Takeyoshi. Particularly influential [is] his popular book *Nihonjin no hō ishiki* … in the title of which he coined the phrase 'Japanese legal consciousness,' …"[10] he was treating Kawashima as a narrator, rather than advocate of the view. Furthermore, in his subsequent works, Haley had little engagement with Kawashima, including his definitive magnum opus, *Authority without Power*, where Kawashima was referenced only once,[11] not even treated as an opponent. It seems to me that the conventional reading of Haley's 1978 article misses a very important point embedded in his discussion of myth-making in Japan: Haley's interest was not any myth-making or myth-making in abstract, but rather a particular form of myth-making, in a particular period of history in Japan.

This demands closer reading of Haley's 1978 article. As noted earlier, in probing into the 1930s, Haley analyzed a list of statutes in 1920s and 1940s Japan on conciliation:

---

framework is heavily indebted to Ludwig Wittgenstein, *see*, CLIFFORD GEERTZ, *id.*, Chapter 1. Karl Manheim seems clearly visible in many of the above works, *see*, KARL MANNHEIM, IDEOLOGY AND UTOPIA: AN INTRODUCTION TO THE SOCIOLOGY OF KNOWLEDGE (Louis Wirth & Edward Shils trans. 1954).

[8] Kiyoshi Igarashi [五十嵐清], *Seio hōgakusha ga mita nihon hō* [西欧法学者が見た日本法] [*Japanese Law from Western Legal Scholars' Perspectives*], in GENDAI HIKAKU HŌGAKU NO SHOSŌ [現代比較法学の諸相] [ASPECTS OF MODERN COMPARATIVE LAW] 271–92 (Tokyo: 2002) (tracking debates about "Japanese legal consciousness" between Western and Japanese scholars from 1978 to the 1990s); Setsuo Miyazawa, *Taking Kawashima Seriously: A Review of Japanese Research on Japanese Legal Consciousness and Disputing Behavior*, 21 LAW & SOC'Y REV. 219 (1987, No. 2); KAHEI ROKUMOTO [六本佳平], HŌSHAKAI GAKU [法社会学] [SOCIOLOGY OF LAW] 272-73 (Tokyo: 1986).

[9] John O. Haley, *Reluctant Litigant*, *supra* note 2, at 360.

[10] *Id*. Kawashima was also referenced in footnotes 5 and 7, *id.*, at 361.

[11] JOHN O. HALEY, AUTHORITY WITHOUT POWER: LAW AND THE JAPANESE PARADOX 175 (1991).

- Land Lease and House Lease Conciliation Law (No. 41, 1922)
- Farm Tenancy Conciliation Law (No. 18, 1924)
- Labor Dispute Conciliation Law (No. 57, 1926)
- Commercial Affairs Conciliation Law (No. 42, 1926)
- Monetary Claims Temporary Conciliation Law (No. 26, 1932)
- Agricultural Land Adjustment Law (No. 67, 1938)
- Personal Status Conciliation Law (No. 11, 1939)
- Special Wartime Civil Affairs Law (No. 63, 1942)

Haley noted that Kawashima "relie[d] heavily on the enactment of these statutes in arguing that the Japanese have been loath to litigation. Yet there is nothing to suggest that they were the product of popular demand for alternative to litigation more in keeping with Japanese sensitivities."[12] Furthermore, Haley continued, "… Kawashima's views are perhaps accurate so long as limited to description of the attitudes of those who came into power in the late 1920s and 1930s rather than the Japanese people as a whole.…"[13] Haley, it seems, makes a subtle but important distinction between Kawashima as a narrator of the culturist approach and those advocates of that approach.

The point became clear in Haley's 1982 sequel to the 1978 piece: "The Politics of Informal Justice: The Japanese Experience, 1932–1942,"[14] where he specifically discussed the debates between the traditionalists (the neo-Confucianist ruling elites such as Yatsuka Hozumi [穂積八束]) who asserted traditional moral values in Japan – the "virtuous ways and beautiful customs" [*junpu bizoku*, 淳風美俗] on the one hand; on the other, lawyers who questioned the ruling elites and advocated for formal adjudication in courtrooms. The challenge was in vain, conciliation was introduced in family disputes, then spilled to land disputes between landlords and tenants, then to labor and commercial disputes, "… by the end of the 1930s nearly all civil disputes had become subject to conciliation."[15] This echoes Haley's 1978 article that conciliation was forced upon people who were otherwise willing to choose trial. "Indeed, from the first conciliation statute to the last, the

---

12 John O. Haley, *Reluctant Litigant*, *supra* note 2, at 373.

13 *Id.*

14 John O. Haley, *The Politics of Informal Justice: The Japanese Experience, 1932–1942*, *in* II. THE POLITICS OF INFORMAL JUSTICE 125–47 (Richard Abel ed. 1982) [hereinafter, *Informal Justice*]. This article was incorporated into Haley's book, JOHN O. HALEY, AUTHORITY WITHOUT POWER, *supra* note 11, at 83–119 (Chapter 5, "Lawsuits and Lawyers: The Making of a Myth").

15 John O. Haley, *Informal Justice*, *id.*, at 136.

central purpose of proponents was to ensure that dispute outcomes reflected Japanese morals rather than law."[16] Kawashima, even as narrator, was almost forgotten in the 1982 article;[17] rather, Haley's target of criticism was largely those proponents of the 1920s and 1940s. As suggested earlier, this was also the case with Haley's book *Authority without Power*. For those who read Haley's work as a debate with Kawashima on the culturist approach, Haley's works after 1982 may present a hard case. The other way to read Haley is that he distinguishes two different kinds of culturist approach: traditionalists like Yatsuka Hozumi were the advocates of conciliation with an anti-modernist agenda, using culture as a justification for the conservative and even fascist move in prewar Japan;[18] Kawashima's culturist approach in postwar Japan, however, represented a modernist self-critical view with the agenda of introducing liberal ideas and reforms in Japan.

(ii) Two Kinds of Myths

In postwar Japan, Kawashima, together with his associates and allies Hisao Ōtsuka [大塚久雄], and Masao Maruyama [丸山眞男], represented a modernist intellectual movement that embraced at the

---

[16] John O. Haley, *Informal Justice*, *supra* note 14, at 137.

[17] Kawashima was only referenced once, John O. Haley, *Informal Justice*, *supra* note 14, at 141.

[18] Henderson commented that a small number of jurists in 1930s Japan showed "certain affinity to Nazi ideas" on the administration of justice, including their envisioned roles of *chōtei*, *see*, DAN FENNO HENDERSON, CONCILIATION AND JAPANESE LAW: TOKUGAWA AND MODERN 215–17 (1965). It is important to note that Haley recognized that conciliation statutes may have benefited debtors or tenants economically because "the [1896 Civil] code placed landlords in an even more favorable legal position." *see*, John O. Haley, *Informal Justice*, *supra* note 14, at 133. Thus, Haley resisted the Marxist temptation to label an explicit class bias on the conciliation statutes in Japan; rather, as Haley saw it, the challenges of conciliation came from the tension between the failures in reforming the formal law and the political unwillingness to impose it by judicial process: "This 'sense of crisis' [in the 1920s] prompted various attempts at substantive reform, all of which failed. Yet the significant political actors agreed that to resort to the formal legal process was not a suitable means for resolving rural tenancy disputes." *Id.*, at 135. Haley was influenced by Ann Waswo, *see*, Ann Waswo, *The Origins of Tenant Unrest*, *in* JAPAN IN CRISIS: ESSAYS ON TAISHŌ DEMOCRACY 374–97 (Bernard S. Silberman & H.D. Harootunian eds. 1974); ANN WASWO, JAPANESE LANDLORDS: THE DECLINE OF A RURAL ELITE (1977).

same time Max Weber and Karl Marx.[19] He inherited the modernization project from his mentors before the war, Sakae Wagatsuma [我妻栄] and Izutarō Suehiro [末弘厳太郎], who were influenced by Rudolf von Jhering and Eugene Ehrlich. However, Wagatsuma and Suehiro did not agree with each other on conciliation.[20] When World War II was over, Kawashima joined the Temporary Judicial Investigation Council [臨時司法制度調査会] under the Supreme Commander for the Allied Powers (SCAP) to work on civil law reform.[21] It was from his experience in the Council that Kawashima started a close encounter with American legal and sociological thinking. In 1950, under the auspices of a SCAP program, he visited the United States for the first time, and met Hans H. Gerth at the University of Wisconsin-Madison, and Talcott Parsons at Harvard.[22] Though, as before the war, his interest in the sociology of law was primarily driven by the desire to improve civil law in Japan, his vocabulary now was more flavored with the modernization theory of Parsons and the Parsonianized Max Weber. In a series of international

---

19 RIKKI KERSTEN, DEMOCRACY IN POSTWAR JAPAN: MARUYAMA MASAO AND THE SEARCH FOR AUTONOMY (1996); ANDREW BARSHAY, THE SOCIAL SCIENCES IN MODERN JAPAN: THE MARXIAN AND MODERNIST TRADITIONS (2004), Chapter 7 "Imagining Democracy in Postwar Japan: Maruyama Masao as a Political Thinker;" Yoshiyuki Matsumura, *The Works of Takeyoshi Kawashima*, 22 LAW & SOC'Y REV. 1037–42 (1988, No. 5). For autobiographical notes of Kawashima, *see*, TAKEYOSHI KAWASHIMA, ARU HŌGAKUSHA NO KISEKI [ある法学者の軌跡] [A LEGAL SCHOLAR'S PATH] (Tokyo: 1997).

20 Wagatsuma was skeptical of conciliation, while Suehiro was clearly in favor of conciliation, *see*, Sakae Wagatsuma, *Shihō no hōhōron ni kansuru ichi kōsatsu* [私法の方法論に関する一考察] [*A Perspective of Private Law as Methodology*], first published in 1927, reprinted in KINDAIHŌ NI OKERU SAIKEN NO YŪETSUTEKI CHII [近代法における債権の優越的地位] [THE SUPERIOR STATUS OF OBLIGATIONS IN MODERN LAW] 475–560 (Tokyo 1953); IZUTARŌ SUEHIRO, NŌSON HŌRITSU MONDAI [農村法律問題] [LEGAL ISSUES IN RURAL JAPAN] 320–33 (Tokyo: 1924); IZUTARŌ SUEHIRO, MINPŌ KŌWA [民法講話] [SPEECHES ON CIVIL LAW] 21–33 (Tokyo: 1926).

21 KAWASHIMA, A LEGAL SCHOLAR'S PATH (1997), *supra* note 19, at 211. Judge Alfred C. Oppler, who chaired both the Courts and Law Division in the Government Section as well as the Legislation and Justice Division of the Legal Section of SCAP, remembered Kawashima as "a courageous critic of the feudal features of Japanese society," *see*, ALFRED C. OPPLER, LEGAL REFORM IN OCCUPIED JAPAN: A PARTICIPANT LOOKS BACK 77 (1976). In 1961, Kawashima reported to a symposium titled "Post-war Democratization in Japan," sponsored by the United Nations Education, Science and Cooperation Organization (UNESCO), *see*, Takeyoshi Kawashima, *Law*, 13 INT'L SOC. SCI. J. 21 (1961, No. 1).

22 KAWASHIMA, A LEGAL SCHOLAR'S PATH (1997), *supra* note 19, at 217.

conferences in the early 1960s, Kawashima showed intensive interest in modernization theory and regarded cultural change as a necessary component of that overall change.[23] Arthur Taylor von Mehren noted during the 1961 conference at Harvard: "A recurrent problem in the conference discussions was the proposition that in traditional Japanese society (and, to a lesser extent, today) relatively little reliance is placed on the formal legal order as an agency for adjusting disputes and channeling human energy and capacity." Thus, "[i]n general, the Japanese participants seemed to see in law a major instrument for moving their society still closer to the industrialized democracies of the West."[24] However, as in other conferences, those views were not as convincing for the American participants at the conference: "[t]he opinions of the American participants on these issues were more varied and less assured."[25]

Haley's "debate" with Kawashima is similar to the debates in the above conferences. However, for most American observers on Japan, debate with the liberal/modernist advocates from postwar Japan was secondary, compared to their discovery of myth-making in prewar Japan. Haley's 1978 and 1982 articles can be read as an integral part of a broader intellectual move in Japan studies in the United States, largely in line with Clifford Geertz's interpretive theory of culture in anthropology. The year 1982 also saw the publication of an edited volume by historians Tetsuo Najita and J. Victor Koschman, *Conflict in Modern Japanese History: The Neglected Tradition* (1982),[26] covering

---

[23] These conferences included: the Conference on Modern Japan of the Association for Asian Studies in January 1962 at Bermuda, an earlier preparation conference from August 29 to September 2, 1960, at Hakone [箱根], Japan, and the Conference on Japanese Law at Harvard Law School in September 1961. Two collection of the papers of these conferences were published: LAW IN JAPAN: THE LEGAL ORDER IN A CHANGING SOCIETY (Arthur Taylor von Mehren ed. 1963) (a collection of papers presented at Harvard Conference, including Kawashima's contribution); CHANGING JAPANESE ATTITUDES TOWARD MODERNIZATION (Marius B. Jansen ed. 1965) (paper presented at the Bermuda Conference, including Maruyama's contributions). Kawashima recorded and reflected on his participation of these conferences in his autobiographical notes, *see*, KAWASHIMA, A LEGAL SCHOLAR'S PATH 261–92 (1997), *supra* note 19.

[24] Arthur Taylor von Mehren, *The Legal Order in Japan's Changing Society: Some Observations*, 76 HARV. L. REV. 1170 (1963), at 1177.

[25] *Id.*

[26] Tetsuo Najita, *Introduction: A Synchronous Approach to the Study of Conflict in Modern Japanese History*, *in* CONFLICT IN MODERN JAPANESE HISTORY: THE NEGLECTED TRADITION 3–21 (Tetsuo Najita & J. Victor Koschman eds. 1982).

a wide range of topics in the theme of invented tradition. From this point on, there emerged in the United States a large body of literature following this line of thinking on labor relations and land reform in prewar Japan, and the intellectual history of the Meiji and Tokugawa periods.[27] Thus we now have a clearer picture of this prewar general ideology, which ultimately evolved to the far-right extremism that was publicly hostile to the Western ideals in liberal democracy.[28] Tetsuo Najita and H.D. Harootunian pointed out, "Western conceptions of legal reason and rational cultural norms, often conveyed in the idiom of progress, rationalism, modernization, or simply Westernization, all came under scrutiny and were invariably modified but more often rejected as extensions of structures of power aimed at extending Western interests."[29] It was in this period, the notion of "harmony" (*wa*, 和) gained currency, and together with the emperor system, unique attributes helped Japan distinguish itself from Europe and the United States.[30] In law, "harmony" was forced upon citizens under the myth of "reluctant litigant".[31]

---

27 *E.g.*, CAROL GLUCK, JAPAN'S MODERNS MYTHS: IDEOLOGY IN THE LATE MEIJI PERIOD (1985); ANDREW GORDON, THE EVOLUTION OF LABOR RELATIONS IN JAPAN: HEAVY INDUSTRY, 1853–1955 (1985); ANDREW GORDON, LABOR AND IMPERIAL DEMOCRACY IN PREWAR JAPAN (1991); SHELDON M. GARON, THE STATE AND LABOR IN MODERN JAPAN (1987); W. DEAN KINZLEY, INDUSTRIAL HARMONY IN MODERN JAPAN: THE INVENTION OF A TRADITION (1991); HARRY HAROOTUNIAN, THINGS SEEN AND UNSEEN: DISCOURSE AND IDEOLOGY IN TOKUGAWA NATIVISM (1988); JAPAN'S COMPETING MODERNITIES: ISSUES IN CULTURE AND DEMOCRACY, 1900–1930 (Sharon A. Minichiello ed. 1998); MIRROR OF MODERNITY: INVENTED TRADITIONS OF MODERN JAPAN (Stephen Vlastos ed. 1998); HARRY HAROOTUNIAN, OVERCOME BY MODERNITY: HISTORICAL SURPLUS AND THE SEARCH FOR CULTURAL AUTHENTICITY IN INTERWAR JAPAN (2000).

28 Tetsuo Najita & H.D. Harootunian, *Japanese Revolt against the West: Political and Cultural Criticism in the Twentieth Century*, *in* MODERN JAPANESE THOUGHT 207–72 (Bob T. Wakabayashi ed. 1998).

29 *Id.*, at 210.

30 Kimio Itō, *The Invention of Wa and the Transformation of the Image of Prince Shōtoku in Modern Japan*, *in* MIRROR OF MODERNITY 37–47 (Stephen Vlastos eds. 1998), *supra* note 27, at 45.

31 John O. Haley, *Reluctant Litigant*, *supra* note 2; Frank K. Upham, *Weak Legal Consciousness as Invented Tradition*, *in* MIRROR OF MODERNITY 48–64 (Stephen Vlastos ed. 1998), *supra* note 27 (a study of the lawsuits brought by Burakumin from *hozu* village, now part of Kameoka City, Kyoto Prefecture).

II. THE RETURN OF ANTI-MODERN MYTHS IN CHINA

Prewar Japan and Republican China had many interactions and shared views,[32] including the anti-modern myths in "harmony." After all, it is convenient for the ruling elites on both sides that the Japanese kanji *wa* and Chinese word *he* is the same script! A civil procedure regulation of 1923, promulgated by the Beijing Beiyang Government, granted the power to the judges to mediate the dispute at any stage of the trial process.[33] In 1930, Republican China passed its own Civil Mediation Act [民事调解法],[34] and in 1935, the Code of Civil Procedure [民事诉讼法],[35] replacing the 1930 statute on mediation. Article 409 of the new Code made mediation a required process before a civil trial was initiated.[36] Civil procedure statutes in Republican China were largely modeled on Japan's, and a number of the most influential commentators were either educated by Japanese advisors in China or in Japanese universities, thus Japan's influence was prominent.[37] Even though the

---

[32] GERMAINE A. HOSTON, THE STATE, IDENTITY, AND THE NATIONAL QUESTION IN CHINA AND JAPAN (1994); THE CHINESE AND THE JAPANESE: ESSAYS IN POLITICAL AND CULTURAL INTERACTIONS (Akira Iriye ed. 1980).

[33] "Regulations Relating to Civil Procedure," [民事诉讼条例] 1921, Beijing, in THE REGULATIONS RELATING TO CIVIL PROCEDURE OF THE REPUBLIC OF CHINA (Peking: 1923). Article 446 of the Regulations provides: "Irrespective of the stage of the proceedings reached, the court may, at any time during the course of debate, attempt to induce the parties to come to a compromise, and may cause a commissioned judge or a judge acting on request to do the same." *Id.*, at 100.

[34] Minshi Tiaojie Fa [Civil Mediation Act], January 11, 1930, passed by Legislative Yuan, and promulgated on January 20, 1930, 5 LI FA YUAN KONG PAO [立法院公报] 431 (No.14). Article 2 of the Act: "Any family dispute or other civil dispute under the jurisdiction of the trial courts, unless it has been dealt with by mediation or that a mediation officer has decided that it is unsuitable for mediation, cannot be brought to the court. Party to other disputes may also apply for mediation."

[35] Zhonghua Min'guo Minshi Susong Fa [Code of Civil Procedure of Republic of China], passed by Legislative Yuan and promulgated on February 1, 1935, 19 LI FA YUAN KONG PAO [立法院公报] 121 (No. 67).

[36] Article 409 of the 1935 Code, *id.*, requires that certain disputes, such as lease of real property and employment relations, must have gone through mediation (by the court) before a lawsuit can be brought to the court. WU XUEYI [吴学义], MINSHI SUSONGFA YAOLUN [民事诉讼法要论] [AN INTRODUCTION OF CIVIL PROCEDURE LAW] 211–12 (Shanghai: 1942); GUO XINGCUN [郭杏邨], MINSHI SUSONG FA [民事訴訟法] [CIVIL PROCEDURE LAW] 32 (Shanghai: 1936).

[37] He Qinhua [何勤华], *Zhongguo Jindai Minshi Susong Faxue de Dansheng*

political state was not always as effective as its counterpart in Japan, the Kuomintang ruling elites adopted the same rhetoric in Republican China. Hu Hanmin [胡汉民], chair of the Legislative Yuan, spoke for many in 1929 when he commented to the national legislature in support of the civil mediation bill: "Our country always values modesty, and people are ashamed of involving in fight in the courtroom …"[38]

In the areas occupied by the Communists during the Anti-Japanese War (1937–1945) and Civil War (1945–1949) periods, mediation was also encouraged, though colored with a combination of Chinese traditional values as well as revolutionary spirits. The revolutionaries, however, did not have a uniform policy on whether mediation should be mandatory in judicial process or not. A 1943 regulation on mediation in Shan-gan-ning Border Regions required that all civil cases and most criminal cases go through mediation before trial.[39] In 1944, Xie Juezai [谢觉哉], then President of the Border Region High Court, gave special instruction to lower courts on mediation: "There must be complete consent from both parties. No coercion, not even a bit, is allowed."[40] He warned, "[i]n encouraging mediation, departures [from principles] may occur, namely, parties may be forced to accept mediation, so that the cadre has a higher number of mediations to report. This should not be tolerated. We must be vigilant on this."[41] In 1945, the problem of over-emphasis on mediation was caught in an internal debate between Border Area leaders, and Xie Juezai's more moderate views prevailed

---

yu Chengzhang [中国近代民事诉讼法学的诞生与成长] [*The Birth and Development of Civil Procedural Law Studies in Recent History*], FALÜ KEXUE [法律科学] [SCIENCE OF LAW] 85 (2004, No. 2).

[38] Liu Xinjie [刘昕杰], *Yihe Weigui: Min'guo Jiceng Minshi Jiufen de Tiaojie* [以和为贵：民国基层民事纠纷的调解] [*Value Harmony: Mediation in Civil Dispute Resolution in Republican China*], SHANDONG DAXUE XUEBAO [山东大学学报] [SHANDONG UNIVERSITY REVIEW] (2011, No. 4).

[39] Article 2 of Shan-gan-ning Bianqu Min Xing Shijian Tiaojie Tiaoli [陕甘宁边区民刑事件调解条例] [Regulations on in Criminal and Civil Mediations in Shan-gan-ning Border Regions], promulgated in June 1943, reprinted in SHAN-GAN-NING BIANQU FALÜ FAGUI HUIBIAN [陕甘宁边区法律法规汇编] [LAWS AND REGULATIONS IN SHAN-GAN-NING BORDER REGIONS] 497–98 (Xi'an: 2010). However, Article 7 of the same regulation also provides that mediation should be based on consent of the parties, and that no governmental officials, grass root organizations or family members may force mediation upon parties. Interestingly, Article 7 does not include court or judges in its prohibited list.

[40] XIE JUEZAI RIJI [谢觉哉日记] [XIE JUEZAI DIARY] 622 (Beijing: 1984), entry of May 11, 1944.

[41] *Id.*

temporarily.[42] It was in the midst of this internal debate that Ma Xiwu [马锡五], a judicial cadre, emerged as a model, known as "Ma Xiwu Trial Method."[43] After the People's Republic was founded, Ma was appointed as Vice President of the Supreme People's Court in 1954, and his name became an icon for mediation in Mao's China. Like Xie Juezai, Ma was explicitly against coercive mediation. In a public speech in 1950, Ma reiterated that "[m]ediation must be voluntary for both parties. No coercion is allowed. Policy, laws and regulations shall be followed, progressive customs be considered favorably." Further, "[m]ediation is not a required process for parties to file lawsuits. One must be patient for parties to embrace [mediation], so as to reduce litigation, and enhance unity among the people. …"[44]

This debate continued in subsequent years. In the 1960s, mediation was often forced upon citizens in Mao's China.[45] After the Cultural Revolution, the 1982 Civil Procedure Code (for Trial Use) tried to moderate the tune by stating the principle as "The people's court, in trial process, shall give priority to mediation; when mediation fails, judgment shall be rendered in timely fashion" (Article 6). The 1991 Civil Procedure Code represented a further step. Article 9 set more explicit limits on mediation: "In civil proceedings, the people's court shall promote mediation in accordance with the principle of voluntariness and legitimacy; a court decision shall be made promptly when mediation has

---

42 WANG SHIRONG [王世荣], ET AL., XINZHONGGUO SIFA ZHIDU DE JISHI – SHAN-GAN-NING BIANQU GAODENG FAYUAN (1937–1949) [新中国司法制度的基石 – 陕甘宁边区高等法院] [THE FOUNDATIONS FOR THE JUSTICE SYSTEM IN NEW CHINA: THE SHAN-GAN-NING BORDER REGION HIGH COURT 1937–1949] (Beijing: 2011), at 244; ZHANG XIBO [张希波] & HAN YANLONG [韩延龙], ZHONGGUO GEMING FAZHISHI [中国革命法制史] [HISTORY OF REVOLUTIONARY LEGAL SYSTEM IN CHINA] (volume I) (Beijing: 1987), at 518–19.

43 Jiang Shigong [强世功], *Quanli de Zuzhi Wangluo yu Falü de Zhilihua – Ma Xiwu Shenpan Fangshi yu Zhongguo Falü de Xin Chuantong* [权力的组织与法律的治理化 – 马锡五审判方式与中国法律的新传统] [*Organization Web of Power and Law's Instrumental Use: Ma Xiwu Trial Method and China's New Tradition in Law*], 3 BEIDA FALÜ PINGLUN [北大法律评论] [PEKING UNIVERSITY LAW REVIEW] 1 (2000, No. 2).

44 Ma Xiwu, *Guanyu Shenpan Zhidu yu Qunzhong Luxian Wenti de Fayan* [关于审判制度与群众路线问题的发言] [*Speech on Issues concerning Judicial Trial and the Mass Line*], SHANDONG ZHENGBAO [山东政报] [SHANDONG NEWS IN POLITICS] 60–61 (Dec. 1950).

45 Stanley B. Lubman, *Mao and Mediation* (1967), *supra* note 1; Jerome Alan Cohen, *Chinese Mediation on the Eve of Modernization* (1966), *supra* note 1.

failed."[46] In subsequent years, the judiciary moved toward more formal judicial processes: procedures were emphasized, evidence rules became more detailed, professional qualification of judges was standardized, military-type uniforms were replaced by judicial robes, and even gavels were introduced. Professionalism became a central value.[47] The "Ma Xiwu method" was largely absent in academic journals, until the introduction of "harmonious society" in 2006.

(i) "Harmonious Society" and Mediation

On October 11, 2006, the Sixth Plenary Session of the 16th Communist Party of China (CPC) Central Committee adopted the "Resolution on Some Major Issues Regarding the Building of a Harmonious Socialist Society." Following the Party's Sixth Plenary in 2006, the Supreme People's Court issued in January 2007 "Several Opinions,"[48] where SPC emphasized that "the judiciary's fundamental task is to mitigate social tensions, enhance social stability, promote social harmony and fulfill social justice." In order to handle a large number of cases effectively, SPC stated, there must be "multiple mechanisms for dispute resolution" and they should be efficient and convenient for the parties involved. In civil adjudication, it meant a stronger judicial policy in encouraging mediation in the trial process, i.e., that a case "be mediated so far as it is possible." Mediation covers not only the areas of family disputes, minor disputes between neighbors, but also land disputes, environmental

---

46 Stanley B. Lubman, *Dispute Resolution in China after Deng Xiaoping: "Mao and Mediation" Revisited*, 11 COLUM. J. ASIAN L. 229 (Fall 1997, No. 2); Fu Hualing, *Understanding People's Mediation in Post-Mao China*, 6 J. CHINESE L. 211 (Fall 1992, No. 2).

47 Yu Xingzhong, *Judicial Professionalism in China: From Discourse to Reality*, *in* PROSPECTS FOR THE PROFESSIONS IN CHINA 78–108 (William P. Alford, Kenneth Winston & William C. Kirby eds. 2011); Shumei Hou & Ronald Keith, *China's Supreme People's Court within the "Political-legal System"*, *in* THE JUDICIALIZATION OF POLITICS IN ASIA 163–83 (Bjorn Dressel ed. 2012); Benjamin L. Liebman, *China's Courts: Restricted Reform*, 191 CHINA Q. 620 (Sep. 2007).

48 Zuigao Renmin Fayuan [最高人民法院] [The Supreme People's Court], *Guanyu wei Goujian Shehuizhuyi Hexie Shehui Tigong Sifa Baozhang de Ruogan Yijian* [关于为构建社会主义和谐社会提供司法保障的若干意见] [*Several Opinions on Providing Judicial Safeguard to Socialist Harmonious Society*], Doc.2 (2007), January 15, 2007, GAZETTE OF THE SUPREME PEOPLE'S COURT OF THE PEOPLE'S REPUBLIC OF CHINA [中华人民共和国最高人民法院公报] 15 (2007, No. 3).

pollution, personal injury cases, medical malpractice, labor disputes, and village governance. "Grand mediation" emphasizes integration of three kinds of mediation: grass roots level mediation by the local people's mediation committee, mediation by governmental agencies, and mediation in the judicial process.[49] For the sake of limited space, this chapter's focus is on the last kind.

Mediation is offered in every stage of the judicial process: the judiciary often tries to mediate the dispute when the complainant comes to the court to file a complaint, at pre-trial process, and during trial. The Civil Procedure Code, amended in August 2012, even allows mediation in appellate process (Article 172). The 2012 amendment consolidates several aspects of judicial mediation that have been conducted on an experimental basis since 2004. First, priority to mediation is added, even though Article 9 remains intact. Article 122 provides: "When a civil dispute filed by parties to the people's court is suitable for mediation, mediation may be applied, unless it is refused by parties." In practice, this means a court may self-initiate mediation from the moment the complaint is filed in the court. During the whole judicial process, the judges would "recommend" mediation relentlessly to the parties.

Second, the legal status of mediation agreements is also clarified. This is an issue that has long troubled judges as well as mediators outside the courtroom. Mediation would not be effective if all it did was to merely reach another agreement; on other hand, however, it may not be realistic to treat a mediation agreement as final or as an arbitral award. The first legislative step was the People's Mediation Act (PMA), enacted in August 2010.[50] Article 33 of the PMA creates a process for the parties to seek judicial confirmation (司法确认) by the people's court within 30 days after a mediation agreement is concluded. Once it is confirmed by the court, an enforcement order may be directly

---

[49] Jieren Hu, *Grand Mediation in China: Mechanism and Application*, 51 ASIAN SURVEY 1065 (Nov.–Dec. 2011, No. 6); Liming Wang, *Characteristics of China's Judicial Mediation System*, 17 ASIA PAC. L. REV. 67 (2009); Michael Palmer, *Compromising Courts and Harmonizing Ideologies: Mediation in the Administrative Chambers of the People's Courts in the People's Republic of China*, NEW COURTS IN ASIA 251–76 (Andrew Harding & Penelope (Pip) Nicholson eds. 2010).

[50] Zhonghua Renmin Gongheguo Renmin Tiaojie Fa [中华人民共和国人民调解法] [People's Republic of China People's Mediation Law], August 28, 2010, passed by the Standing Committee of the National People's Congress, taking effect on January 1, 2011. For an English translation, *PRC People's Mediation Law*, 25 CHINA LAW & PRACTICE 51 (Mar. 2011, No. 2).

sought from the court if the other party defaults. The 2012 amendment to the Civil Procedure Code added two articles, Articles 194 and 195, on judicial confirmation of mediation agreements. On its appearance, Article 194 largely repeats PMA Article 33, discussed earlier. A crucial difference, however, is that Article 194 uses a broad term – "mediation agreement" – which could cover all kinds of mediation agreements; while PML Article 33 applies only to agreements concluded as result of intervention by the grassroot people's mediation committee. In other words, Article 194 extends judicial confirmation to all mediation agreements.[51] Under Article 195, the court may confirm validity of a mediation agreement, rending it directly enforceable; if the court does not confirm validity of the agreement, parties may modify it by concluding another agreement, or to file a formal complaint at the court.

(ii) The Anti-modern Myth

Behind the above legislative change and the flooding of mediation cases is an anti-modern myth in the making, since the call in 2004 for "harmonious society." Mediation is often labeled as "Eastern Virtue" (东方经验). Minister of Justice Wu Aiying [吴爱英] was quoted as saying mediation is a further development of the cultural heritage from an "Eastern tradition" that values harmony.[52] Despite the ideological conflicts in the past and colossal atrocities during times of war, and despite the internal debates in the Border Regions, those statutes are now described as a neat and linear evolution of legal norms leading to their present form, as if no lessons other than historical continuity can be learned from the past.

---

[51] A case decided by the Beijing No. 2 Intermediate People's Court addresses this issue. *Hejie Xieyi Lüxing Butong de Chengxu hui Chansheng Butong de Falü Xiaoli* [和解协议履行不同的程序会产生不同的法律效力] [*In Enforcing Settlement Agreements, Different Processes May Lead to Different Results*], RENMIN FAYUAN BAO [人民法院报] [PEOPLE'S COURT DAILY], Aug. 21, 2013, at 8. Also, Wang Yaxin [王亚新], *Minshi Susong Fa Xiugai yu Queren Tiaojie Xieyi Anjian Chengxu* [民事诉讼法修改与确认调解协议案件程序] [*Amendment to the Civil Procedure Code and Procedures for Judicial Confirmation of Mediation Agreements*], RENMIN FAYUAN BAO [PEOPLE'S COURT DAILY], Jan. 18, 2012, at 7.

[52] XINHUA MEIRI DIANXUN [新华每日电讯] [XINHUA DAILY TELEGRAPH], Oct. 7, 2006, at 1.

Some of the prominent advocates of the Ma Xiwu methods are officials in the judiciary from China's heartland areas. Hao Hongtao, President of the High Court in Gansu Province in northwestern China, for example, quickly linked "harmonious society" with the Ma Xiwu methods in an article published in the *People's Court Daily*.[53] The same newspaper started reporting the "successful" experiences in mediation across China. In Henan Province, central China, the High Court led by President Zhang Liyong began to promote the Ma Xiwu method in lower courts in Henan Province.[54] The return of the "Ma Xiwu method" presents itself in terms of populist justice, thus anti-formalism, and often anti-West.[55] It promises simplicity that had been lost in the procedures, justice that had been unfulfilled, as well as native authenticity that had been obscured by foreign concepts. It insists that heartland China (the location of the "Border Regions" during the 1930s and 1940s) represents the "true" characters of China today. Based on that premise, this body of literature stresses that China is still predominantly a rural society. In its mythical sense, "rural China" is a symbol for uncontaminated identity, a source of real strength, virtue, and pride. Thus, according to the advocates, the "rule of law" modeled on Western-style formal law (especially the Anglo-American adversary system) does not fit the "character" of Chinese society. In this discussion, Ma Xiwu's concerns about over-using mediation are forgotten; rather, the only function of the "Ma Xiwu method," as an icon, is to safeguard "harmony" against any disturbance to the status quo.

III. CONCLUSION

For the ruling elites in China today, "harmonious society" is a particularly attractive concept, and mediation is a preferred tool to achieve it. This chapter has tried to sketch a comparison between the mediation campaigns in China today and conciliation (*chōtei*) in prewar

---

53 Hao Hongtao [郝洪涛], *Hongyang Ma Xiwu Shenpan Fangshi, Cujin Sifa Hexie* [弘扬马锡五审判方式促进司法和谐] [*Spreading Ma Xiwu Method, Promoting Harmony in Judicial Process*], RENMIN FAYUAN BAO [PEOPLE'S COURT DAILY], Mar. 16, 2007.

54 *Zhang Liyong: Huajie Maodun bu Zaihu Fangshi Youduotu* [张立勇：化解矛盾不在乎方式有多土] [*Zhang Liyong: Mitigating Tensions by Ma Xiwu Method*], FAZHI RIBAO [LEGAL DAILY], Nov. 6, 2009, at 3.

55 Benjamin L. Liebman, *A Return to Populist Legality?* (2011), *supra* note 1.

Japan. Further details will be required to make the comparative study complete, but it seems clear enough that the key resemblance lies in the fact that in both countries mediation is legally forced upon citizens and such coercion is justified by a cultural claim – harmony. Even though coercion is well recognized in current literature on China's mediation campaigns, the claim made in this chapter – resemblance with prewar Japan – gives us a much clearer historical sense. In fact, prewar Japan is a lot like today's China: first, rapid industrialization for half a century (from the Meiji Restoration to the 1930s in Japan; from the end of Cultural Revolution to the 2000s in China) led to enormous social tensions; second, an old ruling elite unwilling to engage in political reform thus to accommodate different political interests; third, emboldened by economic success, the ruling elites entertained the notion of Self in cultural/identity terms and fantasized the Self as a superior alternative to the Western models. When combined, all these elements led to a deliberate policy of departing from the formal/modern law imported from the West, justified in cultural terms.

Questions may still be raised, however: for example, would mediation campaigns in China today be more properly compared with postwar, instead of prewar, Japan? After all, it has been well argued that conciliation continued in postwar Japan and was often deployed by conservative forces in the name of harmony.[56] To answer the question, we must return to earlier discussion of Professor John O. Haley's comments on Takeyoshi Kawashima, where two kinds of cultural claims were distinguished and treated differently. Liberal intellectuals like Kawashima pushed for further reform in postwar Japan. In 1951, prewar conciliation statutes were abolished and replaced by the new Law for Conciliation of Civil Affairs (Law No. 222, 1951).[57] Judges were still conservative in general, but the judicial forum became more accessible. Plaintiffs in high-profile cases such as the Minamata litigations were often supported by progressive lawyers associated with the Japan Communist Party or the Socialist Party.[58] It is also not a pure coincidence that Kawashima's popular book *Nihonjin no hō ishiki* was

---

[56] Frank K. Upham, Law and Social Change in Postwar Japan (1987).

[57] For an English translation, The Law of Civil Procedure 209–19 (Tokyo: 1959).

[58] Frank K. Upham, *supra* note 56, at 38 and 55 (discussing the role of Japan Communist Party in Minamata litigations). Other examples include Sanrizuka [三里塚] citizens' movement against the New Tokyo International Airport, *see*, David E. Apter & Nagayo Sawa, Against the State: Politics and Social Protest in Japan (1984).

published in 1967, the same year the first Minamata lawsuit was filed. Access to the judicial process, however limited in postwar Japan, is still missing in China today. Most recently, China's lawyer activist Xu Zhiyong was convicted of the crime of "gathering a crowd to disturb public order" in Beijing.[59] Xu and his law firm played an active role in organizing plaintiffs in China's 2008 Sanlu milk powder civil lawsuits, but he is not tolerated. In this aspect, China's mediation campaigns are more reminiscent of prewar Japan, when conciliation was used in part to prevent citizens from organizing themselves.[60] Therefore, the legal "innovation" in the judicial process in China today is in fact a return of the ancien regime.

---

[59] *China Sentences Xu Zhiyong, Legal Activist, to 4 Years in Prison*, N.Y. TIMES, January 27, 2014.

[60] ANN WASWO, JAPANESE LANDLORDS 94–134 (1977), *supra* note 18.

3.4 Judicial activism in China

Vai Io Lo

I. INTRODUCTION

Judicial activism versus judicial restraint is a perennial theme in legal literature. Based on the principle of separation of powers, judicial activism frequently carries a negative connotation, while judicial restraint is championed as the antidote for unbridled discretion. Since China launched economic reforms in the late 1970s, the Chinese judiciary has undertaken various reforms, especially in terms of the qualification of judges, the judicial processes and the role of the court in society. Indeed, the past three decades witnessed an oscillation of advocacy, between inquisitorial and adversarial trial proceedings, between professionalism and populism, and between activism and passivism. In recent years, Chinese judges have been urged to be active, rather than passive or neutral, in executing their responsibilities. Considering the currency and relevancy of "active judicature" (*nengdong sifa*), this chapter attempts to investigate judicial activism in China. Toward this end, the following discussion is composed of three sections.

To situate the Chinese experience in a comparative context, section II provides a succinct account of judicial activism as understood in common law countries. Section III discusses judicial activism with Chinese characteristics, focusing on judicial interpretations (*sifa jieshi*) and "active judicature" and highlighting the Chinese characteristics, even though the present study is not intended to be a comparative analysis. Taking the discussion to a more general level, section IV draws conclusions in light of China's ongoing efforts to build an effective legal system.

II. JUDICIAL ACTIVISM IN COMMON LAW COUNTRIES

In 1947, Schlesinger coined the term "judicial activism" in a magazine article, but he did not really define the parameters of the term.[1] Over the years, advocates of judicial activism tend to regard it as progressive judicial conduct responding to changing economic, political and social circumstances, while critics of judicial activism tend to characterize it as judicial impropriety usurping the power of other branches of government. Since judicial activism has an elusive meaning, various attempts, mainly in the form of either describing its major attributes or developing an analytical model, have been made to elucidate the nebulous concept of judicial activism. These attempts can be exemplified as follows.

Generally, judicial activism is deemed to have occurred where the court, in adjudging a dispute or hearing an appeal, invalidates statutory provisions, overrules case precedents, or formulates public policies, whether or not due to ideological or political considerations.[2] The labeling of a judge as an activist based on these kinds of conduct is analogous to making a diagnosis based on distinct symptoms. Green, however, argues that judicial activism is "the abuse of unsupervised power that is exercised outside the bounds of judicial role," and that judicial activism does not necessarily promote progressive ideologies or individual rights, because activism occurs whenever a judge has violated cultural standards of a judicial role.[3] In other words, judicial activism is judicial conduct that exceeds what judges are empowered or expected to do.

To provide structure to the concept of judicial activism, Canon has identified six dimensions in a multi-directional model for assessing the

---

[1] Arthur M. Schlesinger, Jr., *The Supreme Court: 1947*, FORTUNE, Jan. 1947, at 73.

[2] *See, e.g.*, Frank B. Cross and Stefanie Lindquist, *The Decisional Significance of the Chief Justice*, 154 U. PA. L. REV. 1665, 1701 (2006) (a commonly invoked measure of judicial activism is the Court's willingness to invalidate statutes); Ernest A. Young, *Judicial Activism and Conservative Politics*, 73 U. COLO. L. REV., 1139, 1144 (2002) (defining judicial activism as departing from text and/or history, departing from judicial precedent, etc.); Bradley C. Canon, *Defining the Dimensions of Judicial Activism*, 66 JUDICATURE 236, 238 (1982–1983) (judicial activism is seen as a significant court-generated change in public policy).

[3] Craig Green, *An Intellectual History of Judicial Activism*, 58 EMORY L. J. 1195, 1222, 1226–27 (2009).

activism of the US Supreme Court, including majoritarianism, interpretive stability, interpretive fidelity, substance/democratic process distinction, specificity of policy and availability of an alternative policymaker.[4] Under this model, activism occurs where judicial reviews result in policies replacing those made by democratically elected representatives; judicial decisions overrule case precedents or existing doctrines; judicial interpretations of constitutional or statutory norms are inconsistent with their plain meaning or the legislative intent; judicial decisions have an impact on substantive policies rather than affecting the democratic political processes; and judicial decisions generate new policies directing or preempting other governmental agencies.[5]

Building on Canon's model, Cohn and Kremnitzer have developed a multi-dimensional model of judicial activism, which is comprised of three visions (traditional, deviation from social consensus or social equilibrium, and protection of core values) and 17 parameters (judicial stability, interpretation, majoritarianism and autonomy, judicial reasoning, threshold activism, judicial remit, rhetoric, obiter dicta, comparative sources, judicial voices, extent of decision, legal background, legislative reaction, administrative reaction, judicial reaction, public reaction and value-content).[6] For example, under

---

4 Majoritarianism refers to the degree to which policies adopted through democratic processes are judicially negated. Interpretive stability refers to the degree to which earlier court decisions, doctrines, or interpretations are changed. Interpretive fidelity refers to the degree to which constitutional provisions are interpreted contrary to the legislative intent or the clear implications of the language used. Substance/democratic process distinction refers to the degree to which judicial decisions make substantive policies rather than affect the preservation of democratic political processes. Specificity of policy refers to the degree to which judicial decisions establish policies instead of leaving discretion to other agencies or individuals. Availability of an alternative policymaker refers to the degree to which judicial decisions supersede serious consideration of the same problems by other governmental agencies. Canon, *supra* note 2, at 239.

5 *Id.* at 240–47.

6 Under the traditional vision, judges are considered activists when they change the law, overstep their role of resolving disputes, or make decisions on policy issues. Parameters 1 to 12 are used to assess activism. Under the "deviation from social consensus or social equilibrium" vision, activism refers to the extent of judicial deviation from the social consensus or social equilibrium that emerges in the constitutional network in reaction to the decision. Parameters 13 to 16 are used to assess activism. Under the "protection of core values" vision, activism refers to judicial departure from the protection of core values or extensive involvement in areas that will not have implications on core values. Parameter 17 is used to assess activism. Margit Cohn and Mordechai

the traditional vision, judges who employ purposive interpretation or expand jurisdiction into areas formerly immune from intervention are deemed activist.[7] Under the "deviation from social consensus or social equilibrium" vision, judicial decisions that are subsequently annulled by the legislature are deemed activist.[8] Under the "protection of core values" vision, judicial intervention in a value-free context is highly activist.[9] By treating the judiciary as an actor in a complex politico-institutional network engaging in constitutional dialogues, this model not only assesses where a judicial decision lies on the continuum of activism and restraint, but also unfolds the relative activism of individual cases, judicial eras or subject matters.[10]

Accordingly, the preceding discussion reflects that judicial activism is a fluid concept and, as such, provides fertile ground for academic debate and legal scholarship. Green's definition of judicial activism hinges on the role of the judiciary. The role of the judiciary is derived from its designated powers and functions which, in turn, depend on the state structure, as well as the economic, cultural and social circumstances of the jurisdiction concerned. Given the variety of political structures and the consequential roles of judiciaries, judicial activism can have different meanings among jurisdictions. From this perspective, it will be instructive to examine what constitutes judicial activism in China.

III. JUDICIAL ACTIVISM WITH CHINESE CHARACTERISTICS

In China, judicial activism is achieved through two major avenues, interpretation of statutory provisions and adjudication of individual cases. Now and then, the Supreme People's Court (SPC) issues judicial interpretations to provide lower courts with guidance in their application of statutory provisions.[11] In 2009, Wang Shengjun, the

---

Kremnitzer, *Judicial Activism: A Multidimensional Model*, 18 CAN. J. L. & JURISPRUDENCE 333, 336 & 340–52 (2005).

7 *Id.* at 341–42.

8 *Id.* at 347.

9 *Id.* at 352.

10 *Id.* at 337–38.

11 *E.g.*, Zuigao Renmin Fayuan Guanyu Shenli Renshen Sunhai Peichang Anjian Shiyong Falu Ruogan Wenti De Jieshi [The Supreme People's Court's Explanation of Several Questions regarding the Application of Law in Adjudging Cases on Compensation for Bodily Harm] (promulgated on 4 December 2003).

President of the SPC, said that "active judicature" was an indispensable choice for the courts to serve the whole situation of economic and social developments.[12] Since then, "active judicature" has become a judicial policy, which Chinese judges have conscientiously followed in adjudging disputes.

(i) Interpretation of Statutory Provisions

Under the Chinese Constitution, the Standing Committee of the National People's Congress (NPC) has the power to interpret the Constitution and basic laws.[13] The NPC authorizes the SPC to issue interpretations on questions concerning the specific application of laws and decrees in adjudicatory work.[14] The SPC maintains that its judicial interpretations are legally binding.[15] In issuing judicial interpretations, the SPC aims at either providing specificity to broad, undefined or vague statutory provisions, whether in terms of general application or applicability to particular types of cases, or expanding or limiting the scope of statutory provisions to deal with new issues arising from changing economic and social circumstances. Judicial activism, therefore, is inevitable because an interpretation resulting in new legal norms or changing existing ones exceeds the mere application of law in adjudging disputes. Two examples of judicial activism concern the division of property upon dissolution of marriage and the burden of proof in medical malpractice cases.

---

[12] Liang Zhang, *Wang Shengjun: Nengdong Sifa Shi Fayuan Biran De Xuanze [Wang Shengjun: Active Judicature Is an Indispensable Choice for the Courts]*, FAZHI RIBAO, 1 Sept. 2009, available at http://www.npc.gov.cn/npc/xinwen/fztd/sfgz/2009-09/01/content_1516819.htm.

[13] Zhonghua Renmin Gongheguo Xianfa [Constitution of the People's Republic of China] (adopted by the National People's Congress on 4 December 1982 and amended in 1988, 1993, 1999 and 2004), art. 67.

[14] Quanguo Renmin Daibiao Dahui Changwu Weiyuanhui Guanyu Jiaqiang Falu Jieshi Gongzuo De Jueyi [The Standing Committee of the National People's Congress' Resolution regarding the Strengthening of Legal Interpretive Work] (adopted on 10 June 1981), art. 2.

[15] Zuigao Renmin Fayuan Guanyu Sifa Jieshi Gongzuo De Ruogan Guiding [The Supreme People's Court's Several Provisions regarding Work on Judicial Interpretation] (promulgated on 1 July 1997), art. 4; Zuigao Renmin Fayuan Guanyu Sifa Jieshi Gongzuo de Guiding [The Supreme People's Court's Provisions regarding Work on Judicial Interpretation] (promulgated on 23 March 2007), art. 5.

In 2001, the NPC substantially amended the Marriage Law, allowing a married couple to own both joint property and individual property.[16] In its first interpretation, the SPC explained what "equal right to handle" joint property meant and stated that individual property would not be converted into joint property as a result of marriage.[17] In its second interpretation, the SPC stated that housing leased by one spouse before marriage but purchased with joint property after marriage should be treated as joint property, despite that the property was registered under the name of one spouse; and that if the parents financed the purchase of housing prior to (or after) marriage, the property should be treated as an individual (or joint) gift, unless otherwise stated.[18] In its third interpretation, the SPC further explained how immovable property should be divided where the couple failed to reach an agreement. For example, where the parents of one spouse financed the purchase of an immovable property after marriage and the property was registered under the name of that spouse, the property should be treated as individual property; and where the parents of both spouses financed the purchase of an immovable property but the property was registered under the name of one spouse, the property would be co-owned according to the respective financial contributions of their parents.[19] Thus, in response to the increasing incidence of divorce,[20] the SPC

---

[16] Zhonghua Renmin Gongheguo Hunyin Fa [The Marriage Law of the People's Republic of China] (adopted by the National People's Congress on 10 Sept. 1980 and amended on 28 April 2001), arts. 17 & 18.

[17] Zuigao Renmin Fayuan Guanyu Shiyong Zhonghua Renmin Gongheguo Hunyin Fa Ruogan Wenti De Jieshi (1) [The Supreme People's Court's Explanation of Several Questions regarding the Application of the Marriage Law of the People's Republic of China (1)] (promulgated on 24 December 2001), arts. 17 & 19.

[18] Zuigao Renmin Fayuan Guanyu Shiyong Zhonghua Renmin Gongheguo Hunyin Fa Ruogan Wenti De Jieshi (2) [The Supreme People's Court's Explanation of Several Questions regarding the Application of the Marriage Law of the People's Republic of China (2)] (promulgated on 26 December 2003), arts. 19 & 22.

[19] Zuigao Renmin Fayuan Guanyu Shiyong Zhonghua Renmin Gongheguo Hunyin Fa Ruogan Wenti De Jieshi (3) [The Supreme People's Court's Explanation of Several Questions regarding the Application of the Marriage Law of the People's Republic of China (3)] (promulgated on 4 July 2011), art. 7.

[20] In 2012, there were more than 3.1 million cases of divorce in China, an increase of 8 per cent from the previous year. Cui Hong, *Zhongguo Lihunlu Zengfu Shinianlai Shouchao Jiehunlu [China's Increase in Divorce Rate Exceeds Marriage Rate the First Time in Ten Years]*, ZHONGGUO FUNU BAO [CHINA WOMEN POST], 26 June 2013, available at http://acwf.people.com.cn/n/2013/0626/c99013-21970906.html.

has issued three interpretations in a span of ten years to provide lower courts with guidance on the distribution of property. Although these interpretations aim at increasing judicial efficiency and reducing litigation cost, the gradual diminution of marital property has been criticized for promoting the re-feudalization of marriage.[21]

Similarly, in "Several Provisions Regarding Evidence in Civil Litigation," the SPC stated that in adjudging disputes involving infringement of rights caused by medical conduct, the medical establishment had to prove the lack of causal relationship between the medical conduct and the harm, as well as, the non-existence of fault.[22] This interpretation was the origin of the so-called inverted burden of proof in medical malpractice cases. Generally, the plaintiff in a tort case carries the burden of proof, but the defendant in a medical malpractice case has to prove the lack of causation and the non-existence of negligence. If the defendant fails to do so, it will be inferred that the plaintiff's harm results from the defendant's fault. With such an interpretation, the SPC shifted the burden of proof from the claimant to the defendant. This activist interpretation was to help victims of medical malpractice who had limited access to medical information and records and were in a disadvantageous position vis-à-vis medical establishments. In 2009, the NPC enacted the Law on Liabilities for Infringement of Rights (or the Torts Law), which did not codify the judicially initiated inverted burden of proof, but provided that a medical establishment, which had been at fault, was liable to a patient who had suffered harm.[23] However, the medical establishment was presumed to have fault if it had violated laws, administrative regulations or rules, or diagnosis and treatment standards; concealed or refused to supply relevant medical information and materials; or fabricated, altered or

---

[21] Shigong Qiang, *Sifa Nengdongxia De Zhongguo Jiating – Cong Zuigao Fayuan Guanyu Hunyinfa De Sifa Jieshi Tanqi [The Chinese Family under Active Judicature – Speaking from the Supreme People's Court's Judicial Interpretations regarding the Marriage Law]*, 2011(1) WENHUA ZONGHENG [BEIJING CULTURAL REVIEW] 24 (2011).

[22] Zuigao Renmin Fayuan Guanyu Minshi Susong Zhengju De Ruogan Guiding [The Supreme People's Court's Several Provisions regarding Evidence in Civil Litigation] (promulgated on 6 Dec. 2001), art. 4. The word "and" is used in the Provisions, but it seems that the lack of causation or the absence of fault should exonerate the defendant.

[23] Zhonghua Renmin Gongheguo Minshi Qinquan Zeren Fa [The Law on Liabilities for Infringement of Rights of the People's Republic of China] (adopted by the National People's Congress on 26 December 2009), art. 54.

destroyed relevant medical records.[24] As a result, the general principle of "who asserts a claim is to produce evidence"[25] should also apply in medical malpractice cases.

(ii) Adjudication of Individual Disputes

Although "active judicature" became a formal judicial policy in 2009, similar practices had existed in the revolutionary base and in the 1950s.[26] Literally, the term *nengdong* in "active judicature" means active, dynamic, adaptable or elastic. As such, "active judicature" provides a conceptual basis for judges to go beyond the mere application of law. Taking all relevant factors into account, Chinese judges are authorized to go beyond doctrinal analysis and to exercise creativity to achieve innovative resolutions of social conflicts. To a limited extent, "active judicature" is analogous to the "common-law attitude" of adjudication where judges try to find the most desirable resolutions and avoid any impediments to their achievement.[27] However, "active judicature" is more than attaining the resolution of disputes.

To understand "active judicature," the first inquiry is what has triggered the recent efforts to promote it as a formal policy. There are four major reasons. First, owing to the global financial crisis, the people's courts have the mission to safeguard social harmony and stability and to ensure the steady growth of the economy.[28] Second, there has been a surge in litigation, that is, there are more cases (demand) than judges (supply), and new types of cases have arisen as a

---

[24] *Id.* art. 58.

[25] Zhonghua Renmin Gongheguo Minshi Susong Fa [The Civil Procedure Law of the People's Republic of China] (adopted by the National People's Congress on 9 Apr. 1991 and amended in 2007 and 2012), art. 64.

[26] Dongchuan Luo and Guangyu Ding, *Woguo Nengdong Sifa De Lilun Yu Shijian Pingshu [Commentary on the Theory and Practice of Our Country's Active Judicature]*, 287–88 FALU SHIYONG [JOURNAL OF LAW APPLICATION] 15, 19 (2010).

[27] Green, *supra* note 3, at 1250 (quoting Justice Antonin Scalia).

[28] Luo and Ding, *supra* note 26, at 19; Guopeng Xu and Chenguang Wang, *Paihuizai Xianquan Yu Fangquan Zhijian – Shehui Zhuanxing Shiqi Dui Sifa Linian De Tansuo [Lingering between Restricting Power and Giving Power – Examination of Judicial Philosophy during a Period of Social Transformation]*, 35(1) XIANDAI FAXUE [MODERN LAW SCIENCE] 28, 29 (2013).

result of China's rapid economic and social transformations.[29] Third, since the adversarial system has been excessively relied upon, judges who are too passive and maintain neutrality have produced absurd adjudicative outcomes that are contrary to moral standards and common sense, thus impairing the credibility of the judiciary[30] Fourth, "active judicature" can fill the gaps between the law and the social and economic realities.[31] Against this backdrop, one key question is what "active judicature" aims to achieve.

Since the people's courts have political, legal and social responsibilities, they are "to serve the whole situation" (*fuwu daju*) and "to administer justice for the people" (*sifa weimin*).[32] To fulfill these mandates, "active judicature" has three objectives: (1) service (carrying out adjudicatory functions through policy consideration, balancing of interests and harmonious judicature to meet the needs of fostering economic development, safeguarding social stability, promoting social harmony, protecting the rights and interests of the people, etc.); (2) initiative (taking initiatives to launch investigation and research, responding to the demands for administration of justice, extending the adjudicatory functions, participating in social governance, etc.); and (3) high efficiency (planning in advance, resolving embryonic conflicts in light of economic and social developments, etc.).[33] As a result, to implement state and party policies,[34] Chinese judges are to assist in maintaining economic growth, people's livelihood and social stability (the so-called *sanbao*), prevent full-blown conflicts, and speedily resolve social contradictions.

To put "active judicature" into action, the people's courts are urged to conduct research to understand the sources of social conflicts and formulate corresponding preventive or tackling measures, open channels for receiving submissions on the administration of justice, engage in "mediation first and combining mediation with adjudication" (*tiaojie youxian tiaopan jiehe*) to resolve disputes, establish litigation mechanisms for the convenience of the people (such as mobile

---

[29] Xu and Wang, *supra* note 28, at 29; Pixiang Gong, *Dangdai Zhongguo Nengdong Sifa De Yiyi Fenxi [The Analysis of the Significance of Active Judicature in Contemporary China]*, 2010 (5) JIANGSU SHEHUI KEXUE [JIANGSU SOCIAL SCIENCE] 100, 105–6 (2010).

[30] Xu and Wang, *supra* note 28, at 29; Gong, *supra* note 29, at 101.

[31] Xu and Wang, *supra* note 28, at 29; Gong, *supra* note 29, at 108.

[32] Luo and Ding, *supra* note 26, at 17.

[33] Luo and Ding, *supra* note 26, at 18; Gong, *supra* note 29, at 103.

[34] Gong, *supra* note 29, at 105.

stations for filing lawsuits, circuit courts and legal aid), strengthen communication with the people to seek public opinions (such as live broadcasts of trials and email or post boxes for opinions), link litigation and non-litigation means to diversify dispute resolution mechanisms, pursue the uniform application of law (especially through the issuance of judicial interpretations), establish cooperative mechanisms to execute judgments, create mechanisms to summarize trial experiences so as to provide judges with guidance, and participate in the innovation of social governance.[35] In regard to how "active judicature" has operated in practice, it will be useful to examine outstanding "active judicature" cases.

In November 2012, from 358 cases that had taken effect between January 2008 and August 2011 nationwide (301 civil and commercial cases, 28 criminal cases, 18 administrative cases and 11 enforcement cases), the SPC selected 100 outstanding "active judicature" cases, from which it further selected the ten most outstanding.[36] Of the ten most outstanding cases, the subject matter concerned bankruptcy reorganization (3), trademark infringement and unfair competition (1), fraud (1), loan contract (1), copyright infringement (1), residential demolition and settlement (1), trading of financial derivatives (1) and administrative disposition (1).[37] Each case had a brief description of the facts, followed by a commentary on what kind of "active judicature" the court had achieved. In essence, apart from applying the relevant legal rules, those courts had acted beyond their adjudicatory role to prevent social disharmony and instability, thereby attaining the so-called unity of social, legal and political effects. For illustration, the following highlights should serve the purpose.

In one case, a large food company filed for bankruptcy re-organization. The court actively assisted the bankrupt company in finding a strategic investor who would pay off its debts and agreed to give priority to its workers in the case of recruitment. Moreover, the court worked with the courts in six provinces to overcome the difficulties associated with the transfer of shares from its existing

---

35 Luo and Ding, *supra* note 26, at 19–22; Gong, *supra* note 29, at 107–8; Xu and Wang, *supra* note 28, at 30.

36 *Zuigao Renmin Fayuan Gongbao Quanguo Fayuan Shida Jianxing Nengdong Sifa Linian Youxiu Anli [The Supreme People's Court Promulgated the Nation's Ten Most Outstanding Cases Implementing the Concept of Active Judicature]*, RENMIN FAYUAN BAO [THE PEOPLE'S COURT POST], 17 November 2012, at 1.

37 *Id.* at 2–3.

shareholders to the investor. The court was praised for reorganizing the company in compliance with the law and extending its adjudicatory functions to undertake non-judicial tasks to produce an outcome maintaining economic development and social stability.[38]

In another case, the debtor company and the guarantee company were unable to repay a bank loan of 60 million renminbi. The loan was subsequently purchased by a foreign company, which filed a lawsuit against both companies. Based on the principle of "mediation first and combining mediation with adjudication," the court conducted mediation with the assistance of the local government and the agency that managed state assets. The mediation not only resolved the dispute in question and three other related cases, but also dealt with two other loans not yet claimed in the lawsuit. The court was praised for protecting the rights of a creditor, preventing the outflow of state assets, and resolving the placement of workers in a state-owned enterprise.[39]

Furthermore, in a copyright infringement case, an entertainment company received the exclusive license to transmit and broadcast the programs of a television channel on its website. However, those programs were made available to the customers of 20 Internet bars without the company's permission. Upon accepting a series of cases, the court conducted a research study, published a report on copyright infringement by Internet bars, convened a symposium that generated five judicial recommendations and ten judicial reminders, and held a press conference. In the end, 172 cases filed with two courts were resolved by either mediation or withdrawal. The court was praised for curing not only the "symptoms," but also the "causes," of copyright infringement by Internet bars, producing a set of guiding opinions on these types of cases, and saving judicial resources by forming joint committees to mediate the disputes.[40]

Consequently, under "active judicature," the role of judges is more expansive than the application of law to the facts to reach a decision. Judges are encouraged to be people-oriented and innovative such that existing disputes can be resolved quickly and potential disputes can be prevented, whether by litigation or alternative dispute resolution, or both. Moreover, courts are urged to conduct proactive research to understand what judicial services will be needed in light of local economic and social developments. As illustrated above, some judges have proficiently executed the mandate to "resolve the case and

---

[38] *Id.* at 2.
[39] *Id.* at 3.
[40] *Id.*

end the matter" (*anjie shiliao*). Nonetheless, owing to insufficient theoretical guidance and standards, some courts have overemphasized the expansion of their powers and functions, ignored judicial rules, and conducted "blind" or arbitrary "active judicature."[41] Likewise, some courts overemphasized mediation, so their judges pushed for mediation, which might run counter to the intentions of the parties and damage the legal rights and interests of the parties.[42]

(iii) The Chinese Characteristics

Whether judicial activism, as understood in common law countries, exists in China is controversial. In common law countries, judges provide new constitutional and statutory interpretations, invalidate statutory provisions or develop public policies based on their moral or political conviction, which is occasioned by the adjudication of, or appeal in, individual cases. In China, however, the SPC issues interpretations whenever it deems appropriate and responds to specific inquiries raised by lower courts through the issuance of answers (*pi fu*). Even so, the formulation of public policies also occurs through the SPC's promulgation of judicial interpretations. In contrast, under "active judicature," judges have a mandate to implement policies formulated by the state or party and to actively prevent and speedily resolve disputes. In adjudicating disputes, judges should not make law,[43] so judicial interpretations play a complementary role by providing guidance and fostering the uniform application of law. Since Chinese judges are just trying to fulfill their mandate, they have not exceeded their prescribed role. As such, it can be argued that "active judicature" is not the equivalent of judicial activism as understood in common law countries. Indeed, although judicial activism carries a negative connotation in common law countries, "active judicature" is acclaimed in China.

In common law countries, judicial activism often deals with or is associated with judicial lawmaking or judicial review of administrative acts or statutory provisions. For example, in the US, individual judges are engaged in unsupervised judging,[44] and the US Supreme Court

---

41 Luo and Ding, *supra* note 26, at 22; Xu and Wang, *supra* note 28, at 30.

42 Xu and Wang, *supra* note 28, at 30.

43 Xu and Wang report that some judgments have generated new legal rules, which are subsequently adopted by the Supreme People's Court in judicial interpretations. Xu and Wang, *supra* note 28, at 32.

44 Green, *supra* note 3, at 1223.

makes the final determination in constitutional reviews. Both cases stem from ad hoc decisions grounded on individual courts' exercise of discretion. On the contrary, judicial interpretation and "active judicature" in China entail judicial construction of law or judicial intervention prior to, during, or even after judicial proceedings. While the NPC Standing Committee is empowered to interpret the Constitution, judges in the courts of first instance are encouraged to creatively engage in "active judicature" within the bounds of law. Since "active judicature" is a basic orientation for all courts and judges,[45] judicial activism in China is a largely top-down, coordinated and purposive initiative.

IV. CONCLUSIONS

Judicial activism occupies a significant spot in the interface between law and society. Where there are statutory lacunae or vagueness or the access to legal services is limited, it is imperative for judges to make judgments that can deliver actual justice or are responsive to the changing circumstances of society. In doing so, the judiciary often develops new legal norms or changes existing ones, promotes the rights of the marginalized, or contributes to the formulation of public policies. Indeed, this phenomenon is prevalent in many jurisdictions.[46] Considering China's rapid economic and social changes and the increasing polarization of society as a result of uneven distribution of wealth, the need for judges to be activist is particularly acute.

Judicial activism through the issuance of statutory interpretations does not raise too much concern, unless the Chinese judiciary resorts to this avenue to bestow unwarranted legislative power on itself. If judicial interpretations do not accord with legislative intent or result in judicial abuse of discretionary power, the NPC can turn to legislative enactment or amendment to rectify the negative outcomes. Nonetheless, two concerns have emerged from the development of "active judicature." First, since judges have the mandate to prevent and speedily resolve disputes, many of them have overstepped their adjudicatory role, whether proactively or reactively, to work with enterprises and governmental agencies to find solutions to various

[45] Gong, *supra* note 29, at 103.

[46] For example, from 1940 to 1970, California experienced a redefinition of judicial role due to economic and political developments. Green, *supra* note 3, at 1247.

types of disputes. This kind of extra-adjudicatory activities can be an obstacle to China's aspiration to become a rule-of-law country, because a neutral, independent judiciary is a key component of the rule of law and undertaking tasks beyond the interpretation and application of law will cause judges to become entangled in non-judicial matters and susceptible to administrative interference. Nonetheless, the rule of law is predicated on liberal democracy, while China espouses "democratic centralism" and the highest state organ is the NPC, to which the judiciary is accountable.[47] Moreover, despite the fact that the Constitution confers judicial power solely on the judiciary, it is still controversial whether China embraces separation of powers or merely separation of functions, and whether China practices judicial independence or merely adjudicatory independence. Although judges in common law countries are not immune from politics, the role of the Chinese judiciary is more complex, which further confounds the issue of judicial independence. In fact, how much negative impact "active judicature" will have on the development of an independent judiciary remains to be seen.

Second, even assuming that "active judicature" is a check on excessive reliance on the adversarial system and will not have a negative impact on the attainment of an independent judiciary, it may hinder China's ongoing efforts to professionalize and enhance the quality of its judges. It is because judges may, under the guise of "active judicature," press for mediated compromises and avoid the rigorous legal reasoning required in adjudicating disputes. Moreover, if lower-court judges implement "active judicature" indiscriminately for promotion and recognition purposes, the outcome will be judicial abuse of discretionary power. Ideally, the judiciary should maintain neutrality and propriety, and arbitrary decisions under the guise of "active judicature" will undermine judicial competence and credibility, which, in turn, can decelerate the progress of legal reforms in China. Accordingly, the crucial question is: What kind of system must be in place to monitor and supervise the implementation of "active judicature" and to prevent excessive or indiscriminate activism?[48] In this connection, the recent campaign for open judicature (*sifa gongkai*) may alleviate the potential drawbacks of "active judicature," because

---

[47] Constitution, *supra* note 13, arts. 3 & 128.

[48] Although Luo and Ding maintain that "active judicature" has a high level of uniformity because it is organized and implemented systematically and subject to direction and supervision, they also discuss the need for "active judicature" to be standardized. Luo and Ding, *supra* note 26, at 18 & 22.

the people's courts are to establish platforms to make adjudicatory processes, adjudicatory documents, and enforcement progress transparent.[49] Even so, unless the "mediation first and combining mediation with adjudication" policy will lose its endorsement, it is imperative to have a monitoring and supervisory system to ensure the proper implementation of "active judicature."

Although it can be argued that China is developing its own legal culture by adopting the policy of "active judicature," introducing a system of guiding cases (*zhidaoxing anli*),[50] and issuing judicial interpretations to facilitate the uniform application of law, it can also be argued that in pursuing "active judicature," the judiciary has resumed its pre-reform position as, or is continuing to be, an administrative arm of the state. Since the development of the judicial role does not occur outside the relevant political and social contexts, it is understandable for Chinese judges to execute their prescribed role to assist in the implementation of state and party policies. Even so, how far will "active judicature" go? The Third Plenary Session of the 18th Central Committee of the Communist Party of China called for the rapid building of a "just, highly efficient and authoritative" socialist system of judicature,[51] so will judicial activism play any role in achieving this endeavor?

On the path of judicial reform, Chinese-style judicial activism as manifested in judicial interpretation and "active judicature," along with the launch of a system of guiding cases and the promotion of

---

[49] Zuigao Renmin Fayuan Guanyu Tuijin Sifa Gongkai Sanda Pingtai Jianshe De Ruogan Yijian [The Supreme People's Court's Several Opinions regarding the Establishment of Three Large Platforms for Promoting Open Judicature] (promulgated on 21 November 2013).

[50] Basically, judicial decisions are selected to illustrate how specific legal norms should be applied or how certain types of disputes have been resolved. Decisions are recommendable if they have attracted widespread attention from society; they are difficult, complicated or of first impression; etc. The Adjudicatory Committee of the Supreme People's Court discusses the recommended cases and decides which ones should be published. In adjudging similar cases, the people's courts at various levels "should refer to" the guiding cases. Zuigao Renmin Fayuan Guanyu Anli Zhidao Gongzuo De Guiding [The Supreme People's Court's Provisions regarding the Work on Guiding Cases] (promulgated on 26 November 2010), arts. 2, 6 & 7.

[51] Zhonggong Zhongyang Guanyu Quanmian Shenhua Gaige Ruogan Zhongda Wenti De Jueding [CPC Central Committee's Decision on Several Important Questions regarding the Comprehensive Deepening of Reforms] (adopted by the 3rd Plenary Session of the 18th CPC Central Committee on 12 November 2013).

open judicature, will certainly contribute to the institutional growth of the judiciary. To an extent, these policy initiatives also reflect that the Chinese judiciary is searching for direction, building identity, and engaging in positioning in the national polity. Although the judiciaries in jurisdictions that do not have well-established legal systems may be pursuing the same, the Chinese judiciary stands out in sharp relief, especially due to its nascent state and China's rapid economic and social transformations.

3.5 The role of courts in "making" Islamic law: South and Southeast Asia

Clark B. Lombardi

Many chapters in this volume explore how Asian courts have been usurping the traditional prerogatives of legislatures and bureaucracies and are finding ways to "make law." In this chapter, I will discuss what may seem an even more startling phenomenon. Judges in South and Southeast Asia are not merely poaching on the traditional turf of legislators and bureaucrats. They are sometimes poaching as well on the traditional turf of religious scholars.

Until fairly recently, Sunni Muslims believed that interpretive authority in questions of religious law lay with scholars trained in the classical Islamic sciences and that this authority was located primarily outside the judiciary. Thus, when faced with open questions of Islamic law, judges were generally expected to seek an advisory opinion from eminent independent scholars. Once the private scholars had provided an interpretation of the law, judges would apply this rule to the case at bar. Today, however, in some parts of Muslim Asia, judges do not rely on religious scholars to interpret Islamic law or to identify new rules where Islamic law has hitherto been silent. Particularly in constitutional courts, many judges who do not have classical religious training are refusing to defer to scholarly opinions about the law. Rather, these judges are developing and applying rules of Islamic law that they are developing for themselves. In this chapter, I will explore how this phenomenon developed and how it has been manifesting itself in three countries in Muslim Asia. I will also briefly consider some of the implications of this development.

I. BACKGROUND

Much of Asia is peopled by Muslims; indeed, it is in South and Southeast Asia that one finds the largest Muslim countries in the world by population.[1] The vast majority of South and Southeast Asian Muslims are members of the Sunni sect. In a number of these countries, constitutional cases regularly appear in which questions of Sunni Islamic law arise. In some cases, Muslims believe that the question of what Islam requires has long been settled. In others, however, no settled rule has emerged. Faced with this type of case, courts would once have been expected to seek guidance from scholars about what rule of law to apply. Today, they often choose not to seek this guidance.

Until recently, Sunnis assumed that Islamic law could only be properly interpreted by classically trained religious scholars known as the *fuqaha'* (singular *faqih*).[2] The Sunni *fuqaha'* were trained and organized through independent self-regulating guilds. After training with one or more established members of the profession, an aspiring *faqih* received a license to interpret law. Now recognized as a member of the scholarly profession, he would struggle to establish his place in a hierarchy of scholars. Lower-ranked scholars were expected to follow the guidance of their superiors. While they could answer easy questions for themselves, they would have to seek guidance on difficult questions from higher-ranked scholars.[3]

Scholars started at the lower level of the hierarchy. Ambitious ones sought to establish a reputation that would allow them to rise in the hierarchy. If they did, they could become figures who did more than learn and apply established law. They would also establish new law in places where the law was unsettled.

As a practical matter, judicial service was not a way to build a scholarly reputation. Judicial work often involved resolving questions of

---

1 *See* PEW RESEARCH RELIGION AND PUBLIC LIFE PROJECT, *The Future of the Global Muslim Population* (January 27, 2011), *available at* http://www.pewforum.org/2011/01/27/the-future-of-the-global-muslim-population/.

2 *See, e.g.*, DEVIN STEWART, ISLAMIC LEGAL ORTHODOXY: TWELVER SHIITE RESPONSES TO THE SUNNI LEGAL SYSTEM 15 (1998); Clark B. Lombardi and R. Michael Feener, *Why Study Islamic Legal Professionals*, 21 PAC. RIM L. & POL'Y J. 1, 5–7 (2012).

3 *See, e.g.*, WAEL B. HALLAQ, SHARI`A: THEORY, PRACTICE, TRANSFORMATIONS 52 (2009); Muhammad Khalid Masud, Brinkely Messick and David S. Powers, *Muftis, Fatwas, and Islamic Legal Interpretation*, *in* ISLAMIC LEGAL INTERPRETATION: MUFTIS AND THEIR FATWAS 3, 8–15 (Muhammad Khalid Masud, Brinkely Messick and David S. Powers eds., 1996).

fact rather than law. Furthermore, elite scholars feared that anyone who served as a government official would inevitably face temptations and pressures that would weaken their objectivity and cloud their judgment. Thus, the most effective way to earn respect from one's colleagues was to excel in teaching, writing and to provide, for free, impressive advisory opinions (*fatwas*) on open questions of law. As a result, most of the leading scholars chose not to take government positions as bureaucrats or judges. Instead, they focused on providing free advisory opinions on difficult questions of Islamic law.[4]

The reluctance of elite scholars to join the judiciary affected profoundly the way that rules of Islamic law developed in the Muslim legal system. When a government developed "Islamic" laws to apply in their courts, they took one of two paths.[5] First, they might appoint lower-level scholars as judges to resolve disputes according to Islamic law as interpreted by their guild. This was not, one must stress, judge-made law. Judges were expected to focus on fact-finding and to applying settled rules of Islamic law. When faced with complicated questions of law or unprecedented situations, they would not develop a new Islamic rule of decision for themselves. Rather, they would seek advisory opinions (*fatwas*) from eminent independent scholars and would follow the rules established by those scholars. Second, rulers might issue statutes. When doing so, they were supposed to ensure that the statutes were drafted in a manner that eminent independent scholars outside the judiciary would accept as consistent with core principles of Islamic law.[6]

As the modern era dawned, social trends seemed to push judges even farther from any role in making law. During the eighteenth and nineteenth centuries, Muslim empires and kingdoms throughout the world were conquered and replaced by colonial states and, following them, nation states. These new types of state radically revised their legal systems. Importantly, most countries replaced the bulk of their indigenous laws with transplanted European laws and established Western-style courts to administer them – staffing these courts with judges trained primarily in European law. Only in a few areas, such

---

[4] *See, e.g.*, NOEL J. COULSON, A HISTORY OF ISLAMIC LAW 121–23 (1964); HALLAQ, *supra* note 3, at 151, 172; KNUT S. VIKOR, BETWEEN GOD AND THE SULTAN: A HISTORY OF ISLAMIC LAW 6–10 (2005).

[5] For this and what follows, see CLARK B. LOMBARDI, STATE LAW AS ISLAMIC LAW IN MODERN EGYPT: THE INCORPORATION OF THE SHARI`A INTO EGYPTIAN CONSTITUTIONAL LAW 49–54 (2006).

[6] *Id.*; *Cf.* VIKOR, *supra* note 4, at 185–91.

as family law, states instructed judges to apply laws derived from the Islamic tradition. Generally, governments did not believe that judges could be trusted properly to determine what Islamic law required (even with advice from eminent scholars). Accordingly, many chose to codify Islamic family law and instructed judges to apply the codes using the standard rules of statutory construction.[7]

As the twentieth century progressed, two developments began to change Muslim attitudes about Islamic authority. As a result, it became possible for judges without significant classical training to assert that they had authority to delve into contested questions of Islamic law and to derive for themselves answers to these questions. The first development was the Islamic revival. The second was the rise of Islamic modernism and other non-traditional theories of Islamic interpretation.

In the twentieth century, many Muslims began to demand an end to the practice of transplanting Western laws into their legal system.[8] They called for their government to return to the practice of reviewing all state law to ensure it was consistent with core principles of Islamic law and, where it was not, to reform the law. Although such demands for Islamization were invariably controversial, they attracted over time powerful popular and political support. Under pressure from Islamists, many states committed themselves, at least to some degree, to Islamize their law.[9] This development brought new urgency to the question of whether the state should continue to rely on the *fuqaha*'s interpretation of Islamic law. As the Islamic revival picked up speed, in the second half of the twentieth century a growing number of Muslims were arguing that the modern Islamic state needed to look beyond the opinions of the *fuqaha*'.

---

[7] Some countries gave jurisdiction over Islamic law to secular state courts. Because judges in these courts had little, if any, training in Islamic law, such states tended to codify the Islamic rules to be applied. They instructed judges to interpret and apply the laws according to the standard rules of statutory construction. Other countries established specialized courts to hear these cases but seemed to have doubts about whether judges would identify correctly Islamic rules of decisional Islamic law. They worried that scholars did not have enough training to identify settled rules or even to recognize which scholars they could trust to develop settled rules. Accordingly, even countries with Islamic courts increasingly chose to codify the law. VIKOR, *supra* note 4, at 225–28. *Cf.* HALLAQ, *supra* note 3, at 367–69.

[8] *See generally*, Ira M. Lapidus, *Islamic Revival and Modernity: The Contemporary Movements and the Historical Paradigms*, 40 J. Econ. & Soc. His. of the Orient 444, 444–60 (1997).

[9] See the surveys in HALLAQ, *supra* note 3, 473–499.

During the eighteenth and increasingly during the nineteenth century and early twentieth centuries, some Sunni Muslims in different parts of the Muslim world began to argue that it was time for Muslims to abandon traditional methods of interpreting Islamic law. Anti-traditionalists did not agree about what should replace traditional thought. Some were partisans of rigid scriptural literalism. Others favored methods of reasoning inspired by nationalist legal scholars on the European continent. Yet others advocated methods of reasoning that were heavily influenced by utilitarianism.[10] Importantly, many of these new methods could be performed by figures with modern "Western" legal training. Indeed, in some cases it would seem that they could best be performed by such figures.

As the Muslim world underwent colonization and modernization, social, political and technological developments together facilitated the spread of this untraditional, modern thought. Groups such as the members of Egypt's Muslim Brotherhood, Pakistan's *Jama'at-i-Islami* and Indonesia's *Muhamadiyya* all championed "modernist" views that would permit judges to assert a far greater role in interpreting Islamic law than traditional theory would have given them. While modern thinkers did not displace traditionalists entirely, they established significant pockets of resistance to traditional understandings of Islam and to the idea that only classically trained scholars could be trusted authoritatively to interpret Islamic scriptures and determine what rules God expected humans and their governments to follow.

As a result of these developments, constitutional court judges throughout the Muslim world found themselves with new opportunities to speak, if they wanted to do so, on questions of Islamic law. Increasingly, it seems, they wanted to. In many parts of the Muslim world, including South and Southeast Asia, judges seized on the opening that this left them to weigh in on contested questions of Islamic law. They insisted that if the state were to be constrained in any way to respect Islamic norms, it should follow Islamic norms *as understood by judges*.

---

[10] *See generally*, Charles Kurzman, *Introduction* to MODERNIST ISLAM, 1840–1940: A SOURCEBOOK 3–27 (Charles Kurzman ed. 2002). For extended studies of the rise of debates in particular countries, see R. MICHAEL FEENER, MUSLIM LEGAL THOUGHT IN MODERN INDONESIA (2007); LOMBARDI, STATE LAW AS ISLAMIC LAW IN MODERN EGYPT: THE INCORPORATION OF THE SHARI'A INTO EGYPTIAN CONSTITUTIONAL LAW, *supra* note 5, at 58–119.

II. INCENTIVES FOR JUDGES IN MUSLIM ASIA TO ADDRESS QUESTIONS OF ISLAMIC LAW

Among the Asian constitutional court judges who are interpreting Islamic law for themselves and are not deferring to classically trained religious scholars, some are surely animated by a personal commitment to modernist Islamist sensibilities. They believe state law should be developed in a manner that respects Islam and believe that judges without classical training are eminently well qualified to determine what Islam requires. However, even some judges who are *not* personally vested in an Islamist vision of the modern state seem to feel that it is important to hear cases involving Islamic law and to use these cases to weigh in on what Islamic law requires. To understand some of the complex reasons why constitutional court judges in Muslim Asia could feel pressured to assert a new role in interpreting Islamic law, one might reflect upon a rather remarkable story in modern Pakistan.

In 1960, an eminent Pakistani judge looked with despair upon the constitutional regime in his country. A.R. Cornelius was a Pakistani Catholic. He was a strong proponent of the liberal rule of law and was about to rise, by dint of seniority, to the position of chief justice on the Pakistani Supreme Court.[11] These were frustrating times for anyone who believed judges should be empowered to ensure that a government respected liberal values. Pakistan had recently undergone a military coup, and the new military regime had stripped the courts of their traditional power to enforce individual rights.[12] In two Supreme Court cases challenging the constitutionality of the military's action, every judge except Cornelius had held that the jurisdiction stripping was "legal" and that the court must refuse to enforce fundamental rights.[13] His colleagues had uniformly declared themselves powerless to defend the liberal rule of law.

---

[11] For biographical details of Cornelius and analyses of his work, see RALPH BRAIBANTI, CHIEF JUSTICE CORNELIUS OF PAKISTAN: AN ANALYSIS WITH LETTERS AND SPEECHES 1–66 (1999); S.M. Haider, *Preface* to A.R. CORNELIUS: LAW AND JUDICIARY IN PAKISTAN (S.M. Haider ed., 1981) 1–45; Clark B. Lombardi, *Can Islamizing a Legal System Even Help Promote Liberal Democracy?: A View from Pakistan*, 7 U. St. Thomas L.J. 649, 649–91 (2010).

[12] *See* LAWRENCE ZIRING, PAKISTAN AT THE CROSSCURRENT OF HISTORY 68–90 (2003); PAULA R. NEWBERG, JUDGING THE STATE: COURTS AND CONSTITUTIONAL POLITICS IN PAKISTAN 69–109 (1995).

[13] *State v. Dosso and Another*, (1958) PLD (SC) 533 (Pak.); *Province of East Pakistan v. Mehdi Ali Khan*, [1959] P.L.D. (S.C.) 387 (Pak.).

It was not that Cornelius's fellow judges approved of unrestrained authoritarianism. Rather, they feared they had no ability at this point to resist the military's act. If they challenged the military and asserted the right to enforce fundamental rights, the military would dissolve the court.[14] This raised the question of whether the judiciary and legal profession could do anything to reestablish its power to act as a liberal check on government. Reflecting on this question, the court's only non-Muslim came up with what many might consider a surprising conclusion. Observing that the most politically engaged part of the population were not liberals, but rather Islamists, he insisted that the judiciary and the legal profession should engage in a two-part project. First, they should ally themselves with the call to Islamize the legal system and they should demand that judges be empowered to enforce it. At the same time, they should actively engage in public discourse about what Islam required and they should argue for an interpretation of Islam that was, in broad terms, consistent with liberal values.

Many Pakistani liberals thought Cornelius's proposal absurd. They pointed out that the vast majority of Islamists (traditionalist *fuqaha'* and lay modernist Islamists alike) were deeply illiberal. Cornelius countered that the Arab world also contained strong, illiberal factions. Nevertheless, some leading Arab judges and legal scholars had developed sophisticated theories of Islamic law that went a long way toward harmonizing Islam with many liberal values. Notwithstanding resistance from some quarters, legal reform in the Arab world was incorporating many of their ideas. Noting that some of Pakistan's revered founders had also wanted to harmonize Islam with modern, liberal values, Cornelius argued that Pakistanis would probably be willing to embrace a similar vision if courts could demonstrate one to them. Admittedly, Islamic forms of liberalism might differ at the margins from traditional European liberalism. Nevertheless, he insisted, it was still an attractive vision and if the judiciary and legal profession committed themselves to articulating and defending it, it would be a compelling one. Once the public embraced their vision, even the most authoritarian government would have to respect it. Even if they were not personally committed to Islam, generals would fear public outrage if the government flagrantly defied a rule its overwhelmingly Muslim subjects considered to be divinely imposed.

Embedded in Cornelius's thinking are several important insights that would over time come independently to be adopted by other important

---

[14] NEWBERG, *supra* note 12, at 77–78; Lombardi, *Can Islamizing a Legal System Even Help Promote Liberal Democracy?*, *supra* note 11, at 664.

judges in Muslim Asia. First, courts are heavily dependent on their moral authority. In countries where the people understood morality in Islamic terms, the judges will improve both individual and government compliance with their law if the people believe it is consistent with Islamic values. Second, as a result of changing attitudes toward Islamic authority, judges have an opportunity to enter debates about what Islam requires and to shape popular understandings of Islam. Third, while courts were today struggling against secular autocrats, they might in the future face a different foe. Over time, Islamists might be able to leverage their growing popular support and take political power – imposing an illiberal government that justified its rule in Islamic terms. If so, the judiciary's only hope of imposing liberal restraints would be in a compelling argument that Islam itself required governments to respect liberal values. As the power of Islam has grown, judges throughout the Muslim world appear independently to have developed very similar insights.

III. EXAMPLES OF RECENT CONSTITUTIONAL COURTS' INTERPRETATION OF ISLAM IN MUSLIM ASIA

(i) Pakistan

Justice Cornelius's argument in favor of a judicial engagement with Islamic thought did not bear immediate fruit in Pakistan. Most members of the Pakistani high judiciary and leaders of the Pakistani Bar in the 1960s simply did not believe that liberalism and Islam could ever be harmonized in a way that was sufficiently liberal for them. In 1971, the military government fell and was replaced by a popularly elected leader who made strategic concessions to Islamist parties, but was generally hostile to conservative Islamist programs.[15] His rise temporarily seemed to vindicate all those who had said that it was unnecessary for legal liberals to engage with and possibly make concessions to conservative Islamists. But Cornelius had the last, albeit bitter, laugh.

---

[15] *See* STEPHEN P. COHEN, THE IDEA OF PAKISTAN 76–83 (2006).

As Cornelius had feared, long-term trends had given Islamist political movements tremendous latent power.[16] Once displaced from power, authoritarian factions within the military began to flirt with the illiberal Islamists that liberals had long failed to court. In 1977, a military dictator took power and decided to legitimize his new regime in Islamic terms – allying himself with the illiberal factions that were, for all practical purposes, the only serious Islamic voice in the country.[17] General Zia al-haq opportunistically reached out to illiberal Sunni *fuqaha'* and Islamists and in keeping with a long-held demand revised Pakistan's constitution to require that all Pakistani law respect Islamic law.[18] He then enacted statutory reform that reflected their deeply illiberal vision of Islam's requirements.[19]

Belatedly, an ever-growing number of legal liberals in Pakistan, both in the judiciary and the bar, saw the wisdom of adopting the position that Cornelius had long espoused – even if they failed to acknowledge his influence.[20] Even before the coup and amendment of the constitution to require governmental respect for Islam, some judges had adopted the Cornelius-esque position that given the apparent commitment of the Pakistani people to Islam, the Pakistani constitution should be interpreted through an Islamic paradigm.[21] After the amendment took place, judges became aggressive in arguing that Islam, properly understood, precluded many of the government's illiberal acts and even precluded some of the new self-styled "Islamic" laws that the government was imposing. During the 1970s and 1980s the government was trying to impose by statute an illiberal vision of the state that was justified by the writings of illiberal Sunni *ulamā* and illiberal lay Islamists. During this period, the judiciary engaged in a parallel,

---

16 COHEN, *supra* note 15, at 75–76.

17 *See* ZIRING, *supra* note 12, at 157–203; *Cf.* COHEN, *supra* note 15, at 84–86.

18 *Id.*

19 *Compare generally* ASMA JAHANGIR AND HINA JILANI, THE HUDOOD ORDINANCES: A DIVINE SANCTION? (1990), *with* Rashida Patel, ISLAMIZATION OF LAWS IN PAKISTAN? (1986), *and* Charles Kennedy, *Islamization in Pakistan: Implementation of the Hudood Ordinance*, 28 ASIAN SURVEY 307, 312–13 (1988).

20 *See* Clark B. Lombardi, *Islamism as a Response to Emergency Rule in Pakistan: The Surprising Proposal of Justice A.R. Cornelius*, *in* EMERGENCY POWERS IN ASIA: EXPLORING THE LIMITS OF LEGALITY 436, 461–62 (Victor V. Ramraj and Arun K. Thiruvengadam eds., 2010).

21 MARTIN LAU, THE ROLE OF ISLAM IN THE LEGAL SYSTEM OF PAKISTAN 15–20 (2006).

25-year experiment in which they began to develop and, where they could, impose their liberal vision. They justified their rulings on the basis of a liberal modernist vision of Islam. Indeed, in one notable case, the Supreme Court's "Shariat Appellate Bench" overturned a new criminal statute that imposed traditional Islamic punishments for fornication on the grounds that it was contrary to "Islamic law." The judges on the Court explicitly stated that, to their mind, the *fuqaha'* had for centuries been misreading a particular scriptural passage. And conservative Islamists were misreading it too.[22] It would be hard to come up with a more striking example of Islamic law being defined by judges rather than jurists.[23] Outraged, Pakistan's military dictator fired the judges who had issued the decision and installed a bench that reversed it.[24] Having decisively won that battle, however, Zia al-Haq and his allies were unable conclusively to win the war.

In the 1990s and on into the present, Pakistan's higher judiciary has consistently held that Islam, properly understood, requires that the government be checked by an independent judiciary that must determine, among other things, whether the government's laws are consistent with Islam.[25] This has been widely accepted by most Islamists, including many who favor socially illiberal policies.[26] More controversially, the courts have argued that Islam requires the government to adopt policies that are socially liberal. In the wake of the judge's revolt of the late 1990s, an event that re-established the power of the judiciary vis-à-vis the executive, the Supreme Court has made some particularly bold interpretations of Islamic law. Recently, it again voided a provision of an "Islamic" criminal statute that imposes a punishment consistent with classical *fiqh* and favored by almost all members of the *ulamā*. They did so on the grounds that, *contra* to the

---

22 *Hazoor Buksh v.The Government*, (1981) PLD (FSC) 145 (Pak.).

23 As it turns out, Zia al-Haq, the military dictator ruling Pakistan at the time of this decision, found this decision intolerable. Having staked his legitimacy on a claim to be more "Islamic" than his democratic opponents, and having trumpeted the voided law as proof of his fidelity to Islam, he could ill afford to have the law struck down as anti-Islamic. Accordingly, he dismissed the judges on the Court and replaced them with a new set of judges who reversed the decision and reinstated the law that was favored by the *ulamā*. Nevertheless, this type of state override was unusual.

24 *Government of Pakistan v. Hazoor Buksh*, (1983) PLD (FSC) 255 (Pak.).

25 *Al Jehad Trust v. Federation of Pakistan*, (1996) PLD (SC) 324 (Pak.). For a discussion of the case, see LAU, *supra* note 21, at 103–5.

26 See for example, the discussion of the powerful *Jama'at-i-Islami*'s ideology in COHEN, *supra* note 15, at 176–178.

ulamā, no authentic *hadith* requires this punishment, and imposing the punishment harms the public interest.[27] More recently, it has issued a ruling stating that an Islamic state must provide conjugal visits for prisoners[28] and must institute affirmative action programs for transgender Pakistanis.[29]

Not all Pakistanis agree with the Pakistani court's interpretations of Islam any more than all Americans agree with the U.S. Supreme Court's interpretation of American law. Nevertheless, many Islamists, like the *Jama'at-i-Islami* continue to be staunch supporters of the idea that the judiciary should be the institution entrusted with the power to interpret the law.[30] They instead call for the appointment of judges who embrace a conservative interpretation of Islam. As Cornelius had hoped, then, Islamization in Pakistan and the aggressive moves by Pakistani judges to play a role in shaping Islamic discourse have promoted judicial empowerment. To date, it has also promoted liberalism. It remains to be seen whether the next generation of judges will continue to promote liberal values or whether a new generation will embrace a more illiberal vision of Islam and the requirements it places on the state.

---

[27] *See Shariat court rules whipping for drinking un-Islamic*, DAWN, May 29, 2009, http://dawn.com/news/891627/shariat-court-rules-whipping-for-drinking-un-islamic.

[28] *Marital Visits for Pakistan Jails*, BBC NEWS ONLINE, Aug. 28, 2009, http://news.bbc.co.uk/2/hi/south_asia/8226803.stm.

[29] This decision was reported by Basim Usmani: *Pakistan to Register 'Third Sex' Hijras: A court ruling follows a bid to improve life for Pakistan's impoverished transgender, transvestite and eunuch community*, THE GUARDIAN, July 18, 2009, http://www.theguardian.com/commentisfree/2009/jul/18/pakistan-transgender-hijra-third-sex. This case, it must be stressed, was brought by an Islamist. Although it was resolved on the ground that the law violated the equal rights provisions of the Pakistani Constitution, rather than the Islamization provisions, it reflects an implicit claim that granting rights to this community was not inconsistent with Islamic values – a position that traditional Islam would probably not have recognized and that contemporary conservative Islamists disagree with.

[30] Parties more closely tied to the *ulamā* may be less supportive, but from my survey of the Pakistani English language press, there is no indication that they have called for revolutionary change in the structure of the system by which "Islamic law" is administered in Pakistan. Rather, they call for the appointment of judges who are liable to interpret *nusus* (rules announced in scripture) and the demands of public welfare in a manner that is more closely aligned with their views.

(ii) Malaysia and Indonesia

South Asia is not the only part of Asia where one finds countries with majority Muslim populations nor the only region in which constitutional judges have begun to assert the ability to interpret Islamic law for themselves without deferring to the views of religious scholars. In Southeast Asia, Indonesia and Malaysia (as well as Brunei) are majority Muslim. Each has been undergoing a period of Islamization in which conservative Islamists have argued for illiberal positions and have justified these positions by reference to the opinions of conservative Islamic clerics. There is no evidence that any judges in these countries were familiar with Cornelius. Independently, however, they seem to have realized that their liberal decisions will be more powerful if they make a point to speak in terms that resonate with Muslims. This is particularly true when the case is one that rules against Islamists who have justified their positions in Islamic terms. When faced with a case that requires them to resolve a contested question of Islamic law (and even in some cases that don't necessarily require this) constitutional courts have issued decisions that rely on the judges own, generally liberal, interpretation of Islamic law.

Judicial engagement with Islamic law in these countries does *not* come about as the result of so-called 'repugnancy cases.' The constitutions of Malaysia and Indonesia do not explicitly require the state to legislate in accordance with Islamic values, and the judiciaries in these countries have bucked calls from Islamists to read an implicit Islamization requirement into the constitution. Nevertheless, the judiciaries in both Malaysia and Indonesia hear cases that invite judicial discussion of Islam's requirements. One sees this trend particularly in litigation over religious freedom in which Muslims claim that state law is preventing them from acting in accordance with Islamic law. Many judges appear to feel they should take advantage of the opportunities that these cases present. They have resolved the cases in a manner that lets them weigh in on national debates about what Islamic law requires of states and individuals – justifying state law in Islamic terms even when it is not necessary to do so.

The Malaysian and Indonesian states restrict behavior that at least some Islamists think is religiously required; restricting, for example, some Islamic dress and limiting men's rights in marriage. Islamists have challenged such laws in court, arguing that they violate their rights under the religious freedom provisions of the constitution. In theory, Malaysian judges faced with claims of this sort could resolve them as U.S. courts do. Feeling themselves ill-equipped to decide what religions require, U.S. judges have decided that they must simply accept a litigant's good faith understanding of their religious obligation. Generally, U.S. courts review the law to see whether the state's interest in having its law applied outweighs citizens' interest in religious freedom.[31] In practice, however, Malaysian courts have avoided this approach. One assumes that this is because resolving this claim would suggest that the state is free to violate Islamic law to the same extent that it is free to violate the rules of other religions. Irrespective of whether judges personally accept this principle (one assumes that they are divided on the question) they seem loath publicly to endorse it. In an environment where Islamists are powerful, courts seem to fear that adopting such a position will needlessly alienate important subsets of the population. Thus, when faced with a claim by Muslims that obeying state law would force them to act in a way that is inconsistent with sharia, the courts have asked whether the Muslim has correctly understood what Islam requires.

The most famous recent example of this was the "Serban case," a case that after generating enormous controversy was decided by Malaysia's Federal Court, the highest appeals court in the national legal system.[32] The plaintiffs in this case were Muslims who had been expelled from school for wearing turbans – something that was not permitted under the dress code. Arguing that the turban was required under Islamic law, they brought suit under the Malaysian constitution's religious freedom provisions.[33] The trial court controversially held that the constitution implicitly required special solicitude for Muslim practice and it enthusiastically embraced the plaintiff's interpretation of Islamic law. Its opinion clearly reflected Islamist sensibilities, suggesting that Islamist attitudes were growing in society and even in the lower judiciary.[34] Reflecting the higher judiciary's continuing skepticism about Islamism, an intermediate court reversed, arguing that Islam did not receive heightened protection over other religions, and, furthermore, that judges

---

31 *See generally, e.g. Employment Division v. Smith*, 494 U.S. 872, 879 (1990).

32 For background and analysis of the underlying dispute and lower court decisions, see Li-Ann Thio and Jaclyn Ling-Chen Neo, *Religious Dress in Schools: The Serban Controversy in Malaysia*, 55 INT'L & COMP. L.Q. 671, 671–88 (2006).

33 *Id.*

34 *Meor Atiqulrahman bin Ishak v. Fatimah bte Sihi* [Meor #1], (2000) 5 MLJ 375, decision of Aug. 6, 1999 (High Court Seremban, Malaysia) [Meor Trial]; *See also* the analysis in Thio & Neo, *supra* note 32.

should play no little role in deciding what Islam required.[35] It drew upon a free exercise model developed by the Indian courts. In deciding whether a religious practice was protected by constitutional guarantees of religious freedom, judges should ask only whether there was objective evidence that the majority of citizens who followed that religion accepted the practice in question as one "essential to the religion." If so, it gets significant protection.

While the appellate court's approach has its attractions, it has some risks in a society where a Muslim majority is becoming pious and politically powerful. It suggests indifference on the part of the judiciary to questions of Islamic legitimacy – a posture that risks delegitimizing the judiciary in the eyes of the public. Furthermore, in a world where Muslims are debating what Islam requires, it cedes the microphone to conservative Islamists. It refuses to challenge their interpretation of Islam as a religion inconsistent with the liberal order. Surely bearing this in mind, Malaysia's highest court, the Federal Court, upheld the appeals court's dismissal of the case, but used subtly different reasoning.[36]

The Federal Court dodged questions of whether Islam had a privileged position in Malaysia and instead challenged the litigants' interpretation of Islam. Muslim plaintiffs have a right to follow all religious practices, not just ones "essential to the religion." However, the amount of protection will depend upon the centrality of the practice to the religion. When it comes to evaluating whether God will reward Muslims for engaging in a certain practice, judges are permitted to seek advice from religious scholars identified as qualified by the state. Nevertheless, the court is absolutely clear about its authority finally to determine what the answer is. "Who is to decide? Of course it has to be the court when the matter comes before the court."[37] And in this case, the court decides to dismiss views that many *fuqaha*' considered long-settled.

---

35 *Fatimah Binti Sihi v. Meor Atiqulrahman*, (2005) 2 MLJ 25, judgment of Dec. 11, 2004 (Court of Appeal Putrajaya, Malaysia) [Meor Appeal #1].

36 *Meor Atiqulrahman v. Fatimah*, (2006) 4 MLJ 605, decision of 12 July 2006 [Meor Final Appeal], *also available at* http://www.ipsofactoj.com/appeal/2006/Part5/app2006(5)-002.htm. For criticism on the Malaysian bar website that the Federal Court should not have weighed in on what Islam requires, see Charles Hector, Opinion, *Serban Case: A Blow to Freedom of Religion and Child Rights*, THE MALAYSIAN BAR (AUG. 9, 2006), http://www.malaysianbar.org.my/members_opinions_and_comments/opinion_serban_case_a_blow_to_freedom_of_religion_and_child_rights_.html.

37 *See* Meor Final Appeal, *supra* note 36.

The court characterizes them as "the views of traditional jurists, the turban-wearing scholars from turban wearing communities."[38] Abjuring these, it looks to the writings of Hashim Kamali, an important, liberal modernist Islamic intellectual based in Malaysia. Relying on his work and the justices' own observations of Muslim behavior, the court determines that wearing a turban is at most a marginal aspect of Islamic practice. Indeed, the Court suggests, it is so marginal that the state's interest in order clearly outweighs any interest the individual plaintiffs had in wearing the turban.

Malaysian judges are not the only judges in Muslim Southeast Asia who are forced to resolve religious freedom cases filed by Muslims. Nor are they the only judges who use these cases as an opportunity to weigh in on open questions of Islamic law. When the Indonesian constitutional court was confronted recently with freedom of religion claims brought by Muslims, they have decided not to follow the lead of the U.S. courts or the Indian courts – courts that resolve freedom of religion claims without subjectively determining what the law requires.[39] Instead, the court held that it is perfectly appropriate for its judges to rely on their own judgment as to whether Islam actually requires the behavior at issue. The court then rejected a Muslim's claim that Islam's restrictions on polygamy violated his right to live according to Islamic values. In the process, the court considered and rejected an eminent, classically trained scholar's conclusion that Islam gave Muslim men broad latitude to marry more than one wife. Following the lead of modernist Islamic thinkers, it argued that traditional Islamic thinkers had misunderstood Islam's requirements, and that Islam placed significant restrictions on men's right to take a second wife and that the Indonesian law did not create any restrictions that were not already present in Islam.[40]

In short, Islam is becoming ever more deeply embedded in the world view of Malaysia's and Indonesia's Muslims. In this environment, constitutional courts have been faced with claims that implicate questions of Islamic law. In some of these cases, courts can resolve these cases without deciding the Islamic question, either by avoiding the question entirely or by deferring on the Islamic question to established scholars. Nevertheless, they are increasingly choosing to do neither of these things. Rather, judges are putting themselves forward as authoritative interpreters of what Islam requires from the state and, indirectly, of how far one can reconcile Islam and liberalism. In so

---

[38] *Id.*

[39] Mahkamah Konstitusi, Decision Number 12/PUU-V/2007.

[40] *Id.*

doing, they are usurping a role that 100 years ago would have been considered inappropriate for someone of their training, a role that would have been left to eminent, classically trained scholars operating (for the most part) outside of government service.

IV. CONCLUSION AND IMPLICATIONS

Social changes in the modern world have made it possible, for the first time, for constitutional court judges to claim that they have the authority to interpret Islamic law on their own. At the same time, judges have started to feel new pressures to assert this claim. In the current era of Islamization, Islamism is extremely powerful in many countries. Laws and legal opinions that are publicly understood to be consistent with Islam are more likely to be respected both by individuals and by the government itself. In this environment, judges on constitutional courts are increasingly reaching out to decide cases involving Islam that they could theoretically avoid, and sometimes are even resolving them in ways that gratuitously reach Islamic questions. As they do so, they are weighing in on disputed questions about what Islam requires and generally trying to develop an interpretation that reconciles Islam with other constitutional principles to which the judges are committed – often principles associated with liberalism.

Many in Muslim Asia continue to contest either the new judicial role in defining Islamic law for the state or the interpretation that the current generation of judges is promoting. It remains to be seen whether constitutional court judges will fully establish themselves as authoritative interpreters of Islamic law or, alternatively, whether, as the price of being taken seriously, constitutional court judges will have to retreat from the forcefully liberal positions that they have hitherto tended to promote. It is possible that a new generation of judges will be more conservative than the last. One way or another, though, the rise of constitutional court judges as an important voice on questions of Islamic law is one well worth watching. It will affect the trajectory of both Islamic thought and of constitutionalism in the Muslim world. It is also possible that it will prove to be at the leading edge of a trend toward the integration of judicial and religious interpretation in other parts of Asia.

Buddhism has been written into the constitutions of several Asian states. Today, these Buddhism provisions are generally not considered to have formal effect in these countries. They certainly are not thought to create a judicially enforceable requirement that state law respect something called "Buddhist law." However, Buddhism is resurgent in a number of these countries, and some illiberal Buddhist political movements are demanding that Asian states align their policies with an illiberal interpretation of Buddhist values. It is worth considering the possibility that if such trends continue, then in the distant future, liberal constitutional court judges in such countries may feel pressures analogous to those faced by their colleagues in the Muslim world during a period of sustained Islamic revival. They may feel obliged to opine on fundamental questions of Buddhist morality and the restrictions it places on the legislative freedom of a self-styled Buddhist state. Only time will tell whether, through this process, judges will begin to "make" a new form of Buddhist law.

3.6 Limitations on the termination of fixed-term employment contracts: Judicially created rules and their codification in Japanese law

Ryuichi Yamakawa[1]

I. INTRODUCTION

With a focus on instances of judicially created norms, this chapter will analyze the limitations on an employer's right to refuse the renewal of fixed-term employment contracts under Japanese labor law. Part II will provide an overview of the legal status of fixed-term employment contracts and will identify problems with statutory law before the amendments to the Labor Contract Act in 2012. Additionally, Part II will provide a comparative analysis of Japanese law with regards to fixed-term employment contracts. Part III of this chapter will describe case law that effectively restricted an employer's right to refuse the renewal of employment contracts under certain circumstances. Part IV will then examine new provisions of the Labor Contract Act, which codifies existing case law, point out its significance and examine remaining issues with respect to changes in Japan's labor market that influenced the amendment. To conclude, Part V will highlight the significance of judicially created legal norms regarding the limitations on an employer's right to refuse the renewal of fixed-term employment contracts.

[1] This chapter is a product of the research project, "A Research on the Comprehensive Legislative Policy for Issues Regarding Atypical Employment," supported by JSPS KAKENHI (Grant-in-Aid for Scientific Research (Scientific Research B)), Project Number 23330018. The author wishes to thank Satoko Nagahara, Managing Partner, La Paz Group (J.D., Keio University Law School) for her helpful assistance in completing this chapter.

II. THE LEGAL STATUS OF FIXED-TERM EMPLOYMENT CONTRACTS

(i) Limitations on Contract Termination Rights

According to a basic principle of contract law, pacta sunt servanda, the parties to a fixed-term employment contract must maintain contractual relationships until the expiration of the contract. Therefore, unless there is a compelling reason for an exception, neither party may terminate the contract before the end of the contract period.[2] Paragraph 1 of Article 17 of the Labor Contract Act embodies and thus effectuates this legal principle in stating that under a fixed-term employment contract, an employer shall not discharge the employee during the contract term unless there is a compelling reason to prematurely discharge the employee. At the same time, in order to avoid infringing an employee's freedom of occupation, paragraph 1 of Article 14 of the Labor Standards Act limits the length of contract terms. Specifically, the maximum length of an employment contract is generally three years and is extended to five years for certain jobs in the professional field and for seniors over the age of 60.

(ii) Employees' Lack of Employment Security after the Expiration of a Fixed-Term Contract

Unlike open-ended employment contracts, fixed-term employment contracts automatically terminate upon the specified expiry date and are generally nonrenewable. Thus, a worker in a fixed-term employment contract is in a precarious position because the worker becomes effectively unemployed upon the expiration of the contract. Indeed, this lack of employment security is considered a basic feature of a fixed-term employment contract, along with the binding force of the contract during the contract term. For a long time, Japanese labor law did not have any statutory regulations to protect fixed-term contract employees from such limited employment security.[3] As will be discussed below, it

---

2 MINPŌ [CIVIL CODE] art. 628.

3 RŌDŌ KEIYAKU HŌ [LABOR CONTRACT ACT], Law No. 128 of 2007, art. 17, para. 2 (providing, "With regard to a fixed-term labor contract, an employer shall give consideration to not renewing such labor contract repeatedly as a result of prescribing a term that is shorter than necessary in light of the purpose of employing the worker based on such labor contract." Although this provision is intended to provide employment security to workers in fixed-term

was case law that first came to provide certain protections for fixed-term contract employees who had a reasonable expectation of contract renewal.

(iii) Comparative Analysis of Labor Laws[4]

Many European countries have adopted labor market regulations to provide fixed-term contract workers with some level of employment security. Most notably, some European countries such as France and Germany categorically prohibit fixed-term employment arrangements unless there are reasonable grounds for the justification, such as the inherently temporary nature of the employment. In other words, these countries have adopted a legal policy adhering to the principle that employment contracts should not be fixed-term. As explained below, the premise of such regulations is that workers in open-ended employment contracts are protected from termination without cause. However, there have been some opposing views contending that such "entrance regulation" would reduce the vitality of the labor market and hinder the opportunity for job creation.[5]

On the other hand, other countries, such as Sweden, have abandoned such "entrance regulation" and instead have established legal rules that allow the conversion of a fixed-term employment contract to an open-ended contract under certain circumstances, e.g., after several renewals. Such legislation, referred to as "exit regulation," is aimed at promoting relative employment security for certain workers who continue to work under fixed-term employment contracts. Similarly, France and Germany have adopted this "exit regulation" in cases where the expiration of a fixed-term employment contract is permitted.

In contrast, Japan did not adopt "entrance" or "exit" regulations for fixed-term employment contracts until the amendments to the Labor Contract Act in 2012, which effectively adopted the "exit regulation."

---

employment contracts, this provision does not provide an enforceable right to such workers. *See* TAKASHI ARAKI ET AL., SHŌSETSU RŌDŌ KEIYAKUHŌ [Detailed Commentary on Labor Contract Act] 157 (2008)).

4 *See generally* Seminar Report, The Japan Institute for Labor Policy and Training, *Labor Policy on Fixed-term Employment Contracts* (May 2010), http://www.jil.go.jp/english/events/100308_report.htm.

5 *See* Takashi Araki, *Yuki Rōdō Keiyaku Kisei no Rippou Seisaku [Legislative Policies Regarding Fixed-term Employment Contract]*, *in* RŌDŌ HŌGAKU NO TENBŌ [Perspectives on Labor Law Theories] 165–68 (Takashi Araki, Masahiko Iwamura, and Ryuichi Yamakawa ed., 2013).

Thus, before the amendments to the Labor Contract Act, workers in fixed-term employment contracts faced considerable employment insecurity, whereas open-ended contract workers enjoyed employment contracts with indefinite terms and greater job security through the abusive dismissal doctrine. Although the Civil Code of Japan does not include a specific provision stating that an employer shall not discharge an employee without good cause, courts have developed such a position through case law. Specifically, courts have established the rule that an employer's discharge constitutes an abuse of right if such a discharge lacks an objectively reasonable cause or is deemed inappropriate from the viewpoint of society.[6] Currently, this case law is codified in Article 16 of the Labor Contract Act. Similarly, many European countries have adopted statutory regulations addressing discharge without good cause in open-ended employment contracts.

Meanwhile, in many US states, the at-will employment doctrine applies to open-ended employment contracts, and an employer may discharge an employee for good cause, bad cause, or even without cause. As a result, even workers who enter into open-ended employment contracts do not enjoy considerable employment security.

In comparison with the law in Europe and the United States, Japanese law has a distinctive feature. Specifically, in Japan, there was a large gap in the level of employment security between open-ended workers, who were protected under the abusive dismissal doctrine, and fixed-term workers, who were not protected under the "entrance" or "exit" regulations. The only protection that such fixed-term workers could rely on was case law that established the abusive dismissal doctrine. This doctrine applied, mutatis mutandis, to an employer's refusal to renew a fixed-term contract when (1) the fixed-term employment contract is deemed to be in fact an open-ended employment contract or (2) there is a reasonable expectation from the worker that the contract would be renewed. The next section explores this case law.

---

[6] For an explanation on the abusive dismissal doctrine, see generally Ryuichi Yamakawa, *From Security to Mobility? Changing Aspects of Japanese Dismissal Law, in* LAW IN JAPAN: A TURNING POINT 483–520 (Daniel H. Foote, 2007).

III. LIMITATIONS ON THE TERMINATION OF FIXED-TERM CONTRACTS

(i) Background

As explained earlier, fixed-term employment contracts automatically terminate at the expiration of the stipulated contract term. In Japan, however, the renewal of fixed-term employment contracts is quite common since there is no legal limitation on the use of fixed-term employment contracts. According to a survey conducted by the Ministry of Health, Labor, and Welfare in 2011, 40.3% of enterprises that hired workers under fixed-term employment contracts renewed such contracts three to five times; 21.5% of such enterprises renewed fixed-term employment contracts six to ten times; and 15.5% of such enterprises renewed fixed-term employment contracts 11 times or more.[7] Consequently, it would be reasonable for some fixed-term employment contract workers to expect a renewal of their contracts, especially in cases where an employer had repeatedly renewed a worker's fixed-term employment contract.

(ii) The Expansion of Employment Security in Fixed-Term Contracts

The repeated renewal of fixed-term employment contracts has a long history in Japan. In the 1950s,[8] the manufacturing industry employed a number of so-called 'temporary workers' under fixed-term employment contracts. This employment practice was criticized because such temporary workers lacked sufficient job security and faced a comparatively lower standard of working conditions in comparison with so-called 'genuine workers,' i.e., regular workers, who were employed under open-ended employment contracts.

---

[7] Kōsei Rōdō Shō [Ministry of Health, Labor, and Welfare], *Heisei 23 Nen Yūki Rōdō Keiyaku ni Kansuru Jittai Chōsa (Jigyōsho Chōsa) [2011 Survey on the Fixed-Term Employment Contract (Enterprise Survey)]*, *available at* http://www.mhlw.go.jp/toukei/list/dl/156-2a-1.pdf (last visited Nov. 29, 2013) (Japan).

[8] *See* Keisuke Nakamura, *Honkō, Shagaikō, Rinjikō [Regular Workers, Workers from Outside of Firm, Temporary Workers]*, 443 Nihon Rōdō Kenkyū Zasshi [The Japanese Journal of Labour Studies] 40 (1997).

As the economy developed, Japan continued to experience a very tight labor market until the 1970s and thus, employment contracts for such "temporary workers" were renewed many times. While some of these "temporary workers" became "genuine workers," others were denied a renewal of their contracts. These latter workers sued their employers, claiming that their contracts had been converted to open-ended employment contracts (transformation theory) or alternatively, that they were at least entitled to a similar level of job security compared to "genuine workers." In response to such claims, courts extended the abusive dismissal doctrine to fixed-term employment contracts, but rejected the transformation theory.

1. Overview of relevant case law

In explaining the need to protect workers from employers' unreasonable refusal to renew fixed-term employment contracts, the Supreme Court of Japan analogized a notice of refusal to renew to a notice of dismissal. In a leading 1974 case called the "Toshiba Yanagicho" case,[9] the Supreme Court held that a notice of refusal was largely equivalent to a notice of dismissal in a situation where a fixed-term employment contract was virtually an open-ended employment contract. Specifically, the Supreme Court's interpretation in this case resulted from the fact that the "temporary workers" were granted repeated renewals of their employment contracts, where the process of renewal was a mere formality, and were engaged in the same job as the "regular workers."

Accordingly, when a notice of refusal to renew is equivalent to a notice of dismissal, the doctrine of abusive dismissal applies, mutatis mutandis, to the notice of refusal. Therefore, a notice of refusal shall be regarded as an abusive exercise of an employer's right if the refusal lacks objectively reasonable cause or is deemed inappropriate from the viewpoint of society.

In another important decision in the 1986 "Hitachi Medico" case,[10] the Supreme Court granted comparable protection to workers in fixed-term employment contracts who had reasonable expectations for renewals of their employment contracts, despite the fact that their contracts were not effectively equivalent to open-ended employment contracts. This was because the fixed-term contract workers' duties were different from the duties of the regular workers. Additionally,

---

[9] Saikō Saibansho [Sup. Ct.] Jul. 22, 1974, Shō 45 (o) no. 1175, 28 Saikō Saibansho Minji Hanrei Shū [Minshū] 927 (Japan).

[10] Saikō Saibansho [Sup. Ct.] Dec. 4, 1986, Shō 56 (o) no. 225, 486 Rōdō Hanrei 6 (Japan).

unlike the situation in the "Toshiba Yanagicho" case, the employer and the employees together made a determination whether each employee's employment contract would be renewed or terminated at the end of the contract term, although the renewal process was simpler at the contract term's end than compared to the time of initial hiring.

The "Hitachi Medico" decision also clarified how, mutatis mutandis, the abusive dismissal doctrine applied to fixed-term employment contracts. The Supreme Court upheld the lower court's decision in holding that in cases where an employer's refusal to renew a fixed-term employment contract lacks objectively reasonable cause or is deemed inappropriate from the viewpoint of society, the fixed-term contract would be legally deemed renewed. This conclusion revealed that the Supreme Court did not adopt the transformation theory because the Supreme Court held that a fixed-term contract continued to be the fixed-term contract even when an employer's refusal to renew would be impermissible as an abuse of the employer's right. In contrast, the Court's adoption of the transformation theory would have led to the conclusion that an employment contract transformed into an open-ended contract when an employer repeatedly renewed a fixed-term employment contract.

2. Significance and remaining issues

For the reasons stated above, case law effectively extended the scope of the abusive dismissal theory in unreasonable refusals to renew a fixed-term employment contract when (1) the fixed-term employment contract in question is virtually an open-ended employment contract, or (2) the employee has a reasonable expectation that the contract will be renewed. Such case law is significant as it functions, to a certain degree, to bridge the gap in the level of employment security between open-ended employment contract workers and fixed-term employment contract workers.

Furthermore, such case law illustrates an example of judicial activism of Japanese courts in the creation of legal norms. As stated above, fixed-term employment contracts theoretically automatically terminate upon expiration and thus, do not allow any room for an action equivalent to discharge. However, in order to provide fixed-term workers with employment security when it is reasonable for such workers to expect a renewal of their contracts, Japanese courts have analogized an employer's discharge to an employer's notice of the contract's expiration. It is important to note that the abusive dismissal doctrine itself originated out of case law, where the court relied on the general principle of the prohibition of abuse of rights under the Civil Code, although Article 627 of the Civil Code does not restrict an employer's right to discharge under an open-ended employment contract provided that notice is given two weeks in advance.[11] Therefore, Japanese courts have extended a judicially created legal norm to a different but similar situation.

However, it should be noted that several issues remain. First, because this legal norm is a product of case law, it is not widely known among workers, employers and especially small-size enterprises with little legal expertise. Second, the application, mutatis mutandis, of the abusive dismissal doctrine and its legal outcome when a refusal to renew an employment contract deemed unreasonable are not easy to understand from a theoretical point of view. Third, it is not easy to foresee when an employee working under a fixed-term employment contract is deemed to have a reasonable expectation of its renewal. Although several significant factors have been extracted from judicial decisions,[12] it is ultimately left to the judge to consider each relevant factor and to make a determination on a case-by-case basis. Lastly, the protection against an unreasonable refusal to renew a fixed-term employment contract is only available to workers who, at least, have reasonable grounds to expect the renewal of their contract. Thus, those workers who do not have such reasonable expectations cannot enjoy such protection.

IV. CODIFICATION OF CASE LAW

(i) Overview of the 2012 Amendments to the Labor Contract Act

The Labor Contract Act was substantially amended in 2012. The purpose of the amendments was to provide greater protection to employees with fixed-term employment contracts. The need for an amendment was driven by the ever-increasing numbers of atypical employees. For instance, in 1984, non-regular workers comprised 16.4% of all workers but by 2012, the percentage more than doubled to 35.2%.[13] To clarify, atypical employment not only includes employment based on fixed-term

---

[11] *See generally* Yamakawa, *supra* note 6, at 484–88.

[12] *See* Ryuichi Yamakawa, Shin Kihon Hō Konmentāru: Rōdō Kijunhō Rōdō Keiyakuhō [New Commentaries on Basic Laws: Labor Standards Law & Labor Contract Law] 425 (Satoshi Nishitani 2012).

[13] Ministry of Health, Labor and Welfare, *Hiseiki Koyō no Genjō wa Dou Natte Iruno [Present Situation of Atypical Employment]*, *available at* http://www.mhlw.go.jp/seisakunitsuite/bunya/koyou_roudou/part_haken/genjou/.

contracts, but also part-time employment and temporary work. Because part-time employment and temporary work contracts are often based on fixed-term employment contracts, the fixed-term employment contracts play a critical role in the atypical labor market.

Furthermore, the need for an amendment was made even more apparent in 2008, when the Lehman shock devastated Japan's labor market and negatively impacted workers with fixed-term employment contracts. To illustrate, the number of refusals to renew fixed-term employment contracts rose from 5291 in October 2008 to 45 041 in December 2008.[14] Accordingly, there were increasing demands to provide better employment security for fixed-term workers.

(ii) New Provisions of the Labor Contract Act

The 2012 amendments to the Labor Contract Act contain three new provisions.[15] First, Article 18 provides that workers who have renewed a fixed-term employment contract at least once in the past and who have been working for more than five years reserve the right, upon application, to convert the contract into an open-ended employment contract. To note, this Article was influenced by the law of certain aforementioned European countries, and aimed to provide greater employment security to workers in fixed-term employment contracts. Additionally, this legal scheme extends to workers who have no reasonable expectation of renewal of their fixed-term employment contracts.

Upon electing to convert a fixed-term employment contract into an open-ended employment contract, an employee is granted virtually identical working conditions as before the conversion, unless otherwise stipulated in the new employment contract or other norms. Therefore, workers whose employment contracts are converted into open-ended contracts do not necessarily procure the same working conditions as their regular, i.e., official, full-time counterparts.

---

[14] Kazuo Yoshida, *Koyō Chōsei no Suii to Hiseiki Rōdōsha [Trend of Reduction-in-Force and Atypical Workers]*, BUSINESS LABOR TREND 61 (Apr. 2009).

[15] The Ministry of Health, Labor, and Welfare issued the interpretative guidance on the 2012 amendments to the Labor Contract Act. *See* Kihatsu [Circular] no. 0810-2, Aug. 10, 2012, *available at* http://www.mhlw.go.jp/seisakunitsuite/bunya/koyou_roudou/roudoukijun/keiyaku/kaisei/dl/h240810-02.pdf.

Furthermore, often a fixed-term employment contract will stipulate restrictions on an employer's right to exercise discretion in the management of fixed-term workers. For example, parties to a fixed-term employment contract sometimes stipulate that the employer may not transfer the employee to a different location or position, despite the fact that such a transfer is usually permitted in the case of regular workers in open-ended employment contracts. Indeed, such a contractual stipulation remains even after the conversion from a fixed-term to an open-ended employment contract. However, it should be noted that disputes sometimes arise if an employer tries to modify such stipulations through change of work rules. Such disputes are resolved under Article 7 or 10 of the Labor Contract Act, which provide for the effect of work rules.[16]

Second, Article 19 codifies case law that restricts an employer's unreasonable refusal to renew a fixed-term employment contract. Third, Article 20 prohibits an employer from taking advantage of an employee's fixed-term status by imposing unreasonable working conditions on such a worker. Indeed, the working conditions of workers in fixed-term employment contracts were often unreasonable due to the fixed-term workers' comparatively weaker bargaining power. Specifically, fixed-term workers tended to refrain from demanding reasonable working conditions because they feared that such demands would prompt their employer to refuse a renewal of their contracts, either at the time of negotiation for a renewal or at some unspecified future date.

Under Article 20, working conditions set out in a fixed-term employment contract will be deemed reasonable and thus honored if such working conditions are based on (1) a worker's substantive duties or (2) changes to a worker's tasks or workplace. In other words, Article 20 provides that when determining whether working conditions are unreasonable, a worker's substantive duties and changes to a worker's tasks or workplace will be key factors to consider.

(iii) Provisions of Article 19

Article 19 of the Labor Contract Act, as amended, provides as follows:

When an employee in a fixed-term employment contract proposes for a new fixed-term employment contract prior to its expiration or after its

---

[16] For more details regarding the effect of work rules in Japan, see ARAKI, *supra* note 3, at 90–108, 113–37.

expiration without delay, and when the employer's refusal to accept the proposal lacks reasonable cause from either an objective viewpoint or from the viewpoint of society, the employer must accept such proposal under the same working conditions as those set out in the previous fixed-term employment contract, if:

1. the previous fixed-term employment contract had been renewed at least once and from the general viewpoint of society, the employer's refusal to renew the contract at the time of its expiration would be considered equivalent to a dismissal or termination of an open-ended employment contract, or
2. the employee in the fixed-term employment contract had reasonable grounds to expect a renewal of the contract at the time of its expiration.

It is clear that Article 19 codified case law regarding the limitations on an employer's right to refuse a renewal of a fixed-term employment contract.[17] In fact, the Labor Policy Council had proposed an amendment to the Labor Contract Act codifying such case law.[18] Specifically, condition 1 of Article 19 originates from the lines of cases represented by the Toshiba Yanagicho case, and condition (2) is based on the line of cases represented by the Hitachi Medico case. Accordingly, to better appreciate Article 19, it is important to understand the underlying precedential case law. For instance, Article 19's provision that a fixed-term employment contract is deemed to have been renewed when an employer's refusal to renew the contract is impermissible came from the court's judgment in the Hitachi Medico case.

Due to this codification, case law restricting an unreasonable refusal to renew a fixed-term employment contract is now embodied in current statutory law and thus, will lead to better recognition among employers and workers. Additionally, the codification resolves the theoretical quandary that arose when the courts extended, mutatis mutandis, the application of the abusive dismissal doctrine from open-ended employment contracts to fixed-term employment contracts.

---

17 *See* Kihatsu [Circular] no. 0810-2, *supra* note 15, at 5-5(2) I.

18 Rōdō Seisaku Shingikai, Rōdō Jōken Bunkakai [Labor Policy Council, Working Conditions Division], *Yūki Rōdō Keiyaku no Arikata ni Tsuite [On the Status of Fixed-Term Employment Contracts], available at* http://www.mhlw.go.jp/stf/shingi/2r98520000022m7s-att/2r98520000022m99.pdf.

On the other hand, Article 19 added a new condition not embodied in aforementioned case law, i.e., an employee's proposal for a new fixed-term employment contract. Under relevant case law, if an employer notifies an employee of a refusal to renew the employee's employment contract, the employee could take the case to court and allege that such a refusal was impermissible. Indeed, such case law did not condition relief on a requirement that the employee proposed a renewal of the contract or a new fixed-term employment contract. Instead, contract law was the impetus behind this proposal requirement, and the Labor Contract Act added this condition rooted in contract law, whereby a contract is only concluded by the parties' proposal and acceptance.

However, because Article 19 was intended to codify aforementioned case law, it is important not to construe this proposal requirement as a new burden on those workers who rely on Article 19 for relief. Specifically, Article 19 allows an employee to propose a new fixed-term contract after the expiration of the previous contract, so long as such proposal is made without delay. Additionally, according to the Ministry of Health, Labor, and Welfare, an employee will be deemed to have met the proposal requirement when an employee uses a trade union to protest a refusal to renew or when an employee files a suit in court alleging that the refusal was impermissible.[19]

(iv) Significance and Remaining Issues

Article 19 of the Labor Contract Act is significant because it codified the judicially created legal norms on the limitations of an employer's right to refuse the renewal of a fixed-term employment contract. At the same time, however, Article 18 of the Labor Contract Act provides workers in fixed-term contracts with the right to convert a fixed-term contract into an open-ended contract as a means to provide such employees with great employment security. The question thus arises whether Article 18 renders Article 19 redundant.

Originally, courts built this case law around Japanese law that, unlike European countries, lacked sufficient regulations to protect fixed-term workers from undue employment insecurity. However, now that the Labor Contract Act provides workers with the right to convert a fixed-term contract into an open-ended contract under Article 18, it is only natural to question whether Article 19 is in fact necessary. However, it is still necessary to have regulatory safeguards in place to

---

19 *See* Kihatsu [Circular] No. 0810-2, *supra* note 15, at 5-5(2) E.

prevent an employer from unreasonably refusing to renew a fixed-term employment contract because some fixed-term employees may choose to continue fixed-term employment without opting to convert their employment contracts into open-ended contracts. In addition, Article 19 may prove critical in cases where an employer refuses to renew a fixed-term employment contract, and the employee fails to meet the requirement necessary to obtain the right of conversion, e.g., where the accumulated period of the employee's employment term does not exceed five years.

For the reasons stated above, labor law in Japan now includes a unique combination of regulations to protect employees in fixed-term employment contracts. For instance, Article 18, which was imported from European law, provides employees with the right of conversion whereas Article 19, which was fashioned out of case law, prevents employers from unreasonably refusing to renew a fixed-term employment contract. To note, these two regulations may complement each other.

Still, some problems stemming from case law remain. One problem is the lack of predictability in knowing when an employee is considered to have a reasonable expectation of renewal of a fixed-term employment contract. Article 19 does not address this issue and thus, this determination is left to the courts to decide on a case-by-case basis.

Furthermore, there is growing controversy over the so-called "last renewal clause." In negotiating a renewal of a fixed-term employment contract, some employers insert a "last renewal clause" into the new contract, which stipulates that "this renewal is the last and there is no more renewal." Such a practice raises the question whether an employee, who reasonably expected a contract renewal, is deemed to have lost this reasonable expectation when an employer inserts a "last renewal clause" into the new fixed-term employment contract. Although some cases prior to the 2012 amendments found that these employees in fact lost this reasonable expectation, paragraph 2 of Article 19 maintained this uncertainty by merely stating that an employee's reasonable expectation that a fixed-term contract would be renewed must exist at the expiry date of the contract.

At present, the Supreme Court has not addressed this issue.[20] However, some lower court decisions before the 2012 amendments held that an employee's genuine agreement to a "last renewal clause" would be considered a voluntarily waiver of the right to claim reasonable

---

[20] For a general trend of lower court decisions, see SHIN KIHON HŌ KONMENTĀRU, *supra* note 12, at 425–26.

expectation of a renewal and thus, the employer could refuse the renewal without a reasonable cause.[21] On the other hand, other lower courts held that when an employer merely announced a "last renewal clause" without an employee's affirmative consent, the employee could still claim a reasonable expectation of renewal at the time prior to such an announcement.[22] Lastly, there is an emerging debate over when an employee is deemed to have "genuinely agreed" to a "last renewal clause" and when an employee is deemed to have "voluntarily waived" a reasonable expectation of the renewal.[23] Because such there is no consensus on these issues, this controversy will likely continue.

V. CONCLUSION

As noted earlier, workers in fixed-term employment contracts lack employment security because such workers automatically lose their employment upon the expiry date of the contract term. Japanese law did not provide limitations on an employer's right to refuse the renewal of a fixed-term employment contract or provide workers with the right to convert a fixed-term employment contract into an open-ended employment contract. In reaction, the courts created legal norms that effectively restricted an employer's right to refuse the renewal of a fixed-term contract under certain circumstances. The courts applied, mutatis mutandis, the abusive dismissal doctrine to fixed-term employment contracts, and such case law later became codified into statutory law.

The 2012 amendments to the Labor Contract Law codified case law that addressed an employer's unreasonable refusal to renew a fixed-term employment contract. In addition to the codification of the abusive dismissal doctrine, the 2012 amendments illustrate the development of Japanese law through the codification of case law.

---

[21] *E.g.*, Tōkyō Chihō Saibansho [Tōkyō Dist. Ct.] Feb. 17, 2012, Hei 21 (wa) no. 12681 (Honda Giken Kōgyō case), 2140 RŌDŌ KEIZAI HANREI SOKUHŌ [UPDATE REPORT ON LABOR AND ECONOMY] 3 (Japan).

[22] *E.g.*, Tōkyō Chihō Saibansho [Tōkyō Dist. Ct.] Dec. 25, 2008, Hei 19 (wa) no. 27403 (Rikkyō Jogakuin case), 981 RŌDŌ HANREI 63 (Japan).

[23] *See* Ryuichi Yamakawa, *Rōdō Jōken Henkō ni Okeru Doui no Nintei [Finding of Employee's Consent in the Change of Working Conditions]*, *in* RŌDŌ HŌGAKU NO TENBOU [Perspective of Labor Law Theory] 257–83 (Takashi Araki 2013).

From a comparative law perspective, the 2012 amendments to the Labor Contract Law adopted a European-style regulation of fixed-term employment contracts in providing workers in fixed-term employment contracts the right to convert their contracts into open-ended employment contracts. This example highlights the influence of foreign labor law on Japanese labor law, and such foreign influence is abundant in other areas of Japanese law.[24]

Overall, as illustrated in Figure 3.6.1 below, the present legal ordering of fixed-term employment contracts under Japanese labor law is an interesting combination of regulations with origins in both case law and foreign law.

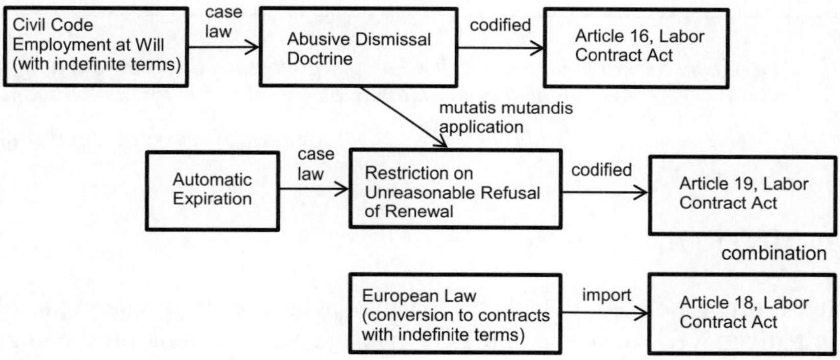

Figure 3.6.1 Development of regulation of termination regarding fixed-term employment contract

[24] For the influence of foreign law on Japanese collective labor relations law, see Ryuichi Yamakawa, *Strangers When We Met: The Influence of Foreign Labor Relations Law and its Domestication in Japan*, 4 PAC. RIM L. & POL'Y J. 363–94 (1995).

3.7 Goddess of justice without a blindfold: How do Japanese judges treat *pro se* litigants?

Kyoko Ishida[1]

The reason for not having a blindfold on our goddess is that we want judges to open their eyes and find the best solution for each litigant.

Member of Supreme Court staff

I. INTRODUCTION

It is often pointed out that Japanese judges exercise strength of initiative over parties in the case management of civil proceedings regardless of the fact that the Japanese Code of Civil Procedure (CCP) does not provide court contempt or any other strong sanctions.[2] In fact, in addition to providing the general authority to control court proceedings,[3] the CCP provides judges with the authority to clarify facts through the questioning of parties[4] and to recommend

---

[1] The author thanks the Legal Research Institute for inviting me to their research project and allowing me to publish the results of the survey here. Needless to say, all things written here are solely my own opinion and independent from the Institute. I also thank the Asian Law Center for giving me the opportunity to publish this article. In particular, I would like to thank Lisa Elizabeth Tamaki and Junji Kitagawa who kindly supported my publication.

[2] *See, e.g.*, Koichi Miki, *Roles of Judges and Attorneys under the Non-Sanction Scheme in Japanese Civil Procedure*, 27 HASTINGS INT'L & COMP. L. REV. 31 (2003).

[3] MINJI SOSHŌHŌ [MINSOHŌ] [C. CIV. PRO.] art. 148.

[4] MINJI SOSHŌHŌ [MINSOHŌ] [C. CIV. PRO.] art. 149, para. 1, *translated in* http://www.japaneselawtranslation.go.jp/law/detail/?re=02&x=0&y=0&co=01&kn[]=%E3%81%BF&ky=code+of+civil+procedure&page=7 (last visited November 10, 2013). Article 149 (1) of the CCP provides that "the presiding

settlement,[5] and these provisions legitimize the judges' strong leadership in proceedings in Japan. A topic of discourse among practitioners, one explanation for this practice is that there are many cases in which one party or both parties are *pro se* litigants (a party without a representing attorney), and therefore judges have to exercise strong leadership over the parties so that the proceedings go smoothly and efficiently. There had been, however, no quantitative survey on how Japanese judges actually treated *pro se* litigants until the Legal Research and Training Institute under the Supreme Court of Japan conducted a survey on *pro se* litigation for the first time in 2011.[6] While there have been several surveys conducted in Japan about Japanese civil procedure from the litigants' point of view,[7] the significant feature of this survey was that the respondents were professional judges who were actually handling *pro se* litigation. The survey collected 285 samples in total and presented the first empirical foothold in the discussion about case management of *pro se* litigation in Japanese courts. In this short chapter, I will introduce an overview of the survey and discuss major findings.

---

judge, on the date for oral argument or a date other than that date, in order to clarify the matters related to the suit, may ask questions of a party or encourage him/her to show proof with regard to factual or legal matters."

5 MINJI SOSHŌHŌ [MINSOHŌ] [C. CIV. PRO.] art. 89, *translated in* http://www.japaneselawtranslation.go.jp/law/detail/?re=02&x=0&y=0&co=01&kn[]=%E3%81%BF&ky=code+of+civil+procedure&page=7 (last visited November 10, 2013). Article 89 provides that "the court, irrespective of to what extent a suit has progressed, may attempt to arrange a settlement or have an authorized judge or commissioned judge attempt to arrange a settlement."

6 Complete report is available in Japanese. *See* 64-3 SHIHŌ KENSHŪJO [LEGAL RESEARCH AND TRAINING INSTITUTE], SAIKŌ SAIBANSHO [SUP. CT.], *Honninsosho ni kansuru jisshoteki kenkyu* [*Empirical Research on Pro Se Litigation*], *in* SHIHŌKENKYŪ HŌKOKUSHO [JUDICIAL RESEARCH REPORT] 1 (2013) (hereinafter Survey Report).

7 With the cooperation of the Supreme Court of Japan, three empirical surveys were conducted in 2000, 2006, and 2011. Reports of these surveys are available in Japanese: SHIHŌ SEIDO KAIKAKU SHINGIKAI, MINJI SOSHŌ RIYŌSHA CHŌSA HŌKOKUSHO [REPORT OF SURVEY ON USERS OF CIVIL LITIGATION], http://www.kantei.go.jp/jp/sihouseido/tyousa/2001/survey-report.html (last visited Sept. 20, 2013); MINJI SOSHŌSEIDO KENKYUKAI, 2006 NEN MINJI SOSHŌ RIYŌSHA CHŌSA [SURVEY ON USERS OF CIVIL LITIGATION IN 2006] (2007); and MINJI SOSHŌSEIDO KENKYUKAI, 2011 NEN MINJI SOSHŌ RIYŌSHA CHŌSA [SURVEY ON USERS OF CIVIL LITIGATION IN 2011] (2012).

II. WHY DOES *PRO SE* LITIGATION MATTER?: A GENERAL OVERVIEW OF *PRO SE* LITIGANTS AT THE DISTRICT COURT LEVEL

Before discussing the survey, I will briefly explain why *pro se* litigation matters in the Japanese judiciary. Even though the number of attorneys (*bengoshi*), who are the only professionals that can represent clients in district courts,[8] is increasing rapidly as a result of the Justice System Reform,[9] there are a substantial number of parties who do not retain an attorney and appear in court by themselves.[10] Figure 3.7.1 shows the changes in the number of attorneys and the number of general disputes at district courts based on attorney representation from 2003 to 2012. Although the number of attorneys has increased greatly, from 19 508 in 2003 to 32 088 in 2012, the ratio of cases in which both parties are represented by an attorney is only 37.6 per cent

---

[8] In Japan, there are several kinds of license holders who are authorized to practice law within a certain scope. The justice system reform starting in 2001 expanded the scope of practice for those lawyers other than attorneys, and today judicial scriveners (*shihō shoshi*) can represent clients in summary courts that handle disputes involving less than 1.3 million yen. At the district court level, however, only attorneys can represent a client. Representation of clients outside of court for disputes that should be handled in district courts is also prohibited under the Attorney Act as an unauthorized practice of law. Bengoshi hō [Attorney Act], Law No.205 of 1949, art. 72. *See* Kyoko Ishida, *The Glowing Influences of "Lawyer Substitutes" on Citizens' Access to Legal Services*, 27 WASEDA BULL. COMP. L. 15 (2009).

[9] The Justice System Reform started in 2001 upon publication of the Recommendation of the Justice System Reform Council. JUSTICE SYSTEM REFORM COUNCIL, RECOMMENDATIONS OF THE JUSTICE SYSTEM REFORM COUNCIL (June 12, 2001), *translated in* http://www.kantei.go.jp/foreign/policy/sihou/singikai/990612_e.html (last visited Sept. 9, 2013). While the Recommendation proposed an expansive law reform, one of the major targets was the reform of the legal profession system. Based on the Recommendation, graduate-level law schools were introduced, and the number of those who could pass the national bar examination was greatly expanded. Accordingly, the total number of attorneys rapidly increased. *See* Setsuo Miyazawa, *Successes, Failures, and Remaining Issues of the Justice System Reform in Japan: An Introduction to the Symposium Issue*, 36 HASTINGS INT'L & COMP. L. REV. 313 (2013).

[10] The problem of "access to legal services" in Japan is also an important and interesting issue today. This is, however, out of the scope of this chapter, and I will analyze the survey data from this point of view at another opportunity.

(63 302 cases out of 168 230 cases in total) – the majority of cases brought to district courts are *pro se* litigation cases in the sense that either one party or both parties do not have an attorney.

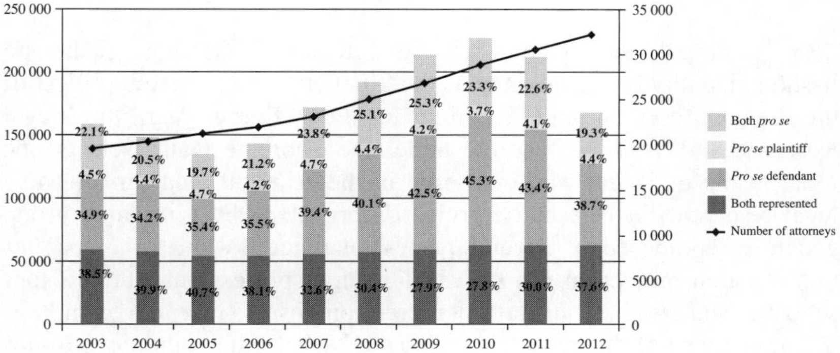

Sources: Breakdown of district court cases obtained using search engine from *Shihō Tōkei* [*Judicial Statistics*], SAIBANSHO [COURTS IN JAPAN], http://www.courts.go.jp/search/jtsp0010 (last visited Sept. 9, 2013). Statistics on number of attorneys from JAPAN FEDERATION OF BAR ASSOCIATIONS, WHITE PAPER ON ATTORNEYS 2012, at 45 (2012), *available at* http://www.nichibenren.or.jp/library/en/about/data/WhitePaper2012.pdf.

Figure 3.7.1 Changes in the number of attorneys and breakdown of general disputes at district courts based on attorney representation from 2003 to 2012

Due to this large percentage of *pro se* litigation cases, it is far from rare for district court judges to face a litigant without an attorney. How do they then treat these litigants? Do they treat them differently from those litigants represented by an attorney? How is the burden on judges and the judicial staff in treating these litigants different from the burden in treating litigants with an attorney? Finally, what is the problem with having so many *pro se* litigants in court, and what kind of policy implication, if any, could arise from such a problem? The answers to all of these questions require an empirical survey on judges who actually handle such cases in court, and the survey discussed below was conducted in order to examine these questions.

III. AN EMPIRICAL SURVEY ON *PRO SE* LITIGATION – ITS RESEARCH DESIGN AND MAJOR FINDINGS

(i) Research Design

"An Empirical Survey on Pro Se Litigation" (Honnin soshō no jisshōteki kenkyū) was adopted as the 2010 civil law research project of the Legal Research and Training Institute. Every year, the Legal Research and Training Institute under the Supreme Court selects one topic in the civil area and one topic in the criminal area for intensive legal research. Each research project is organized by a research group generally composed of several professional judges and scholars. For this research project on *pro se* litigation, four professional judges, four scholars, and two judicial staff members composed a research team.[11]

The purpose of this research was to study the actual conditions of *pro se* litigation objectively and empirically by sending out a questionnaire to those judges who actually handled *pro se* cases.[12] Specifically, the questionnaire targeted judges who had a case that met the following conditions: (a) the case had held more than three oral hearings (except for hearings held on the date the judgment was given) or at least one preparatory proceeding to arrange issues and evidence; (b) one or both parties were *pro se*; (c) the claim was not about the return of an overdue loan, the eviction from a public apartment, or the return of a scholarship; and (d) the case had concluded between the 20th and the 31st of January 2011.[13] Condition (a) ensured that the case involved was a substantive dispute, and condition (c) aimed to exclude fixed pattern litigation cases that ended in settlement or withdrawal more than in ordinary disputes.

---

[11] The author also participated in this research group as part of the research support staff.

[12] In order to learn about the practice of case management in *pro se* litigation in depth, the team also had the opportunity to hear about the real practice of handling *pro se* litigants from chief judges of the Tokyo District Court and the Osaka District Court. Furthermore, the team sent out a short questionnaire composed of 12 questions to high court judges who had handled an appealed *pro se* litigation case. Forty-seven samples were collected from the high court judges. This information is available in the Survey Report, *supra* note 6. This chapter, however, focuses on the results of the questionnaire survey conducted among district court judges.

[13] *Id.* at 2–3.

The questionnaire was composed of 76 questions divided into the following ten parts: Part 1 "General Questions," questioning the respondent's thoughts or policy in case management;[14] Part 2 "Burden of Clerks in General," asking about the clerks' burden in general in *pro se* litigation;[15] Part 3 "Case Information," asking for details of the case that was the object of the questionnaire;[16] Part 4 "Burden of the Clerk and Information about the Parties," questioning whether the burden of the clerk was heavier compared to general litigation, where both parties were represented by an attorney, and asking for the attributes of the parties;[17] Part 5 "About the Complaint, Answer, Preparatory Documents, and Documentary Evidence," questioning whether the documents submitted by the *pro se* party were sufficient and whether the judge or the clerk gave any support to the party;[18] Part 6 "About the Issue Arrangement Proceedings," questioning how the respondent managed the issue arrangement proceedings and whether any special measures were taken due to the fact that one or both parties did not have an attorney;[19] Part 7 "About the Witness Examination Stage," questioning how the respondent handled the witness examination proceedings and whether any special measures were taken due to the fact that one or both parties did not have an attorney;[20] Part 8 "About the Settlement Stage," questioning whether the respondent recommended settlement to the parties and, if so, how the *pro se* litigant reacted;[21] Part 9 "About the Judgment and Withdrawal Stage," questioning the respondent whether it was easier to write a judgment in this case compared to a case where both parties were represented by an attorney;[22] and Part 10 "About the Conclusion of the Case," questioning the respondent whether the conclusion of the case might have been different if the *pro se* litigant had retained an attorney.[23]

---

14 Questions 1–7 on the Questionnaire for district court judges (*Chihōsai-bansho saibankan ni kansuru ankēto*). *Id.* at 43–45.

15 Question 8. *Id.* at 46.

16 Questions 9–20. *Id.* at 47–50.

17 Questions 21–30. *Id.* at 51–53.

18 Questions 31–41. *Id.* at 54–58.

19 Questions 42–50. *Id.* at 59–63.

20 Questions 51–55. *Id.* at 64–66.

21 Questions 56–62. *Id.* at 67–70.

22 Questions 63 and 64. *Id.* at 71.

23 Questions 65–76. *Id.* at 72–78.

In total, samples were collected on 285 cases, including 83 cases in which the plaintiffs were the *pro se* litigants, 169 cases in which the defendants were the *pro se* litigants, and 33 cases in which both parties were the *pro se* litigants.[24]

(ii) Major Findings

While the questionnaire asked about the expansive aspects of *pro se* litigation, here I will focus on the following three major issues: (a) how the general policies of individual judges on case management of *pro se* litigation matter in their daily case management; (b) whether any special measures were taken for *pro se* litigants; and (c) whether the respondent judge believed that the result of the case would have been different had the *pro se* litigant been represented by an attorney.

1. How general policies of individual judges matter in their daily case management

Question 3 asked whether the respondents support the following two ideas: (a) "the judge should provide an easy and careful explanation about the proceedings to *pro se* litigants, bearing in mind that they are not professional attorneys"; and (b) "the judge should actively give suggestions to *pro se* litigants about how to organize their case legally and how to present their claims and evidence, bearing in mind that they are not professional attorneys." The respondents were asked to answer using a four-point scale: "Agree," "Somewhat agree," "Somewhat disagree," and "Disagree." The majority seemed to support the idea of practicing special care for *pro se* litigants: as to Question (a), 65.4% of the respondents answered "Agree," and 30.7% answered "Somewhat agree"; and as to Question (b), 8.3% of the respondents answered "Agree," and 48.0% answered "Somewhat agree." Yet, here we can see some differences between the answers for (a) and (b). While most of them did not oppose the idea of giving a careful explanation to *pro se* litigants in Question (a), 43.7% of the respondents did not support

[24] Raw data was deposited with the Social Science Japan Data Archive at the Social Science Institute, University of Tokyo (Japanese only). It will be available in the database at SOCIAL SCIENCE JAPAN DATA ARCHIVE, https://ssjda.iss.u-tokyo.ac.jp/en/ (last visited Sept. 14, 2013), after the internal proceedings are completed. As of November 2013, the hard copy of the Survey Report is the only version available to the public.

the idea of giving active suggestions on litigation strategy in Question (b).[25]

Question 5 asked about the respondents' daily practice in *pro se* litigation: (a) "I provide an easy and careful explanation about the proceedings to *pro se* litigants, bearing in mind that they are not professional"; and (b) "I actively give suggestions to *pro se* litigants about how to organize their case legally and how to present their claims and evidence, bearing in mind that they are not professional." Here, too, the respondents were asked to answer using a four-point scale: "Yes," "Generally yes," "Generally no," and "No." The answers to these questions show a similar result to Question 3: as to Question (a), 57.5% of the respondents answered "Yes," and 40.2% answered "Generally yes"; and as to Question (b), 7.5% answered "Yes," and 51.2% answered "Generally yes." Similar to the difference in the results for Questions 3(a) and 3(b), the majority gave a kind explanation to *pro se* litigants, but 41.3% of the respondents declined to give active suggestions about litigation strategy in practice.[26]

Table 3.7.1 Cross-table of Q3(a) and Q5(a)

Q3(a) "Court should provide an easy explanation"			Q5(a) "I provide an easy explanation."				
			Yes	Generally yes	Generally no	No	Total
	Agree	Count	152	31	0	0	183
		%	83.1%	16.9%	0.0%	0.0%	100.0%
	Somewhat agree	Count	8	87	0	0	95
		%	8.4%	91.6%	0.0%	0.0%	100.0%
	Somewhat disagree	Count	2	2	4	0	8
		%	25.0%	25.0%	50.0%	0.0%	100.0%
	Disagree	Count	0	0	0	2	2
		%	0.0%	0.0%	0.0%	100.0%	100.0%
Total		Count	162	120	4	2	288
		%	56.3%	41.7%	1.4%	0.7%	100.0%

Note: Fisher's Exact Test: p=0.00 (2-sided)

25 In Question 3(b), 36.6% of the respondents answered "Somewhat disagree," and 7.1% answered "Disagree."

26 In Question 5(b), 35.0% of the respondents answered "Generally no," and 6.3% answered "No."

Table 3.7.2 Cross-table of Q3(b) and Q5(b)

Q3 (b) "Court should actively give suggestions"			Q5 (b) "I actively give suggestions" Yes	Generally yes	Generally no	No	Total
	Agree	Count	18	3	0	0	21
		%	85.7%	14.3%	0.0%	0.0%	100.0%
	Somewhat agree	Count	1	141	0	0	142
		%	0.7%	99.3%	0.0%	0.0%	100.0%
	Somewhat disagree	Count	0	6	96	3	105
		%	0.0%	5.7%	91.4%	2.9%	100.0%
	Disagree	Count	0	1	4	15	20
		%	0.0%	5.0%	20.0%	75.0%	100.0%
Total		Count	19	151	100	18	288
		%	6.6%	52.4%	34.7%	6.3%	100.0%

Note: Fisher's Exact Test: p=0.00 (2-sided)

Tables 3.7.1 and 3.7.2 show a cross-table of the results for Questions 3 and 5. It may not be surprising to have the results statistically prove a co-relationship between the respondents' general policy and their daily practice. This means that when a judge supports the idea of practicing special care for *pro se* litigants, he or she tends to actually practice such special care.

However, why do some judges refrain from supporting or even taking special care for pro se litigants? Questions 4 and 6 asked those who answered in the negative to (a) and/or (b)[27] why they did not support or actually practice special care for *pro se* litigants, providing four possible reasons, to be answered respectively using a four-point scale: (a) "If they file an action without retaining an attorney, the court can expect that the litigants have certain knowledge in substantive and procedural law" (hereinafter "certain knowledge is expected"); (b) "If they file an action without retaining an attorney, they should be responsible for bearing the result" (hereinafter "self-responsibility"); (c) "The court has no time to give special treatment due to their heavy caseload" (hereinafter "heavy caseload"); and (d) "In order not to raise a question of objective equality and fairness" (hereinafter "consideration

[27] This means that the targeted respondents for these questions are those who answered "Somewhat disagree" or "Disagree" in Question 3 and "Generally no" or "No" in Question 5.

of fairness"). Table 3.7.3 shows the results of these questions. Self-responsibility and consideration of fairness seem to be the major reasons the respondents had for not supporting the policy and/or for not practicing special care for *pro se* litigants.

Table 3.7.3 Results of Questions 4 and 6: Why the respondent does not support or practice special care for pro se *litigants*

	Q4 Reason for not supporting the policy in Q3				Q6 Reason for not doing the practice in Q5			
	Agree	Somewhat agree	Somewhat disagree	Disagree	Agree	Somewhat agree	Somewhat disagree	Disagree
(a) Certain knowledge is expected	3 (2.7%)	18 (16.8%)	46 (41.1%)	45 (40.2%)	3 (2.8%)	17 (15.9%)	39 (36.4%)	48 (44.9%)
(b) Self-responsibility	53 (47.3%)	58 (51.8%)	1 (0.9%)	0 (0.0%)	53 (49.5%)	53 (49.5%)	1 (0.9%)	0 (0.0%)
(c) Heavy caseload	0 (0.0%)	13 (11.6%)	31 (27.7%)	68 (60.7%)	0 (0.0%)	14 (13.1%)	28 (26.2%)	65 (60.7%)
(d) Consideration of fairness	49 (43.8%)	51 (45.5%)	9 (8.0%)	3 (2.7%)	48 (44.9%)	46 (43.0%)	7 (6.5%)	6 (5.6%)

2. Measures taken especially for *pro se* litigants

Question 46 asked whether the respondent took any special measures in the proceedings to arrange issues and evidence for *pro se* litigants that would not have been taken if the party had been represented by an attorney. Specifically, the question asked whether the following nine measures were taken for the *pro se* litigant, considering the fact that he or she did not have an attorney:[28] (a) "the respondent asked the *pro se* litigant to clarify the matter, which was not clearly asserted at the time but could be organized as a reasonable claim if the court reasonably interpreted the explanation and evidence submitted by the *pro se* litigant"; (b) "the respondent orally explained to the *pro se* litigant the concrete issues that should be stated in a preparatory brief and advised him or her to submit such a document"; (c) "the respondent handed the *pro se* litigant a list of concrete issues that should be stated in a preparatory brief and advised him or her to submit such a document"; (d) "the respondent made a statement for the *pro se* litigant based on

[28] The questionnaire clarifies that the respondent should mark "No" if such a measure would have been necessary even if the party was represented by an attorney.

his or her oral and written statement"; (e) "the respondent handed the *pro se* litigant a sample form of an explanatory document to be attached with evidence"; (f) "the respondent concretely suggested to the *pro se* litigant that he or she submit a particular documentary evidence"; (g) "the respondent handed the *pro se* litigant a sample form of a statement"; and (h) "the respondent handed the *pro se* litigant a sample form of a document to request to call a witness and/or a list of questions to be asked during the witness examination"; and (i) "the respondent suggested or advised the *pro se* litigant to request to call a specific person (including the party himself or herself) for witness examination."

Question 53 asked about a similar issue in witness examination. Namely, the respondents were asked whether the following five measures were taken for the *pro se* litigant, considering the fact that he or she did not have an attorney: (a) "the respondent requested the *pro se* litigant submit a detailed list of questions that would be asked at the direct examination"; (b) "the respondent requested the *pro se* litigant submit a detailed list of questions that would be asked in the cross examination"; (c) "the court conducted the first direct examination of the *pro se* litigant"; (d) "the court conducted the first direct examination of the witness whom the *pro se* litigant requested to examine"; and (e) "the court conducted the cross examination instead of the *pro se* litigant against the witness whom the opposing party (with an attorney) requested to call as a witness."

Table 3.7.4 shows the results of Questions 46 and 53. It may be surprising that 38.9% of the respondents answered that they had written a statement by themselves for the *pro se* litigant after hearing the *pro se* litigant's oral statement or reading the documents submitted by him or her, and 37.5% of the respondents orally explained the concrete issues that should be stated in the preparatory brief of the *pro se* litigant. Other notable points are that 87.9% of the respondents conducted the first direct examination of the *pro se* litigant, and 32.1% conducted the cross-examination instead of the *pro se* litigant against the witness of the opposing party. Article 202 (1) of the CCP provides the order of examination as follows: the party who has requested the examination, the other party, and the presiding judge.[29] However, paragraph (2) of the same Article also allows the court to change this order after hearing the opinions of the parties.[30] In *pro se* litigation, many judges applied this

---

[29] MINJI SOSHŌHŌ [MINSOHŌ] [C. CIV. PRO.] art. 202, para. 1.

[30] MINJI SOSHŌHŌ [MINSOHŌ] [C. CIV. PRO.] art. 202, para. 2. Although this particular provision is provided for the examination of witnesses, it is also applied to the examination of the parties.

exception under paragraph (2) for the direct examination of the *pro se* litigant and conducted the first examination, and roughly one-third of the respondents conducted the cross examination of the witness of the opposing side instead of the *pro se* litigant.

Table 3.7.4 Whether special measures were taken for pro se *litigants in the proceedings to arrange issues and evidence and for witness examination*

	Yes		No	
	Count	%	Count	%
Q46 (a) Asked the *pro se* litigant to clarify the matter that was not clearly asserted at the time but could be organized as a reasonable claim	66	22.9%	219	76.8%
Q46 (b) Orally explained to the *pro se* litigant the concrete issues that should be stated in a preparatory brief	107	37.5%	178	62.5%
Q46 (c) Handed the *pro se* litigant a list of concrete issues that should be stated in a preparatory brief	18	6.3%	267	93.7%
Q46 (d) Made a statement for the *pro se* litigant based on his or her oral and written statement	111	38.9%	174	61.1%
Q46 (e) Handed the *pro se* litigant a sample form of an explanatory document to be attached with evidence	78	27.4%	207	72.6%
Q46 (f) Concretely suggested to the *pro se* litigant that he or she submit a particular documentary evidence	72	25.3%	213	74.7%
Q46 (g) Handed the *pro se* litigant a sample form of a statement.	28	9.8%	257	90.2%
Q46 (h) Handed the *pro se* litigant a sample form of a document to request to call a witness and/or a list of questions for the witness examination	46	16.1%	239	83.9%
Q46 (i) Suggested or advised the *pro se* litigant to request to call a specific person (including the party himself or herself) for witness examination	41	14.4%	244	85.5%
Q53 (a) Requested the *pro se* litigant submit a detailed list of questions that would be asked at the direct examination	33	26.2%	93	73.8%
Q53 (b) Requested the *pro se* litigant submit a detailed list of questions that would be asked in the cross-examination	6	4.8%	120	95.2%
Q53 (c) Conducted the first direct examination of the *pro se* litigant	102	87.9%	14	12.1%
Q53 (d) Conducted the first direct examination of the witness whom the *pro se* litigant requested to examine	9	36.0%	16	64.0%
Q53 (e) Conducted the cross-examination instead of the *pro se* litigant against the witness of the opposing party	35	32.1%	74	67.9%

The results above show a tendency among the responding judges to take necessary measures in expediting the proceedings or in finding the truth for the *pro se* litigants such as orally explaining concrete issues to be stated in the brief, documenting what the *pro se* litigants orally stated, conducting the first examination of the *pro se* litigant, or even conducting the cross examination instead of the *pro se* litigant. Interestingly, these answers to Questions 46 and 53 do not show a clear statistical co-relationship with the answers to Question 3 on the respondents' general policy of *pro se* case management.[31]

Questions 56 to 62 were about the settlement stage. Of the respondents, 177 (62.1%) suggested that the parties hold a settlement conference, and 134 (47.0%) actually held a settlement conference.[32] Question 62 asked whether the respondent would have definitely recommended settlement if the *pro se* litigant had retained an attorney. Of the respondents, 211 (74.0%) answered "Yes." This number is 12% larger than the number of respondents who actually suggested holding a settlement conference. The fact that a party does not retain an attorney seems to become an obstacle for the court when recommending settlement. In fact, in the answers for Question 61, which asked the reason for not suggesting a settlement conference, 53 (35.1%) respondents answered "Yes" to the reason "the *pro se* plaintiff had no willingness at all to settle the case,"[33] and 92 (60.9%) respondents answered "Yes" to the reason "the *pro se* defendant had no willingness at all to settle the case" (See Table 3.7.5).[34] If these *pro se* litigants had retained an attorney, the attorney could have taken on the role of an intermediary between the court and the party and given reasonable advice to the party about what could be gained through settlement.

---

31 I examined the co-relationship by using a cross-table analysis of the answers to Q46 and 53, and Q3 by replacing the answers to Q3 into a two-point scale. Although the majority of the results did not show a co-relationship, there were four exceptions: Q46 (a) and Q3 (b) (Chi-Square Test, $p=0.00$); Q46 (b) and Q3(a) (Fishers' Exact Test, $p<0.1$(2-sided)); Q46 (f) and Q3 (a) (Fisher's Exact test, $p<0.1$(2-sided)); and Q46 (f) and Q3 (b)(Chi-Square Test, $p<0.5$). In these couples, the respondents tended to take special measures when they supported practicing with special care for *pro se* litigants.

32 Question 56 (a) asked "Did you suggest the parties hold a settlement conference?" Question 56 (b) asked "Did you actually hold a settlement conference?"

33 Question 61 (a) required a Yes or No answer to the statement "The *pro se* plaintiff had no willingness at all to settle the case."

34 Question 61(b) required a Yes or No answer to the statement "The *pro se* defendant had no willingness at all to settle the case."

Table 3.7.5 Q61 Reasons for not suggesting a settlement conference

	Yes		No	
	Count	%	Count	%
Q61 (a) The *pro se* plaintiff had no willingness at all to settle the case	53	35.1%	98	64.9%
Q61 (b) The *pro se* defendant had no willingness at all to settle the case	92	60.9%	59	39.1%
Q61 (c) The *pro se* litigant had problems understanding or communicating with the judge and others	36	23.8%	115	76.2%
Q61 (d) I could not decide whether I should recommend settlement for this case	7	4.6%	144	95.4%
Q61 (e) This case was not suitable for settlement	69	45.7%	82	54.3%

3. Whether the result would have been different if the *pro se* litigant had retained an attorney

Question 71 asked whether the respondent thought the results would have been different if the *pro se* litigant had retained an attorney (*See* Table 3.7.6). It is notable that 17.9% of the respondents answered that there was a possibility the *pro se* litigant could have had an advantageous result if he or she had retained an attorney. This means that even though many judges take various measures for the *pro se* litigants, bearing in mind that they are not professional, they also recognize the limitation of their ability to support *pro se* litigants.

Table 3.7.6 Q71 Whether the respondent thought the results would have been different if the pro se *litigant had retained an attorney*

	Yes		No		Don't know	
	Count	%	Count	%	Count	%
Q71 (a) There is a possibility that the *pro se* litigant could have had an advantageous result	51	17.9	186	65.3	48	16.8
Q71 (b) There would be no advantageous or disadvantageous result	160	56.1	59	24.2	56	19.6
Q71 (c) There is a possibility that the *pro se* litigant could have had a disadvantageous result	1	0.4	234	82.1	50	17.5

IV. DISCUSSION

(i) Pursuit of Substantive Justice with Caring, Speedy Proceedings and Procedural Fairness

The survey results show several interesting points. First of all, just as the symbol of justice in the Supreme Court of Japan does not have a blindfold on,[35] many judges treat *pro se* litigants differently from parties with an attorney. Judges provide special care for *pro se* litigants, such as suggesting what should be written in their briefs, writing a statement based on their oral statement, or even conducting the cross-examination instead of them. It would appear that this style of treatment is aimed at the pursuit of substantive justice and in order to speed along proceedings.

After the Justice System Reform, a strong pressure on the first instance court arose to accelerate proceedings.[36] How to manage *pro se* cases is one of the important keys in expediting the speed of the case disposition overall. However, this does not mean that Japanese judges do not care about procedural fairness. The survey results show that a substantial number of respondents do not generally give suggestions concerning litigation strategy on the grounds that it could impair the fairness of the proceedings. The fact that Japanese judges try to pursue substantive justice, speedy proceedings, and procedural fairness at the same time can easily impose a heavy burden and a psychological dilemma.

(ii) Cost of Having So Many *Pro Se* Litigants

Regardless of whether the ultimate goal is substantive justice or speedy proceedings, the survey results show that Japanese judges incur substantial costs in *pro se* case management.[37] Many of them provide

---

[35] While the goddess of justice generally has on a blindfold, as *Themis* from Greek mythology does, the goddess that is located in the entrance hall of the Supreme Court of Japan does not have a blindfold. Yet, she does have a balance and a sword in both hands, as the goddess of justice generally does.

[36] Soshō no jinsokuka ni kansuru hōritsu [Act on the Expediting of Trials], Law No. 107 of 2003, art. 2. The Act on the Expediting of Trials was enacted in 2003. Article 2 provides that all first instance courts are encouraged to complete all cases within two years.

[37] The survey results also show the heavy burden of court clerks. Survey Report, *supra* note 6, at 77.

special care for *pro se* litigants, and such treatment requires additional time and imposes a greater workload and psychological burden compared to what is required for a party with an attorney. Who owes these costs? They are owed not only by the individual judge confronting a *pro se* litigant but also by the public because the judiciary is a public infrastructure. In this respect, too, the current situation brings unfairness in terms of cost sharing: Those who pay the cost for retaining an attorney also have to pay the public cost for *pro se* litigants. While one of the major purposes of the Justice System Reform was to establish a fair and self-responsible society by expanding the number of attorneys,[38] this has not been achieved yet in terms of case management in civil litigation.

The survey results also show that there are a substantial number of cases in which the *pro se* litigants could have obtained a better result if they had retained an attorney. This means that, for these cases, the support of the judges could not bring the *pro se* litigants what they could have gained with an attorney, regardless of how much cost the judges incurred in case management. While this shows the reasonable limitation of the court, which should be a fair dispute resolution institution, it also shows the fact that the judiciary cannot bring justice for those *pro se* litigants without the support of a private legal professional.

(iii) Policy Implication

Even with this overview of the survey results, some abstract policy recommendations are possible. First of all, we need to consider a way to decrease the burden on the court of having so many *pro se* litigants. There are two different methods to achieve this goal. One is to decrease the number of *pro se* litigants. Although the Justice System Reform expanded the amount of legal services,[39] we need to examine why there are still so many *pro se* litigants in court and if there is a way of decreasing their numbers. The other method is to figure out measures

---

38 The Justice System Reform Council, *supra* note 9.

39 In addition to increasing the number of attorneys, for example, Sōgō hōritsu shienhō [Comprehensive Legal Support Act], Law No. 74 of 2004 was enacted in 2004, and this act enabled the establishment of comprehensive legal services all over Japan in both civil and criminal matters by institutionalizing, for the first time, "staff attorneys" who were employed by the quasi-governmental institution.

to efficiently treat *pro se* cases while maintaining procedural fairness.[40] From this survey, we can explore what typical burdens the judges or the courts facing *pro se* litigants have to owe. Through careful examination of the survey results, we can figure out a way to improve the efficiency of pro se case management.

Second, a more theoretical debate is necessary on how much support from the court for *pro se* litigants is justifiable, especially after the Justice System Reform. As stated, judges and courts are a public infrastructure. While it is undisputable that both substantive justice and procedural justice are invaluable elements in legal dispute resolution, these values can conflict with each other easily in individual cases. How much procedural justice can a judge sacrifice for the sake of realizing substantive justice? Does expansion of the number of attorneys through the justice system reform justify or mandate the court's respect for procedural justice more than before? Based on the reality shown in the survey results, practitioners and academics need to engage in discussions on this theoretical aspect.

V. CONCLUSION

In this short chapter, I discussed the first survey on how Japanese judges treat *pro se* litigants. Just as the statue of justice at the Supreme Court of Japan has her eyes open, the survey results show that Japanese judges truly do pay serious attention to substantive justice by providing special care for *pro se* litigants. At the same time, however, the results show that they do care about the fair treatment of the parties as well, and thus this imposes upon them a substantial cost and creates a dilemma in *pro se* case management.

This survey is the first empirical survey on Japanese judges, and its value cannot be impaired by the fact that the number of samples was relatively small.[41] There are still many aspects to be examined in depth

[40] The problem of having so many *pro se* litigants is recognized even in the United States. For example, the California State Court Task Force tackled this problem and published an action plan in 2004. JUDICIAL COUNCIL OF CALIFORNIA, STATEWIDE ACTION PLAN FOR SERVING SELF-REPRESENTED LITIGANTS (2004) *available at* http://www.courts.ca.gov/documents/self replitsrept.pdf (last visited Sept. 20, 2013).

[41] Right after the Legal Research Institute requested all district courts to cooperate with this survey, the 2011 Great East Japan Earthquake (*Higashi nihon daishinsai)* occurred. It was practically difficult to raise the number of samples during such an emergency.

from these survey results in order to present a concrete recommendation for reform of the judicial system. Hopefully this chapter will trigger closer inspection of this important survey and contribute to the enrichment of the study of the Japanese judiciary.

PART IV

Legal transplants and the influence of Japanese law in Asia

4.1 The influence of Japanese law on Taiwan law

Tay-Sheng Wang

I. THE SHAPING OF TAIWAN LAW

Taiwan law means, in this chapter, the law existing in Taiwan since 1895, when Taiwan became a colony in the prewar Japanese Empire. The periods of Dutch and Spanish rule (1624–1662) and Koxinga regime's rule (1661–1683) were so short in Taiwan's history that the ruled had not yet shaped their own political identity. For the next 212 years (1683–1895), Taiwan was ruled by a local government of imperial China and there was almost no Taiwanese political or cultural identity during that time.[1] However, since 1895 a modern-style legal system was brought to Taiwan by the Japanese colonialists. More importantly, Taiwan became a specific jurisdiction within the whole Japanese empire, having its own laws and court system different from that of metropolitan Japan.[2] The term, and concept of, "Taiwan law" thus emerged. Although Taiwan was regarded as a province of Republican China between 1945 and 1949, Taiwan has been constituted a de facto independent state since 1949, as mentioned below. Therefore, the law in Taiwan, officially named the Republic of China ("ROC") law, can be called "Taiwan law" in the international community.[3]

---

[1] Taiwan did not acquire provincial status under the rule of Qing Dynasty until 1885. *See* Robert Gardella, *From Treaty Ports to Provincial Status, 1860–1894*, in Murray A. Rubinstein ed., TAIWAN: A NEW HISTORY (Armonk, N.Y.: M.E. Sharpe, 1999), 187. On briefly discussing the history of Taiwan before 1895, see TAY-SHENG WANG, LEGAL REFORM IN TAIWAN UNDER JAPANESE COLONIAL RULE (1895–1945): THE RECEPTION OF WESTERN LAW 14–26 (Seattle, WA: University of Washington Press, 2000).

[2] *See* TAY-SHENG WANG, *supra* note 1, at 36–56, 63–89.

[3] "Taiwan" is more well known in the international community than "the Republic of China" or "ROC." *See also* CHANG-FA LO, THE LEGAL CULTURE AND SYSTEM OF TAIWAN 1–4 (The Netherlands: Kluwer International, 2006).

Taiwan law is a member of the civil law family, of which the sources of positive law are statutes. The provisions in statutes are in essence the products of the legislature, in which various political forces make their compromise; however, they are written by legal terminology and often need to be interpreted for general application to individual cases in accordance with legal theories. Scholars who are familiar with legal theories thus play important roles in shaping positive law. The authoritative legal interpretations are ultimately made by the court by applying statutes to regulate related parties in a society. Accordingly, in order to answer to what extent Japanese law influences Taiwan law, we have to examine not only legal provisions in the law books but also political circumstances for legislation and the characteristics of legal scholars and the legal profession in Taiwan. In addition, this chapter will further discuss legal practices in Taiwanese society in order to explore Japanese law elements in the daily lives of people.[4]

II. JAPANESE INFLUENCE ON TAIWAN'S LEGISLATION

"Taiwan" is the name used by the majority of Taiwanese people to identify their country in today's Taiwan, but it is not the official name of the country in the positive law of Taiwan. The main reason for this is that current positive law in Taiwan was put into effect by the government of Republican China, which was overthrown by the present Chinese government, the People's Republic of China ("PRC"), in 1949. However, the PRC did not take over Taiwan in 1949. The sovereignty of Taiwan is still a controversial issue in international law. In any event, since 1949, the Taiwan authorities have referred to their country, whose territory comprises Taiwan only, by China's former name, the Republic of China (ROC).

Nevertheless, Japanese laws have a close tie with Taiwan in history because the majority of people in Taiwan experienced a modern-style legal system for the first time during the 50-year period of Japanese

[4] Generally discussing the relationship among provisions in statutes, legal theories, legal interpretations in administrative and judicial cases, and application of law in daily lives of people, see TAY-SHENG WANG, JUYOU LISHI SIWEI DE FAXUE: JIEHUO TAIWAN FALU SHEHUI SHI YU FALU LUNZHENG [Jurisprudence with Historical Thinking: Combination of Taiwanese Social History of Law and Legal Reasoning] 3–30 (Taipei: the author, 2010).

colonial rule (1895–1945). Japanese law was no longer the positive law in Taiwan after 1945 when Republican China took over Taiwan on behalf of the Allies after World War II. The influence of Japanese laws, however, continued to grow in postwar Taiwan because the newly implemented ROC laws were deeply impacted by Japanese laws. At the beginning of the 20th century, Qing China employed Japanese legal scholars to compile Chinese modern-style codes, promote Chinese legal education, and allowed a large number of Chinese students to study law in Meiji Japan. Republican China promulgated its civil code, criminal code, the code for civil procedure, and the code for criminal procedure from 1929 to 1935. Those basic codes of the ROC law were in appearance modeled on civil law countries, especially Germany, but in fact directed by Japanese law and legal theories, which were dominated by German jurisprudence.[5] Unfortunately, those ROC codes had poor levels of enforcement in Republican China and were rejected by the Chinese people in 1949, after they had been effective in China for 20 years at most. In contrast, ROC law has been well implemented in Taiwan partly because Taiwanese society was relatively familiar with modern-style laws during Japanese colonial rule,[6] and has been effective in Taiwan since 1945, so for the past 69 years.

Since 1950, both Taiwan and Japan have had a close political relationship with the USA.[7] It is therefore convenient for Taiwan law to imitate Japanese laws because the two countries share the same legal values. Occasionally, it appears that Taiwan law attempts to adopt American institutions, but it is actually modeled on Japanese law. The 1995 trust law of Taiwan is an example. When Taiwan law tried to adopt the principles of US trust law, the case law in the US legal system, it was actually modeled on Japanese trust law, because Taiwan

---

5 *See* Dan F. Henderson, *Japanese Influences on Communist Chinese Legal Language*, in Jerome A. Cohen ed., CONTEMPORARY CHINESE LAW: RESEARCH PROBLEMS AND PERSPECTIVES (Cambridge, MA: Harvard University Press, 1970), 158–87.

6 *See generally* TAY-SHENG WANG, *supra* note 1, at 174–83.

7 The outbreak of the Korean War caused a reversal of US policy toward Taiwan, from abandoning the island, to Communist China's takeover, to guaranteeing Taiwan's protection through US military deployment in 1950. By the end of 1951, a US embassy replaced the American Consulate General in Taipei, Congress passed a bill providing $300 million in aid to Taiwan, and a US general headed a Military Assistance Group on the island. *See* DENNY ROY, TAIWAN: A POLITICAL HISTORY 112, 116 (Ithaca, NY: Cornell University Press, 2003).

law like Japanese law is rooted in civil law traditions.[8] Since 2003, Taiwan law has, to a large extent, followed US-style procedure for criminal justice. The incentive for this legislation, however, is to imitate Japanese criminal procedural law that was reformed to adopt American institutions during the American occupation period.[9]

Another example is Japanese laws for codifying Taiwan's legal practice, which originated from Japan under colonial rule. Japanese *ne-teito* (fixed mortgage), by which the debtor furnished security for an undetermined number of debts within a fixed amount, was a traditional practice in Japan and became prevalent in Taiwan due to Japanese rule. The ROC Civil Code made in China did not include such practice, but it was regarded as customary law and held valid by postwar Taiwanese courts.[10] The 2007 revision of the ROC Civil Code has expressly added this practice, called "maximum-amount mortgage," by referring to Japanese law.

III. JAPANESE INFLUENCE ON TAIWAN'S LEGAL THEORIES

Legal scholars in colonial Taiwan were almost all Japanese and they left Taiwan after 1945. Only a very small number of native Taiwanese jurists, who were trained in Japanese laws in the colonial days, became members of the first generation of Taiwan's legal scholars that emerged in the postwar era. Most of Taiwan's first-generation legal scholars were those people who had received their legal education in Republican China. However, Japanese legal books were often translated into Chinese and welcomed by law students in China under the administration of the

---

[8] *See* TZU-CHIANG CHEN, TAIWAN MINFA YU RIBEN ZHAIQUAN FA ZHI XIANDAI HUA [Taiwanese Civil Law and the Modernization of Japanese Law on Obligations] 180 (Taipei: Angle Publishing Co., 2011).

[9] The former head of Taiwan's Supreme Court said that Taiwan courts suggested the adoption of postwar Japanese criminal procedural law, in which prosecutors had a heavy burden to prove defendants guilty in the trial, to urge Taiwan's prosecutors to be more prudent in deciding whether to charge the suspected or not, so that the number of lawsuits in the court could decrease. *See* DIVISION ON JUDICIAL ADMINISTRATION, JUDICIAL YUAN ed., TAIWAN FAJIE QIXIU KOUSHU LISHI, DIER JI [The Oral History of the Elder in Taiwan's Legal Community, Vol. II] 202, 205–06 (Taipei: Judicial Yuan, 2006).

[10] *See generally* Tay-sheng Wang, *Chapter 4: Taiwan*, in Poh-Ling Tan ed., EAST ASIAN LEGAL SYSTEMS: LAW, SOCIETY AND PLURALISM IN EAST ASIA 156 (Sydney: Butterworths, 1997).

Peking government (1912–1928). The legal terminology and theories influenced by prewar Japan were frequently used to interpret the provisions of newly enacted ROC codes under the administration of the Nationalist government (1928–1948). It is not surprising that legal scholars from Republican China often cited Japanese laws or decisions to interpret the meaning of provisions in ROC law. As a consequence, the legal theories of Taiwan's first-generation legal scholars basically follow the direction of Japan's legal community.[11]

Many of Taiwan's second-generation legal scholars, emerging after the mid-1960s, went to European countries, especially Germany, for advanced studies in law. They directly learned European legal theories and criticized the traditional ones borrowed from Japan's legal scholars. Although some of the second-generation scholars went to Japan for advanced studies, what they learned were postwar, not prewar, Japanese law and legal theories. Generally speaking, Japanese laws and legal theories had dominance over Taiwan's legal community from the 1950s to the 1970s. In the 1980s, the influence of Japanese laws and legal theories on Taiwan law remained as strong as German or American laws. Japan's influence gradually decreased in the 1990s because most of Taiwan's third-generation legal scholars, emerging after the mid-1980s, studied law in Germany or the USA and the number of those scholars who studied law in Japan decreased. Taking into consideration Taiwan's fourth-generation legal scholars, emerging after 2000, the majority are those legal scholars who went to Germany (and other European countries) or the US (and the UK) for advanced studies, and the minority are those legal scholars who received their Ph.D. education in Japan or Taiwan.[12] Nevertheless, in comparative law studies in today's Taiwan, Japanese laws are always referred to.

In sum, partly because the number of Taiwanese law students studying in Japan has decreased, Japanese laws have lost their original influence upon Taiwan law. If a Taiwanese law student who wants to pursue a Ph.D. degree in Japan is required to study German law or US law, he or she may think it would be better to go to Germany or the United States for advanced studies. On the other hand, Japanese laws are still attractive to Taiwanese law students. As mentioned above,

---

[11] *See* Tay-sheng Wang, *Sige Shidai Xingsu Ercheng De Zhanhou Taiwan Faxue* [Jurisprudence of Postwar Taiwan Shaped by Four Generations], TAIDA FAXUE LUNCONG [NTU LAW JOURNAL], 40: special issue (Oct. 2011), 1372–82, 1396–1400. On the legal theories of civil law, see TZU-CHIANG CHEN *supra* note 8, at 343, 346.

[12] *See* Tay-sheng Wang, *supra* note 11, at 1400–03, 1405–07.

Japanese laws remain the main source of Taiwanese legislation. If a Japanese law becomes the model for Taiwan law, the provisions of this Taiwan law are ordinarily interpreted with reference to Japanese law and decisions. Training in Japanese law is thereby needed for the enforcement of Taiwan law. Moreover, the situation of Japanese society often repeats itself in Taiwanese society about a decade later. Japanese law, which was enacted to resolve these social problems, is very useful for Taiwan law in order to deal with similar social problems.

IV. JAPANESE INFLUENCE ON TAIWAN'S JUDICIAL DECISIONS

Anyone familiar with the decisions of Japanese courts will notice the similarity in the form of writing between the decisions of Japanese courts and their counterparts in Taiwan courts. This similarity, however, did not result from Japanese colonial rule in Taiwan, but from the Japanese influence on the writing style of decisions in the courts of Republican China. In fact, all of the Japanese judicial officials left Taiwan after 1945. There were few Taiwanese judges in colonial days, although they continued to be judicial officials in postwar Taiwan. Therefore, the judicial culture in postwar Taiwan, including the notorious corruption in the past, was derived from Republican China rather than prewar Japan.[13]

The legal interpretation of ROC law in postwar Taiwan, on the other hand, was indeed to a large extent influenced by Japanese law and legal theories. Most importantly, those decisions of the courts in Republican China, which present Taiwanese courts must follow, were made under the strength of the influence of Japanese laws and legal theories, as discussed above. In addition, many elite judicial officials familiar with the Japanese language in colonial days were educated by ROC law in postwar Taiwan. They frequently read Japanese materials when they had difficulty resolving legal issues under ROC law.

A retired judge of Taiwan's Administrative Supreme Court said that the education she had received in colonial days had been Japanese, and thus she had absorbed a large number of Japanese legal theories on administrative law by the time of her appointment as judge in the administrative court, largely because only a few of the materials written in Chinese discussed administrative law. She further pointed

---

13 *See* TAY-SHENG WANG, *supra* note 1, at 179–81.

out that there were at least six judges in the Administrative Supreme Court who often read Japanese theories and decisions. According to her observation, the administrative court of Taiwan became gradually inclined to adopt German law and theories after several Taiwanese legal scholars had studied in Germany and had written many articles introducing those theories, moreover, the Grand Justices had also adopted many of the German legal theories as well.[14] It is obvious that the attitude of Taiwanese courts depends on the mainstream proposition in academic circles. Therefore, the influence of Japanese laws on Taiwanese courts did prevail in the past but has decreased recently.

V. JAPANESE INFLUENCE ON THE LEGAL LIVES OF TAIWAN'S PEOPLE

Having fought against the Japanese in World War II, the KMT (Kuomintang, Chinese Nationalist Party) regime, who took over Taiwan in 1945, wanted to eliminate the Japanese legacy in Taiwanese society in the postwar era. The KMT regime, however, massacred thousands of native Taiwanese in the 228 Incident in 1947 and enforced martial law in Taiwan from 1949 to 1987.[15] Consequently, many native Taiwanese, unlike most Koreans who also experienced Japanese colonial rule before 1945, became friendly to the Japanese on the grounds that Japanese colonialists were not so "bad" in contrast to the Chinese KMT regime.[16] In addition, many of the legal practices were actually introduced by Japanese colonialists into the daily lives of the native Taiwanese, and they had already become accustomed to them. If no external force existed to prohibit them from adopting those legal practices, people were inclined to continue them.

The continuity of legal practices brought by the Japanese could be found in Taiwanese society. For example, a contract relating to

---

[14] *See* DIVISION ON JUDICIAL ADMINISTRATION, JUDICIAL YUAN ed., TAIWAN FAJIE QIXIU KOUSHU LISHI DISI JI [The Oral History of the Elder in Taiwan's Legal Community, *Vol. IV*] 190–91 (Taipei: Judicial Yuan, 2008).

[15] *See generally* Tay-sheng Wang, *The Legal Development of Taiwan in the 20th Century: Toward A Liberal and Democratic Country*, 11(3) PAC. RIM L. & POL'Y J. 531, 536–38 (2002).

[16] It should also be noted, however, that most Mainlanders, who migrated from the Chinese mainland to Taiwan during the 1945–1950 period and dominated Taiwan's politics before the 1990s, were usually unfriendly to the Japanese. Moreover, many native Taiwanese who supported the KMT regime had the same attitude as most Mainlanders.

prostitution in colonial Taiwan was included in the public notary documents of a Taiwanese district court in 1912.[17] According to this agreement, a Japanese person "borrowed" 320 dollars from another Japanese person who ran the prostitution industry in Taiwan, and the daughter of this borrower in return for the money had to become a prostitute for a period of four years. It is astonishing that such an agreement involving the sale of a human body was considered legal so that it was included in the public notary documents in the colonial court. It is also very shocking to find that, according to a newspaper report, a similar contract was entered into in Taiwan in 1958, when ROC law would have been in effect in Taiwan for over ten years. In fact, the colonial government did promulgate a regulation allowing this kind of prostitution contract during the period between 1910 and 1918.[18] It seemed, however, that the abolition of this regulation did not impede the spread of such a prostitution contract in Taiwan. Surprisingly, this legacy of Japanese law further survived in postwar Taiwanese society.

The legal transaction for real estate further illustrates the Japanese legacy in Taiwan. The colonial authorities introduced the Japanese scrivener (*shiho daisho nin*, *shiho shoshi* after 1935) system to the Taiwanese when they enacted a new law that required registration in certain legal transactions relating to land in 1905. Most Taiwanese were unfamiliar with not only the Japanese language but also the modern private law, but were still willing to employ a scrivener to deal with such a registration in the colonial, namely Japanese, government. A scrivener had to present an employee's "officially recognized seal" (*in kan*) to prove that he made the registration on behalf of a specific employer. Accordingly, the Japanese system of "officially recognized seals" appeared in colonial Taiwan as well.[19] Furthermore, the Taiwanese

---

[17] The decisions of civil and criminal cases and the public notary documents of four district courts in colonial Taiwan during the period from 1895 to 1945 can be found in "Taiwan Colonial Court Records Archives." The pictures of these archives are stored in the National Taiwan University Library and open to academic researchers after acquiring approval. *See* http://tccra.lib.ntu.edu.tw/tccra_develop/

[18] *See* Shih-fang Lin, *Jiuzi Mailuo Yanhua Jie: Rizhi Shiqi Taiwan sheqing Hangye Zhong De Funu Renshen Maimai* [Selling Daughter to Be a Prostitute: the Sale of Body of a Female in the Prostitute Industry in Colonial Taiwan], 23 J. WOMEN'S & GENDER STUD. (NATIONAL TAIWAN UNIVERSITY), 93, 119–23, 128–29 (2007).

[19] *See* TAY-SHENG WANG, TAIWAN FU DE SHIJI BIANGE [Transformation of Taiwanese Law in the Twentieth Century] 353–54, 357–58 (Taipei: Angle Publishing Co., 2005).

frequently wanted to borrow money from modern-style banks, which emerged in Taiwan for the first time and were always managed by the Japanese at that time, for buying real estate. It was common for him or her to provide the aforementioned "maximum-amount mortgage," a Japanese legal practice, as a security for a loan. The various transactions relating to real estate were quite common in colonial Taiwan, and the Japanese systems of scrivener, officially recognized seal, and maximum-amount mortgage naturally became prevalent and were also used in other types of business transactions among Taiwanese people.

Although no counterparts existed in ROC law, these legal practices deriving from Japanese law remained welcome in postwar Taiwanese society. The ROC legal system originally created in China did not include the Japanese-style scrivener, so the scrivener, in fact a member of the legal profession, was no longer regulated by the government. Under pressure from practicing lawyers, the Taiwan government has since 1970 forbidden the practice of scriveners. Nonetheless, the Taiwanese people have never stopped employing scriveners in legal transactions for real estate and so on. In 1981, the Taiwan government created a system of "a licensed agent for land registration" to legalize a scrivener.[20] However, many scriveners are still active in Taiwanese society without a license. On the other hand, the government in postwar Taiwan continued to offer the "officially recognized seal" upon popular application. In the 2000s, the Taiwan government tried to stop this service on the ground that it was not provided in ROC law. This suggestion immediately encountered popular objection and was finally abandoned. Almost at the same time the maximum-amount mortgage was included in the Civil Code, as discussed above. Nevertheless, very few people in today's Taiwan recognize that these legal practices are influenced by Japanese law because for a long time official education in Taiwan has ignored Taiwanese social history in the Japanese colonial rule period.

VI. CONCLUSION

Taiwan was not merged into Communist China in 1949, but became a de facto country and implemented the law of Republican China. This allowed Japanese law to continue to influence Taiwan law after its 50-year colonial rule in Taiwan. However, since the 1960s Taiwan law began to directly borrow legal institutions or theories from Germany

---

20 *See* TAY-SHENG WANG, TAIWAN FALU SHI GAILUN [General Discussion on Taiwanese Legal History] 235–37 (Taipei: Angle Publishing Co., 4th edn., 2012).

and the United States. Especially after the democratization of Taiwan in the 1990s, Taiwan law has developed its own characteristics and it no longer merely learns from Japanese law and legal theories. In any event, the influence of Japanese law does exist in the legal lives of Taiwanese in an unidentified way. To make comparative studies on Taiwan law and Japanese laws is definitely significant for both countries.

4.2 Corporate law and corporate law scholarship in Korea: A comparative essay

Kon Sik Kim[1]

I. INTRODUCTION

Korea's stellar economic performance during the last four decades of the 20th century is well known and widely admired. Other segments of Korean society have been moving forward in step with its economic progress. Not only cars and smart phones, but also movies and pop singers symbolize the elevated status of Korea in the global market. Korea's corporate law, however, largely lagged behind the business sector. Its corporate statutes played no significant role until the end of the last century.

The situation, however, changed dramatically as the country fell into a financial crisis in 1997. The crisis was, for better or worse, generally regarded as a consequence of Korea's poor corporate governance. Under pressure from international institutions such as the International Monetary Fund (IMF) and the World Bank, the Korean government embarked on improving corporate governance by, among other things, revamping its corporate statutes. The post-crisis corporate law reforms advanced the relevance of corporate law in the business community, and, in turn, contributed to a rapid growth of corporate law practice. In the process, however, corporate law scholars have played no significant role, as discussed later.[2] On the contrary, corporate law scholarship has been influenced by these developments.

---

[1] This chapter draws partly on my previous article published in Korean, titled "*Our Corporate Law and Corporate Legal Scholarship in the 21st Century: Its Limits and Challenges*" JUSTICE No. 92 239–52 (2006). This article is funded by the Seoul National University Law Foundation in 2014.

[2] *See infra* Part III(i).

The purpose of this chapter is to review the transformation of corporate law in Korea during the last two decades from a comparative perspective. The term "corporate law" here is used in a broader sense, encompassing the capital market law. During the same period, the corporate statutes have been amended eight times,[3] and a wide range of provisions have been introduced or amended. This chapter will not purport to describe any individual provision or principle in detail.[4] Instead, this chapter will survey more general features of corporate law and corporate legal scholarship in Korea, with a special emphasis on forces shaping the current statutes.

Korean corporate law has undergone a substantial change since the financial crisis in 1997, which will be reflected in the organization of this chapter. Part II will discuss the status of corporate law and corporate law scholarship prior to the financial crisis. Part III will then survey post-crisis developments related to corporate law. Part IV will examine post-crisis corporate law scholarship. Part V will address challenges of future corporate law reform.

---

[3] They were amended in 1995, 1998, 1999, 2001, 2009 (twice), 2011, and 2014.

[4] There is now a growing body of literature in English on individual topics of Korean corporate law. Since the crisis, I have published the following papers: *Invigorating Shareholder Derivative Actions in South Korea*, in Dan W. Puchniak et al. eds., THE DERIVATIVE ACTION IN ASIA 189–217 (2012) (with Hyeok-Joon Rho); *Corporate Legal Personality and Corporate Loss in Korean Law*, in Stefan Grundmann et al. eds., Unternehmen, Markt und Verantwortung (De Gruyter, Festschrift für Klaus J. Hopt zum 70. Geburtstag am 24. August 2010); *The role of judges in corporate governance: the Korean experience*, in Hideki Kanda et al. eds. TRANSFORMING CORPORATE GOVERNANCE IN EAST ASIA (2008); *Transplanting Audit Committees to Korean Soil: A Window into the Evolution of Korean Corporate Governance*, 9 ASIAN-PAC. L. & POL'Y J. 163 (2007); *Revamping Fiduciary Duties in Korea: Does Law Matter to Corporate Governance?*, in Curtis Milhaupt ed., GLOBAL MARKETS, DOMESTIC INSTITUTIONS, 373–99 (2003) (with Joongi Kim); *Establishing a New Stock Market for Shareholder Value Oriented Firms in Korea*, 3 CHI. J. INT'L L. 277 (Fall, 2002) (with Stephen Choi).

II. PRE-CRISIS CORPORATE LAW AND CORPORATE LAW SCHOLARSHIP

(i) Genesis: Overwhelming Influence of Japanese Law

Although sporadic efforts had been made to introduce a modern legal system even before Korea was colonized by Japan in 1910, it was not until the beginning of Japanese rule that a full-fledged set of modern statutes was applied in Korea. During the colonial period (1910–1945), the Japanese government applied its own statutes in Korea with some adaptation. Japan's Commercial Code, which contained corporate statutes, was one of those Japanese codes. The Japanese Commercial Code, originally adopted in 1899 and later revised in 1911 and 1938, was heavily influenced by German law.

When the Korean government was established in 1948, one of its initial tasks was to replace the existing Japanese laws with its own laws. Due to the political and social turmoil caused by the Korean War, the legislation project could not proceed as planned. The new Commercial Code came into force only in 1963, almost 20 years after liberation from Japanese control. Although Koreans wanted to reconfirm Korean independence in the field of legislation, they could not achieve their aspiration in the field of commercial law at least. The Commercial Code was not substantially different from its Japanese counterpart. Although Korea and Japan started following different paths in corporate law legislation around the new millennium, their corporate statutes as of 1963 were identical in most, if not all, respects. Like their Japanese counterpart, the new statutes incorporated some elements of US practice. They adopted, for example, the concepts of authorized capital, boards of directors and shareholders derivative suits.

(ii) Irrelevance of Corporate Law

As most of the codes enacted in the early days were modeled after codes of Western countries, a substantial gap existed between law and reality in Korea. Corporate law was no exception. A primary reason for this incongruity may be the reality that the corporate form, appropriate for large, publicly held firms, was adopted by a wide range of firms, even by a sole proprietor with modest capital.

The corporate statutes were of little relevance in Korea's efforts to develop its economy. Their irrelevance may be due to two conceptually distinct but related factors: concentrated ownership and debt financing.

In the beginning of the economic growth in the 1960s, firms relied overwhelmingly on debt financing. As founding entrepreneurs did not need to issue shares to outsiders, they could maintain an absolute majority of the shares. As early as the late 1960s, the government began its efforts to foster a capital market and virtually forced major firms to carry out IPOs (Initial Public Offerings). Although the ownership portion of founding entrepreneurs was gradually on the decrease, they still held on average slightly more than 20 percent of the shares in the early 1980s. Their effective control, however, was much stronger than the official figure suggested, due to the widespread practice of "disguised IPO," in which entrepreneurs parked their shares in the accounts of their subordinates or relatives.

The corporate statutes were mainly designed to restrain agency problems arising from the conflicts between managers and shareholders. Most of the statutes were rarely invoked in the presence of a controlling shareholder. Firms were managed in almost complete disregard of corporate formalities. It was customary not to hold a board meeting even in the largest firms. An officer would prepare only the minutes of the board meeting, using the seals deposited by the directors. In smaller firms, even the general shareholders meeting (GSM) was often dispensed with. In such firms, the distinction between the firm itself and the controlling shareholder was often disregarded and the controlling shareholder would sometimes usurp corporate funds for personal purposes. These kinds of irregularities did not receive attention until a formal complaint was filed by a disgruntled shareholder.

(iii) Corporate Law Practice

The irrelevance of corporate law resulted in a small number of corporate law cases. Even in the 1980s, corporate law cases were not only scant but also involved a limited number of fact patterns, such as failure to comply with requirements for a resolution at the GSM. Underdeveloped corporate law deterred the sophistication of local law practice. Until the end of the 1970s, practicing lawyers were basically solo practitioners specializing in litigation. Although a few law firms emerged in the 1970s, they were primarily serving foreign clients doing business in Korea. Even major corporate law disputes were handled by solo practitioners, not law firms. Also, it was quite unusual for a domestic firm to retain a lawyer in the absence of a dispute.

(iv) Corporate Law Scholarship

The irrelevance of corporate law naturally had an effect on the nature of legal scholarship. Especially in the earlier period of economic growth, legal scholars devoted themselves to accurately understanding the foreign concepts. A typical academic paper dealt with a corporate law principle or doctrine, touching upon its foreign origin. Instead of pursuing the principle's actual or potential applications in real life, scholars tended to devote themselves to importing new theories developed in foreign countries. This kind of aloofness on the part of corporate law scholars may be understandable because there were few pressing corporate law issues at that stage. A measure of such aloofness, however, still remains among legal academics to this day.

(v) Growth of Minority Shareholders

With the expansion of economy and the progress of democracy in the late 1980s, the government had to reduce intervention in resource allocation and rely more on market mechanisms. The government made further efforts to develop the capital market and to encourage firms to rely more on equity financing. Firms also felt the need to rely on the capital market. Firms have been expanding rapidly during the 1970s and 1980s, but they could not continue to borrow because their debt equity ratio was already too high and the government's pressure became stronger. Another factor in favor of equity financing was the growth of Korea's capital market. As the growing middle class were seeking investment opportunities other than bank deposits, the capital market was becoming more attractive for large firms as a cheaper source of funds.

As firms started issuing shares, the relative holdings of controlling shareholders were bound to decline. In the 1990s, the portion of controlling shareholders fell to 10 percent on average. The sudden increase of non-voting preferred shares in the late 1980s may be regarded as an attempt by controlling shareholders to bolster their decreasing shares. Far more popular among controlling shareholders was a scheme to use shares held by affiliated firms. By this time, virtually all large firms belonged to a business group, commonly called a *chaebol*. Controlling shareholders maintained their ultimate control by means of widespread intra-group shareholdings. As shown later, this phenomenon more or less continues to this day, forming the most distinctive feature of Korea's corporate governance.

With the decrease of shares directly owned by the controlling family, the gap between the cash-flow right and the control right grew. This is the classic situation in which conflict between the controlling shareholders and minority shareholders arises. Despite the growing presence of outside investors, the behavior of the controlling family changed little. They exercised absolute control in their business empire. As their cash-flow right dwindled, they now had more incentive to engage in so-called 'tunneling' activities, which aggravated the already poor reputation of *chaebol* among the general public.

(vi) Lethargy of Corporate Law

It was clear even in the early 1990s that the existing corporate statutes fell short of addressing these changed business realities. Minority shareholders had no effective remedies against tunneling activities of the controlling family. Nevertheless, there was no sign of change in corporate statutes, nor in corporate law scholarship. It was widely known that every *chaebol* had a single controlling shareholder, often called a "chairman" or *chongsu*, at the top. Few scholars, however, attempted to do research as to whether or not the existing statutes were adequate to constrain the behavior of the chairman. Nor was there an earnest proposal to stem the possibility of abuse by changing the statutes.

The first major revision of the corporate statutes took place in 1984, more than 20 years after the code was enacted. The 1984 revision strengthened the power of the statutory auditor by empowering him to supervise operational as well as accounting matters. Provisions were introduced to control cross-shareholdings and to allow stock dividends. Carefully following the revisions adopted in Japan, the 1984 revisions were not geared to the challenges of corporate governance facing Korea.

The second opportunity to revamp the corporate statutes came in 1995. By this time, the problem of *chaebol* chairmen had become more acute and the inadequacy of the corporate statutes more obvious. No significant attempt was made, however, to address the problems of *chaebol* in the 1995 revision. Although the 1995 revision did introduce the appraisal remedy for dissenting shareholders, it was already available to shareholders of a listed firm under the then-existing Securities Transaction Law.

(vii) Players in the Corporate Law Revision Process

Why did those corporate law revisions fail to respond to the changing realities? The answer to this question may be related to the actual process of corporate law reform. Corporate law revision was, and still is, carried out by the Ministry of Justice (MOJ), a ministry dominated by prosecutors. Prosecutors were generally not interested in, and had no expertise in, corporate law issues. Although the MOJ recently established a separate section for commercial law matters, only one junior prosecutor is normally assigned for the corporate law revision. As a result, the MOJ has been heavily relying on the corporate law committee dominated by senior law professors. By 1995, corporate governance was a hot topic not just in the US but also in other parts of the world. Even in Korea, a small group of scholars started publishing papers on the subject, but the corporate governance discourse failed to attract attention from those senior academics.

Before the committee embarks on a revision process, the MOJ routinely seeks opinions from various related institutions, most of which are closely aligned with the business interests. In 1995, there was virtually no institution claiming to advocate for the interests of investors in Korea. Neither the ruling party nor the opposition parties were as yet interested in appealing to general investors. So when the academic members of the corporate law committee failed to perceive the perils of the *chaebol* structure, the voice of minority shareholders was completely lost in the legislative process.

Korea thus wasted the last opportunity to reinvigorate its corporate statutes before the financial crisis hit the country in 1997.

III. POST-CRISIS DEVELOPMENTS

(i) Post-crisis Corporate Governance Reforms

The 1997 financial crisis called attention to the importance of corporate law reforms for the first time in Korea. Although the exact cause of the crisis may be hard to determine, it was widely accepted by the general public that poor corporate governance of *chaebol* was a major factor leading the country to the crisis. Indeed, it was in 1997 that the term "corporate governance" was casually used by the media for the first time in Korea. Under pressure from the IMF and the World Bank, Korea had to go through a broad range of reforms, many of them in the area of corporate law. For example, large listed firms are required to fill a majority of board seats with outside directors, and to establish an audit committee, instead of a statutory auditor. Threshold shareholding requirements for the rights of minority shareholders have been substantially relaxed to make it easier for minority shareholders to exercise their rights. Now, for example, a shareholder with 0.01 percent of the shares, not 5 percent under the pre-1998 law, can file a derivative suit against directors.

As discussed later, the corporate statutes have been revised several times after the crisis. The most recent and comprehensive revision was undertaken in 2011. Now, the focus of the 2011 revision was shifted from corporate governance to allowing more leeway to firms in structuring and operating their business enterprises. For example, the scope of securities that firms can issue has been expanded.

As a consequence of the series of law reforms, Korea's corporate law has become closer to that of developed countries such as the US at least in substance. And, at the same time, the relevance of corporate law has been strengthened in the economic community. This has led to dramatic changes in corporate law practice. Two examples of such changes will be introduced here: the rise of court cases and the growth of law firms.

(ii) Rise of Corporate Law Cases

With the democratization of Korea in the late 1980s came the explosion of litigation. Lawsuits increased dramatically. Corporate law cases were no exception. Since the financial crisis, corporate law cases further increased. This trend stands out in a corporate law casebook. The 2013 edition of a leading casebook on corporate law[5] covers 246 Supreme Court decisions altogether. Table 4.2.1 shows the distribution of the decisions by year. The number of decisions announced during the period 2001–2010 is more than the number of the decisions announced during the period 1961–2000.

A similar phenomenon is observed in the field of capital market law. A textbook on capital market law[6] discusses 91 Supreme Court decisions. Table 4.2.2 shows that more than half of them (57 out of 91) were those announced during the period of 2001–2010.

---

[5] KON SIK KIM ET AL., CORPORATE LAW (4th ed. 2013).

[6] KON SIK KIM & SUNSEOP JUNG, CAPITAL MARKET LAW (2d. ed. 2010).

Table 4.2.1 *Supreme Court decisions by year: Corporate law*

Period	Number of decisions
1960s	2
1970s	16
1980s	28
1990s	52
2001–2010	123
2011–2012	25
Total	246

Table 4.2.2 *Supreme Court decisions by year: Capital market law*

Period	Number of decisions
1960s	1
1970s	5
1980s	2
1990s	26
2001–2010	57
Total	91

(iii) Growth of Law Firms

A byproduct of the explosive increase in the number of corporate law disputes is the rapid rise of law firms in Korea. A few small-scale law firms emerged in Korea only in the late 1970s. Kim & Chang, the largest law firm in Korea, had only two founding lawyers until the mid-1970s. The firm had grown to 101 as of November 1997, when the crisis hit Korea. It continued to expand to 483 as of 2013, a more than four-fold expansion during the 15-year period.

Kim & Chang is not the only law firm that grew during the post-crisis period. Table 4.2.3 shows the number of lawyers at the top ten law firms in Korea.

The number of law firms also increased during the same period. Only a limited number of them had existed up until the end of 1970s. Even in the mid-1990s, when the term "law firm" became known to the general public, there were only four law firms with 50 to 100 lawyers each in Korea. The number of law firms has grown from fewer than 100 in 1996, to 185 in 2000, to 461 in 2009, and to 724 in 2013.[7] The

[7] Sung-Soo Hong, *Growth of Law Firms and Change in Professional Ethics*,

Table 4.2.3 Top 10 Law firms in Korea (March 2013)

Rank	Firm	Number of lawyers
1	Kim & Chang	483
2	Bae, Kim & Lee	298
3	Lee & Ko	296
4	Shin & Kim	249
5	Yoon & Yang	228
6	Yulchon	198
7	Barun	139
8	Logos	98
9	Jipyong & Jisung	97
10	Hwang Mok Park	96

Source: Ministry of Justice, Korea (March 2013)

rapid advance of law firms transformed the configuration of Korea's legal profession almost completely. Until the end of 1970s, virtually all the lawyers were solo practitioners specializing in litigation. As of 2013, 13,216 lawyers are now practicing in Korea, 6,146 of them, almost half, are affiliated with law firms.[8]

Although not all the law firm lawyers specialize in corporate law, a significant number of them deal with corporate and capital market law. Even in the late 1980s, corporate law disputes were generally handled by solo practitioners. It is now rare, however, to find a high-profile case not represented by a major law firm.

IV. POST-CRISIS CORPORATE LAW SCHOLARSHIP

(i) Role of Corporate Law Scholars

What kind of role did corporate law scholars play in this transformation of corporate law? Not much. As discussed earlier, the MOJ's corporate law committee has been dominated by law professors. The two pre-crisis revisions in 1984 and 1995, and the original statutes enacted in

Law & Society Vol. 41, 145, 158 (2011) (in Korean): Korean Bar Association Website (http://www.koreanbar.or.kr) (visited on August 28, 2013).

[8] Korean Bar Association Website (http://www.koreanbar.or.kr) (visited on August 28, 2013).

1962, were the brainchild of corporate law scholars, not the MOJ and not the National Assembly. In the revisions (1998, 1999, and 2001) immediately following the financial crisis, however, the MOJ adopted a more aggressive posture, putting pressure on the committee's academic members to be more amenable to reform measures.[9]

In order to secure financial support from international institutions such as the IMF and the World Bank, the government made a commitment to take reform measures recommended by them. Thus, the MOJ had no option but to push ahead with promised reforms. Members of the corporate law committee were generally reluctant to adopt many of the reform measures. For example, the proposal to introduce an audit committee was opposed by most members, and by senior legal scholars in particular.[10] Proposals to lower the minimum par from 5000 Won to 100 Won (Art. 329(4))[11] and to eliminate the requirement for the minimum number of incorporators (Art. 288) were also in dispute.

Hostility toward these reform measures was widely shared by other members of the legal academy. Why they came to have such a negative view toward the reform measures is not clear. Some of them may have felt uncomfortable with what struck them as a wholesale import of Anglo-American concepts into the corporate statutes. Or, such hostility was possibly due to the prevailing academic mindset of corporate law scholars.

(ii) Lack of Functional Analysis

During the crisis, legal academics were largely unable to come up with their own reform measures to remedy defects of the existing statutes. Impetus and insights for reform came from outside the legal academy. This inability may be at least partly due to the lack of functional analysis in the mainstream corporate legal scholarship.

A functional approach to law aims to develop a menu of solutions for a social problem. Thus, the starting point of a functional analysis is to identify the problem. The next step is to search for effective solutions. This is the stage where comparative law may come to play a role. The last step of this functional analysis is to assess the effectiveness of

---

[9] I joined the committee from the 1998 revision.

[10] I headed a working committee responsible for drafting provisions related to board committees including an audit committee.

[11] Under the current statutes, a corporation may issue even no-par stocks.

an adopted solution in addressing the problem. From the functional perspective, the value of a country's corporate law provisions depends not on their theoretical consistency, but on their effectiveness in handling pressing corporate law tasks of the country.

This kind of functional approach, however, has been very weak, if not totally absent, in Korea. The prevalent attitude was to regard corporate law as a system of immutable concepts. Legal scholars tended to focus on solutions rather than problems. Although things are changing now, scholars still tend to pay more attention to the details of an individual legal doctrine than to how it actually affects the problem. For example, a number of papers have been published on the provision on self-dealing (Art. 398), few of them attempt to reveal its limits in addressing problems actually arising from the *chaebol* context.

(iii) Overcoming the Dogmatic Mode of Research

A functional analysis may start from overcoming the conventional mode of research, which was heavily tilted toward dogmatic reasoning. It requires legal scholars to pay more attention to facts rather than concepts. Legal scholars have so far turned away from empirical research. As most of them are not equipped with skills necessary for empirical research, it is too much to expect them to engage in empirical research like their counterparts in the US. They should be encouraged, however, to take advantage of a growing body of empirical research based on Korean data.

A functional analysis is employed to affect the behavior of corporate actors. In this regard, even a corporate law scholar needs to take an interdisciplinary approach. The law and economics approach to corporate law is now well known among Korean scholars. A small but growing number of young scholars have expertise in finance and accounting. From now on, however, perspectives of other disciplines, such as political science and psychology, will be of help.

So far such an interdisciplinary research has been rare. There are grounds for optimism, however. The first factor is the influence of the corporate law scholarship in the US, which is heavily imbued with a variety of interdisciplinary research. Every year, an increasing number of young Koreans visit leading law schools in the US. When they come back and join the legal academy, they are expected to practice what they have studied in the US.

The second factor may take longer to stir up a change. Following Japan, Korea started a US-style law school system in 2009. Unlike in

Japan, a majority of incoming students are those who have specialized in non-law subjects such as social sciences and engineering. The new breed of lawyers is expected to have much less difficulty and psychological inhibition in practicing empirical methods in their legal research.

V. CHALLENGES OF CORPORATE LAW REFORM

A functional approach in corporate law will be essential for enhancing the level and relevance of corporate law scholarship in future. Efforts of legal scholars alone will not bring a better corporate law regime, however. There are two sizeable obstacles to corporate law reform. The first is the difficulty of the *chaebol* problem. The second is the political environment. In sum, the first relates to the technical difficulty of coming up with a set of effective solutions, and the second relates to the difficulty of implementing those solutions in the existing political environment.

(i) Difficulty of the *Chaebol* Problem

The ownership structure of large Korean firms is often characterized as controlling minority shareholder (CMS) structure. A CMS effectively controls the whole business group by means of extensive inter-company shareholdings. A number of major *chaebol* have converted into a holding company structure. But if both the controlling shareholder of the holding company and the holding company itself usually hold far less than 50 percent in the individual firms in the group, the CMS problem remains, although in a less serious form, in the holding company structure.

Figure 4.2.1 shows the size of internal ownership in the top ten *chaebol* in Korea. Internal ownership here refers to the sum of shares held by the CMS and those held by member firms.

Figure 4.2.1 shows the three basic features of Korea's CMS structure. First, the CMS's direct holdings are extremely low, less than one percent in 2012. Second, the CMS exercises absolute control by means of holdings of member firms. Third, despite persistent criticism of this disparity between the CMS's cash-flow right and the control right, the CMS structure has remained stable over the last two decades.

The CMS structure allows all the member firms to maintain a long-term perspective without too much focus on short-term profits. This

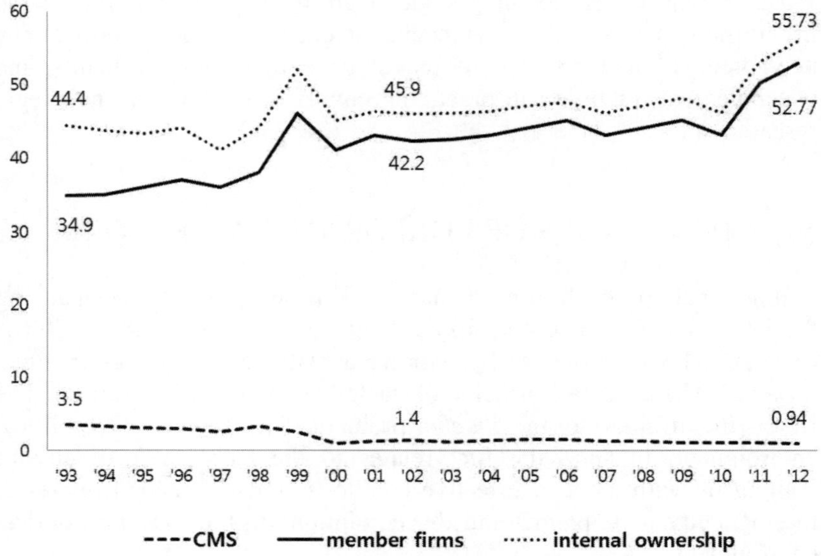

Source: Fair Trade Commission, Press Release, July 2, 2012

Figure 4.2.1 Changes in the size of internal ownership in the top ten chaebol *(unit: %)*

aspect is often touted as a principal advantage of the current *chaebol* structure. On the other hand, the CMS structure is prone to abuse. The most well known example of such abuse is so-called 'tunneling' by the CMS.

In Korea, tunneling is believed to take place on two occasions. First, the CMS engages in tunneling to enable his heirs to accumulate funds for securing control. The CMS has developed a variety of tactics. In the 1990s, a popular tactic was to issue or transfer equity securities to his heirs at low prices. Some CMS were held liable for damages and even went to jail for such tactics. Even Chairman Lee of Samsung narrowly avoided conviction by the 6–5 decision at the Supreme Court a few years ago.

After the danger of issuing equity securities was made clear, the CMS took a more cautious approach. They turned to what Koreans call "concentrated awarding of contracts," a scheme of favoring heirs in awarding contracts. This practice became so widespread that it is difficult to find a *chaebol* that has not engaged in this practice. Although this practice recently gained much notoriety even among the general public, it has not been easy to restrain this practice as a technical matter.

The second instance where a *chaebol* engages in tunneling activities is when it tries to save a distressed member firm. In theory, of course, it is possible for the CMS to let the firm go bankrupt. As a practical matter, however, it has been, and still is, very difficult to cut off such a troubled subsidiary for various reasons: the detrimental effect on the group reputation, sanctions by creditor banks, and dampening employee morale, for example. Even if salvaging the distressed firm can be justified for business reasons, it is very difficult to allocate the financial burden fairly among the member firms. There is a risk that the CMS may be convicted for breach of trust if he is found to have made a wrong decision.[12]

Tunneling can be eliminated if *chaebol* groups are disbanded or intra-group transactions are banned altogether. Neither of the two can be an option at the moment. Korea has not yet found an effective solution for this problem, which does not seem so serious in other developed economies.

(ii) Political Environment

As discussed above, it is technically difficult to get at a set of effective measures for the *chaebol* problem. Even if the legal academy manages to come up with a policy solution, it may be difficult to pursue it depending on the political environment.

The battlefield of corporate governance reform now appears heavily tilted in favor of *chaebol*, which wields influence over major players in Korean society such as politicians, bureaucrats, mainstream media, and academics. On the contrary, only a small number of intellectuals and liberal politicians can be counted as critics of *chaebol*. What can change the balance of power between the two forces is the general public, who feel rather ambivalent about the *chaebol*'s dominance in Korea. Feeling proud of the success of *chaebol* in the global market place, they feel, at the same time, uncomfortable with the abuse of power by the CMS. The mood changes swiftly. Depending on the political mood of the time, a particular reform bill may or may not pass.

---

[12] The risk is not just theoretical, but real. A chairman of a Top 10 business group was convicted for these salvaging transactions and sentenced to four years' imprisonment.

Until the mid-1990s, the general public was not interested in corporate law. The corporate statutes were almost entirely left to the discretion of a small number of scholars. As the statutes became more relevant to corporate actors including the CMSs, room for political intervention also grew. Under these circumstances, two types of risk exist with respect to corporate law reform. The first type of risk is that a desirable bill is blocked by political forces. The second type of risk is that an unreasonable bill is passed due to political forces. There are many instances of the first type of risk, which are relatively well known. The second type of risk is constantly emphasized by the allies of *chaebol*. The second type of risk is also real, and may be quite serious given the difficulty of discovering a set of adequate measures. For the time being, however, the second type of risk is not likely to materialize according to the current political atmosphere.

VI. CONCLUDING REMARKS

Until the 1980s, corporate law in Korea was a rather quiet, and even dull, field of law. With the financial crisis in 1997 as a turning point, corporate law has evolved into an exciting, even creative, field of law. It has been changing from a received system of concepts and doctrines, to a set of solutions designed for problems of the business community. As it gains relevance, however, corporate law has been subject to political pressure. Prior to the financial crisis, corporate law reform had attracted little public attention. A recent corporate law reform bill[13] promoted by the MOJ was discussed in the editorial section of major daily newspapers, and even at the dinner President Park had with business leaders. Political intervention is just a fact of life in a corporate governance reform in developed countries such as the US, Germany, and Japan. As it moves along the road to a developed economy, Korea is becoming similar to other developed countries in this respect as well.

---

[13] I did not participate in the drafting process.

4.3 Judicial innovation in Chinese corporate law

Donald Clarke

I. INTRODUCTION

What does "judicial innovation" mean in the Chinese context? In this chapter, I shall use the term to mean actions by courts to substantially modify substantive or procedural rules (generally set forth in a statute) that would otherwise apply, or to fill a vacuum by providing such substantive and procedural rules where they simply cannot be said to already exist.

It is sometimes said that Chinese courts may not and do not innovate in this sense; that they are required to hew closely to statutory norms in deciding the cases before them. This view, owing more to ideology than to observation, has never really been tenable. First, Chinese courts, like other courts, sometimes simply must fill in gaps because they are required to decide a case one way or the other. At times they have done so quite creatively. Second, the Supreme People's Court (the "SPC"), and to a lesser degree provincial-level courts, have a practice of issuing rules of general application both in the context of particular cases and, more importantly, in the abstract, untethered to any particular case. Whether the SPC and other courts should do this is debated in China;[1] the point here, however, is that they *do* do it. These rules can be public or internal.[2] They can put meat on the bones of existing law, prohibit what

---

1 The literature on this subject is vast. For a recent comprehensive treatment, see Ji Changlong (季长龙), Guifanxing Sifa Jieshi de Fayuan Diwei Yanjiu (规范性司法解释的法源地位研究) [A Study on the Status of Normative Judicial Interpretations as Sources of Law] (unpublished PhD dissertation, People's University of China, 2008).

2 *See* Nicholas Howson, *Corporate Law in the Shanghai People's Courts, 1992–2008: Judicial Autonomy in a Contemporary Authoritarian State*, 5 E. Asia L. Rev. 303, 336–37 (2010).

existing law seems to allow, or allow what existing law does not seem to allow (through silence or explicit prohibition), in addition to simply instructing courts to change course on some issue.[3] As we shall see, such rules can derogate substantially from otherwise applicable rules, and thus in such cases deserve the label of innovation.

In an important 2010 article, Nicholas Howson reported his findings that Shanghai courts engaged in extensive innovation (as I have defined it) in the realm of corporate law prior to 2006, when a new version of the Company Law came into effect, and to a lesser extent after that.[4] They adjudicated claims for which no plausible basis was provided by legislation, administrative rule, or even SPC document, such as breach of fiduciary duty, veil-piercing, derivative suits, promoters' liability, dividend distributions, employee stock ownership holding entities, and the contribution of services as equity.[5] They even approved a single-shareholder company (something not possible under the pre-2006 Company Law) while admitting that it had "some degree of illegality."[6] In short, Howson observed the Shanghai courts, contrary to stereotype, acting

> with creativity and power to affirm equitable procedures and legal claims to serve "justice," stretch the application of law (again to provide "justice"), dismiss form to privilege function, "make law" based upon their autonomous conception of who or what the statutory framework is designed to serve, devise non-statutory legal standards for application of corporate law doctrine, and create remedies out of whole cloth.[7]

While Shanghai may not be representative of what courts around the country actually do, there is no question that courts can innovate if they wish and that they have actually done so, although not necessarily always in plaintiff-friendly ways. In the remainder of this chapter, I shall look at judicial innovations in a few selected areas and offer some concluding thoughts at the end.

---

3 *See id.* at 331.
4 *See id.*
5 *See id.* at 339–45.
6 *Id.* at 364.
7 *Id.* at 349.

II. VEIL-PIERCING

China's first company law – that is, a law covering the organization of business entities with limited liability for investors who might be non-state entities – came into effect in July 1994.[8] That law stipulated limited liability for investors and contained no exceptions; it did not contain a concept of veil-piercing until it was revised in 2005 (effective in 2006). Nevertheless, the same concerns that have moved courts in other jurisdictions to develop a concept of veil-piercing (making investors liable for corporate debts when considerations of fairness would seem to call for it) moved the court system in China as well to develop such a concept.

Quite early in the post-Mao era, despite the absence of a general corporation statute, many entities came into existence bearing the name of "company" and purporting to have limited liability. Some of these entities were formed pursuant to one of two documents issued in 1992 by the State Commission on the Reform of the Economic System that constituted a kind of proto-company law.[9] Others seem to have had no legislative basis at all; they existed because the body forming them had the political clout to get them registered as companies at the local branch of the State Administration of Industry and Commerce.[10] In 1992 alone, before the Company Law existed, 480,000 new companies were registered.[11]

---

[8] Zhonghua Renmin Gongheguo Gongsifa (中华人民共和国公司法) [Company Law of the People's Republic of China] (promulgated by Standing Committee of the Eighth National People's Congress, Dec. 29, 1993, effective Jul. 1, 1994), http://www.pkulaw.cn/fulltext_form.aspx?Gid=7672.

[9] *See* Gufen Youxian Gongsi Guifan Yijian (股份有限公司规范意见) [Opinions on Standards for the Companies Limited by Shares] (promulgated by No. 31 [1992] Order of the State Commission for Restructuring the Economic System (SCRES), May 15, 1992, effective May 15, 1992), http://www.lawinfochina.com/display.aspx?id=6466; Youxian Zeren Gongsi Guifan Yijian (有限责任公司规范意见) [Opinion on Standards for Limited Liability Companies] (promulgated by State Commission on Reform of the Economic System, May 15, 1992, effective May 15, 1992), http://www.lawinfochina.com/display.aspx?id=6462.

[10] *See generally* Donald C. Clarke, *How Do We Know When an Enterprise Exists? Unanswerable Questions and Legal Polycentricity in China*, 19 COL. J. ASIAN L. 50 (2005 [2006]).

[11] *See* Xianchu Zhang, *Piercing the Company Veil and Regulation of Companies in China*, *in* LEGAL DEVELOPMENTS IN CHINA: MARKET ECONOMY 130, 130 (Guiguo Wang & Zhenying Wei eds., 1996).

Many of these companies were undercapitalized; the common term for them was "briefcase company." They might enter into contracts, take an advance payment, and disappear. In a different economy, perhaps, creditors would know how to take action to protect themselves. They could perform due diligence such as credit checks, and insist on personal guarantees from sole shareholders. But these were the early days of economic reform in China, and to many people, the very word "company" signaled something large and solid. Thus, frauds (often perpetrated by governmental entities that established the companies) were widespread, and presented a problem that the courts could not evade.

The problem existed because China had a concept of limited liability before it had a company law. The concept can be found, for example, in the provisions regarding "legal persons" (*faren*) in Chapter 3 of the 1986 General Principles of Civil Law (the "GPCL"). The principle established there (although, surprisingly, not explicitly spelled out) is that creditors of legal persons (of which companies are an example) cannot look beyond the assets of that legal person. To qualify as a legal person, an entity must satisfy certain conditions, including the ability to bear civil liability independently.[12] This condition has never been understood to mean, however, that an entity loses its limited-liability status precisely when it becomes meaningful, *i.e.*, when it cannot pay all its debts. Instead, it must be understood as a kind of capitalization requirement, similar to another provision requiring legal persons to have "the necessary property or funds." Although the GPCL require no specific minimum capitalization amounts, the Company Law does, using the term "registered capital."

Perhaps due to the drafters' inexperience, the GPCL do not specify that an investor or promoter in an indebted entity is liable when the requirements of legal personality are not met. Various misdeeds on the part of the legal person can be visited on the head of the "legal representative," but that is the person running the legal person, not the investor who benefits financially from its misdeeds. Thus, some judicial creativity was necessary.

The early appearance of something akin to veil-piercing appears in case decisions. In 1991, the SPC partially pierced the veil when it held a local government liable (but only to the extent of uncontributed

---

[12] *See* Zhonghua Renmin Gongheguo Minfa Tongze (中华人民共和国民法通则) [General Principles of Civil Law of the People's Republic of China] (promulgated by National People's Congress, Aug. 27, 2009, effective Aug. 27, 2009), Art. 37, http://www.lawinfochina.com/display.aspx?lib=law&id=1165.

registered capital) when the company it established had no capitalization and the local government had transferred assets out of the company just before a judgment in favor of the plaintiff creditor was to be executed.[13] This is not genuine piercing, however – it is merely requiring the investor to fulfill a duty it had already undertaken but not yet performed.

In 1992, the SPC affirmed a lower court decision to order a county government to repay the debts of a company it had established when it was found that the company had no capitalization. Moreover, the county government had collected a debt owed to the company, and company employees came from the county government and returned to it upon dissolution.[14] The factors apparently important to the SPC are similar to the factors used by US courts to justify piercing: inadequate initial capitalization and failure of the investor to treat the company as a separate entity.

In another 1992 case, the SPC found a government entity liable for the debts of a subordinate company where the government entity, a minority shareholder, had failed to contribute any capital and had directly caused the subordinate company to commit the act incurring the liability.[15] This again is not exactly piercing; it can be understood as a finding that the governmental entity was in fact the party that committed the act incurring the liability, so no theory of piercing is necessary.[16]

To be sure, the SPC did not seem to develop a consistently applied doctrine of veil-piercing and there were some steps backward or sideways.[17] Ultimately the SPC came out with a formal pronouncement (the "Reply")[18] in this area in March 1994, before the Company Law had even come into effect. The Reply in effect codified, but did not go beyond, the SPC's pre-1994 jurisprudence in this area. It was a response

---

13 *See* Zhang, *supra* note 11, at 135 (discussing Ping Ding case).

14 *See id.* at 134–35 (discussing Yue Hai Import-Export Company case).

15 *See id.* at 135 (discussing Union of Victory Oil Refinery case).

16 This theory was applied by the Supreme Court of the United States in *United States v. Bestfoods*, 524 U.S. 51 (1998).

17 There is insufficient space here to go into the details. *See generally* Zhang, *supra* note 11, at 135–37.

18 Zuigao Renmin Fayuan Guanyu Qiye Kaiban de Qita Qiye bei Chexiao Huozhe Xieye Hou Minshi Zeren Chengdan Wenti de Pifu (最高人民法院关于企业开办的其他企业被撤销或者歇业后民事责任承担问题的批复) [Supreme People's Court's Response to Questions Regarding Civil Liability After Company Revocation or Liquidation] (promulgated by the Supreme People's Court, Mar. 30, 1994, effective Mar. 30, 1994), http://www.chinabaike.com/law/zhishi/yf/1423239.html.

to a request for instructions from the Guangdong provincial court in a case involving the responsibility of an enterprise for the debts of a dissolved enterprise it had established. In the Reply, the SPC upheld in general the principle of limited liability for investors in enterprises with legal person status on the basis of Article 48 of the GPCL. It also instructed, however, that the parent enterprise could be held liable to creditors for any difference between the enterprise's official registered capital and the amount the parent had actually contributed.[19]

Although this Reply has been characterized by some Chinese commentators[20] as providing for piercing the veil – in Chinese terms, "negating corporate personality" – in fact it is but a small step toward genuine veil-piercing. It gives creditors something they already had a right to expect and makes the parent enterprise liable for an amount it already agreed to pay, but no more. The Reply also states that where an enterprise does not meet the criteria for legal person at all, the body that established it is liable for its debts.[21] This, too, is not quite veil-piercing or the negation of corporate personality. It is denying that corporate personality ever existed. It states that the courts will hold the parent directly liable for the debts because the grounds for not doing so – the existence of a limited-liability entity standing between the parent and the creditors – are not present.

Indeed, that veil-piercing theory is precisely the wrong lens with which to view the Reply is clear from a 2001 SPC Reply[22] on whether

---

19 *See id.* at Para. 1(2).

20 *See*, *e.g.*, Yan Zeping (阎泽平), *Woguo Faren Renge Fouren Zhidu Xianzhuang ji Lifa Gouxiang* (我国法人人格否认制度现状及立法构想) [*Observations and Legislative Ideas Regarding China's Current Corporate Personality Denial Regime*], HEBEI FAXUE (河北法学) [HEBEI LEGAL STUDIES], No. 1, 1999, at 76, 76; Du Bo (杜博), *Gongsi Farenge Fouren Yuanli yu Woguo Sifa Shijian* (公司法人格否认原理与我国司法实践) [*Principles of Corporate Personality Denial and Their Judicial Applications in China*], *in* ZHONGGUO MINSHANGFA SHIWU LUNTAN LUNWENJI (中国民商法实务论坛论文集) [COLLECTED ESSAYS FROM THE CHINA COMMERCIAL AND CIVIL LAW AFFAIRS FORUM] 257, 261 (2001).

21 *See id.* at Para. 1(3).

22 Guanyu Shenli Jundui, Wujing Budui, Zhengfa Jiguan Yijiao, Chexiao he yu Dangzheng Jiguan Tuogou Qiye Xiangguan Jiufen Anjian Ruogan Wenti de Guiding (最高人民法院关于审理军队、武警部队、政法机关移交、撤销企业和与党政机关脱钩企业相关纠纷案件若干问题的规定) [Regulations on Several Issues of Adjudicating Disputes Involving the Enterprises Handed Over or Closed Down by the People's Liberation Army, the Armed Police Force, and the Political-Legal Organs and the Enterprises Separated from the Party and Government Organs] (promulgated by the Supreme People's

a parent has *unlimited* liability for debts in cases of inadequate or no capitalization. In other words, if the difference between paid-in capital and registered capital is X, and there are several creditors whose total claims are more than X, is the parent obliged to pay X to each creditor in each lawsuit, or is it discharged from further obligations once it has paid X? Some cases had apparently opted for the former rule;[23] the 2001 Reply settled the question in favor of the latter.[24] Thus, nothing like piercing is going on here. It is simply a question of remedying an initial failure to pay in promised capital.[25]

In short, much of what we see can be thought of as courts simply enforcing the terms of a statute; we see only cautious, small steps beyond the letter of the statute. Although innovation is usually thought of as something that favors plaintiffs as courts create new causes of actions and new remedies, here its effect is more ambiguous. The courts are policing contributions to registered capital and illegitimate transfers of assets out of the reach of creditors, but are unwilling to go all the way to robust veil-piercing. This approach by courts provides support for the view of courts as primarily enforcers of public law norms and only secondarily concerned with adjusting private rights. The capitalization requirement is one imposed by state law. To be sure, it is imposed in part in a belief that large capitalization requirements protect creditors. But I believe the capitalization requirements of the Chinese Company

Court, Mar. 20, 2001, effective Mar. 23, 2001), http://china.findlaw.cn/fagui/p_1/38243.html.

[23] *See* Song Xiaoming, Zhang Yongjian & Liu Min, *Zuigao Renmin Fayuan Guanyu Shiyong Zhonghua Renmin Gongheguo Gongsifa Ruogan Wenti de Guiding (Er) de Lijie yu Shiyong* (*最高人民法院关于使用中華人民共和國公司法若干問題的規定（二）的理解与适用*) [*Interpretations and Application of the Regulations on Several Issues Regarding the Application of the PRC Company Law (II)*] in MINSHANGSHI SHENPAN ZHIDAO [GUIDE ON CIVIL AND COMMERCIAL TRIAL] 26, 37 (Xi Xiaoming ed. 2008, Issue 2), *cited in* Xi Chao, *Piercing the Corporate Veil in China: How Did We Get There?*, 5 J. BUS. L. 413, 416, n. 22 (2011).

[24] *See* 2001 Reply, *supra* note 22, Art. 10.

[25] Similarly cautious is a Shanghai Higher-Level People's Court instruction on the same subject. *See* Shanghai Shi Gaoji Renmin Fayuan Guanyu Shenli Sheji Gongsi Susong Anjian Ruogan Wenti de Chuli Yijian (上海市高级人民法院关于审理涉及公司诉讼案件若干问题的处理意见) [Opinion of the Shanghai Superior People's Court on Several Questions Regarding Corporate Litigation Cases] (promulgated by the Shanghai Superior People's Court, Jun. 12, 2003, effective Jun. 12, 2003), http://www.sh148.org/law04/law04/10161.htm. Like the SPC documents, this document sets forth detailed rules that cannot be derived from any statutory language.

Law – requirements that are completely disproportionate to those of other countries, whether developed or not[26] – stem also from a purely public-law policy of putting barriers in the way of corporate formation, which in turn stems from a belief that corporations are things to be carefully watched and regulated, not necessarily things to be encouraged with the most convenient possible legal regime. And even if we return to the first reason – the desire to protect creditors – the fact is that courts often did not protect creditors once the state-required capitalization had been paid.

III. MISLEADING DISCLOSURES IN SECURITIES LAW

Another example of defendant-friendly judicial innovation can be found in Chinese securities law. Here, the Chinese court system has cut back on what would seem to be rights unambiguously granted under statute.

In its original 1998 version, as well as following a major revision effective in 2005, China's Securities Law gives persons the right to sue for a number of violations, including insider trading,[27] market manipulation,[28] and misleading disclosures.[29] Yet lawsuits on these claims have been few. It is implausible to suppose that this is because of the lack of violations in the Wild West of China's stock markets. A more likely explanation is judicial innovation in favor of defendants.

The first lawsuit on any of those claims appears to have occurred in 1996 – before a Securities Law even existed – in the case of *Liu Zhongmin vs. Bohai Group*.[30] In that case, the plaintiff bought shares

---

26 For example, the Company Law at present requires a minimum capitalization of 5 million *yuan* for stock companies. The minimum capitalization required for companies of this kind in the OECD countries is far less: about $42,000 in Germany, and in Delaware, of course, nothing at all.

27 *See* Zhonghua Renmin Gongheguo Zhengquanfa (中华人民共和国证券法) [Securities Law of the People's Republic of China] (promulgated by Standing Committee of the National People's Congress, Jun. 29, 2013, effective Jan. 1, 2006), Art. 73, http://www.lawinfochina.com/display.aspx?id=14878. The corresponding section of the previous Securities Law, promulgated in 1998, is Article 67.

28 *See id.* at Art. 77 (Art. 71 of 1998 Securities Law).

29 *See id.* at Art. 69 (Art. 63 of 1998 Securities Law).

30 The case is discussed in Hui Huang, *Private Enforcement of Securities Law in China: A Ten-Year Retrospective and Empirical Assessment,* 61 AM. J. COMP. L. 757, 760 (2013). *See also* Hui Huang, *Zhongguo Zhengquan Minshi*

following the company's issuance of a misleading semi-annual financial report and sold them after they dropped following exposure of the misleading information. He lost on the grounds of failure to prove a causal link between his loss and the defendant's misrepresentation.

Very little subsequently happened in the realm of shareholder litigation until 2001, when a spate of corporate scandals led to a number of civil suits seeking compensation for Securities Law violations. The prospect of legal actions with tens of millions of potential plaintiffs seems to have unnerved the authorities, and the Supreme People's Court responded between 2001 and 2003 with a set of three circulars that imposed severe limits on private securities litigation.

The first circular, in 2001, was an instruction to China's courts to simply stop accepting all civil cases seeking compensation for misconduct in securities markets.[31] The stated rationale was that the Securities Law provided inadequate guidance on important elements of securities litigation and that courts should wait until the Supreme People's Court issued such guidance. As this instruction simply nullified rights to compensation specifically granted by the Securities Law, the SPC came under a great deal of criticism, and in response it issued a second circular in early 2002.[32] This circular purported to lift the restriction on cases of misleading disclosure, but continued the ban on lawsuits sounding in market manipulation or insider trading. According to one scholar, while some courts began accepting cases, all were stayed pending the issuance of further instructions from the SPC.[33]

Suopei Diyian: Liu Zhongmin Su Bohai Jituan An (中国证券民事索赔第一案刘中民诉渤海集团案) [*The First Case in Chinese Securities Civil Actions: Liu Zhongmin v. Bohai Group*], XINLANG CAIJING (新浪财经) [SINA FINANCE], Mar. 9, 2011, http://finance.sina.com.cn/stock/t/20110309/19219500855.shtml.

31 *See* Zuigao Renmin Fayuan Guanyu She Zhengquan Minshi Peichang Anjian Zhan Buyu Shouli de Tongzhi (最高人民法院关于涉证券民事赔偿案件暂不予受理的通知) [Supreme People's Court Notice on Temporarily Not Accepting Securities Cases Involving Civil Suits for Damages] (promulgated by the Supreme People's Court, Sep. 21, 2001, effective Sep. 21, 2001), www.law-lib.com/law/law_view.asp?id=16373.

32 *See* Zuigao Renmin Fayuan Guanyu Shouli Zhengquan Shichang Yin Xujia Chenshu Yinfa de Minshi Jiufen Anjian Youguan Wenti de Tongzhi (最高人民法院关于受理证券市场因虚假陈述引发的民事侵权纠纷案件的通知) [Notice on Issues Relating to the Acceptance of Civil Cases in Tort Arising out of False Representations in Securities Markets] (promulgated by the Supreme People's Court, Jan. 15, 2002, effective Jan. 15, 2002), www.law-lib.com/law/law_view.asp?id=16956.

33 *See* Huang, *supra* note 30, at 760–61.

Those further instructions finally came in 2003 in the form of a third circular.[34] That circular set forth detailed provisions on the hearing of misrepresentation suits, but did not lift the ban on suits for market manipulation or insider trading. A judicial document issued to courts internally some time after a nationwide meeting on civil adjudication in May 2007 has apparently now broadened the scope of permissible claims to include market manipulation and insider trading, but other procedural hurdles established by the earlier circulars still apply.[35]

The chief impediment to private securities litigation by the set of SPC circulars and instructions is the imposition of what is in effect a requirement that plaintiffs get a key to the courthouse from a state agency. The plaintiff must be able to point to an official punishment, criminal or administrative, imposed by the China Securities Regulatory Commission or some other state agency. Even those who support this prerequisite as a matter of policy admit that it has no basis in statutory law and was in effect simply made up by the SPC.[36] No clearer

---

34 *See* Zuigao Renmin Fayuan Guanyu Shenli Zhengquan Shichang Yinxujia Chenshu Yinfa de Minshi Peichang Anjian de Ruogan Guiding (最高人民法院关于审理证券市场因虚假陈述引发的民事赔偿案件的 若干規定) [Several Provisions on the Adjudication of Civil Suits for Damages Arising out of False Representations in Securities Markets] (promulgated by the Supreme People's Court, Jan. 9,2003, effective Jan. 9, 2003), www.law-lib.com/law/law_view.asp?id=42438.

35 *See* Luo Peixin (罗培新), *Qianzhi Chengxu Quliu Kunjing* (*前置程序去留困境*) [*Difficulties over Whether to Eliminate or Keep the Precondition Procedure*], CAIJING [*Finance*], No. 19, 2007, at 28; Wu Xiaofeng (吴晓锋), *Neimu Jiaoyi, Caozong Shichang Minshi Peichang Anjian Huzhiyuchu* (*内幕交易 操纵市场民事赔偿案件呼之欲出*) [*Civil Compensation Cases for Insider Trading and Market Manipulation About to Appear*], RENMIN WANG (人民網) [PEOPLE'S NET], Nov. 18, 2007, http://npc.people.com.cn/GB/6543957.html.

36 *See* Luo Peixin (罗培新), *Zhengquan Minshi Peichang: Zheng Jian Hui bu Cha, Fayuan bu Shen?* (**证券民事赔偿：证监会不查，法院不审？**) [*Civil Lawsuits for Damages in Securities Cases: Will Courts Not Try the Case if the Securities Regulatory Commission Doesn't Investigate?*], CAIJING (财经) [FINANCE AND ECONOMICS], Sep. 11, 2007, http://www.caijing.com.cn/2007-09-11/100029938.html. For other criticism the SPC for simply making up this barrier without any statutory foundation, see, *inter alia*, Lu Li, *Zhengquan Minshi Peichang Ruogan Wenti Tantao – Jianping Zuigao Renmin Fayuan Guanyu Shenli Zhengquan Minshi Peichangan de Ruogan Guiding* (*证券民事赔偿若干问题探讨——兼评最高人民法院关于审理证券民事赔偿案的若干规定*) [*Discussion of Several Problems Regarding Securities Civil Compensation – Comments on Several Supreme People's Court Regulations on Hearing Securities Civil Compensation*], JINRONG YANJIU (金融研究) [JOURNAL OF FINANCIAL RESEARCH], No. 3, 2004, at 22.

refutation can be found of the oft-repeated bromide that Chinese courts may not, and in fact do not, go beyond narrowly confined interpretation of law all the way to making law.

IV. DERIVATIVE ACTIONS

Derivative actions show Chinese courts unambiguously innovating in favor of plaintiffs. Since 2006, derivative actions have been statutorily available under China's Company Law.[37] But before then, courts had already allowed such actions many times.

The first known case is the 1994 Zhangjiagang Fiber Company case.[38] In that case, the SPC stated that it would be permissible in principle for the Chinese investor in a Chinese-foreign equity joint venture (the "JV") to represent the JV in suing a vendor to the JV (and a related party to the foreign investor in the JV).[39] In other lawsuits following the Zhangjiagang Fiber Company case, courts accepted derivative actions several times, while occasionally rejecting them.[40]

The judiciary was also busy in its quasi-legislative capacity.[41] In December 2002, a senior Supreme People's Court judge stated publicly

---

[37] *See* Company Law, *supra* note 8, at Art. 152.

[38] Guanyu Zhongwai Hezi Jingying Qiye Duiwai Fasheng Jingji Hetong Jiufen, Kongzhi Heying Qiye de Waifang yu Maifang You Lihai Guanxi, Heying Qiye de Zhongfang Ying Yi Shei de Mingyi Xiang Renmin Fayuan Qisu Wenti de Fuhan (最高人民法院关于中外合资经营企业对外发生经济合同纠纷,控制合营企业的外方与卖方有利害关系,合营企业的中方应以谁的名义向人民法院起诉问题的复函) [Reply Letter on the Issue of in Whose Name the Chinese Party to a Chinese-Foreign Equity Joint Venture Should Bring Suit When the Joint Venture Has an Economic Contract Dispute with an External Party and the Foreign Party Controlling the Joint Venture Has a Relationship of Interest with the Seller] (promulgated by the Supreme People's Court, Nov. 4, 1994, effective Nov. 4, 1994), http://www.people.com.cn/zixun/flfgk/item/dwjjf/falv/9/9-1-4-01.html [hereinafter *SPC Reply on Derivative Suits*].

[39] The case is discussed in Donald C. Clarke, *Law Without Order in Chinese Corporate Governance Institutions*, 30 NW. J. INT'L L. & BUS. 131, 192–93 (2010).

[40] *See id.* at 193–95; Donald C. Clarke & Nicholas Howson, *Derivative Actions in the People's Republic of China*, *in* THE DERIVATIVE ACTION IN ASIA: A COMPARATIVE AND FUNCTIONAL APPROACH 243 (Dan W. Puchiak, Harald Baum & Michael Ewing-Chow eds. 2012).

[41] This paragraph draws substantially on Clarke & Howson, *supra* note 40, at 261–63.

that courts should accept derivative suits.[42] Although a lower court later called such remarks "for reference" only and refused to consider them a basis for accepting a derivative suit,[43] there is little doubt that the court system, and not just individual courts, was institutionally taking note of the problem. From late 2002 to 2004, for example, provincial-level courts in Zhejiang, Jiangsu, Shanghai, and Beijing all issued documents permitting derivative suits in courts under their jurisdiction, and describing their implementation in great detail.[44] This level of detail strongly suggests that local-level courts were in fact accepting and adjudicating derivative lawsuits well before 2006.

---

[42] *See Gao Fayuan Fuyuanzhang Li Guoguang Biaoshi: Xiaogudong Gao Dagudong Fayuan Ying Shouli* (高法院副院长李国光表示：小股东告大股东法院应受理) [*Supreme People's Court Vice President Li Guoguang Indicates That Courts Should Accept Suits by Small Shareholders Against Large Shareholders*], BEIJING YULE XINBAO (北京娛樂新報) [BEIJING RECREATION NEWS], Dec. 12, 2002, http://news.sohu.com/58/64/news204906458.shtml.

[43] *See Shouli Gudong Daibiao Susong Wei Bei Shouli* (首例股東代表訴訟未被受理) [*First Shareholder Representative Suit Is Not Accepted*], SHANGHAI ZHENGQUAN BAO (上海證券報) [SHANGHAI SECURITIES NEWS], Apr. 22, 2003, http://101.stock888.net/030422/100,101,78015,00.shtml; *see also* Qian Weiqing (钱卫清), *Gongsi Susong: Gongsi Sifa Jiuji Fangshi Xin Lun (6)* (公司诉讼——公司司法救济方式新论 (6)) [*Corporate Litigation: A New Discussion of Methods of Judicial Remedies for Companies (6)*], CHINALAWINFO.COM, May 23, 2003, http://article.chinalawinfo.com/article/user/article_display.asp?ArticleID=25304.

[44] *See* Z. Zhang, *Making Shareholder Derivative Actions Happen in China: How Should Lawsuits Be Funded?,* 38 H.K. L.J. 520, 523 n. 28 (2008) (citing Guanyu Gongsifa Shiyong Ruogan Yinan Wenti de Lijie (关於公司法使用若干疑难问题的理解) [Understandings on Several Difficult Issues Regarding the Application of Company Law] (promulgated by Zhejiang Higher-Level People's Court, No. 2 Civil Division, Dec. 2002), *available at* http://bit.ly/1eBZX0P); *Guanyu Shenli Sheji Gongsi Susong Anjian Ruogan Wenti de Chuli Yijian (Yi)* (关於审理涉及公司诉讼案件若干问题的处理意见) [Opinions on Adjudicating Cases Regarding Corporate Litigation (No. 1)] (promulgated by Shanghai Higher-Level People's Court, No. 2 Civil Division, June 12, 2003), *in* GONGSIFA YINAN WENTI JIEXI (DI SAN BAN) (公司法疑难问题解析（第3版）) [COMPANY LAW ISSUES: PROBLEMS AND ANALYSIS (3RD EDITION)] 231 (Shanghai Higher-Level People's Court ed. 2006), *available at* http://bit.ly/1oz5oXe; Guanyu Shenli Gongsi Jiufen Anjian Ruogan Wenti de Zhidao Yijian (Shixing) (关於审理公司纠纷案件若干问题的指导意见 (施行)) [Guiding Opinions on Several Issues on Adjudicating Corporate Dispute Cases (Trial Implementation)] (promulgated by Beijing Higher-Level People's Court, Feb. 9, 2004), *in* GONGSIFA YINAN WENTI JIEXI (DI SAN BAN) (公司法疑难问题解析 (第3版)) [COMPANY LAW ISSUES: PROBLEMS AND ANALYSIS (3RD EDITION)] 236 (Shanghai Higher-Level People's Court ed. 2006), *available at* http://bit.ly/1f5oYpS.

In addition to approving the 1994 Zhangjiagang Fiber Company case, the SPC in 2003 distributed for comment a draft regulation that substantially re-wrote the Company Law and provided, among other things, for a derivative suit mechanism.[45]

V. CONCLUSION

This brief canvassing of judicial innovation in corporate law has one unsurprising result and one intriguing result. The unsurprising result is that Chinese courts do innovate. The result is unsurprising because courts have to resolve the disputes that come before them.[46] The applicable law will not always be clear. In that case, courts are left with no choice but to innovate. We even see courts innovating to reach a result unambiguously contrary to that called for by existing law.[47] The interesting questions then are: how openly and boldly do they do so? What principles, if any, guide their innovation?

The intriguing result is that innovation seems to go in both directions: it can be both defendant-friendly and plaintiff-friendly. Judicial innovation is usually thought of as something that expands the realm of causes of action, and is therefore plaintiff-friendly. But Chinese courts have innovated in some decidedly plaintiff-unfriendly ways,

---

45 *See* Guanyu Shenli Gongsi Jiufen Anjian Ruogan Wenti de Guiding (Yi) (Zhengqiu Yijian Gao) (关于审理公司纠纷案件若干问题的规定 (一) (征求意见稿)) [Regulation Regarding Several Problems on Hearing Company Dispute Cases (First) (Comment Draft)] (promulgated by the Supreme People's Court, Nov. 4, 2003, effective Nov. 4, 2003), http://www.chinacourt.org/public/detail.php?id=88551. The draft regulation never made it to the stage of formal issuance, and was made moot by the 2006 Company Law.

46 As we can see in the area of misleading disclosures, Chinese courts sometimes have the option of "resolving" a dispute by simply refusing to hear it, which is in effect a ruling in favor of the defendant. Yet those cases, at least sometimes, rise to a level of visibility where they can be studied. At other times, of course, they will remain invisible.

47 In 2004, for example, the Guangxi provincial-level court prohibited courts under it from taking cases in a number of sensitive categories. This door-barring was completely without statutory basis. *See Guangxi bu Shouli 13 Lei Ruoshi Qunti An; Sheng Gao Yuan Cheng You Guoqing Jueding* (*广西不受理13类弱势群体案 省高院称由国情决定*) [*Guangxi Refuses to Accept 13 Categories of Cases Relating to Disadvantaged People, High Court Asserts It Is Decided by the Situation of the Country*], ZHONGGUO QINGNIAN BAO (中国青年报) [CHINA YOUTH DAILY), Aug. 24, 2004, *available at* http://news.qq.com/a/20040824/000070.htm.

especially in the area of securities litigation. At the same time, they have been perhaps surprisingly generous to plaintiffs suing derivatively and for breaches of fiduciary duty, although of course we have no way of knowing how many such cases were rejected by courts before they ever rose to the level of visibility.

How can these different approaches be reconciled? I can only suggest some tentative hypotheses here as the subject of future research. First, the courts' well-known conservatism and aversion to anything that could get out of control might explain defendant-friendly innovation in securities litigation without corresponding defendant-friendly innovation elsewhere. Second, we might expect to see more innovation when it is consistent with a state regulatory agenda and less when it is purely in the service of protecting plaintiffs' rights. This might explain the stunted innovation we see in the realm of veil-piercing. Third, when the parties seem evenly matched, courts may often show themselves quite willing, contrary to stereotype, to do whatever is necessary to achieve substantial justice. That is what we seem to see in the derivative suit cases.

A further question for research is the relationship between formal innovation in the form of normative documents issued by the Supreme People's Court and innovation in the everyday adjudicatory work of lower courts. It might be thought that the latter constituted the raw material, or at least the inspiration, for the former, but in some cases formal SPC interpretations follow so closely on the heels of promulgated legislation that they could not have been based on judicial practice and experience.[48]

[48] *See* Chen Su (陈甦), *Sifa Jieshi de Jiangou Linian Fenxi* (司法解释的建构理念分析) [*An Analysis of the Structural Concept of Judicial Interpretations*], FAXUE YANJIU (法学研究) [STUDIES IN LAW], No. 2, 2012, at 3.

4.4 The influence of US and Japanese laws upon Indonesian law

Kurnia Toha

I. INTRODUCTION

Long before colonialists arrived in Indonesia, villages throughout the archipelago applied their own norms and rules. Communities in a range of regions coexisted peacefully based on values existing in those respective communities. These rules were unwritten and uncodified.[1]

After colonialism came to Indonesia, different rules of law were implemented in different classes of communities. For Europeans, European law was implemented, while for Indonesians, including foreign easterners – those of Chinese, Arab, or Indian descent – customary laws were implemented, except if they voluntarily submitted themselves to the Western legal system. In addition, there was Islam's Sharia law, applicable to Muslim/Islamic Indonesian people, in particular pertaining to marital and inheritance law.[2]

Subsequent to independence, the Indonesian elite aspired to reform the laws applicable in Indonesia in order for them to become modern law.[3] Legal development from 1945 during the Sukarno period and up to 1966 had not seen much transformation as independence was followed by a period of consolidation and more focus was placed on development in the political field. After the rule of President Suharto, which began in 1967 and continued until 1998, the focus was on economic development. During this period of economic development, Indonesia operated an open-door policy on foreign investment and

---

1 Sudargo Gautama, *Contract Law*, *in* CURRENT DEVELOPMENT OF LAWS IN INDONESIA 33 (1999).

2 MAHADI, S.H., BRIEF DESCRIPTION OF THE CUSTOMARY LAW SINCE RR YEAR 1854 2 (3rd ed., 2003).

3 DANIEL S. LEV, LAW AND POLITICS IN INDONESIA, THE SUSTAINABILITY AND TRANSFORMATION 7 (1990).

international cooperation. In order to encourage rapid economic development and foreign investment, it was necessary to reform laws so as to conform with international economic policy. Erman Rajagukguk has stated that economic globalization would have an enormous impact in the field of law, namely that globalization of law would take place. Therefore, it would become necessary to harmonize the laws of states through standardization in reference to international agreements or by following the model of industrial countries.[4] Furthermore, Hikmahanto Juwana said that law amendment in Indonesia should be undertaken: first, within the framework of reforming outdated laws. As the law had been presented during the Dutch colonial era, as a consequence of the European class and those who had already submitted to Dutch law, the implementation of Western civil law based on the principle of concordance was mostly the same as the law in the Netherlands. Subsequent to independence, by the transitional provisions of the 1945 Constitution, those laws belonging to Dutch heritage, which were initially only for Europeans and the European equivalents, had remained in force, including for those indigenous Indonesian people awaiting the replacement of those laws by new laws. Laws of Dutch heritage, largely made in the 19th or in the early 20th century, were developed under colonial conditions, and therefore required reform in accordance with the advancement of the state and the nature of independence. Besides those laws of Dutch heritage, following its independence the Indonesian government also enacted new laws and regulations, some of which may also require amendment and renewal due to the passage of time, development, and scientific advancement. In my opinion, the reformation of these outdated laws, essentially laws of Dutch heritage, ought also to be encouraged because of the desire for liberation from the influence of the colonial period, as well as from the influence of the supremacy of law. One monumental instance of the effort made to reform colonial law into national law, based on existing customary law and getting to the root values that existed in Indonesian communities, was the birth of Act No. 5 of 1960, concerning Basic Regulations on Agrarian Principles. With the enactment of Act No. 5 of 1960, the agrarian regulations set forth in Book II of the Civil Code were repealed and declared invalid. Another example is Act No. 1 of 1995, on the issue of the limited liability company,

---

[4] Erman Rajagukguk, *Indonesian Development under Economic Globalization: The Reform of Investment Law*, *in* Koesnadi Hardjasoemantri and Naoyuki Sakumoto ed., CURRENT DEVELOPMENT OF LAWS IN INDONESIA 66–67 (1999).

which officially revoked an existing regulation of the limited liability company contained in the Commercial Code of the Dutch colonization legacy. Act No. 1 of 1995 contains principles for companies, and these principles are frequently adopted by developed countries, including companies in the United States.

The second reason for the amendment of laws and regulations should be in the framework of the implementation of international agreements. The amendment of laws in Indonesia is also done to implement international agreements, which have been consented to and ratified by Indonesia.[5] Various laws and regulations were amended to adjust to international agreements, among others were laws related to Intellectual Property Rights, namely Act No. 6 of 1982 concerning Copyrights, which revoked the Copyrights Laws of the Dutch Colonial Government of 1912. This Copyright Act was subsequently amended by Act No. 7 of 1987 and re-amended by Act No. 12 of 1997. Another regulation that was necessary to adjust to international agreements is Act No. 6 of 1999 on Patent. This Act repealed the patent law of the Dutch colonial government of 1912. Act No. 6 of 1989 was amended by Act No. 13 of 1997 on the Amendment of Act No. 6 of 1989, concerning Patent. Later, Act No. 21 of 1961 concerning Company Trademark and Trade rescinded the Trademark Law, the heritage of the Dutch colonial government of 1912, which was then amended by Act No. 19 of 1992 and re-amended by Act No. 14 of 1997.[6] Many of these laws were amended again after the economic crises in 1998.

The third reason, to enhance foreign investment,[7] was that when Suharto became president, economic development became the first priority. With the limitation in domestic investment, consequently, economic development was expected to be supported by the in-flow of foreign investment. In order to attract foreign investors to invest in Indonesia, it required economic stability, security, and needed to be supported by the laws that could protect the interests of such foreign investment. Therefore, many types of regulations in the economic sector were issued, such as Act No. 14 of 1967 on Banking, Act No. 1 of 1967 on Foreign Investment, and Act No. 11 of 1967 on Mining. Subsequently, these laws and other regulations were amended several

---

[5] Hikmahanto Juwana, *A Survey on the Influence of International Economic Policy on Indonesian Laws: Implementation and Problems*, *in* Koesnadi Hardjasoemantri and Naoyuki Sakumoto ed., CURRENT DEVELOPMENT OF LAWS IN INDONESIA 212 (1999).

[6] *Id.* at 212.

[7] *Id.* at 214.

times. After the economic crisis of 1998, they were amended again to adjust to the need for development.

The fourth reason for making amendments to the regulations is for the purpose of bringing them in line with international issues.[8] As a member state of the United Nations and part of the international community, Indonesia cannot avoid international issues such as issues concerning the protection of human rights of the indigenous people and the environment. As a result, Act No. 4 of 1982 was issued on the Environment, which was amended by Act No. 23 of 1997. Provisions on the Recognition for the Rights of Indigenous People are stipulated in Act No. 41 of 1999 and in the Ministerial Regulation of the State Minister of Agrarian/Head of National Land Agency Republic of Indonesia No. 5 of 1999.

Finally, the last reason why amendments to the laws and regulations should be issued is the fulfillment of the needs of the nation of Indonesia, which is becoming an industrialized country.[9] As a state that is actively developing in all spheres of life, it needs to be supported by laws and regulations required of an industrial state; i.e., Act No. 5 of 1999 on the Prohibition of Monopolistic Practices and Unfair Business Competition. The substance of this Act is nearly similar to the comparable Laws among industrialized countries, as well as the Law on Intellectual Property Rights, Labor Law, Consumer Protection Law, Capital Market Law, the laws governing privatization, the laws governing Money Laundering, etc.

Encouragement for the law reforms has been vigorously voiced by academics and non-governmental organizations, especially in supporting the development of the protection of human rights, the protection of people's rights such as the rights of indigenous people, gender equality, consumer protection, indigent rights protection, corruption eradication, and bureaucratic reform. In support of the development, including the development and reformation of the laws as well as the regulations, Indonesia ought to cooperate and receive assistance from international agencies such as the World Bank, Asian Development, IMF, and aid from developed countries, such as the US and Japan.

As a result of this international cooperation, agencies influencing each other cannot be avoided, and in the field of law as well. In

---

[8] *Id.* at 214–15.

[9] Hikmahanto Juwana, *A Survey on the Influence of International Economic Policy on Indonesian Laws: Implementation and Problems*, *in* Koesnadi Hardjasoemantri and Naoyuki Sakumoto ed., CURRENT DEVELOPMENT OF LAWS IN INDONESIA 208 (1999).

the framework of the law development mentioned there are several opinions regarding the transformation of law in Indonesia. Firstly, there are schools of law whose opinion was that the development of Indonesian law should be based on original Indonesian law, by promoting customary laws into the national law. The second opinion is that the development of Indonesian law should be come about by way of developing a colonial law that has been reviewed, based on the principles contained in the Five Principles (*Pancasila*). The third opinion needs a limited codification and unification. Related to the field of culture and religion, as far as possible, it should be unchanged or remain, while the fields related to economy, such as contracts, business entities, trade, banking, taxation, capital market, intellectual property rights and finance, can be set forth in the legislation.[10]

In order to obtain a more comprehensive portrait regarding the reformation process of law in Indonesia, further clarity in regard to the history of Indonesian law, and how the American and the Japanese laws influenced the development of Indonesian law, needs to be explored.

II. THE HISTORY OF INDONESIAN LAW UNTIL INDEPENDENCE

Prior to the Dutch entering Indonesia in the 1500s, the Indonesian people applied customary law. Customary law was not written in the sense of the written form of regulations and they were different from one area to another.[11] Although the customary laws were divergent from one to the other, it did not mean there were no similarities between various areas of customary laws. The differences and similarities in customary laws established a legal system that is different from Western law.[12] Further, Van Vollenhoven stated that there actually were similarities where such customary laws could be passed, and the differences were actually merely regarding things that were not

---

[10] SOETANDYO WIGNJOSOEBROTO, FROM COLONIAL LAW TO NATIONAL LAW 234–38 (1994).

[11] VAN VOLLENHOVEN, THE FINDING OF CUSTOMARY LAW, Leiden, 1928, translated by KITLV and Djambatan, 1981, at 3.

[12] Sudargo Gautama, *Contract Law*, *in* Koesnadi Hardjasoemantri and Naoyuki Sakumoto eds., CURRENT DEVELOPMENT OF LAWS IN INDONESIA 33 (1999). *See also* R. VAN DIJK, INTRODUCTORY TO INDONESIAN CUSTOMARY LAW 8 (1982).

important.[13] Furthermore, Van Vollehhoven, who was regarded as the Father of Customary Law, divided the regions of Indonesia into 17 territories of customary law. There are several characteristics in customary laws, namely that customary laws retain their traditional nature. Customary laws are living norms and adopted by traditional communities in villages, which are maintained and inherited for generations. The second characteristic is that customary laws can be evolving, due to the influence of life and the change in life that always comes about. Customary law is the living law, hence customary law is changing in accordance with the development of such communities, respectively. The last characteristic is that customary laws have adaptability since they are not written and not codified. Therefore, given that customary laws are inherited from generation to generation and decided by meetings of the traditional elders, customary laws are very flexible in order to adapt to the advancement and needs of their communities.[14]

After the Dutch entered the country, under Article 75 of Regering Reglement (the Dutch Constitution), different laws were implemented between community classes in Indonesia. European law was applied to the European class, whereas religious law, Indonesian class institutions, customs or customary laws were applied to classes of Indonesian people, including foreign easterners (of Chinese, Arab, or Indian descent). Communities of those of Indonesian, Chinese, Arab, or Indian descent could have the law applicable to Europeans applied to them if they voluntarily submitted to European civil law.[15] In addition to differences in applicable laws, there were also different judiciaries. There were judiciaries for the European class and indigenous and village judiciaries for small alliances like a village or neighborhood.[16]

During the Japanese period of occupation from 1942 to 1945, there was not much change in the legal field. The Japanese government removed the multiple judiciaries, so there was simply a single judiciary for all community classes in Indonesia. However, many differences in civil law remained: there was Western civil law, customary civil law, and Islamic/Sharia civil law.[17]

---

13 Van Vollenhoven, *supra* note 11, at 14.

14 R. VAN DIJK, INTRODUCTORY TO INDONESIAN CUSTOMARY LAW 10 (1982).

15 MAHADI, SH. BRIEF EXPLANATION ON THE CUSTOMARY LAW SINCE RR YEAR OF 1854 2 (3rd ed., 2003).

16 *Id.* at 29.

17 DANIEL S. LEV, LAW AND POLITICS IN INDONESIA, A SUSTAINABILITY AND TRANSFORMATION 2 (1990).

Even before Indonesian independence many nationalist elites defined the future of Indonesia, which was marked by rapid economic and social progress. Similarly, with those applicable laws, the customary law as viewed by leaders deemed it inadequate and due for renewal, heading for a new and modern law.[18] Daniel S. Lev stated that the main activator for the growth of a new law in Indonesia was social and economic modernization. In addition there were also other important reasons, which included the willpower of elite groups in Indonesia to insure that prevailing Indonesian law could be acceptable internationally.[19] This is in line with the opinion of Professor Sudargo Gautama, who said that customary law has the main objective of meeting the needs of closed communities, rural communities, which have not yet engaged in world trading activities. He stated further that customary law in its original form is not suitable for global trading.[20] In general, this opinion is true, and thus in the case of applying customary law to modern and international economic activities, it naturally requires adjustments.

Subsequent to independence in 1945, there was a very strong desire to change the legacy of Dutch colonial law into national law. Even though the will to replace colonial law with one appropriate to Indonesia was strong, in the first decade after independence no significant law reforms were implemented, partly because development under President Sukarno and during the consolidation period was marked by political conflicts as well as government succession at that time.[21] For example, in 1960 Act No. 5 of 1960 on Basic Regulations of Agrarian Principles was created, which repealed the Civil Code Book II on Material Objects. This Act is considered compliant with the living values of Indonesian communities and applied to all classes of citizens in Indonesia, putting an end to the pluralism of laws that regulated agrarian laws applied to classes of citizens in Indonesia. This agrarian law remained valid until recently and was based on values of traditional laws and was pro-indigent.[22]

Although there was a yearning for change in applicable laws, significant law transformation in Indonesia only came about when Suharto became president in 1966. In contrast to President Sukarno, who emphasized political development, Suharto was more focused

---

18 *Id.* at 7.

19 *Id.* at 7.

20 Sudargo Gautama, *supra* note 1, at 37.

21 ZULKARNAIN DJAMIN, ECONOMIC DEVELOPMENT IN INDONESIA, SINCE THE FIRST *REPELITA* (5-Year Development Plan) 1 (2nd ed., 1993).

22 Daniel S. Lev., *supra* note 17, at 87.

on economic development. Concerning this economic development, with domestic sources of capital limited, as a consequence economic development was based on international cooperation, foreign loans,[23] and foreign investment. Because of economic development and the need to attract foreign investment, it was necessary to make changes or enact laws that could ensure the realization of foreign investment. Thus, there were various laws promulgated relating to economic activities such as the Law on Foreign Investment Act No. 1 of 1967, Act No. 14 of 1967 on Banking that was later amended by Act No. 7 of 1992, Act No. 13 of 1967 on the Central Bank, Act No. 5 of 1967 on Forestry, and Act No. 11 of 1967 on Mining. By means of this variety of legislation, economic development in Indonesia started to achieve results. There was plenty of investment, either domestic investment or foreign investment, coming into Indonesia, so that economic development activities were not only carried out by state-owned enterprise/regional enterprise, but also by private parties. These ranges of legislation were subsequently amended or replaced by new laws in accordance with the essence of development.

Massive changes to legislations happened again after the economic crisis and the fall of President Suharto in 1998. As part of Indonesia's commitment to the IMF, civil society, and academic pressure, numerous laws specifically related to economic activities and the enforcement of human rights were amended or new laws enacted, such as Act No. 10 of 1998 concerning an Amendment to Act No. 7 of 1992 on Banking, Act No. 41 of 1999 on Forestry, which replaced Act No. 5 in 1967, Act No. 5 of 1999 concerning Prohibition of Monopolistic Practices and Unfair Business Competition, Act No. 37 of 2004 on Bankruptcy and Debt Repayment Obligations Delay, which replaced the Bankruptcy Law of the colonial era. Then, laws on Intellectual Property Rights were also amended by the issuance of new laws, namely, Act No. 15 of 2001 on Trademarks, Act No. 14 of 2001 on Patent, and Act No. 19 of 2002 on Copyright. Next, Act No. 25 of 2007 on Investment replaced Act No. 1 of 1967 concerning Foreign Investment as amended by Act No. 11 of 1970 on the Amendment and Supplement to Act No. 1 of 1967 concerning Foreign Investment, and Act No. 6 1968 on Domestic Investment, which was amended by Act No. 12 of 1970 on the Amendment and Supplement to Act No. 6 of 1968 on Domestic Investment. With the new investment law, there is no longer a distinction between provisions for domestic investment and foreign investment. Another rule also changing is Act No. 40 of 2007

---

[23] Didik J. Rachbini, Economy of Debt Politics 23 (2001).

on Limited Liability Companies, which replaced Act No. 1 of 1995 on Limited Liability Companies, to make it more suited to the needs of development and the rules prevailing in developed countries and industrial countries.

Although there have been numerous new regulations in the field of economic laws, the Dutch substantive criminal law was still in effect until recently. Indeed, attempts have been made to prepare a new law, but more than 20 years later it has not been completed. However, in the sector of criminal procedural law, there are new criminal procedure regulations subsequent to the enforcement of Act No. 8 of 1981 on Criminal Procedural Law. This new Criminal Procedure Law revoked the Dutch Colonial Criminal Procedure Law. As for civil law, although the Civil Code is still prevailing, specifically the laws relating to economic activities have been replaced by new legislation, which is specific and only regulates certain sectors, such as Banking Law, Limited Liability Company Law, Mortgage Law, Capital Market Law, Copyright Law, Trademark Law, Patent Law, Money Laundering Law, Anti-Monopoly Practice Law, and Unfair Business Competition Law.

III. THE INFLUENCE OF US LAW UPON INDONESIAN LAW

As a developing country, Indonesia is actively involved in development, either in economic, social, political, security or legal areas. Consequently, in line with rapid economic development, the law should be able to accommodate the changing landscape and even be the determinant and facilitator of development toward better and fairer conditions. In the framework of this development, the cooperation with alliance countries is unavoidable, including cooperation with the United States.

Indonesian–American cooperation has taken place over quite a long period, more than 70 years, commencing before independence and lasting until recently. As a superpower country in politics, economics and military matters, America is a very important partner for Indonesia. The United States is an export market for Indonesian goods and became the third-largest country in direct investment in Indonesia in 2011, after Japan and China.[24] The non-energy sector's exports from

---

24 http://indonesian.jakarta.usembassy.gov/, A Comprehensive Cooperation USA – Indonesia.

Indonesia to the US are expected to increase. Exports increasing in 2010 and 2011 reached 31 to 49 percent and 15 to 37 percent, respectively. One of the biggest Indonesian import sources is the United States.[25]

Close cooperation between Indonesia and the US is also very influential in law reform in Indonesia. In general, the influence of US law on Indonesian law can occur in a number of ways, including, first, the role of American experts or those studying in American universities who studied Indonesia. Nasir Tamara stated that these experts could be classified within the first generation as Clifford Geertz, Hildred Geertz, Clair Holt, Guy Pauker, and Karl J. Pelzer; the second generation as John Smail, James Siegel, John Sutter, Ruth McVey, Gustav Papayek, Benedict Anderson, Daniel S. Lev, Harry J. Benda, Robert Jay, and Herbert Feith; and the third generation as James Fox, Donald Emerson, William Liddle, Alland Samson, Karl Jackson, and William Frederick.[26] It might be said as well that a number of other experts should also be included, such as Roy Prosterman, who wrote extensively about the land in Indonesia, and Nancy Peluso, who wrote about forestry in Indonesia. The younger generation, too, pays attention, undertaking research and writing about Indonesia; among them are Veronica Taylor, who does a considerable amount of writing and researching about various Indonesian laws, and Celia Lowe who wrote about anthropology and is currently engaged in researching avian flu in Indonesia. The writings and opinions of experts provide an abundant amount of information and a good understanding about Indonesia to the American people and the world in general, especially, in the field of law and political law. Thus, Daniel S. Lev from the University of Washington has had a great deal of influence on the development of Indonesian law. Likewise Veronica Taylor, who once guided many Indonesian students while they were completing masters and doctoral degrees in the field of legal studies at the University of Washington, was very influential on the development of legal thought for the students. The influence of these experts and other experts from universities in America, who are not mentioned here individually, also helped via technical assistance in the instance of Acts prepared by the Indonesian ministry. These experts contribute their thoughts during

---

[25] Center for Regional and Bilateral Ministry of Finance Republic of Indonesia and American Study Programme Graduate Programme University of Indonesia, Study on Bilateral Cooperation Indonesia – United States in Economic and Finance (2012), at 3.

[26] Nasir Tamara, Reviewing Indonesia, the American Influence on Indonesian Scholars 23–24 (1997).

preparation of a law or regulation and also actively contribute their thoughts through seminars in Indonesia.

Second, US law was also adopted through educational cooperation. Globalization has brought changes in many countries including in the education curricula.[27] Through strong cooperation between Indonesia and the US, education has also influenced law school curricula and teaching methods in Indonesia. The US, for Indonesian people, is a very attractive place in which to continue their education, because the quality is very good, the scholarship funding is generous, and they will have a promising future. There are a number of legal experts in Indonesia who have educational backgrounds from America. They are often afterward asked to be lecturers or professors at the best universities in Indonesia, such as the University of Indonesia, Padjadjaran University, the University of Gadjah Mada and Airlangga University. Additionally, many of them become important officials in the government, such as a government minister, the General Directorate, and head of the legal bureau in the ministry. These Indonesian legal experts then teach a great deal of law learned at the American universities to their students, ranging from undergraduate to doctoral programs. Many of these American legal experts' theories are used as references in analyzing legal issues in Indonesia and in scientific works, either in undergraduate law education, master of law, or doctoral programs. Occasionally there may have been a course subject taught prior to an enactment of a regulation, for example, the Anti-monopoly Law, which was taught by Professor Erman Rajagukguk at the University of Indonesia, on applicable law in the United States in 1994, while the Indonesian Law on Anti-monopoly was passed in 1999.

As influential professors in Indonesia, or government officials, these US-educated legal experts must also have important roles in preparing legislation. Some of these legal experts have been greatly influential in law reform in Indonesia, among them are: Professor Moehtar Kusumaatmadja, who taught at the University of Padjadjaran and became Minister of Justice and Minister for Foreign Affairs; Professor Charles Himawan, who introduced the study of economic law, philosophy of economic law, and economic analysis of law; Professor Mardjono Reksodiputro, Professor Arie S. Hutagalung, and Professor Felix Oentoeng Subagyo, who are all lecturers at the University of Indonesia in economic and agrarian law classes, and recognized as well-known law consultants in Indonesia; and Professor Erman Rajagukguk,

---

[27] MARCELO M. SUAREZ-OROZCO & DESIREE BAOLIAN QIN-HILLIARD, GLOBALIZATION CULTURE AND EDUCATION IN THE NEW MILLENNIUM 73 (2004).

who is a professor at the University of Indonesia in economic law and also served as Director General in the Ministry of Justice and Deputy Chief Cabinet Secretary for four presidents. Besides at the university- and government-official level, many of these US-graduated legal experts also become famous and influential legal consultants in Indonesia.

From 1995 until the early 2000s, the US government provided assistance to Indonesia through Ellipse I and II (Economic Law and Procurement Improvement System) Projects. Through these projects, specifically for the education sector, many have graduated with a Masters in US law. These Masters graduates are now distributed throughout Indonesia as either lecturers in various faculties of law or in the ministries and the Business Competition Supervisory Commission. Furthermore, they are also teaching staff development through curriculum development, are lecturers of development by conducting internship programs at leading law schools in Indonesia,[28] lecture during summer courses, act as visiting professors in the US,[29] and provide development of legal education methods.[30] The Socratic method of teaching was introduced and is now widely applied in Indonesia. The essence of this method is to make students actively provide opinions in analyzing a legal case.

Scholarships to study in the US are also given to civil servants of ministry and non-governmental organizations. After their return to Indonesia, they will play an important role in preparing regulations in their ministries. Similarly, members of non-governmental organizations return to Indonesia after college and will actively voice the need for legal reform and legislation.

The influence of American law upon Indonesian law is not only provided through education, expert assistance, and education of officials from various faculties of law at US universities, but also through the process of law enforcement. In law enforcement, many US experts' theories on topics such as Corporate Law enforcement, Banking Law,

---

[28] ADIJAYA YUSUF, SH.LLM. & JOHN W. HEAD, TOPICS ON THE ECONOMIC LAW CLASS AND CURRICULUM (1998). Though this program, lecturers from various universities conduct internship at leading law faculties in Indonesia to compose the syllabus and master the material of law subjects.

[29] This visiting professor program is implemented by sending lecturer staff from a number of law faculties in Indonesia such as UI, UNPAD, UGM, UNAIR, ANDALAS. Moreover, staff of the Indonesian Navy, Ministry of Finance and State Secretary attend many subject courses at Harvard Law School and receive the guidance of professors at Harvard Law School for topics in which they have an interest.

[30] W. LAWRENCE CHURCH, LAW TEACHING AND EDUCATION METHODS (1998).

Capital Market Law, and Legal Prohibition on Monopolistic Practices and Unfair Business Competition are often adopted. Principally, for example, Indonesian Antitrust Law is similar to US Antitrust Law. Similarly, the Law on Limited Liability Company, Banking, Capital Market, and Intellectual Property Rights laws contains similar provisions as in the United States and other developed countries. Similarly the principles of Law No. 2 of 2012 on Land Procurement for Development in the Public Interest, regarding land acquisition for public interest in the United States, especially the principle of due process of law and fair compensation, has been adopted. Although there are differences here and there, these differences were not on principle matters but of the process, and only relating to a small part.

In 2010 there was agreement on the US–Indonesia Comprehensive Partnership, which is a long-term commitment between President Obama and President Yudhoyono to broaden, deepen, and enhance bilateral cooperation between the US and Indonesia. This cooperation broadly covers almost all aspects of development, including the field of education, which is a fundamental matter in the Comprehensive Partnership. In the educational field, cooperation resulted in the development of the Fulbright program, the Community College Initiative, English-language training and the exchange of students, a higher education quality improvement program in Indonesia, and the Higher Education Partnership program. In the legal field, the International Investigative Training Assistance Program (ICITAP) was developed in order to upgrade the capacity and competence of law enforcers in the fight against organized crime, to protect natural resources, forensic, maritime, security, port and border issues. For example, the Office of Overseas Prosecutorial Development Assistance and Training (OPDAT) program provides the rule of law, training for prosecutors, judicial security, counsel for asset confiscation, money laundering, and combating terrorism. The Export Control and Related Border Security program provides maritime law enforcement training. USAID improved the rule of law by strengthening the Supreme Court, improving legal education and improving local NGOs in human rights advocacy. The FBI Legal Attaché conducts joint and parallel investigations with the Corruption Eradication Commission. Training was also given to the Indonesian National Police in order to counter terrorism.[31]

---

[31] http://indonesian.jakarta.usembassy.gov/, A Comprehensive Cooperation USA – Indonesia.

With cooperation in the field of education and law, which is very broad and comprehensive, the future for Indonesian law will involve the participation of a greater number of legal experts and law enforcement practitioners with a US education. Similarly, there will be further transferring of knowledge from US experts through technical assistance, training, seminars and workshops for Indonesian legal experts. Therefore, in the future, the influence of US law on legal developments in Indonesia will retain an equally important role.

IV. THE INFLUENCE OF JAPANESE LAW UPON INDONESIAN LAW

The cooperation between Indonesia and Japan began in 1966. In 1966 Japan also took the initiative to hold a meeting in Tokyo to discuss aid to Indonesia and as a result the Inter-Governmental Group on Indonesia (IGGI) was formed. In the early days of IGGI's formation, Japan and the United States bore the cost of two-thirds of all assistance, while the remaining one-third was charged to other donor countries.[32]

Cooperation between Indonesia and Japan within the last 50 years is very significant in the development of Indonesia. In general, Japan is the largest donor to Indonesia and for Japan, Indonesia is the largest recipient of Japanese aid.[33] Japan has provided significant assistance to lay the foundation for development in economic infrastructure, development in human resources – particularly to support agricultural development – and to facilitate industry, policy and debt relief for development.[34] Japanese aid to Indonesia covers almost every aspect of development, however, and is focused on the fields of, among others, infrastructure, human resource development, education, agriculture, rural development, fulfillment of basic needs, export improvement, and environmental maintenance.[35]

Although Japanese and Indonesian cooperation has been long-standing, intensive cooperation in the field of law has been in operation

---

32 The Japan Embassy in Indonesia, Japanese Economic Cooperation to Indonesia: Policy and Accomplishment (1992), at 5.

33 http://www.id.emb-japan.go.jp/oda/id/whatisoda_02.htm, The History of Japan's Aid for ODA (People with AIDS) in Indonesia.

34 Government of Japan, Country Assistance Program for the Republic of Indonesia (November 2004), at 1.

35 Japanese Embassy in Indonesia, *supra* note 32, at 5.

for the past 15 years.[36] So far, the Japanese aid program has been more focused on sustainable economic development led by private sectors, to create a democratic and fair society as well as support for peace and stability.[37] Therefore, it is not surprising that the influence of Japanese law is not so noticeable in Indonesia. Japanese law's influence upon the development of law in Indonesia is also going through the same process as the influence of US law on Indonesian law, namely through the transfer of knowledge, either by training in Indonesia or in Japan, or through the supply of technical assistance by sending Japanese experts to Indonesia, such as Tsutomu Hiraishi, Sozuburo Mitamayama Kawata and Tamki Kakudo, who have been in Jakarta since 2003. The cooperation is also conducted through the sending of Indonesian students to study at universities in Japan. So far, however, it must be admitted that the emphasis of Japanese assistance to Indonesia has been more on aid for the development of infrastructure, agriculture and subsistence. Similarly for education, it has been more on emphasizing the areas mentioned, and only a little on the field of law. The influence of Japanese law on the development of law in Indonesia is not as great as the influence of US law; nevertheless, there is scholarship assistance for some students to study law in Japan. Assistance for the development of law in Indonesia, particularly concerning Intellectual Property Rights law, was also through the training of lecturers from various universities in Indonesia in order for them to learn about Intellectual Property Rights in Japan. Training and seminars on legal development were also held in Indonesia. Through these collaborations Japanese law also plays an important role in the development of economic law in Indonesia, such as in the field of Intellectual Property Rights[38] and Business Competition law. Japan's assistance in law development in Indonesia can be seen through the support of MITI and JETRO in the APEC Symposium in 2000 on Strengthening Economic Legal Infrastructure.[39]

Indonesian and Japanese legal cooperation, other than through education, is also focused on the changes in the judiciary and

---

[36] A Japanese Contribution to Indonesian Law, http://www.japantimes.co.jp/opinion/2011/04/26/commentary/a-japanese-contribution-to-indonesian-law/.

[37] Government of Japan, Country Assistance Program, *supra* note 34, at 9.

[38] Among others was conducted through a Seminar on Economic Laws and Institutions: Indonesia and Japan, sponsored by JETRO, October 4, 1999. Also the international seminar The Practice of Law Enforcement on IPR, April 20, 2000.

[39] APEC Symposium on Strengthening Economic Legal Infrastructure, July 20–21, 2000.

decentralization.[40] One of the results of the cooperation from Japanese law is court-connected mediation implantation (*Wakai*) in the legal system in Indonesia. It is widely known that there was a backlog of approximately 16 000 cases in the Supreme Court of the Republic of Indonesia. In order to reduce the number of cases in the Supreme Court, the Supreme Court issued Supreme Court Regulation No. 1 of 2008 on Court Connected Mediation, which is basically adopted from the *Wakai* system.[41] We expect that Japan's future assistance will also be enhanced mainly through scholarships to study law at universities in Japan.

V. THE PROBLEM OF IMPLEMENTATION

The adoption of foreign legislation by another country is not a process that runs smoothly by itself. There are values and norms that can be easily absorbed because of universal values, but there are also values that simply cannot be applied in Indonesia due to its differences in culture, stage of development, and legal systems. These norms of foreign laws certainly take time and need socialization to make them understandable and understood by Indonesian legal experts. Aside from the legal norms, which are relatively new for Indonesian legal experts, of course, adjustments to the Indonesian condition, culture, and legal system are also necessary.

We can use the example of anti-trust doctrine and law theory existing in the United States, Japan, and other developed countries in the practice in Indonesia, which has caused much controversy among both academics and legal practitioners. The application of indirect evidence by the Commission for the Supervision of Business Competition is receiving many challenges due to the Indonesian law of criminal procedure and civil procedure that such evidence was not recognized as proof. Similarly, the application of the principles of *per se illegal* and *rule of reason* are new concepts to Indonesian legal experts, so when the principles were introduced in competition law in Indonesia, there were many misunderstandings of the said principles and how they are applied in case adjudication.

Similarly, understanding about gender equality, for some communities in Indonesia, especially those based on patriarchy and matriarchy, is

---

[40] http://www.mofa.go.jp/policy/oda/region/e_asia/indonesia.pdf.

[41] http://www.japantimes.co.jp/opinion/2011/04/26/a-japanese-contribution-to-indonesian-law/, A Japanese Contribution to Indonesian law.

rather difficult to accept. Based on community mores with a matriarchy system, women play a more important role in the family. Similarly, in a society with a patriarchy system, men have a more important role. It does not mean that the two societies do not have protection and that discriminative actions occur; because it is based on local wisdom, a fair settlement mechanism of the applicable legal system does exist.

Adoption of the principle of workers' protection in Act No. 2 of 2004 on Industrial Relations Dispute Settlement has also caused problems in practice. This law was born with technical assistance from the United States through the International Labor Organization. In theory this law is very protective of the rights of labor, but it opens the possibility of labor outsourcing; on the other hand, it is also considered as burdensome for employers. So this law in practice will not be favored by workers or by the companies. The intention of this law is the eventual development of a harmonious relationship between companies and their workers, but it has actually led to many demonstrations everywhere, because law enforcement developed from following the teachings of American legal experts on the application of indirect evidence, *per se illegal*, and *rule of reason*, as well as the principles of the teachings of a single business entity in matters of business competition in Indonesia, was not accepted. The controversy is because of the Indonesian legal system, which is based on written rules, so the law and teachings or doctrines that have been applied overseas, including in the United States and Japan, can only be applied in Indonesia if they have been adopted by law in Indonesia. However, the application of the teachings of foreign legal experts from the US and Japan continues to have an important contribution in the development of laws in Indonesia. These teachings through discussions, decisions of the Business Competition Supervision Commission, and court decisions are gradually beginning to be understood and accepted by Indonesian legal experts.

VI. CONCLUSION

Development of a nation cannot be separated from the cooperation and assistance of the state's companions. With the globalization of the world economy also comes exchange and adoption of values, including the cultural, economic, political, military and legal systems. Economic globalization has also resulted in legal norms. In the process of this change, laws relating to economic activities, international treaties and those related to human rights are areas that make it easier to adopt legal norms from other countries. This is partly because of shared interests and universal values. While legal norms relating to religion and culture, such as marriage laws and inheritance laws, are legal norms that are very difficult to change because the norms referred to come from God, or are based on the local culture. Although, however, laws relating to economic activities and human rights must be easier to adopt as legal norms of another state, because between one state to another state each has different cultural values and different development progress, then these foreign laws, including US and Japanese laws, cannot simply be transplanted.

As Indonesia's largest partners, the United States and Japan have no doubt played a very important role in the development of Indonesia, including law development. With the amount of scholarship funding available, greater numbers of Indonesian people will study in the US. Similarly, its position as a superpower results in the US becoming a favorite destination for Indonesian people who have money to send their children to study there.

With such greater and greater levels of assistance and cooperation, and as developed industrialized countries that are influential in the world, the US and Japan in the future will continue to occupy a more crucial role in the development of and changes in Indonesian law. In order for those laws to be effective and bring justice, laws coming from overseas need socialization and adjustment to the objective conditions of the respective countries, as well as adaption to the prevailing legal system in the related state.

PART V

Legal innovations in intellectual property

5.1 A change of leadership in patent policy and law development? The active role played by Japanese courts in Japan's patent term extension reform

Toshiko Takenaka*

I. INTRODUCTION

In both developed and developing countries, the high cost of healthcare is a serious concern for both policy makers and the public. Because prescription drug costs account for a significant portion of healthcare expenditure, replacing brand-name drugs with their generic equivalents is an effective way to reduce healthcare costs.[1] However, generic drug manufacturers are unable to market the bio-equivalent of a brand-name drug until the patents on the brand-name drug have expired. Marketing of drugs requires approval from a drug regulatory authority, which requires submission of certain data. Generic drug manufacturers cannot perform the clinical trials necessary to develop this data, which requires making and using the brand-name drug to establish bio-equivalency between the brand name and generic drug, until the patent on the

---

* The author would like to thank Mr. Takuya Yasui, a visiting scholar at the University of Washington School of Law (2013–14) for his invaluable input on the examination procedure on pharmaceutical products at the Japan Patent Office. Mr. Yasui with Mr. Junji Kitagaya, who is also a visiting scholar at UW School of Law, served as my research assitances to oversee editing process of this book.

[1] *E.g.*, in the US prescription drugs account for 12% of personal healthcare expenditures. US Department of Health and Human Services Centers for Disease Control and Prevention/National Center for Health Statistics, Health, United States, 2009: With Special Feature on Medical Technology 55 fig. 21 (Jan. 2010).

brand-name drug expires. To expedite the entry of generic drugs into the market, the patent systems in the United States, Japan and member states of the European Union provide immunity for acts related to the development of data necessary for regulatory agency approval.[2]

Brand-name drug manufacturers continue to attempt to extend their market exclusivity in spite of immunity provisions. Brand-name drug manufacturers sue generic drug manufacturers that are performing clinical trials, claiming the generic drug manufacturers' making and using patented drugs for alleged clinical trials are outside the scope of immunity. They also obtain additional patents on the technologies associated with soon-to-expire patents. Such technologies may include new uses, derivatives, formulations and dosages of the drug covered by the soon-to-expire patent. In developing countries where generic drug manufacturers dominate the domestic markets, legislators have introduced anti-evergreening provisions that prevent brand-name drug manufacturers from obtaining the additional patents.[3]

In developed countries such as the United States and Europe, brand-name and generic drug manufacturers compete head to head in their domestic markets. In an environment of aging populations and rising healthcare costs, the public scorns attempts by brand-name drug manufacturers to extend their patent term and market exclusivity. Striking a bargain between the competing interests of brand-name and generic drug manufacturers through legislative reform of drug patent terms is challenging, and courts often play an important role in balancing the competing interests of the drug manufacturers and the public. Recently the US Supreme Court stripped antitrust immunity from brand-name drug manufacturers and instructed lower courts to apply a rule of

---

[2] *E.g.*, the US Patent Act in 35 U.S.C. § 271(e) provides an experimental use exception for acts reasonably related to the development of data necessary to receive approval from the US Food and Drug Administration. Japan Patent Act Art. 69, Para. 1. EU member states introduced an exception comparable to § 271(e) exception through EU Directive relating to veterinary medicinal products. Directive 2001/82/EC on the Community Code relating to Veterinary Medicinal Products, Art. 13, OJ L. 331, 1 (2001) (http://eur-lex.europa.eu/LexUriServ/LexUriServ.do?uri=CONSLEG:2001L0082:20090807:EN:PDF).

[3] *E.g.*, The Patents Act, § 3(d), 2005 (India). The term "evergreening" is used for a strategy to extend the patent term of an about-to-expire patent which covers a product by obtaining multiple patents covering of various aspects of the same product. For an extensive discussion of the anti-evergreening provision in Indian Patent Act see Janice M. Muller, *The Tiger Awakens: The Tumultuous Transformation of India's Patent System and the Rise of Indian Pharmaceutical Innovation*, 68 U. PITT. L. REV. 491 (2007), *available at* http://ssrn.com/abstract=923538.

reason standard when examining antitrust claims regarding pay-for-delay agreements between brand-name and generic drug manufacturers.[4] The EU Commission issued a decision to fine both brand-name and generic drug manufacturers who enter into similar pay-for-delay agreements.[5] In Canada the Supreme Court was willing to reach beyond its traditional authority to find a brand-name drug manufacturer's patent invalid in order to let a generic version enter the domestic market early.[6]

In contrast, in *Takeda Pharmaceutical Company (Takeda) v. Japan Patent Office (JPO)*,[7] the Supreme Court of Japan sided with brand-name drug manufacturers by affirming the conclusion of the Intellectual Property High Court's (IP High Court) decision that would facilitate the extension of brand-name drug patent terms. The IP High Court's decision departed from its precedent of endorsing the JPO's patent term extension (PTE) practice and broke Japan's long-established tradition of allowing bureaucrats such as JPO officials to lead patent law and policy development.[8] To protect public interests, the JPO has long adopted a practice of rejecting PTE applications unless an application is directed to a drug that has a new active ingredient or a new use of an existing drug. Nonetheless the IP High Court struck down JPO's practice and adopted a divergent rule to grant patent term extensions on a broad range

---

[4] "Pay-for-Delay" agreements are arrangements between a brand-name drug manufacturer and a potential genetic competitor in which the brand-name drug manufacturer who owns a patent agrees to pay a sum of money to the competitor and the competitor agrees not to challenge the patent and will not enter the market for a specified period of time. *E.g.*, FTC v. Actavis, Inc., 133 S. Ct. 2223, 186 L. Ed. 2d 343 (U.S. 2013) (ruling on facts that included a generic drug manufacturer who agreed not to enter the market for a specified number of years in exchange for millions of dollars paid to the brand-name drug patent owner).

[5] Press Release, European Commission, Commission fines Lundbeck and other pharma companies for delaying market entry of generic medicines: statement by Vice-President Almunia (June 19, 2013), *available at* http://europa.eu/rapid/press-release_SPEECH-13-553_en.htm.

[6] Teva Canada Ltd. v. Pfizer Canada Inc., 2012 SCC 60, [2012] 3 S.C.R. (revising its 2013 decision to limit its invalidity finding only with respect to the generic drug manufacturer's application under Canada's Patent Medicines Notice of Compliance Regulations, which is the Canadian counterpart of US Hatch-Waxman Act).

[7] Saikō Saibansho [Sup. Ct.] Apr. 28, 2011, Hei 21 (gyō hi) no. 326, 65 SAIKŌ SAIBANSHO MINJI HANREISHŪ (No. 3) 1654; 1348 HANREI TAIMUZU 102; 2115 HANREI JIHŌ 32 (Japan).

[8] Chiteki Zaisan Kōtō Saibansho [Intellectual Prop. High Ct.] May 29, 2009, Hei 20 (gyō ke) no. 10458, 1305 HANREI TAIMUZU 80; 2047 HANREI JIHŌ 11 (Japan).

of patented technology of drug products on which a brand-name drug manufacturer must receive a disposition of approval prior to marketing. Although the Supreme Court affirmed the IP High Court's conclusion of striking down the JPO's PTE practice, it played an intermediary role by limiting its endorsement of the IP Court's holding and allowing the JPO to develop a new practice. Thus *Takeda v. JPO* highlights increased roles played by Japanese courts in enacting patent law and policy.

Takeda v. JPO also highlights the important role played by comparative law in interpreting the Japanese Patent Act (JPA). A recognized need for worldwide patent harmonization along with Japanese judges' interaction with US and European judges has resulted in US patent jurisprudence significantly influencing Japanese patent case law.[9] Significantly, in *Takeda v. JPO* Japan's PTE practice departs from its US and EU counterparts by increasing protection to brand-name drug manufacturers beyond what is available in either the US or Europe. Nonetheless, the influence of foreign law in Japanese patent law is evident because both IP High Court and the JPO examine their US and EU counterparts when developing their PTE practice. Accordingly, this chapter focuses on the roles played by the Supreme Court and IP High Court in reforming Japan's PTE system while examining the influence of *Takeda v. JPO* and comparative law.

II. *TAKEDA V. JPO*

(i) Background: Patent Term Extension System in Japan

In developed as well as many developing countries, the making and selling of drugs is heavily regulated by a government agency. In Japan, the Ministry of Health, Labor and Welfare (MHLW) regulates drug marketing under the Pharmaceutical Affairs Act (PAA), which aims to ensure drug safety.[10] Brand-name drug manufacturers are unable to market their patented drugs unless they receive approval from MHLW under PAA. MHLW requires considerable time to execute a disposition granting approval because drug manufacturers must first conduct clinical

---

[9] Toshiko Takenaka, *Chief Judge Rader's Contribution to Comparative Patent Law*, 7 WASH. J. L. TECH. & ARTS 379 (2012), *available at* http://digital.law.washington.edu/dspace-law/bitstream/handle/1773.1/1127/7WJLTA379.pdf?sequence=4.

[10] Pharmaceutical Affairs Act (Yakujihō), Law No. 145 of 1960, (Aug. 10, 1960).

trials and develop data that establish drug safety, which MHLW must examine prior to issuing its disposition.[11] The patent term on the drug is running during the period the brand-name drug manufacturer is awaiting approval by MHLW to market and sell the drug.

To recoup the lost benefits of patent exclusivity during this period in which brand-name drug manufacturers are unable to market their patented new drugs, Japan introduced a patent term extension (PTE) system in 1988. Under the JPA, the objective of Japan's PTE system is set forth: "Where there is a period during which the patented invention is unable to be worked because approvals prescribed by relevant Acts that are intended to ensure the safety, etc. or any other disposition designated by Cabinet Order as requiring considerable time for the proper execution of the disposition in light of the purpose, procedures, etc., of such a disposition are necessary to obtain for the working of the patented invention, the duration of the patent right may be extended, upon the filing of a request for the registration of extension of the duration, by a period not exceeding five years."[12] To request the extension, brand-name drug manufacturers must file a PTE application, and may receive an extension of patent rights by a period not to exceed five years.[13] However, the Patent Act provides multiple grounds for rejection of a PTE request, including "Where the disposition designated by Cabinet Order is not deemed to have been necessary to obtain for the working of the patented invention which is under the examination for PTE."[14] The JPA's PTE provision did not clarify the definition of such "working" of the patented invention in connection with the "disposition." Accordingly, interpretation of the provision by the JPO and courts has been required.

Where an extension is granted, the effect of the extended patent term is limited; it is effective only against such acts of working of the patented invention for the product that were prescribed by the disposition and prohibited prior to approval by MHLW.[15] JPO's examination practice

---

[11] For a general discussion on Japan's drug market approval process, see National Institute of Health Sciences, Pharmaceutical Administration and Regulation in Japan (Mar. 2011), *available at* http://www.nihs.go.jp/mhlw/yakuji/yakuji-e_20110502-02.pdf.

[12] Japanese Patent Act, Art. 67(2).

[13] Japanese Patent Act, Art. 67(2), 67-2 (2011).

[14] Japanese Patent Act, Art. 67-3 (2011).

[15] Japanese Patent Act, Art. 68-2 (2011).

allows separate product patent for a new use of a known drug product.[16] Where a specific usage of the drug product is prescribed for the new use patent, a disposition was required for market approval of a patented new use of a known drug. The patent term for such patent may be extended only on this new use of the known product and not on the previously known product itself. Where the active ingredient and the use of a newly formulated drug product are the same as those of a previously approved product, the drug manufacturer may need to conduct further clinical trials and seek additional approval from MHLW in order to market the new product.[17] However, the time period necessary for MHLW to execute a disposition on a new formulation of a previously approved product is much shorter than the time period to receive approval on an entirely new product.

Since the introduction of PTEs, the JPO has rejected PTE applications unless the patent under examination is directed to an approved drug product that contains a new active ingredient or a new use of a previously approved drug. This is because the object of the PTE system recites "considerable time" required for getting an execution of a disposal. The PAA categorizes a drug or use of a previously approved drug as a new drug or new use according to the active ingredient of the drug or "efficacy/effect" of the known drug, respectively. Accordingly, the focus of a PTE rejection should be on the active ingredient or efficacy/effect of the drug product at issue.[18] Thus the JPO has interpreted the necessity of disposition provision so as to reject PTEs where a disposition was obtained for a new formulation of a drug product in which the active ingredient and the use of the product are the same as that of a known and previously approved drug. The JPO's interpretation is supported by policies to prevent brand-name drug manufacturers' attempts to extend their market exclusivity. It is also consistent with PTE practice under the US Patent Act and the

---

[16] JAPAN PATENT OFFICE, PATENT AND UTILITY MODEL EXAMINATION GUIDELINES, Part VII Chapter 3 Medicinal Inventions (Oct. 2011), *available at* http://www.jpo.go.jp/tetuzuki_e/t_tokkyo_e/Guidelines/7_3.pdf.

[17] Japan Patent Office, DDS Technologies and Examination under Pharmaceutical Affairs Act (Dec. 2008), *available at* http://www.jpo.go.jp/shiryou/toushin/shingikai/pdf/entyou-wg02_shiryou/entyou-wg_shiryou03.pdf.

[18] Maki Yamada, *Review of Important Supreme Court Decisions*, 53 LAW & TECHNOLOGY 63 (2011).

Supplementary Protection Certificate (SPC) in EU member states.[19] However, in spite of the JPO's interpretation, the JPA does not explicitly require a drug product to be defined according to "the active ingredient or efficacy/effect" as is done in the US and EU.[20] Nevertheless, the Tokyo High Court, which had exclusive jurisdiction over appeals from JPO, endorsed JPO's practice and upheld JPO's rejections of PTE applications under the JPO's interpretation.[21]

In April 2005 Japan's IP High Court was created within the Tokyo High Court as a "semi-independent" court that has its own administrative power and unique organizational structure.[22] The newly created IP High Court continued to uphold the JPO's PTE practice.[23] In many cases coming before the IP High Court the patents and market approvals at issue are directed to new formulations of previously approved drugs that enhance therapeutic gains through improved drug delivery systems.[24] The IP High Court has been reluctant to upset the JPO's established practices regarding newly formulated drug products, stating that new legislation was necessary in order to extend patent terms for dispositions related

---

[19] 35 U.S.C. §156; Regulation (EC) No 1610/96 of the European Parliament and of the Council of 23 July 1996 concerning the creation of a supplementary protection certificate for plant protection products, Article 1, Para. 9, Art. 3, Para. 1 (a) (OJ 1996 L 198, p. 30), *available at* http://eur-lex.europa.eu/LexUriServ/LexUriServ.do?uri=OJ:L:1996:198:0030:0035:EN:PDF.

[20] 35 USC §156(f); Council Regulation (EEC) No 1768/92 of 18 June 1992 concerning the creation of a supplementary protection certificate for medicinal products, Art. 1 (b).

[21] Tokyō Kōtō Saibansho [Tokyo High Ct.] Mar. 5, 1998, Hei 7 (gyō ke) no. 155, 1650 HANREI JIHŌ 137 (Japan); Tokyō Kōtō Saibansho [Tokyo High Ct.] Feb. 10, 2000, Hei 10 (gyō ke) no. 361, 1719 HANREI JIHŌ 133 (Japan).

[22] Toshiko Takenaka, *Success or Failure? Japan's National Strategy on Intellectual Property and Evolution of Its Impact from the Comparative Law Perspective*, 8 WASH. U. GLOBAL STUD. L. REV. 379 (2009), *available at* http://law.wustl.edu/WUGSLR/Issues/Volume8_2/takenaka.pdf.

[23] Chiteki Zaisan Kōtō Saibansho [Intellectual Prop. High Ct.] Oct. 11, 2005, Hei 17 (gyō ke) no. 10345 (Japan); Chiteki Zaisan Kōtō Saibansho [Intellectual Prop. High Ct.] July 19, 2007, Hei 18 (gyō ke) no. 10311, 1980 HANREI JIHŌ 133 (Japan). For a review of cases reviewing JPO's PTE practice, see Naoharu Takeyama, *Overview of the Patent Term Extension System and Recent Judicial Precedents*, YUASA & HARA INTELLECTUAL PROPERTY NEWS, Jan. 2010, at 1, *available at* http://www.yuasa-hara.co.jp/english/news/pdf/ipnews028.pdf.

[24] *See e.g.*, Chiteki Zaisan Kōtō Saibansho [Intellectual Prop. High Ct.] Oct. 11, 2005, Hei 17 (gyō ke) no. 10345 (Japan); Chiteki Zaisan Kōtō Saibansho [Intellectual Prop. High Ct.] July 19, 2007, Hei 18 (gyō ke) no. 10311, 1980 HANREI JIHŌ 133 (Japan); Chiteki Zaisan Kōtō Saibansho [Intellectual Prop. High Ct.] Sept. 27, 2007, Hei 19 (gyō ke) no. 10016 (Japan).

to new formulations of known active ingredients.[25] Patent scholars extensively criticized these IP High Court decisions as being inconsistent with the language of PTE provisions and urged the JPO to grant PTEs regardless of active ingredients or efficacy/effect.[26]

(ii) IP High Court Decision

In *Takeda v. JPO* a brand-name drug manufacturer and patentee, Takeda, filed a PTE application for a patent directed to a drug product that was approved as "Pacif capsule, 30mg."[27] The MHLW disposition granting market approval identifies the drug product's active ingredient as morphine hydrochloride and the efficacy/effect as relieving cancer pains. Prior to seeking the PTE application at issue, another drug manufacturer obtained approval for another drug product, approved as Opso liquid for oral administration, 5mg/10mg, which has the same active ingredient and efficacy/effect as Pacif capsule. According to the JPO's established practice the JPO rejected Takeda's PTE application on the ground that a disposition was not necessary for working of the patented invention under Art. 67-3. The JPO stated that the disposition for Opso liquid enabled marketing of a product with the active ingredient morphine hydrochloride for cancer pains, regardless of the fact that the patent at issue was directed to Pacif capsule's new formulation.

The patentee appealed against the JPO's rejection. The IP High Court found that the JPO erroneously interpreted the JPA and it cancelled the JPO's rejection.[28] It held that the JPO's interpretation is inconsistent with the plain language of the grounds of rejection allowable under the JPA and that the JPO's interpretation effectively revises the JPA's language, which is beyond the JPO's authority. The IP High Court adopted a formalistic interpretation of the JPA, which is in contrast to its precedents that allowed the JPO's pragmatic approach to interpreting the JPA in light of the PTE's objective.

Contrary to its precedents the IP High Court found there was no legislative history produced by the JPO to support the JPO's

---

[25] Chiteki Zaisan Kōtō Saibansho [Intellectual Prop. High Ct.] Oct. 11, 2005, Hei 17 (gyō ke) no. 10345 (Japan).

[26] Yamada, *supra* note 18.

[27] Chiteki Zaisan Kōtō Saibansho [Intellectual Prop. High Ct.] May 29, 2009, Hei 20 (gyō ke) no. 10458, 1305 HANREI TAIMUZU 80; 2047 HANREI JIHŌ 11 (Japan).

[28] *Id.*

interpretation. Rather, the IP High Court restated the objective of the PTE as aiming to recover a period of patent term during which the patentee had intended to market a drug product but was unable to market while waiting for the disposition that was necessary to market the drug product. In light of this objective, a patentee is entitled to a PTE for any patented drug product that required a separate disposition. The court emphasized that the extended term is effective only against the specific drug product and its equivalents that were the subject of the disposition and was unmarketable prior to approval by MHLW. Such a drug product should be defined under the PAA by its dosage, structure and ingredients, but not necessarily by the active ingredient. The court found nothing in the JPA to support the JPO's argument that a drug product must be defined by its active ingredient. To support its interpretation, the IP High Court cited the US Patent Act, which expressly defines the term "drug product" as the active ingredient of the product.[29] In contrast, no definition of a drug product is included in the JPA's PTE provisions. Thus a drug product that is subject to a disposition under the JPA should not be defined solely by its active ingredient during the PTE examination.

In summary, the IP High Court made clear the JPO must establish one of the following facts in order to reject a PTE application due to a lack of a disposition necessary to market a drug product: (1) the disposition does not lift restrictions on the patentee's right to work the patented invention, or (2) the act restricted and addressed by a disposition is not the working of the patented invention. Because the JPO failed to establish either of these facts, the IP High Court canceled the rejection and remanded the case to the JPO to examine the application according to the court's interpretation of the ground of rejection.

(iii) Supreme Court Decision[30]

The Supreme Court of Japan denied the JPO's petition of *jokoku* appeal against a ruling with respect to the IP High Court decision.[30] However,

---

29 35 U.S.C. §156 (f)(2).

30 The Supreme Court of Japan exercises its appellate jurisdiction over either a final appeal or appeal against a ruling. In civil and administrative cases, the grounds for a final appeal are limited to (1) a violation of the Constitution or (2) a significant violation of Civil Procedure. The Supreme Court may exercise its discretion to grant an appeal against a ruling if the appeal is based on one of four grounds listed in the Civil Procedure Code. For the jurisdiction of the Supreme Court of Japan, see Supreme Court of Japan, Overview of the Judicial System

the Supreme Court issued its own opinion, although the opinion was very brief, and agreed with the IP High Court that the JPO erroneously rejected Takeda's PTE application. The Supreme Court did not fully endorse the active role played by the IP High Court in the interpretation of the PTE. The Court agreed only that a patentee is entitled to a PTE where a previously approved drug does not fall within the scope of the patent under the PTE examination. However, if the previously approved drug is outside the scope of the patent on which a PTE application is filed, the disposition of such drug is irrelevant to PTE grant of the patent under examination. The Court was silent on the situation in which a previously approved product does fall into the scope of the patent under the PTE examination, and left the JPO and legislators to clarify the appropriate outcome in such a situation.

III. ANALYSIS

(i) A Change of Leadership?: The Intellectual Property High Court versus the Japan Patent Office

The active role played by the IP High Court can be viewed as a change of leadership in the development of patent law and policy. Since its creation, the Supreme Court endorses the IP High Court's leadership role by affirming almost all IP High Court decisions,[31] and the JPO acquiesced to this leadership change. After the Supreme Court endorsed the IP High Court's decision, the JPO was prepared to implement the Supreme Court's decision and address the issues remaining in the law after the IP High Court's holding. This is a significant departure from Japan's traditional law-making process.

Japan is known for delegating broad authority from the legislature to bureaucrats such as those in the Ministry of Economy, Trade, and Industry (METI) and the JPO.[32] Bureaucrats have taken leadership

---

in Japan (http://www.courts.go.jp/english/judicial_sys/overview_of/overview/index.html).

[31] As of Aug. 30, 2013, among the 268 appeals from IP High Court decisions involving patent rights, the Supreme Court vacated and remanded only one decision and reversed and decided only one decision.

[32] Tom Ginsburg, *Dismantling the "Developmental State"? Administrative Procedure Reform in Japan and Korea*, 4 AM. J. COMP. L. 585 (2001), *available at* http://home.uchicago.edu/~tginsburg/pdf/articles/DismantlingTheDevelopmentalState.pdf.

roles in law and policy development by drafting and implementing legislation and adopting broad statutory language such that details may be provided in formal agency rules and informal administrative guidance.[33] Regarding the Patent Act, the JPO has enjoyed such a leadership role. The PTE provisions at issue in *Takeda v. JPO* highlight the flexibility and discretion given to the JPO through interpretation of broad statutory language in order to achieve certain goals while forgoing extensive legislative procedures. Accordingly the IP High Court, and its predecessors prior to the creation of IP High Court in 2005, traditionally took a hands-off approach and endorsed the JPO's interpretation of PTE provisions in light of its legislative intent. [34] Although the courts acknowledged that the PTE statutory language is broad and ambiguous when compared with US and European PTE provisions,[35] the different roles played by the Japanese and the US/European courts in their respective legal systems may justify such ambiguity.[36] Therefore the Tokyo High Court and IP High Court were reluctant to overturn the JPO's practice.

In the early 2000s there was a push for major reform of the Japanese legal system; however, the consequent reform did not significantly change the degree of deference courts gave to the JPO in interpreting ambiguous PTE provisions. The Japanese government implemented recommendations, which were published by the Judicial System Reform Council in 2001,[37] that led to major revisions in civil procedure. Patent jurisdiction was concentrated in the Osaka and Tokyo district courts and exclusive jurisdiction of patent appeals was granted to the IP High

---

33 YUKIO YANAGIDA ET AL., LAW AND INVESTMENT IN JAPAN: CASES AND MATERIALS 39 (1994).

34 *See e.g.*, Chiteki Zaisan Kōtō Saibansho [Intellectual Prop. High Ct.] Oct. 11, 2005, Hei 17 (gyō ke) no. 10345 (Japan); Chiteki Zaisan Kōtō Saibansho [Intellectual Prop. High Ct.] Nov. 16, 2007, Hei 17 (gyō ke) no. 10184, 1208 HANREI TAIMUZU 292 (Japan); Chiteki Zaisan Kōtō Saibansho [Intellectual Prop. High Ct.] July 19, 2007, Hei 18 (gyō ke) no. 10311, 1980 HANREI JIHŌ 133 (Japan).

35 Chiteki Zaisan Kōtō Saibansho [Intellectual Prop. High Ct.] Oct. 11, 2005, Hei 17 (gyō ke) no. 10345 (Japan).

36 Ginsburg, *supra* note 32, at 4.

37 Justice System Reform Council, Recommendations of the Justice System Reform Council: For a Justice System to Support Japan in the Twenty-First Century, June 12, 2001, *available at* http://www.kantei.go.jp/foreign/judiciary/2001/0612report.html.

Court.[38] Moreover in 2001 the government executed major bureaucratic reforms that merged certain ministries.[39] However METI and JPO were generally unaffected because the creation of the IP High Court did not alter the degree of discretion the Japanese courts' gave to the JPO. Instead the power of the JPO was enhanced by Japan's adoption of pro-patent policies. In 2003 the Basic IP Law was enacted to create the IP Strategy Headquarters in the Cabinet, which began to publish its annual strategy programs charging ministries and agencies, particularly METI and JPO, to implement action plans to enhance patent protection.[40] The IP Strategy Headquarters urged the Supreme Court of Japan to create a special intellectual property court to signify Japan's commitment to IP protection, leading to the creation of the IP High Court.[41] In spite of the government's intent to create a pro-patent court, the IP High Court remained reluctant to interfere with the JPO's leadership in PTE reform until the 2009 *Takeda v. JPO* decision.

Although the changes brought by the judicial and bureaucratic reforms were relatively minimal, an increased power to examine patentability requirements may have encouraged courts to restrain the JPO's leadership. In the *Kilby* decision, the Supreme Court of Japan overturned long-established practices when it endorsed the holding of the Tokyo High Court, which gave Japanese courts power to decide the validity of patents.[42] Consequently accused infringers may raise the invalidity defense where the reason for invalidity is obvious. Prior to *Kilby* Japanese courts followed the traditional German model of refraining from examining patent validity in infringement proceedings, and the JPO thereby enjoyed exclusive power to develop and implement policies related to patentability. After *Kilby* the JPO codified the Japanese courts' newly acquired power over patent validity in the 2005 Patent

---

38 Minji Soshōhōtō No Ichibu Wo Kaisei Suru Hōritsu [Law for Revising Part of the Civil Procedure Law], Law No. 108 of 2003, art. 6, para. 1 (amending Minji Soshōhō [Civil Procedure Law], etc. Law No. 109 of 1998).

39 Junko Kato, *Reforming the Japanese Bureaucracy: Perceptions, Potential and Pitfalls*, 117 ASIA PROGRAM SPECIAL REPORT 34 (Jan. 2004), *available at* http://faculty.washington.edu/pekkanen/Pekkanen%20WWC%20report.pdf.

40 Takenaka, *supra* note 22, at 380.

41 Takenaka, *supra* note 22, at 387.

42 Saikō Saibansho [Sup. Ct.] Apr. 11, 2000, Hei 10 (o) no. 364, 54 SAIKŌ SAIBANSHO MINJI HANREISHŪ (No. 4) 1368; 1032 HANREI TAIMUZU 120; 1710 HANREI JIHŌ 68 (Japan). For a discussion of this case, see Toshiko Takenaka, *A Major Change for Japanese Patent Enforcement*, NEWSLETTER, CASRIP (2000), *available at* http://www.law.washington.edu/Casrip/Newsletter/2000/newsv7i2jp1.pdf.

Act Revision.[43] With the endorsement of bureaucrats and legislatures, Japanese courts began to aggressively participate in the development of patentability law and policy by finding to be invalid more than 50% of the patents issued by the JPO.[44] Additionally some IP High Court decisions led to the review of the JPO's examination guidelines.[45]

Another likely reason for the IP High Court's willingness to interfere with the JPO's patent policy development, particularly within the PTE system, was the government's adoption of pro-medical patent policies. In 2006 Prof. Shinya Yamanaka, an adult stem cells researcher, and his research team successfully generated induced pluripotent stem cells (iPS cells). His research began to attract the attention of the Japanese community, which eagerly awaited news of Prof. Yamanaka's Nobel Prize for Physiology or Medicine. The government felt it was necessary to improve Japan's ability to commercialize on Prof. Yamanaka's research for the benefit of the Japanese medical science industry. Thus the 2008 annual strategic program charged METI and the JPO with conducting PTE reform.[46] The IP Strategy Headquarters also published a report in 2009 that reviewed patent protection of advanced medical science inventions.[47] The report emphasized the importance of drug delivery systems, such as dosage forms and drug formulations, and

---

[43] Japanese Patent Act, Art. 104-3 (2011); *see* Toshiko Takenaka, *Merging Civil and Common Law Traditions in the Patent Validity Challenge System: Japanese Experiences* (July 5, 2011), NOURRITURE DE L'ESPRIT: FESTSCHRIFT FÜR DIETER STAUDER ZUM 70. GEBURTSTAG, p. 271, Horst-Peter Gotting, Claudia Schluter, eds., Nomos Verlagsgesellschaft 2011, University of Washington School of Law Research Paper No. 2011-19, *available at* http://ssrn.com/abstract=1957397.

[44] Shigeo Takakura, *Review of the Recent Trend in Patent Litigation from the Viewpoint of Innovation*, RESEARCH INSTITUTE OF ECONOMY, TRADE & INDUSTRY, IAA, COLUMN 184 (Sep. 3, 2008), *available at* http://www.rieti.go.jp/en/columns/a01_0242.html.

[45] For example, a grant panel decision of IP High Court Heisei 18 (Gyo-Ke), No.10563 given on May 30, 2008) led to a revision of Examination Guidelines for "Amendment of Description, Claims and Drawings (New Matter)" http://www.jpo.go.jp/tetuzuki_e/t_tokkyo_e/amendment_claims_drawings_e.htm.

[46] INTELLECTUAL PROPERTY STRATEGY HEADQUARTERS, INTELLECTUAL PROPERTY STRATEGIC PROGRAM 2008, *available at* http://www.kantei.go.jp/jp/singi/titeki2/keikaku2008_e.pdf.

[47] INTELLECTUAL PROPERTY STRATEGY HEADQUARTERS, PATENT PROTECTION IN THE FIELD OF ADVANCED MEDICAL TECHNOLOGIES (May 29, 2009); Akiteru Tamura, *Patent Protection for Inventions in the Life Sciences and Its Prospect*, 48 PATENT STUDIES (2009), *available at* http://www.inpit.go.jp/content/100049786.pdf.

urged the JPO to review its examination guidelines, which led to a major reform in patentability requirements for medicinal inventions in October 2009.[48]

As part of the METI-JPO deliberative council in 2008, the JPO employed Japan's legal tradition of organizing working groups in order to reform the PTE system.[49] In Japan's policy and law-making process, deliberative councils (*shingikai*) play an important role in allowing for the consideration of the viewpoints of outside experts, who represent various interest groups affected by a law.[50] The PTE Reform Working Group included members representing brand-name and generic drug manufacturers as well as patent academics. The JPO charged the Working Group with discussing whether a revision of current PTE provisions was necessary or a reform could be achieved without a revision. The JPO proposed multiple options for revising the Patent Act including an option to clarify that the disposition required for a grant of a PTE must be a disposition for "a new drug product" as defined by the active ingredient and efficacy/effect under the PAA.[51] A committee member representing brand-name drug manufacturers was fiercely opposed to the JPO's proposal. The member urged the JPO to consider the importance of recent advances in drug delivery systems (DDS), which include a new formulation of a previously known product, and to allow PTEs on patents directed to a DDS technology.[52] This view was reiterated by patent academics. However a member representing generic drug manufacturers supported the JPO's proposal and emphasized the harm to the public interest resulting from the delayed market entry of generic drugs due to extensions on the patent terms of their brand-name counterparts.

---

[48] Japan Patent Office, Revision of Examination Guidelines for Industrially Applicable Inventions and Revision of Examination Guidelines for Medicinal Inventions (Oct. 23, 2009), http://www.jpo.go.jp/tetuzuki_e/t_tokkyo_e/industrially_applicable_medicinal_e.htm.

[49] Japan Patent Office, Patent Term Extension System Reform Working Group, Preliminary Report (Sept., 2009), http://www.jpo.go.jp/iken/pdf/houshiki binrankaitei/torimatome.pdf.

[50] Ginsburg, *supra* note 32, at 10.

[51] Japan Patent Office, Proceeding of Second PTE Working Group Meeting (Dec. 24, 2008), http://www.jpo.go.jp/shiryou/toushin/shingikai/entyou-wg02_gijiroku.htm.

[52] Japan Patent Office, Proceeding of Third PTE Working Group Meeting (Feb. 9, 2009), http://www.jpo.go.jp/shiryou/toushin/shingikai/entyou-wg03_gijiroku.htm; Opinions of Japan Pharmaceutical Manufacturers Association, Feb. 2, 2009 (Material #5 attached to PTE Reform Working Group Preliminary Report), *available at* http://www.jpo.go.jp/shiryou/toushin/shingikai/pdf/entyou-wg03_shiryou/entyou-wg_shiryou05.pdf.

While the working group's discussions had reached an impasse, the IP High Court issued a landmark decision, *Takeda v. JPO*, supporting the brand-name drug manufacturer's view. Because the JPO filed a petition for *jokoku* appeal, the discussion at the Working Group was on hold until the Supreme Court handed down its decision. Upon issuance of the Supreme Court decision, the Working Group's goal was shifted from implementing the JPO's own policy through JPA revision to implementing the Supreme Court's holding.[53] Rather than further insisting on JPA revision, the JPO was willing to modify its PTE practice according to the Supreme Court decision. With respect to the Supreme Court's silence on PTE practice where a previously approved product falls into the scope of the patent under PTE examination, the JPO proposed two options: either a practice that fully implements the IP High Court's interpretation, or a compromise between the JPO and the IP High Court interpretations. The working group adopted the second option, which allows a PTE for every disposition of a drug product unless a previous disposition had previously lifted a restriction on marketing the patented invention at issue for the drug product.

The 2012 revision of the PTE examination guidelines implemented this option after additional commentary from the public was reviewed.[54] To determine whether a previous disposition enabled the patentee to work on the patented invention at issue for the drug product covered by the patent under the PTE examination – and therefore makes the patent ineligible for a PTE grant – the JPO compares a drug product description from the prior disposition with the scope of the patent under PTE examination. A PTE application is rejected "if a person has obtained a disposition for a prior drug product or a prior agricultural chemical (a 'prior disposition') that satisfies the 'matters falling under the matters to define the invention (and the use)' of the drug product or the agricultural chemical that was the subject of the present

---

[53] Japan Patent Office, Proceeding of Sixth PTE Working Group Meeting (Aug. 19, 2011), http://www.jpo.go.jp/shiryou/toushin/shingikai/pdf/encyo_seido_wg_menu/encyou-wg06_gijiroku.pdf.

[54] Japan Patent Office, Revision of the Examination Guidelines for "Patent Term Extension" (Feb. 14, 2012), http://www.jpo.go.jp/iken_e/patent_term_rev.htm. The revised guidelines were challenged again by a brand-name drug manufactuer in *Genentech v. JPO,* Intellectual Prop. High Ct. May 30, 2014, Hei 25 (gyō ke) no. 10195. The Grand Bench of IP High Court cancelled the JPO's rejection under the revised examination guidelines based on the same grounds found in *Takeda v. JPO*. The JPO is expected to file a petition of *jokoku* appeal with the Supreme Court of Japan. Thus, there will be another fight over leadership between the IP High Court and the JPO.

disposition."[55] Under the new PTE guidelines, patentees may be entitled to a PTE for a new formulation of a previously approved drug product because a previous disposition does not allow marketing of the patented invention for the new formulation even where the active ingredient is the same.[56] The revised guidelines also limit the effect of the extended patent term to the product described in the disposition.[57] The revisions made it easier for brand-name drug manufacturers to extend patent terms for new drug delivery systems with new formulations while still limiting the scope of the extended term, which enables earlier entry of generic drugs into the market.

(ii) Influence of Comparative Law

The influence of comparative law in Japan's PTE reform is evident because both the IP High Court and the JPO PTE Working Group examined US and European PTE systems when revising Japan's PTE system. The influence of TRIPs is also apparent in the international harmonization of the minimum requirements for patent grant and enforcement.[58] Moreover patent offices in developed countries, such as the JPO, USPTO, and EPO, are keenly aware of the necessity of harmonizing patent grant requirements in order to enhance collaboration of examination through the patent prosecution highway.[59] Japanese courts and the JPO share a consensus that patent practice should be harmonized with their US and European counterparts where a different approach is not clearly justified.

---

[55] *Id.*

[56] For a discussion of impact of revised PTE guidelines, see Hiroshi Kato, A View on Patent Term Extension System, *available at* http://www.law.nihon-u.ac.jp/publication/pdf/chizai/5/05.pdf at 8.

[57] Junji Tanaka, Revision of Patent Term Extension Examination Guidelines: Background of Revision and Its Impact (Apr. 4, 2012), *available at* http://ushiki-pat.com/index.php/topics-ja/3-topic/19-column2012040401.

[58] Agreement on Trade-Related Aspects of Intellectual Property Rights, Apr. 15, 1994, 1869 U.N.T.S. 299, 33 I.L.M. 1197 [hereinafter TRIPS Agreement], available at http://www.wto.org/english/tratop_e/trips_e/t_agm0_e.htm.

[59] Eric L. Lane, *Building the Global Green Patent Highway: A Proposal for International Harmonization of green Technology Fast Track programs*, 27 BERKELEY TECH. L. J. 1120 (2012); Chun Dongwook, *Patent Law Harmonization in the Age of Globalization: The Necessity and Strategy for a Pragmatic Outcome*, 93 J. PAT. & TRADEMARK OFF. SOC'Y 129 (2011).

Such justification has been found to exist with respect to the PTE system. PTE requirements for drug products are closely connected to drug regulation systems. Although the World Health Organization (WHO) has made an extensive effort to harmonize various elements of drug regulatory activities in UN member states, drug regulation systems differ significantly from one country to another. Reflecting such differences, the requirements for a PTE grant as well as the effect of extended patent terms in Japan, US and European Union countries remain significantly different. Japan's PTE system was created only a few years after the creation of the US PTE system and at a time when EU countries had not yet adopted their PTE system.[60] The JPO acknowledged in *Takeda v. JPO* that it did not intend to introduce a system harmonized with the US PTE when it introduced the bill to establish the Japanese PTE system.

The Japanese PTE system is significantly more brand-name drug manufacturer friendly than either the US system or its EU counterpart, the SPC.[61] Only the Japanese system grants multiple extensions for the same patent whereas the US and EU grant only one extension.[62] The US Patent Act and the EU SPC also include active ingredient limitations to prevent brand-name drug manufacturers from obtaining PTEs on new technologies that are associated with a preapproved drug that has the same active ingredient.[63] In contrast, the Japanese PTE system does not explicitly contain such limitations and the terms of multiple patents may be extended where they cover new use or formulations of the same active ingredient.[64] If the same patent covers multiple drug products that are respectively subject to multiple dispositions, the patent term is extended every time a disposition is made.

The IP High Court made the already brand-name drug manufacturer friendly system even more so by removing the active ingredient limitation developed by the JPO. In contrast, the US and Europe

---

60 Japan Pharmaceutical Manufacturers Association Opinions, *supra* note 52, at 2.

61 For a comparison of PTE systems, see Shunsuke Nakanishi, Overviews and Implementation of Patent Term Extension Systems in Japan, US and UK, 12 (2009), *available at* http://ikkyo-univ.sakura.ne.jp/webs/ipp/consulting project/2009/CP09Nakanishi.pdf; see also Council Regulation (EEC) No. 1768/92 of 18 June 1992 concerning the creation of a supplementary protection certificate for medicinal products [hereinafter "SPC Regulation"], *available at* http://eur-lex.europa.eu/LexUriServ/LexUriServ.do?uri=CELEX:31992R1768:EN:HTML.

62 35 U.S.C. §156(a)(1); SPC Regulation, Art. 1(c).

63 35 U.S.C. §156(f); SPC Regulation, Art. 1(b).

64 See Nakanishi, *supra* note 62.

strongly enforce the active ingredient limitation and have limited PTE opportunities. The US Court of Appeals for the Federal Circuit interprets "active ingredient" broadly to mean an ingredient present in the drug being approved, including any salt or ester of such ingredient.[65] This interpretation excludes PTEs on a new use or formulation of a drug product if the drug product has the same active ingredient of a previously approved drug product. The Court of Justice for the European Union (CJEU) has similarly prevented issuance of an SPC with respect to new uses and formulations.[66]

The domestic drug industry's unique needs and market also justified the JPO's adoption of a PTE system that departs from its US and European counterparts. Japan's generic drug manufacturers have a relatively low profile because Japanese consumers prioritize quality over price, preferring brand-name drugs to generic drugs.[67] In spite of MHLW's campaign to promote generics, the generic drug market share still remains low.[68] MHLW heavily controls both new drugs as well as generic and the price of generic on average of long-listed drug products sold by brand-name drug manufacturers.[69] As a result, the impact of generic drugs remains minor in Japanese market.

Moreover, brand-name drug manufacturers worldwide continue to struggle to develop new drugs, and almost all Japanese brand-name drug manufacturers sell both their brand-name drug as well as the generic equivalent. If Japanese drug manufacturers are unable to extend patent

---

[65] 35 USC §156(f); Glaxo Operations UK, Ltd. v. Quigg, 894 F.2d 392, 394 (Fed. Cir. 1990); PhotoCure Asa v. Kappos, 603 F.3d 1372, 1376 (Fed. Cir. 2010).

[66] C-31/03 (*Pharmacia Italia*), Judgment of the Court (Fifth Chamber) of 19 Oct. 2004, http://curia.europa.eu/juris/liste.jsf?language=en&num=C-31/03; C-431/04 (*Massachusetts Institute of Technology*) Judgment of the Court (Second Chamber) of 4 May 2006, http://curia.europa.eu/juris/liste.jsf?num=C-431/04. For a discussion of these cases, *see* Gordon Wright, Twenty-one Years of SPCs – A Cause for Celebration?, Life Science Intellectual Property Review (Mar. 28, 2013) http://www.lifesciencesipreview.com/article/twenty-one-years-of-spcs-a-cause-for-celebration.

[67] Thomson Reuters, The Japanese Generic Drug Market: Opportunity and Strategies for Success (Sept. 10, 2013), http://thomsonreuters.com/business-unit/science/pdf/ls/newport-japanese-generics.pdf.

[68] Sawai Situation of Generics in Japan (Sept. 10, 2013), http://www.sawai.co.jp/en/generics/index.html.

[69] PWC, Asia-Pacific Pharama & Life Science Newsletter, 7 (March 28) (https://www.pwc.com/en_GX/gx/pharma-life-sciences/publications/asia-pharma-newsletter/assets/pwc-asia-pacific-pharma-and-life-sciences-newsletter.pdf).

terms through patents on new formulations, they may simply give up research and development for new drugs and switch primarily to generic drug manufacturing. IP High Court judges are keenly aware of such issues because METI and JPO frequently invite the judges to participate in *shingikai*.

Although the comparative law has not been used to fully harmonize PTE systems, the influence of the US Patent Act and EU SPC is felt when they are used in the IP High Court to clarify the ambiguity of the Japanese PTE provisions and by JPO in its legislative efforts through the Working Groups. Although the IP High Court favored a more extreme view on PTEs in order to promote medical science patents, the JPO's compromise option was adopted. The final PTE system reflects the influence of the JPO's prior practice that was relatively more in line with the US and EU practice to enforce an active ingredient limitation.

IV. CONCLUSION

The IP High Court may have taken on its unique leadership role in *Takeda v. JPO* because the Court was created to symbolize Japan's commitment to pro-patent policy by modeling the US Court of Appeals for the Federal Circuit, which is known to be a pro-patent court. IP High Court judges frequently share a podium with Federal Circuit judges at international conferences. JPO officials and examiners also attend these conferences and become familiar with the Federal Circuit's leadership in law and policy development as well as the USPTO's practice to follow the guidance of the Federal Circuit's case law. In Japan the JPO has similarly been taking the lead, but it may allow Japanese courts to step in, particularly where the traditional policy development mechanism is deadlocked, as exemplified in *Takeda v. JPO*. Moreover, the IP High Court may be willing to take on a leadership role regardless of the efforts made by the JPO. *Takeda v. JPO* may suggest the time has come to coordinate leadership in patent law and policy development between the Court and the JPO.

Regardless of leadership, comparative law plays an important role in interpreting the JPA and in developing patent examination rules and practice in Japan. Both the IP High Court and JPO's PTE Working Group examined their US and European counterparts when interpreting the language of PTE provisions. Patent harmonization is such a strong policy in Japanese courts and in the JPO that they would not depart from a harmonizing interpretation of the JPA unless it was clearly justified.

5.2 Ethics rather than rights: Reconsidering "transmit rather than create" – Toward a new understanding of Korea's intellectual property rights tradition

Hyung Doo Nam[1]

I. INTRODUCTION

From a Western perspective, Korea, similar to China, has been thought to inadequately protect intellectual property, and there has been ongoing friction regarding intellectual property trade relations. For a considerable time, Korea was annually listed on the United States Trade Representative (USTR)'s Special 301 Report on Intellectual Property Rights Watch List or Priority Watch List.[2] During the negotiation of the Korea–US Free Trade Agreement (KORUS FTA), which was ratified by the Congress of the United States on October 12, 2011, and by the National Assembly of Korea on November 22, 2011,[3] there was substantial disagreement regarding the scope of protection that should be afforded to intellectual property rights.

Professor William P. Alford of Harvard Law School examined the

---

[1] This chapter is a continuation of the article, "韓国の伝統思想に見られる著作権という観念 – Alford教授の意見に対する反論的試論" ["Ideas of Copyright in Korean Intellectual Tradition: Toward a Refutation of Alford's Thesis"], 著作権研究 36号, (日本)著作権法学会 (Dec. 2010), which was published in Japanese. I thank Joongwon Park, J.D. of Georgetown University Law Center, for his help with the translation of a substantial part of this chapter.

[2] Korea has been removed from the Watch List and Priority Watch List since 2009. U.S. Trade Representative, Special 301 Report (2009), *available at* http://www.ustr.gov/about-us/press-office/reports-and-publications/2009.

[3] Free Trade Agreement between the Republic of Korea and the United States of America, *available at* http://www.fta.go.kr/korus/board/diary.asp.

low level of protection afforded to intellectual property rights in China and Taiwan, finding the cause in the countries' common Confucian background.[4] Alford's study, which has been considered a potent theory on the topic,[5] argues that China's traditional focus on the interaction with past orthodoxy rather than originality led to a belief that knowledge should be held communally and thus was the reason an intellectual property system did not develop.[6] A Western scholar's assessment from a Confucian perspective is original and quite convincing. Because Korean culture is similarly deeply rooted in Confucianism, Alford's theory may be applied to Korea as well. However, as 20 years have passed since the publication of Alford's theory, it is questionable whether the Western view of intellectual property rights in the Eastern world is correct as applied to Korea.

For the past 30 years, Korea has achieved miraculous economic development. The Korean economy is ranked 15th in the world by size,[7] and Korea is the US's 7th largest trading partner, ranking between the UK and Brazil.[8] The United States Patent and Trademark Office

---

[4] William P. Alford, To Steal a Book Is an Elegant Offense: Intellectual Property Law in Chinese Civilization, 9–29 (1995).

[5] *See* Jonathan Ocko, *Copying, Culture, and Control: Chinese Intellectual Property Law in Historical Context*, 8 Yale J.L. & Human. 559 (1996) (reviewing Alford, *supra* note 4); Matt Jackson, *Harmony or Discord? The Pressure toward Conformity in International Copyright*, 43 IDEA 607, 618 (2003); Peter Yu, *Piracy, Prejudice, and Perspectives: An Attempt to Use Shakespeare to Reconfigure the U.S.-China Intellectual Property Debate*, 19 B.U. Int'l L.J. 1, 16–21 (2001); Warren Newberry, *Copyright Reform in China: A "TRIPS" Much Shorter and Less Strange Than Imagined?*, 35 Conn. L. Rev. 1425, 1436–38 (2003).

[6] Alford, *supra* note 4, at 25–29. Alford, quoting Confucius's phrase, "I transmit rather than create; I believe in and love the Ancients," points out that Chinese scholars such as Confucius focused on transmission rather than creation and argues that this tradition hindered the development of intellectual property rights. However, it is difficult to agree with Alford's theory because there cannot be mere transmission without creation and because this phenomenon is not unique to China or the East. Indeed, until at least the Middle Ages, this phenomenon was similar in the Western world as well. *See* Jackson, *supra* note 5, at 612–13. I note here that the title of this chapter, "Ethics rather than rights" was inspired by the above phrase used by Confucius.

[7] Based on the IMF's statistics of 2012 Gross Domestic Product. International Monetary Fund, World Economic Outlook April 2013: Hopes, Realities, Risks (Apr. 2013), *available at* http://www.imf.org/external/pubs/ft/weo/2013/01/pdf/text.pdf.

[8] Korea is currently the seventh-largest trading partner of the US with $101.2 billion in total (exports and imports) goods trade during 2012. Top

(USPTO) application and registration numbers show that Samsung is ranked second in the number of US patents assigned, and five Korean corporations are ranked within the top 50,[9] which is indicative of Korea's world-class industrial technology. The past 20 years have shown remarkable change and growth in Korea's culture as well. The "*Hallyu* Syndrome"[10] starting in the 1990s has expanded beyond the Chinese character cultural regions of Asia (China, Japan, Taiwan, Hong Kong, Singapore, Vietnam and Thai) and into the US, Europe, India, the Islam cultural area and even South America.[11] Due to such industrial, technological and cultural developments, Korea can no longer be ignored or dismissed as merely a small country or local economy. Similar to other youth in East Asia, young Koreans are no longer influenced by Confucianism as strongly as past generations. Yet, the influence of Korean traditional ideology such as Confucianism on politics, economy, society and culture is still strong. If we are to accept the claims of Alford, it is not easy to explain the development of the knowledge industry in a Korean society where the traditional ideology of Confucianism emphasizing public ownership prevails. In particular, according to utilitarian logic, development in the industrial technology and culture industries is incentivized through the protection of intellectual property. Korea's industrial growth, despite a tradition of weak protection afforded to intellectual property, challenges the universal validity of the utilitarian theory and, in particular, the incentive theory. It also raises the possibility that there was in fact a tradition of protecting intellectual property in Korea.

In Part II, I will report the fabrication of the justification theory in intellectual property related international commerce and argue that protection of domestic industry is the more honest and practical explanation. In Part III, I will show that, although not as a right,

---

Trading Partners – December 2012, U.S. CENSUS BUREAU, http://www.census.gov/ foreign-trade/statistics/highlights/top/top1212cm.html (last visited Sept. 28, 2013).

[9] IFI CLAIMS 2012 Top 50 US Patent Assignees, IFI CLAIMS PATENT SERVICES, http://ificlaims.com/index.php?page=misc_top_50_2012 (last visited Sept. 28, 2013).

[10] "*Hallyu*" means "Korean wave" in Chinese characters and Korean.

[11] The expression "*Hallyu*" was sufficient when Korean cultural phenomena such as music, movies, dramas, food and clothing were popular in East Asia, especially in Chinese character cultural regions. However, as "*Hallyu*" spread beyond East Asia to the whole world, the expression "K-pop" or "K-culture" was used instead. This change in language shows the strength of Korean culture and the Korean culture industry.

there were social ethics that were against the indiscreet use of others' intellectual property in Korean, as well as Chinese, tradition. Through this study, I caution against the one-sided Western view of traditional Eastern intellectual property rights, and I believe this study will contribute to better-directed future research.

II. POLICY-BASED APPROACH DISGUISED AS A DOCTRINAL APPROACH

When the Berne Convention for the Protection of Literary and Artistic Works (Berne Convention) on copyright law, the first of its kind, was created in the late 19th century, the net exporting countries, such as the UK, France and Germany, preferred a natural rights approach to copyright protection.[12] On the other hand, net importing countries, such as the US and Russia, which were developing countries, preferred a utilitarian approach and thus rejected the Berne Convention and insisted on copyright protection based only on domestic legislation.[13]

The US boasts a record of rapid development, transitioning from a net importer of intellectual property to a net exporter. In the early 19th century, publishers in New York, Philadelphia and Boston reaped massive profits by pirating the works of English authors and later justifying their actions under the utilitarian principle of providing public goods at low costs.[14] This utilitarian stance on intellectual property rights in the US was consistent with its protectionist stance on international trade. However, it is notable because it is entirely contrary to the current US stance emphasizing strong international protection for intellectual property rights, in particular copyrights. The US became the top exporter of copyrights by the end of World War II. According to Paul Goldstein, this structural change seems correlated to the 1947 US proposal of the

---

[12] Although there is a natural rights tradition in the UK, the UK turned to a utilitarian tradition in *Donaldson v. Beckett*, in 1774, when it was ruled that the statutory right was above the common law right. Carla Hesse, *The Rise of Intellectual Property, 700 B.C.–A.D. 2000: An Idea in the Balance*, DAEDULUS 26, 37 Spring 2002.

[13] *Id.* at 40–41.

[14] *Id.* In 1843, for instance, Charles Dickens's novel *A Christmas Carol* sold for the equivalent of $2.50 in the UK, whereas the pirated version sold for six cents in the US. Even Isaac Funk, who reaped large profits from pirated materials, criticized the widespread piracy of the book *The Life of Jesus* as a violation of the eighth commandment's prohibition against stealing and as a "national sin of literary piracy."

Universal Copyright Convention to harmonize the natural rights tradition and the utilitarian tradition.[15] In 1988, the US became a signatory of the Berne Convention and, in contrast to its earlier stance, became a staunch advocate of strengthening policy and legislation to protect intellectual property rights, in particular copyrights. This signals a shift from the initial US focus on "encouragement of learning" for public utility to a new focus on the increase of private profits through the protection of intellectual property rights.[16]

Professor Ha-Joon Chang of Cambridge University criticizes US foreign trade policy vis-à-vis developing countries, saying that the US is forgetting its former status as a developing country and citing the US's earlier stance on intellectual property rights as an example.[17] The crux of Chang's argument is that the pressure applied by current developed countries, such as the US, imposing a stringent system of intellectual property rights on developing countries, is unwarranted since the developed countries were themselves former violators. Accordingly, the US's international commerce policy favoring strong protection of intellectual property rights is largely a policy-based approach aimed to protect the country's domestic industry rather than an approach grounded on a doctrinal basis.

In the latter part of the 20th century, there was a sharp clash among countries over the issue of intellectual property rights. This clash arose from the net importers' lax domestic and international stance on intellectual property protection that was based on the principles of utilitarianism and emphasized the communal nature of intellectual property. This resistance to strong protection is similar to that shown by the US in the 19th century against its more developed counterparts in Europe. Interestingly, since the 1970s, the US has been a staunch

---

15 PAUL GOLDSTEIN, COPYRIGHT'S HIGHWAY: FROM GUTENBERG TO THE CELESTIAL JUKEBOX, 151 (rev. ed. 2003).

16 Hesse, *supra* note 12, at 42.

17 Chang refers to intellectual property rights in his critical evaluation of the economic pressure applied by Western developed countries toward developing countries. This is premised on the criticism that intellectual property rights are being overprotected. HA-JOON CHANG, KICKING AWAY THE LADDER: DEVELOPMENT STRATEGY IN HISTORICAL PERSPECTIVE, 81–85 (2002); HA-JOON CHANG, GLOBALISATION, ECONOMIC DEVELOPMENT AND THE ROLE OF THE STATE 75, 273–301 (2003); HA-JOON CHANG, BAD SAMARITANS: RICH NATIONS, POOR POLICIES, AND THE THREAT TO THE DEVELOPING WORLD, 122–44 (2007). Meanwhile, by arguing that developing countries net-importing cultural goods and technology are similar in status to 19th-century US, Hesse holds a similar view as Chang. Hesse, *supra* note 12, at 44–45.

advocate of strong intellectual property rights protection and has been applying considerable pressure against developing countries through the use of trade sanctions.[18]

In its early stages of economic development, Korea was an importer of foreign technology and culture and provided a low level of intellectual property protection. However, in recent years, Korea has implemented stronger measures to protect intellectual property, almost to the point of being excessive. Korea's patent protection has increased with economic development, and this evolution is similar to its copyright protection, where there has been considerable legal reform through the KORUS FTA and Korea–EU FTA. For example, the protection period for copyrights has been extended from 50 years to 70 years after death,[19] and offenses subject to complaint have been practically eliminated.[20] Moreover, temporary reproduction including temporary storage in electronic form has been acknowledged as a form of reproduction,[21] and in terms of compensation for damages, statutory damages have been partly implemented.[22] As such, the level of protection afforded to copyright has increased. Recently, the problem has become more about excessive protection of copyrights not only in international commerce but also in Korean domestic law.

For example, one Korean case involved a father who uploaded a video of his five-year-old daughter singing a song by a famous Korean singer.[23] The Korea Music Copyright Association (KOMCA), entrusted with the music copyright, set up a claim alleging copyright infringement and requested an injunction and compensation for damages, but later dropped the claim after public outcry. In a turn of events, the father brought suit for a defensive confirmation trial, requesting confirmation that there was no copyright infringement, and a judgment finding no copyright infringement was pronounced and concluded.[24]

Currently, Korean copyright law requires a showing of nearly the same elements for civil compensation for damages, an injunction and criminal punishment. Although there are offenses subject to complaint,

---

[18] Hesse, *supra* note 12, at 44–45.

[19] Jeo jak gwon beop [Copyright Act], art. 39(1) (S.Kor.), *available at* http://eng.copyright.or.kr/.

[20] *Id.* art. 140, *available at* http://eng.copyright.or.kr/.

[21] *Id.* art. 2(22), *available at* http://eng.copyright.or.kr/.

[22] *Id.* art. 125, *available at* http://eng.copyright.or.kr/.

[23] The video file is approximately 53 seconds long. The URL of the video file on the plaintiff's blog is http://blog.naver.com/yang456/140062293006 (last visited Sept. 30, 2013).

[24] Seoul High Court [Seoul High Ct.], 2010Na35260, Oct. 13, 2010 (S.Kor.).

because certain offenses are indictable without complaint in cases where there is a commercial purpose or repeat offenses, it is common for a copyright holder to simultaneously request civil compensation and criminal punishment. Although cases where actual imprisonment is sentenced are rare, it is burdensome for a person to be involved in a criminal proceeding even if the punishment is only a fine. Particularly, there may be significant consequences in the case of adolescents. Copyright holders, by way of the attorneys who represent them, take advantage of this and often make criminal accusations. There have been many instances of copyright holders settling for large sums of money with parents who are afraid of their child being involved in a criminal proceeding.[25] In the Korean judicial system where civil damages awarded are markedly low, copyright holders (and their lawyers) often decide to pursue settlements through criminal accusations rather than through civil compensatory damages. Regrettably, there have been instances of adolescents, unable to arrange enough settlement money, who end up committing suicide or committing further crimes to come up with money.[26] Some unscrupulous copyright holders and related dealers, through their experience with this so-called 'settlement profiting,' found that alleging infringement and settling after making criminal accusations proved more profitable than licensing and inducing the legal use of copyrights. This phenomenon repulsed many Koreans who were trying to adjust to a foreign and transplanted copyright system.

Due to the influence of the US, many intellectual property right holders in Korea have opened their eyes to the protection of intellectual property rights and accordingly, there has been active protection in certain areas with the assistance of scholarship and the courts. One such example is the right of publicity. After the James Dean case,[27] the first

---

[25] Kugjin Kang, *"Sharp Increase in the Number of Accusations Regarding Online Copyrights – Lucrative for Lawyers, Frightening for Users,"* SEOUL SHINMUN (July 30, 2008), http://www.seoul.co.kr/news/newsView.php?id=20080730014005 (last visited Sept. 30, 2013).

[26] Yukyung Kim, *"Beware of 'Online Hunters,'"* HANKYUNG SHINMUN (July 22, 2009), http://www.hankyung.com/news/app/newsview.php?aid=2009072002177 (last visited Sept. 30, 2013).

[27] An heir of James Dean, a famous American actor who died in 1955, brought an action in Korea against a Korean underwear manufacturing company, seeking prohibition on the use of the name and likeness of James Dean and damages arising out of the unauthorized use thereof. The plaintiff based the cause of action on the allegation that the defendant company infringed upon the right of publicity of the deceased, which was a novel cause of action in Korea at

case in Korea where protection under the right of publicity was sought, Korean courts have generally acknowledged the right of publicity.[28] Although there have been cases stating that a civil law country like Korea should not acknowledge an exclusive right such as the right of publicity absent legislation,[29] these cases have become the minority, and most Korean courts thus approve of an extensive right of publicity. Here, the speed and swiftness of such recognition should be noted.[30]

In the US, whether the use of a baseball player's name and game statistics on baseball trading cards infringes the right of publicity has long been a litigated issue.[31] The 1953 *Haelan Laboratories v. Topps Chewing Gum* case[32] was the first case to use the term "right of publicity," and the right of publicity was later affirmed in the 1970 *Uhlaender v. Henricksen* case.[33] However, in the 1996 *Cardtoons v. Major League Baseball* case[34] and the 2006 *C.B.C. v. Major League Baseball* case,[35] the courts held to the contrary. Specifically, these courts concluded that baseball players' names and statistics are "bits of baseball history" and thus, First Amendment protection rights trump the right of publicity.[36]

---

the time. Seoul Western District Court [Seoul District Ct], 94Gahab13831, Aug. 29, 1997 (S.Kor.).

[28] For a study on the history of the right of publicity and the trend in recent court cases in Korea, *see* Hyung Doo Nam, *The Emergence of Hollywood Ghosts on Korean TVs: The Right of Publicity from the Global Market Perspective*, 19 PAC. RIM L. & POL'Y J. 487 (2010).

[29] Seoul Central District Court [Seoul District Ct.], 2002Gadan54093, Oct. 1, 2004 (S.Kor.); Suwon District Court [Suwon District Ct.], 2004Gadan20834, Jan. 13, 2005 (S.Kor.).

[30] Although the court affirmed the right of publicity in the James Dean case, the court did not recognize the post mortem right of publicity. However, nine years later, a Korean court recognized such post mortem right of publicity. Seoul Eastern District Court [Seoul District Ct.], 2006Gahab6780, Dec. 21, 2006 (S.Kor.).

[31] *See* J. Gordon Hylton, *Baseball Cards and the Birth of the Right of Publicity: The Curious Case of Haelan Laboratories v. Topps Chewing Gum*, 12 MARQ. SPORTS L. REV. 273 (2001).

[32] Haelan Laboratories, Inc. v. Topps Chewing Gum, Inc., 202 F.2d 866 (2d Cir. 1953).

[33] Uhlaender v. Henricksen, 316 F.Supp. 1277 (D. Minn. 1970).

[34] Cardtoons, L.C. v. Major League Baseball Players Association, 95 F.3d 959 (10th Cir. 1996).

[35] C.B.C. Distribution and Mktg., Inc. v. Major League Baseball Advanced Media, 443 F.Supp. 2d 1077 (E.D. Mo. 2006).

[36] *Id.* at 1092–93.

In Korea, after a court found that a computer game company violated Korean professional baseball players' right of publicity by using their names in a computer baseball simulation game,[37] recently retired professional baseball players created a separate entity and won a suit against the computer game company.[38] As illustrated through the string of right of publicity cases involving the use of professional baseball players' identities, US courts have recognized the problem of excessive protection and have moved toward protecting First Amendment speech. In contrast, Korean courts, despite having more recently recognized the right of publicity, have afforded more active protection than US courts.[39]

In the area of trademarks, counterfeit products are still widely distributed in Korea, and the level of protection afforded is understandably lower compared to patents or copyrights. One reason for the prevalence of counterfeit products is that many Korean companies in the fashion or goods industries lack global brand recognition.[40] Another reason is the traditional Korean tendency for self-display and craving for display.[41] Although counterfeiting exists in Korea, it is not as serious as in China, and the number of fake products is declining as economic standards improve. Furthermore, consumer consciousness is improving toward the protection of trademarks. In some regards, these changes reflect the success of the US's international commerce policy during the past few decades.

Although there are some unsatisfactory aspects of Korea's intellectual property regime, particularly in the area of trademarks, Korea is no longer a country infringing upon the US's intellectual property rights or inadequately protecting copyrights. Thus, at the bare minimum,

---

[37] Seoul Central District Court [Seoul District Ct.], 2005Gahab80450, Apr. 19, 2006 (S.Kor.).

[38] Seoul Western District Court [Seoul District Ct.], 2010Kahab245, Apr. 21, 2010 (S.Kor.).

[39] Nam, *supra* note 28, at 509–11.

[40] Samsung is the only Korean company ranked as one of the top 100 brands worldwide as of 2013. This is evidence that Korean companies are weaker in the area of global brand recognition compared to the area of patents or copyrights. Brandz Top 100 Most Valuable Global Brands 2013, http://www.millwardbrown.com/brandz/2013/Top100/Docs/2013_BrandZ_Top100_Chart.pdf (last visited Sept. 30, 2013).

[41] This is related to the "status theory" regarding fashion – that because fashion is often a means of distinguishing class, some people choose fashion beyond their economic status due to a desire to raise their social class. *See generally* C. Scott Hemphill & Jeannie Suk, *The Law, Culture, and Economics of Fashion*, 61 STAN. L. REV. 1147, 1156–57 (2009).

Alford's claim is much less convincing today compared to the past. Consequently, Alford's analysis, based on the premise that Korea is infringing upon intellectual property rights, should be reevaluated. In particular, because the US's international commerce policy on the protection of intellectual property is rooted in a policy-based approach intended to protect US domestic industry, it is a pointless exercise to analyze and conclude that other trade countries' traditional ideologies do not support the protection of intellectual property rights. In other words, it is problematic that the US, a country that used to be a significant infringer of intellectual property rights, is pushing for the protection of intellectual property rights in countries that are in a similar situation as the US used to be in and is disguising a policy-based approach as a doctrinal claim.

III. ETHICS RATHER THAN RIGHTS

Under the intellectual property justification theory understanding knowledge as a property right, Alford's assertion that intellectual property rights were nonexistent or insufficiently protected in China or Taiwan is certainly convincing. Indeed, copyright in the form of modern property rights was born only after the 18th-century Enlightenment and the civil revolution of 1789 in France. The Western tradition of individualism at the end of the medieval dark ages, which emphasized the human personality, combined with the flowering of rationalism to create a normative system of rights and duties centered on property rights. During this process, as knowledge became a property right, a normative system of rights and duties centered around knowledge developed into an intellectual property system that included patent law and copyright law. After the 19th century, as the balance of power rapidly shifted to Western countries, countries such as Korea, China and Japan implemented, sometimes involuntarily, Western legal systems, including the intellectual property law system.

With a long history and culture, Eastern countries have accumulated knowledge over an extended period of time and have developed a splendid culture based on this knowledge. The splendid culture of the East would not have been possible absent some standard that permeated throughout intellectual society. Specifically, the standard regulating the communication of knowledge in the Eastern world was not a legal system based on rights and duties like the modern Western world, but an ethics system that emphasized spirit. This standard was in large part due to the strong heritage of collectivism that emphasized society and groups rather than individualism and human personality. Conversely, from Alford's vantage point, this was due to a lack of awareness of the privatization of knowledge through property rights. However, the reason Eastern society was not full of lawless chaos as per the Western-centric view was because there was a different standard that negated the need for regulation through property rights.

In Korea, similar to China, although there was a significant lack of awareness of protecting knowledge or intellectual creations as property rights, there has been a longstanding discussion within the field of academic ethics or order. An ethical approach to intellectual creations is "plagiarism," and this concept has been in existence for a long time in both Korea and China.

It is understood that "plagiarism" originated from the Latin phrase *plagiarius*, meaning "kidnapping/kidnapper." There is a term that corresponds to the term plagiarism in Chinese, Japanese and Korean. Indeed, the term was used in ancient Korean and Chinese documents.[42] In Korea, "plagiarism" was used consistently from the Goryeo dynasty (918–1392) through the Joseon dynasty (1392–1910).[43] For example, Lee Kyu-bo (1168–1241), a leading writer during the Goryeo dynasty, used the phrase *Do*, which means stealing, to refer to the misuse of a predecessor's work.[44] Similarly, Lee Su-gwang (1563–1628), a Silhak (the Realist School of Confucianism) scholar, stated that there were many pieces copied from others in classical literature, and that it was easy to copy others' work but difficult to create an original work.[45] This expression embodies the notion that creation is more valuable than copying, and reveals that Korean traditional thought espoused creation over copying and viewed the wrongful use of others' work as stealing. In particular, Lee Su-gwang introduced the origin of the expression *Seulgab-Dojeok*, which refers to a situation where another person's work is quoted but misused due to a misunderstanding of its original

---

[42] For example, Yu Jongwon (733–819), a writer during the Tang dynasty, used the phrase plagiarism in his work and criticized the unauthorized use of others' work. YU JONGWON, YU JONGWON JIB, 161 (translated by Oh Soohyung, Lee Sukhyung, and Hong Seungjik, Somyung pub., 2009).

[43] Lee Hyesoon, *Traditional Discussion on Plagiarism*, in PLAGIARISM – REFLECTION FROM A HUMANITIES POINT OF VIEW 10–30 (edited by Lee Hyesoon & Jung Hayung, Jibmoondang pub., 2008).

[44] LEE KYU-BO, DONGGUKISANGGUKJIB, vol. III, 244 (translated by Lee Jungsub, Minjok Munhwa Chujinhoe pub., 1978) (1251).

[45] LEE SU-GWANG, JIBONGYUSEOL, vol. I, 331 (translated by Nam Mansung, Eulyu Munhwasa pub., 1994) (1613).

meaning.[46] To illustrate the point, a thief stole a *Seulgab*, a type of women's underwear, but did not know what it was for and wore it on his head, thus becoming a laughingstock.[47] Although the aforementioned perspectives may not be reflective of the entire landscape of Korean traditional thought, it is important to note that Korean culture valued creation over copying and condemned the unauthorized or wrongful use of others' work as stealing.

With regard to the Western world, the birth of copyright law during the 18th century was possible because of the increase in publications. The Enlightenment and the growth of the bourgeois class brought great cultural change in 18th-century Europe. Specifically, the reading population grew from a small select class to a larger middle class, thereby leading to a rapid expansion of the publication industry. This rapid expansion and the resulting rise in pirated publications gave rise to a discussion on copyrights, which led to the birth of copyright law.[48]

Korea, on the other hand, experienced a less dramatic and diverse expansion of scholarship and knowledge compared to the Western world after the Reformation, Renaissance and Enlightenment. This comparative constraint was because Silhak, which flourished in Korea during the 18th and 19th century, was still centered on the study of Confucian classics, even though it expanded the scope of denotation of neo-Confucianism. Although there was great change in Korean academia and culture due to Silhak, it paled in comparison to Europe. Accordingly, because there was not a large enough market for publications and because reading was not sufficiently popularized among ordinary citizens, copyright law did not become a large issue in Korea.

A comparison of two representative Chinese poets, Du Fu (712–770) and Su Dongpo (1036–1101), by Jeong Yak-yong (1762–1836, penname Dasan), one of the most famous Korean philosophers, can be properly understood within this historical context. In his comparison of the two poets, Dasan considered Du Fu a higher-level poet than Su Dongpo because Du Fu's work seemed to originate from the classics, but in an unnoticeable way, whereas Su Dongpo's work seemed noticeably derived from the classics.[49] On a superficial level, Dasan's position

---

46 LEE SU-GWANG, JIBONGYUSEOL, vol. II, 299.

47 *Id.*

48 Hesse, *supra* note 12, at 31.

49 JEONG YAK-YONG, YUBAEJIESEO BONAEN PYUNJI ["Letters from a Place of Exile"], 56 (edited & translated by Park Sukmu, Changbi pub., 2011) (1801–1820).

seems to imply that he supports some forms of plagiarism. However, it is necessary to view Dasan's belief in a larger historical context. For instance Dasan, a major Silhak scholar, wrote a script to the king lamenting the small number of books learned men read in preparation for the state examination.[50] From children to elders, the number of books did not exceed 50. Accordingly, Dasan should not be understood as an endorser of plagiarism without regard to the contemporaneous situation where only a small number of books were available to read.

Furthermore, the traditional Korean reverence for not revealing the source of origin was due to the fact that there was comparably a smaller amount of precedent information available in comparison to today. Due to the severely limited number of people reading classics and the availability of classics to be read, quoting and revealing the source of origin were thought to degrade the standard of poetry and prose. Dasan's belief on using classics as precedent literature in writing was not a reflection of a negative view toward "honest writing." Rather, it was a reflection of the contemporaneous historical context in which both the availability of books and the number of people with access to or command over high-level literature were quite limited. Therefore, it is inappropriate to view Dasan as a defender of plagiarism.

Although Korea did not have a system of rights and duties that protected intellectual creations as property rights, Korea would not have been able to develop a rich and influential culture throughout its long history if plagiarism had been widely permitted. Although intellectual creations were not protected as an exclusive right under a personal property right system, it is clear that there was a longstanding ethical standard prohibiting plagiarism under scholarly ethics. In this regard, Western scholars' analyses, which found that Korea lacked an awareness of intellectual property, overlook this ethical standard and thus are incomplete.

IV. CONCLUSION

As discussed above, much of the philosophical justification theory developed in Western society is in fact based on the protection of domestic industry. Accordingly, an analysis of intellectual property

---

50 JEONG YAK-YONG, GUGYUK DASAN SIMUNJIB ["Dasan's Literature Translated in Korean"], 60–61 (translated by Kim Sinho and Kim Jaeyul, Sol pub., 1996).

protection excessively focused on philosophical theories could lead to trade friction with other countries and would be problematic in terms of global harmonization.

In addition, Korea and other Asian countries that have been accused of inadequately protecting intellectual property rights have in fact had a long cultural tradition rich with intellectual creation. Accordingly, denouncing these countries from a Western perspective for not affording protection to others' knowledge and works is unwarranted. Indeed, these countries have had a culture of respecting others' intellectual creations through social ethics or unwritten academic codes rather than through individual property rights. It is thus important to keep in mind the expression, "ethics rather than rights," when trying to understand Eastern countries and their cultures.

5.3 What are the challenges awaiting the Thai government if the Bayh-Dole Act is adopted in Thailand?

Orakanoke Phanraksa

I. INTRODUCTION

Over the past decade, many developing countries have passed their laws sharing a concept similar to that of the United States (US) Bayh-Dole Act[1] (hereinafter "BD Act"), that ownership of government-funded intellectual property shall vest into grant recipients under certain conditions. The Thai government is moving toward a similar direction, which is to adopt the ownership concept of government-funded research to their intellectual property (IP) system. Whether or not the Bayh-Dole concept is a proper model for developing countries is a key question frequently critiqued by many academics in the US. This chapter argues that the concept of IP ownership alone would not work in a different research and technology transfer enviroment like Thailand. Instead, other factors are required in order to improve the technology transfer system. Unlike the US federal funding agencies that require uniform IP policy with the goal to promote technology transfer from public sectors to industries, the Thai government considers adopting the Bayh-Dole Act concept based on different grounds. There are fewer than ten government funding agencies who play an essential role in promoting good science in Thailand. In most cases, government funding agencies shall co-own funded IP with their grant recipients. Under Thai Patent law, licensing or any assignments of the patent title requires the consent of the co-owner in writing.[2] This frequently creates bureacracy and further delays licensing transactions. To solve this problem, some funding agencies opt

[1] Patent and Trademark Act of 1980 (Bayh-Dole Act), Pub.L. No. 96-517, 98 Stat. 3015 (1980) (codified as amended at 35.U.S.C. §§200–212).

[2] The Thai Patent Act B.E.2522 (A.D.1979) Section 40.

for individual IP management agreements, giving a grant contractor the right to manage the funded IP on their behalf on a case-by-case basis.[3] Although IP management agreements are made available by some funding agencies, whether or not the right to manage such funded IP will pass to the grant contractor is subject to the funding agencies' sole discretion. Moreover, due to the fact that IP management agreement is required by each individual funding agency at different stages of funding processes, this could easily cause confusion and uncertainty to grant applicants who are new or not familiar with the different timeline conditions.

Other grounds remain as to why the BD Act model is considered by the Thai government as a suitable model for the country. In order to articulate and examine these grounds, this chapter is divided into four parts. Part I briefly discusses the Bayh-Dole Act and recent critiques made by academia in the US. This is to reflect issues that Thailand should take into consideration. Part II provides an overview of the technology transfer policy in Thailand. There are three issues discussed in depth in this section. First, the significance of IP ownership and the different types of research activities that render different conditions of this ownership. Funding research is one part of the discussion as it is directly related to the BD Act concept. Furthermore, a form of activity that becomes a frequent channel for the transfer of technology from public to private sectors is a research collaboration. In this section, first, challenges encountered by and between research contractual parties are addressed. Second, key factors to strengthen the technology transfer system are introduced. A research funding system is a critical issue requiring a closer examination. Although empirical studies of licensing activities of government-funded research are rare and unsystematic, a study of the Science Technology and Innovation Policy Office (STI) indicates that a small percentage of government-funded research was commercialized over the past decades.[4] For instance, the oldest funding agency, founded in 1956 and whose IP unit was just established in 2006, has sought out IP protections through different forms of IPs, including patents, petty patents, plant varieties, copyrights, and trademarks. Nonetheless, only 10 out of 92 IPs were licensed with no disclosure of

---

[3] Examples of the key government funding agencies that give the grant recipients the right to manage funded IPs are Thailand Research fund (TRF), National Science and Technology Development Agency (NSTDA), and National Research Council of Thailand (NRCT).

[4] Science, Technology, and Innovation Policy Study titled "Policy Measures to Promote the Thai Intellectual Property System," 2012 (on file with author).

their generated revenue. A statistic for another leading organization functioning as a funding and a research institute reported that only 10% of their accumulative 1888 IPs have been licensed since 1991.[5] This has raised some critical concerns, such as whether existing research grant criteria and reviewing processes are valid in such a way that would promote government-funded research for further utilization, and what are key factors influencing a private sector's interest in acquiring or licensing in government-funded research. Third, the challenges that technology licensing offices often encounter are deliberated. At present, there are mainly ten major universities being sponsored by the Ministry of Education through a project titled "Promoting Technology Licensing Office in Academic Institutions."[6] Although these ten offices have been partially supported by the government since 2006, it does not necessarly imply all of them are doing well in technology licensing. Institutional politics such as different visions and priorities of the university's executive, understanding of university's top management level, and continuation of institutional support play the key roles in the direction of their university technology licensing offices (TLOs). Part III proposes policy considerations for the Thai government. Certain provisions under the BD Act are recommended while special features are proposed to meet an ultimate goal, that is to improve IP management in a public sector and to promote the technology transfer system in Thailand. Part IV delivers a conclusion. For further implementation, some recommendations are also proposed.

II. THE BAYH-DOLE ACT AND RECENT US CRITIQUES

The Bayh-Dole legislation is a model symbolizing IP ownership of government-funded research. The justification behind the passage of the BD Act could be simply elaborated as follows. After World War II, the US government needed to spur their economic growth and strengthen their national competitiveness. The US Congress aimed at fostering technological advancement and commercialization in the industry. In the late 1970s, Congress was involved in a series of legislative debates to design the laws that created a system to transfer

---

[5] *Id.* at 25, 29.

[6] Higher Education Commission Technology Licensing Project Call for Proposal. Available at http://www.ubi.mua.go.th/download/2006050401.pdf (last visited on July 30, 2013).

technology from federal laboratories to the private sector; implemented tax incentives for collaborative work; instituted direct and indirect government support for increased research and development (R&D); and changed government patent policy to promote commercialization of federally funded technology.[7] Most proponents of the BD Act model often cited the figure that illustrates a low rate of federally funded research commercialization, that is "less than 5% of the 28,000 government owned patents were utilized."[8] It was argued that without title to an invention and proper IP protection, a company would not invest the additional time and money necessary to commercialize a product or process for the marketplace.[9] This was mainly because, in general, the government retained title to inventions made with government money.

After three decades of the implementation of the Act, there are a number of studies on the impact of the Act on the US economy, and patenting and licensing practice in US universities. There are both those who believe the BD Act was meeting its goals to promote the utilization of inventions arising from federally supported R&D, "... to promote collaboration between commercial concerns and nonprofit organizations, including universities ..."[10] and those who believe that the US economy has not grown this far because of the existence of the Act. A series of empirical studies on the BD Act that come out positive are from General Accounting Office Reports (GAO). This chapter selects only two main reports to demonstrate the different timing of the surveys done during the mid-1980s and 1990s. The first GAO study found that by 1987 all university administrators questioned indicated that the BD Act had been significant in stimulating business sponsorship of university research, which had grown 74 percent from FY 1980 to FY 1985.[11] It further reported that the private sector was less concerned knowing that universities could take title to federally funded inventions. Then, another study from the GAO also reported that agency and university representatives believed the Act had a positive impact on all stakeholders

---

7 CRS Report RL 32076, *The Bayh-Dole Act: Selected Issues in Patent Policy and the Commercialization of Technology*, by Wendy H. Schacht.

8 Federal Council for Science and Technology. Annual Report on Government Patent Policy (U.S. Government Printing Office, 1976).

9 See *supra* note 7, at 2.

10 35 U.S.C. § 200.

11 U.S. General Accounting Office, Patent Policy: Recent Changes in Federal Law Considered Beneficial, RCED-87-44, April 1987, 3.

involved.[12] In addition, a series of statistical surveys of licensing activities of the Association of University Technology Managers (AUTM) also offers apparent evidence indicating the evolution of university technology licensing. The number of licensing technologies including new products based on university technology has been increasing annually. Since 1980, more than 8778 new firms have been established to develop and market academic research, and 3927 startups still operate as of the end of FY 2011.[13] Furthermore, 670 new companies were formed, 487 of which had their primary place of business in their licensing institution's home state.[14]

Although the success of the BD Act has been saluted by its advocates over the past decades, questions and concerns have been raised as to the truthfulness of this success. These concerns could be divided into two areas. The first area involves the influence of the BD Act on university research norms and the second area involves concerns over the university patenting and licensing practice, which essentially results in limited access to research tools.

(i) Influence of the Bayh-Dole Act on University Research Norms

With respect to the influence of the Act on university research norms, this includes key concerns such as university research toward commercial application, delay in publications as a result of collaboration with the industry, and limited openness and exchange of scientific discoveries. For example, according to the empirical studies most frequently cited to demonstrate delays in academic publications (Blumenthal and Campbell), the studies indicate that approximately 20% of life science researchers delayed publication of their studies more than six months, in particular when such research is associated with patents and commercialization consideration.[15] This delay is even longer than the 30- to 60-day period that the National Institute of Health normally considers appropriate for the purpose of filing a patent. The

---

[12] U.S. General Accounting Office, Technology Transfer: Administration of the Bayh-Dole Act by Research Universities, RCED-98-126, May 1998, 2.

[13] Association of University Technology Managers, AUTM U.S. Licensing Activity Survey Highlights: FY2011. Available at http://www.autm.net/FY_2011_Licensing_Activity_Survey/9920.htm (last visited July 21, 2013).

[14] *Id.*

[15] David Blumenthal, E. Campbell, Melissa S. Anderson, Nancyanne Causino, and Karen Seashore Louis, *Withholding Research Results in Academic Life*, 277 JAMA 1224 (1997).

survey also reported that of the 210 life science companies responding, a third of those companies dispute with their academic collaborators over IP, and 30% noted that conflicts of interest emerged when university researchers were involved with another company.[16]

(ii) University Patenting and Licensing Practices

The second area involves the patenting and licensing practice of universities in the US. Due to the fact that the BD Act allows grant contractors the discretion to file patent protection on government-funded patentable inventions, the number of university patents is rising significantly in particular in the biomedical research field. According to the study by the Boston Consulting Group, new gene patents granted increased from about 400 to 2800 from 1990 to 1999.[17] The number of granted patents to universities expanded from 55% to 73% during that same period of time. Unfortunately, since there is no restriction or guideline on the type of research to patent, this freedom allows the universities to patent their inventions at will. This results in patenting of upstream research tools that may not need patent protection in the first place. A series of studies by the prominent scholars, Arti Rai and Rebecca Eisenberg, argue that the BD Act draws no distinction between inventions that lead directly to commercial products and fundamental advances known as "research tools," which in fact should be placed in the public domain for public interest.[18] Furthermore, although this concern over expansive patenting on research tools is often debated among academia in the US, Sara Boettiger and Alan Bennett have shared a similar concern regarding developing countries' access to basic

---

16 David Blumenthal, Nancyanne Causino, E. Campbell, Karen Seashore Louis, *Relationships between Academic Institutions and Industry in the Life Sciences: An Industry Survey*, 334 New Engl J Med 368–74 (1996).

17 Hamilton Moses III and Joseph B. Martin, *Academic Relationships with Industry*, 285 JAMA, 993 (2001).

18 Arti K. Rai and Rebecca S. Eisenberg, *Bayh-Dole Reform and the Progress of Biomedicine*, 66 L. & CONTEMP. PROBS. 289, 310 (2003). (Arguing that by allowing universities a sole discretion to patent discoveries made under federal funding, instead of spurring innovation, certain patents become barriers to biomedical research and development.) Rebecca S. Eisenberg, *Public Research and Private Development: Patents and Technology Transfer in Government Sponsored Research*, 82 VA. L. REV. 1663–1727 (1996). (Providing historical background of patent and technology transfer policies in the US and pointing out that the effect of the Bayh-Dole Act may be overstated and not as influential to the innovation system as claimed.)

research.[19] The studies by Sampat and other scholars also provide strong cautions for developing countries that are considering adaptation of the Bayh-Dole model.[20] They believe that the US university patenting and licensing activities that have evolved are based on a number of factors.[21] The study by Mowery suggests that the emphasis on the BD Act as a catalyst to increased university–industry cooperation and technology transfer is misleading. Instead, it can also be attributed to the long history of collaboration and knowledge flows between universities and industries in the US.[22]

Following the passage of the BD Act, the US has encountered discussion of those two areas concerned (the influence of Bayh-Dole on university research norms and the concerns about the university patenting and licensing practice that results in limited access of research tools). In many countries, such as South Africa, Brazil, and the Philippines, there is no empirical study suggesting the BD Act model works in a different research environment. The critical comment often made by prominent scholars in the US is that without proper safeguards serving the public interest in those developing countries, the effect of this US-modeled law could turn out to be harmful to their research development processes. In order to explore whether the BD Act concept would work in Thailand we must first understand the next section, which provides the background of the technology transfer system in Thailand.

---

[19] Sara Boettiger and Alan Bennett, *The Bayh-Dole Act: Implications for Developing Countries*, 46 IDEA 261, 278 (2006).

[20] A.D. So, B.N. Sampat, A.K. Rai, Deegan R. Cook, J.H. Reichman, R. Weissman, & A. Kapczynski, *Is Bayh-Dole Good for Developing Countries? Lessons from the U.S. Experience*, 6 PUB. LIBR. SCI. BIOLOGY 2078, 2082 (2008).

[21] David C. Mowery, Richard R. Nelson, B.N. Sampat & Arvids A. Ziedonis, *The Growth of Patenting and Licensing by U.S. Universities: An Assessment of the Effects of the Bayh-Dole Act of 1980*, 30 RESEARCH POLICY 99, 100 (2001).

[22] David C. Mowery, *The Bayh-Dole Act and High Technology Entrepreneurship in U.S. Universities: Chicken, Egg, or Something Else?* Paper prepared for the Eller Center conference on "Entrepreneurship Education and Technology Transfer," University of Arizona, January 21–22, 2005. Available at http://entrepreneurship.eller.arizona.edu/docs/conferences/2005/colloquium/D_Mowery.pdf (last visited on August 2, 2013).

III. OVERVIEW OF TECHNOLOGY TRANSFER POLICY IN THAILAND

At present, the policy aiming at promoting domestic transfer of technology in Thailand could be divided into two categories. The first category involves tax policy aimed at promoting R&D participation in the private sector, for example, the Department of Revenue passed the law that provides a 200% tax deduction for R&D expense.[23] The second category directly involves Thai patent law, which provides that to ensure that an inventor is entitled to benefits arising from their intellectual creation done under the course of employment, he/she is entitled to the remuneration in addition to his/her regular salary.[24] This remuneration concept is applicable to any institution in the public sector.[25] Nonetheless, whether or not government employees would receive this remuneration would be subject to his/her institutional IP policy. The Patent Act leaves government institutions discretion to design their own institutional policy. Other than these two key policies available at the national level, the rest of the technology transfer promotion policy is eventually designed on an institutional basis.

(i) Role of Intellectual Property Ownership

A basic principle of ownership of a Thai patent is that an inventor owns his/her invention unless such work is done under the course of their employment.[26] Unlike patent law, under a course of employment, an author of copyrightable work shall own his/her creation of such work unless otherwise explicitly identified in an employment contract.[27] In Thailand, a type of research transaction that seems to offer most challenges between research institutions/universities and companies is collaborative research. While a company is trying to make the best out of the deal, research institutions/universities want to secure and protect the benefits of their institution as their research is basically funded from tax money. As a consequence, the IP condition becomes an issue that delays the entire process. In particular, if the research collaboration is done with a big company, some deal negotiations and

---

23 The Tax Incentive Order No. 297 (B.E.2539) A.D.1996 and the Revenue Department under the Notification of the Ministry of Finance (No. 3), 1996.

24 The Thai Patent Act B.E.2522 Section 12.

25 *Id.* Section 13.

26 *Id.* Section 11.

27 The Thai Copyright Act B.E. 2537 (A.D.1994) Section 9.

contract preparation could last up to a year. Often, contractual parties prefer not to discuss any issues about IP at an early stage. Their main concern is that negotiation on IP would delay or even stop the deals. In contrast with the researchers' viewpoint, the delay of IP clarification at an early stage could harm the relationship between the parties. For example, there was the licensing case of a patent application related to a dental mini-implant, developed as a result of an informal collaboration between one leading national research laboratory and a group of dentists from three different universities. No document regarding IP ownership and management was arranged at the start of the collaboration. Such a document would have included the right to manage the pending patent and commercialization. After this technology was licensed to a company, technical consultancy relating to the pending patent was required. Since there was no clarification in regard to the roles of the researchers from each institution, limited assistance was provided to the company. The researchers' contribution to this collaboration and the benefit-sharing ratio between each institution was never addressed until the period shortly before the termination of the licensing agreement. This case became an expensive experience for all stakeholders as it took almost two years to clarify all controversial issues, including IP management.

Contract research, on the contrary, is less troublesome. A hirer shall own their contracted research unless explicitly agreed otherwise in writing. As for government-funded research, IP ownership depends on the institutional policy of each funding agency. Apparently, most funding agencies in Thailand shall co-own their funded IPs; however, the IP management agreement could be done separately from a master funding agreement. For instance, one major funding agency would allow the grant recipient the right of IP management only if such request is executed prior to executing the research funding agreement. In contrast, some agencies allow grant recipients to make a request for IP management rights when a patenting or licensing opportunity is anticipated, and this request is flexible to the extent that such request could be done after the completion of the research project. Having said that, the IP agreement could still become an issue and be time consuming. For instance, although the grant recipient is entitled to the right of IP management under the IP management agreement, they are required to receive the consent of the funding agency prior to executing any licensing deals.[28] Moreover, when a higher percentage

---

[28] The Thai Patent Act, *supra* note 2.

of benefit sharing is demanded by a grant recipient or when a grant recipient wants to file a patent application overseas, their request shall go through an executive board of that granting agency for a final decision.[29] A major issue in filing a patent application overseas is the patent cost. Any delay caused by a lengthy process of the IP management agreement would create uncertainty and concerns for a potential licensee, leading to a decision not to license, or would discourage the company's interest in further collaboration with the university/government laboratory. Moreover, when it comes to a research project with multi-sources of funds, this scenario would lead to a complication of the IP ownership issue and a lengthy negotiation process among stakeholders. In brief, the role of IP ownership is vital to some types of research transactions such as collaborative research and in-house research. After a closer examination of the IP ownership concern, the IP management agreement is regarded as an important tool frequently used to prevent any conflicts. Nonetheless, the IP agreement could create uncertainty for the companies, especially when dealing with licensing of government-funded research. The companies need to ensure that their contractual party has the authority to enter into licensing agreements.

(ii) Key Factors to Strengthen the Technology Transfer System

This part discusses four key factors having a considerable influence on promoting technology transfer from the public to the private sectors. According to a study by the Science, Technology, and Innovation Office (STI), four issues are identified as key factors to strengthen the technology transfer system in Thailand. These four factors are 1) IP ownership of government-funded research, 2) privatization of the Thai patent office, 3) the financial mechanism to promote R&D participation from the private sector, and 4) TLO capacity building.[30] IP ownership

---

[29] In Thailand, the patent registration and maintenance fee for non-profit organizations, including universities listed under the Department of Intellectual Property, is waived.

[30] STI Policy Study, *supra* note 4. (The study of STI was a collaborative research project between five funding agencies and the Department of Intellectual Property completed in 2012. The study discusses problems related to the IPRs and proposes four recommendations to the Thai government. Out of the four recommendations, the research team perceives the financial mechanism promoting R&D participation from the private sector most crucial to the current technology transfer system in Thailand.)

was already discussed in a previous section, thus, this part will focus on the financial mechanism and TLO capacity building. With respect to the financial mechanism, throughout the commercialization process there are, mainly, five groups of activities: technology creation, proof of concept, testing and prototyping, pilot scale, and commercialization.[31] A large proportion of innovation in many developing countries occurs in university or public research institutes and Thailand is no exception. The majority of research grants provided for technology creation and proof of concept primarily go to university and public research institutes. It is quite common for Thai Small and Medium Enterprises (SMEs) to join at a later stage or when the university technology matures or becomes more promising. According to the study by the Fiscal Policy Research Institute Foundation, the financial support needed by the private sector starts from the testing and prototyping to commericialization. Due to this demand, the Thai government is gearing toward an idea to establish a venture capital fund. If that is the case, an idea to apply the BD Act may be adopted to this funding type in order to ensure the companies have no concern regarding a complication of IP ownership after receiving the fund.[32]

Regarding TLO capacity building, this chapter argues that although there has been an evolution of TLOs in Thailand since 2006, problems remain that require closer attention from the Thai government. According to the study by Lerson, TLOs could be categorized into four tiers. The first tier goes to TLOs that have been established for longer than ten years and have more than ten personnel in the office.[33] The

---

[31] Krongkan Chadtham Kolkai Thang Kan-ngeun pue Sanab-sanoon Borisat Khanad-klang lae Khanad-yom nai Kanpattana tor yod phon-ngan vichai pai soo Kan sang moolkha puem cheung panich. (Financial policy recommendations to promote R&D participation and commercialization of Small and Medium Enterprises.) Fiscal Policy Research Institute Foundation, commissioned by the Science, Technology, and Innovation Office. September 2, 2013. (Draft in progress.)

[32] At the time of writing, the STI Office and the research team are preparing a policy recommendation for the venture capital fund to submit to the Cabinet for their approval.

[33] Lerson Tanasukarn, Naew-thang Kan sang Kuam Khem-khang hai kae Nuay-ngan Borihan chad-kan lae tai tod technology khong Sa-tha ban vichai lae Sa-tha ban kan Suek sa Thai. (Policy recommendations for the Capacity Building of IP Management and Technology Transfer Offices in Research and Academic Institutions in Thailand.), commissioned by the Science, Technology, and Innovation Office. July 1, 2013. (Draft in progress) (This study is the most updated study regarding the status of TLOs in Thailand. After a decade of

accumulative numbers of patent filings for this group are quite high, compared to the other tiers. One research institution has filed an average of 200 patent applications annually. With respect to the first tier of TLOs, this group could produce 7–10 licensing agreements annually. Some of these licensing deals could generate licensing revenue higher than USD 60,000. This figure of licensing income is considered high and it rarely happens to the other TLO tiers in Thailand.

The next tier covers the TLOs established in or after 2006. These are institutions with approximately 5–6 personnel, and these institutions file an average of 50–70 patent applications annually.[34] The third tier includes the TLOs existing in some government-funding agencies and public research institutions, while the fourth tier covers universities whose TLOs have been established less than three years. The fourth-tiered TLOs file approximately 1–50 patent applications per year, depending on the experience of their personnel.[35] The study further identifies challenges most frequently encountered by the TLOs, and these could be divided into two groups. The first group focuses on the problems in academic and research universities, most of which take the view that the understanding of an institution's top management and continuation of its support are vital to the operation and the developing direction of the offices. The second group includes the IP management units in government-funding agencies. Although some of these funding agencies have a number of IPs, the utilization ratio of such IPs and personnel in IP management is relatively limited.[36] Having discussed the problems above, it indicates the urgency to promote capacity building of TLO personnel, otherwise, the passage of a BD-like Act would jeopardize the use of government-funded research.

IV. POLICY CONSIDERATION FOR THAILAND

At present, the Thai government is considering adopting BD-like legislation in order to accelerate the transfer of government-funded

---

Lerson's latest study about TLO models in Thailand, this study focuses on the practices of TLOs/IP units in 20 institutions, 14 of which are universities, 3 are public research institutes, and 3 are government funding agencies.)

[34] *Id.* at 44.

[35] *Id.*

[36] *Id.* at 45–49. No numbers or details of licensing deals are revealed or discussed in this project study due to confidentiality concerns of the interviewed/surveyed respondents.

research to the private sector. The challenges imposed on the US government in the early 1970s were different from what Thailand has encountered today. Based on a different research environment and a scarcity of technology transfer professionals in Thailand, this chapter argues that the Thai government has to take a holistic approach to develop both legal tools and relevant policies, dealing with infrastructure, including the funding system and human resources.

To start with, it is essential for the government to consider the following issues. First, the need to revisit the Thai research funding system is inevitable. At present, the major six funding agencies are trying to allocate their research funds on a technological cluster basis. With this clustering system, they expect to be able simply to evaluate the entire value chain of each research cluster being managed. In doing so, a huge amount of funding will be allocated to one agency before further distributing the fund to individual grant recipients. Nonetheless, this could lead to more trouble for TLOs representing those institutions involved. This is because there are three tiers of management, starting with the major funding agency, the implementing funding agency, and then multi-grant recipients. Without proper management, the IP would thus be jointly owned by many stakeholders through these multi-layers. Given that the BD Act concept was adopted, limited access to basic research done by those multi-grant recipients is anticipated. Thus, not having a safeguard in place to guarantee access for those granted basic research, including research tools, could result in delaying R&D progress in Thailand. Therefore, a guideline for TLO practice is highly recommended.

The preceding paragraph reflects the requirements to be carried out by the funding agencies. What also needs to be addressed is how to increase R&D participation from the private sector. It is important to have the private sector join the research project at an early stage in order to help shape and fine-tune the invention from the idea to market. Most SMEs come in at the very last stage of technology development due to lower financial risks. The study of the Fiscal Policy Research Institute Foundation points out that among the four categories of their interviewed enterprises, the first three groups (newly established enterprises, small enterprises, and medium enterprises) rank financial support as their top priority. Large enterprises tend to concern themselves more with the confidentiality issue when dealing with outside partners. In this regard, having reviewed other research grant policies involving small business companies in the US, the Small Business and Innovation Research program (SBIR) and Small

Business Technology Transfer program (STTR)[37] as implemented in the US are worth discussing here. Both the SBIR and STTR are three-phase programs, comprising a feasibility/proof concept, a continuation of the research results from Phase 1, and finally a commercialization stage. While a matching fund under the SBIR is provided for US small business enterprises, the STTR is available for research cooperation between small business enterprises and a research institution, requiring the company to perform at least 40% of that R&D and a research institution perform at least 30% of that research project. Since it is the federal government fund, the IP ownership concept under the BD Act is also applied here. Nonetheless, STTR differs from SBIR in several aspects, one significant aspect being to require that both the SMEs and their research partner execute an IP agreement detailing issues like an allocation of intellectual property rights and rights to carry out follow-on research, development, or commercialization activities. As stated earlier, collaborative research becomes a more common way to link government laboratories to the private sector in Thailand. It is anticipated that for a research grant to be available for cooperation between these two stakeholders would be one of the significant tools for driving innovative research in Thailand. Therefore, a detailed study to further examine whether the SBIR and STTR program should be emulated in the research funding system in Thailand is highly recommended.

With respect to human resources, countries considering the BD-like legislation should be prepared to subsidize their TLOs in order to ensure that the university TLOs could handle the funded IP properly.[38] The subsidy should consider relevant costs, including but not limited to the management of IPs and human resource development. Currently, so far as the TLO sponsorship program is concerned, there is only one main source of sponsorship provided by the Higher Education Commission, Ministry of Education. This may be insufficient if the Thai government wants to increase the number of Thai technology transfer professionals.

---

[37] SBIR is a US Government program, coordinated by the Small Business Administration (SBA), in which 2.5% of the total extramural research budgets of all federal agencies with extramural research budgets in excess of 100 million USD are reserved for contracts or grants to small business. A key objective of the program is to encourage domestic small businesses to engage in federal R&D that has the potential for commercialization. Available at http://www.sbir.gov/about/about-sbir. STTR is also coordinated by the SBA and established in order to facilitate cooperative R&D between small business concerns and US research institutions. Available at http://www.sbir.gov/about/about-sttr (last visited on September 6, 2013).

[38] Bhaven N. Sampat, *Lessons from Bayh-Dole*, 468 NATURE 756 (2010).

In addition to the policies to promote the infrastructure above, this part suggests the legal tools that would facilitate the management and commercialization of the government-funded IPs. Having learned from the US experience after its three decades of the implementation of the BD Act, below are the key points the Thai government should take into consideration. First, a transparent procedure in the patenting and licensing by the grant recipients is required. This is to ensure that the inventions discovered are treated properly. At present, numbers of patents are one of the crucial key performance indicators (KPIs) in many universities and most public research institutions in Thailand. A trend or domino effect is apparent when the number of patent filings is set at as high a number as institutional KPIs each year. This phenomenon has already created a bottleneck problem since TLO personnel have to deal with quantitative patenting tasks rather than the qualitative ones. Filing as many patent applications as possible with the patent fee waived by the DIP could easily result in patenting of research that might not have needed protection in the first place, or could result in low-quality patents. Second, a non-exclusive license policy should be promoted by the grant recipients in order to allow open access. In practice, although the non-exclusive license policy is endorsed by many institutions, it has an institutional basis. In particular in the pharmaceutical field, it is often the case that the licensee prefers an exclusive license. It turns out to be only deep-pocket companies who are able to afford such licensing costs. Thus, in order to ensure the balance of viewpoint in how to commercialize government-funded research, the funding agencies would need to come up with a non-exclusive licensing policy. Third, licensing preferences for domestic companies would be to the benefit of the country. The Thai government has to carefully look at the types of domestic preference that they want to foster. According to the study by Mireles, a tiered approach for developing countries was proposed.[39] Although Thai SME business types are not that varied, the proposed model is worth considering. The recommendations are that the first preference is for licensees that would carry out R&D in the country, as well as manufacturing, and would use the technology for the country's benefit; the second preference is for licensees that are manufacturing-based and would use the technology in the country; and finally, if either one of the above preferences could not be met, the license shall go to licensees that would use the technology to

---

[39] Michael S. Mireles, *The Bayh-Dole Act and Incentives for the Commercialization of Government-Funded Invention in Developing Countries*, 76 UMKC L. Rev. 525, 543 (2007).

substantially benefit the country.[40] At least, this policy could be viewed as a safe harbor for both the funding agencies and the grant recipients. Fourth, the retention of the non-exclusive, nontransferable, irrevocable, paid-up license for the government agency to use the government funded IP should not be left out.

Finally, although the IP ownership concept under the BD Act is well taken, it should be carefully crafted in legislation if the government also wishes to emulate the SBIR and STTR programs in the research funding system. Through the commercialization process, if there is any research collaboration between the university/public research institutions and the SBIR-like grant recipients, the IP ownership and IP management condition could lead to a complex negotiation. Therefore, this chapter strongly recommends that the draft legislation clearly state to which funding types the IP ownership concept would be applied and under what conditions.

V. CONCLUSION

Without any precursor studies to examine whether the BD-like legislation works in those forerunner countries whose research environments are similar, many developing countries opt for an option to pass the law retaining salient features of the US system, with the expectation of seeing a development of their technology transfer system prosper. Thailand is on its way to adopt the BD law model like many of those harbingers. However, this chapter argues that there remain other factors in need of serious attention from the Thai government should the BD model be adopted. The chapter has proposed two prongs of policy consideration. The first prong deals with the funding system and infrastructure. The funding system needs to be revisited as it is a beginning point for how the research of the country is to be developed and utilized at a later stage. A middle person linking the R&D to the business world is the TLOs. Therefore, a capacity building of TLO personnel is a must and continuation of the government subsidy for TLO activities is highly encouraged. In order to promote more R&D participation from the private sector, the SBIR and STTR models are worth considering.

With respect to the features of the draft legislation, this chapter proposes to retain certain provisions of the BD Act and add some features to ensure the public interest is served. The suggested provisions

---

40 *Id.* at 544.

are as follows: the requirement of the transparency in patenting and licensing of the grant recipients, the non-exclusive license policy, the licensing preferences for domestic companies, and finally the retention of the rights to use the government-funded research. With this in mind, since there is no "one size fits all" law model, this piece of draft legislation would become a challenge for the Thai policy maker in the near future. What could be done in parallel is to start working on the regulatory implementation to ensure the law could achieve its ultimate goal, that is to accelerate and facilitate IP management within the government-funding agencies and to maximize utilization of government-funded research through a more uniform and systematic management system.

5.4 Public health and pharmaceutical patent protection in Indonesia: The implementation of the TRIPS safeguards and other strategies to increase access to essential medicines[1]

Tomi Suryo Utomo

BACKGROUND

In 1998 Michael A. Heller introduced the term "tragedy of the anti-commons" to describe the situation in which people have limited access to a scarce resource.[2] Even though Heller focuses on property

[1] Portions of this chapter were first published in the article "Pharmaceutical Patent Protection and the Introduction of Generic Drugs in Indonesia in the Post-TRIPS Era – Is Patent Law the Only Factor Affecting the Introduction of Generic Drugs?" 42 IIC 759 (2011).

[2] The definition of the tragedy of anti-commons is "multiple owners are each endowed with the right to exclude others from a scarce resource, and no one has an effective privilege of use." (Michael A. Heller, *The Tragedy of the Anticommons: Property in the Transition from Marx to Markets*, 111 HARV. L. REV. 621, 3 (1998); James J. Buchanan and Yong J. Yoon, *Symmetric Tragedies: Commons and Anticommons*, 43 J.L. & ECON. 1, 1–3 (2000); Francesco Parisi, Norbert Schulz and Ben Depoorter, *Simultaneous and Sequential Anticommons*, YALE LAW SCHOOL JOHN M. OLIN CENTER FOR STUDIES IN LAW, ECONOMICS, AND PUBLIC POLICY YEAR 2003, Paper 279, at http://lsr.nellco.org/cgi/viewcontent.cgi?article=1009&context=yale/lepp (last visited Oct. 5, 2006)); Stephen R. Munzer, *The Common and the Anticommons in the Law and Theory of Property, in* PHILOSOPHY OF LAW AND LEGAL THEORY 152 (Martin P. Golding and William A. Edmundson eds., 2005). This term is a "mirror image"of the Tragedy of Commons introduced by Garret Hardin in 1968 which refers to "a potentially unsustainable situation in which too many owners have the privilege to use a

law in general, many scholars now use that term in other areas of law, including intellectual property law.[3] The exclusive right given to an owner of intellectual property to exclude others from using that property appears to fit with Heller's description. An exclusive right often creates tension between the owner and members of society whose access to the intellectual property becomes limited by law.

The tension between private ownership rights and public access is a key feature of pharmaceutical patents. Protection for medicines, it is argued, is likely to affect access to medicines for people in developing countries. Both before and after the TRIPS Agreement, pharmaceutical patent protection has been a controversial issue within a number of countries.[4] In particular, in the post-TRIPS era, patent protection for medicines has been a concern among WTO members because TRIPS requires members to provide patent protection for processes and products relating to pharmaceuticals.[5] These include protection for pharmaceutical compositions, therapeutic uses, polymorphs, active ingredients, related forms and pharmaceutical processes.[6]

Many developing countries have objected to the inclusion of patent protection for pharmaceuticals within the WTO framework for three primary reasons. First, some developing countries believe that access

---

given resource or *commons* and no one has a right to exclude others." (Shishir K Jha, *Globalization of Intellectual Property Rights and the Enclosure of the Commons,* http://www.ircc.iitb.ac.in/webadm/update/archives/August_2003/glob-shishirl.html (last visited Mar. 3, 2006); Lee Anne Fennell, *Common Interest Tragedies*, 98 NW. U. L. REV. 907, 3–7 (2004); Abraham Bell and Gideon Parchomovsky, *Of Property and Antiproperty,* 102 MICH. L. REV. 1, 6–7 (2003).

3 *See* Michael A. Heller and Rebecca S. Eisenberg, *Can Patents Deter Innovation? Anticommons in Biomedical Research*, 280 SCIENCE 698 (1998), Robert P. Merges, *A New Dynamism in the Public Domain*, 71 U. CHI. L. REV. 183, 1–6 (2004); Anupam Chander and Madhavi Sunder, *The Romance of the Public Domain*, 92 CAL. L. REV. 1331, 1–7 (2004); Mark A. Lemley, *Property, Intellectual Property, and Free Riding*, 83 TEX. L. REV. 1031, 1–6 (2005).

4 For example in South Africa and Brazil, there is a strong movement to refuse the existence of patent law in pharmaceuticals following the national HIV/AIDS epidemic in these countries (*see* JOHN R. THOMAS, PHARMACEUTICAL PATENT LAW 5 (2005).

5 The legal foundation of this obligation is from article 27 of TRIPS which states "... patent shall be available for any inventions, whether products or processes, in all fields of technology, provided that they are new, involve an inventive step and are capable of industrial application."

6 CARLOS M. CORREA, INTEGRATING PUBLIC HEALTH CONCERNS INTO PATENT LEGISLATION IN DEVELOPING COUNTRIES 37 (2000).

to medicines is a human right.[7] They worry that protection will restrict access to essential medicines.[8] Second, some developing countries view protection for pharmaceutical patents as ineffective and have refused to protect intellectual property rights sufficiently when protection was not in their best economic interests and a certain level of technology and development – such as when the Netherlands did not provide patent protection during the 19th century.[9] Third, based on the experiences of some developing countries, such as those of India and Brazil, it is argued that protection will hamper the development of local pharmaceutical companies in developing countries that aim to increase domestic access to medicines.[10] These concerns are understandable because a number of

---

[7] *See* WHO ESSENTIAL DRUG AND MEDICINES POLICY, NETWORK FOR MONITORING THE IMPACT OF GLOBALIZATION AND TRIPS ON ACCESS TO MEDICINES 20 (2001).

[8] *See* DAVID P. FIDLER, INTERNATIONAL LAW AND PUBLIC HEALTH MATERIALS ON AND ANALYSIS OF GLOBAL HEALTH JURISPRUDENCE 259 (2000); WILLIAM CORNISH, INTELLECTUAL PROPERTY OMNIPRESENT, DISTRACTING, IRRELEVANT? 11 (2004). According to the WHO estimation "one third of the world's population lacks access to the most basic medicines, while in the poorest parts of Africa and Asia this figure climbs to one half" (GRAHAM DUKES, THE LAW AND ETHICS OF THE PHARMACEUTICAL INDUSTRY 263 (2006).

[9] *See* Marco C.E.J. Bronckers, *The Impact of TRIPS: Intellectual Property Protection in Developing Countries*, 31 COMMON MKT. L. REV. 1245 (1994); Julio Nogues, *Patents and Pharmaceutical Drugs: Understanding the Pressures on Developing Countries*, 24 J. WORLD TRADE, no. 6, at 81 (1990). Salazar said that Germany excluded chemicals from patentability in a law of 1877 and France in its law of 1844. The reason for this policy at that time was because "it was necessary to reinvigorate an industry that was lagging behind its counterparts in other countries." In addition, the extension to protect pharmaceutical product patents in several developed countries existed when those "achieved a certain level of development of their pharmaceutical industries." France provided protection for pharmaceutical product patents in 1960 and was followed by Germany in 1968, Italy in 1978, Japan in 1976 and Switzerland in 1977 (Silvia Salazar, *Intellectual Property and the Right to Health*, http://www.wipo.int/edocs/mdocs/tk/en/wipo_unhchr_ip_pnl_98/wipo_unhchr_ip_pnl_98_3.pdf (last visited Jan. 7, 2014)); *see also* Ants Kukrus and Raul Kartus, *Issues of Pharmaceutical Products Trade in the European Union in the Global Market Conditions*, http:www.mattimar.ee/publikatsioonid/majanduspoliitika/2007/06.pdf (last visited Jan. 7, 2014).

[10] India has a strong opinion about the impact of pharmaceutical patent protection, particularly pharmaceutical product patents. This opinion can be found in the objectives of the Indian Patent Law of 1970 which abolished pharmaceutical product in that law for the purpose of developing "an independent Indian Pharmaceutical industry." (*see* Carsten Fink, *How Stronger Patent Protection in India Might Affect the Behavior of Transnational*

studies have shown that patent protection for pharmaceuticals increases the price of drugs in developing countries.[11] Higher prices limit the access of the public, particularly the poor, to cheaper drugs.[12]

Reduced access to important medicines has caused domestic conflict in many developing countries, including Indonesia. For the Indonesian government, protection for pharmaceutical patents[13] constitutes a serious public health issue. It must balance its policy of protecting pharmaceutical patents[14] according to the TRIPS Agreement (international standards) and its goal of providing cheaper drugs (domestic developmental policy).[15] Unless the government provides sufficient protection for pharmaceutical patents, it faces sanctions from the WTO for violating the principles of international trade.

Pharmaceutical Industries, at 7, http://elibrary.worldbank.org/doi/pdf/10.1596/1813-9450-2352 (last visited Jan. 7, 2014)). Another example is Brazil, which abolished the protection of pharmaceutical products in 1969 for the purpose of creating a stronger domestic pharmaceutical industry (Srividhya Ragavan, *Can't We All Get Along? The Case for a Workable Patent Model*, 35 ARIZ. ST. L.J. 117, 7 (2003); *see also* Keith E. Maskus and Denise Eby Konan, *Trade- Related Intellectual Property Rights: Issues and Exploratory Results, in* ANALYTICAL AND NEGOTIATING ISSUES IN THE GLOBAL TRADING SYSTEM 402–03 (Alan V. Deardorff and Robert M. Stern eds., 1994).

11 For examples: Nogues (1990, 1993), Challu (1991), Chambouleyron (1995), Watal (1996, unpublished) (*see* UNITED NATIONS CONFERENCE ON TRADE AND DEVELOPMENT, THE TRIPS AGREEMENT AND DEVELOPING COUNTRIES 62 (1996)), and K. Bala and Kiran Sagoo (1999) (K. Bala and Kiran Sagoo, Patents and Prices, http://www.haiweb.org/pubs/hainews/Patents%20and%20Prices.html (April/May 2000).

12 *See* Theresa Beeby Lewis, *Patent Protection for the Pharmaceutical Industries: A Survey of the Patent Laws of Various Countries*, 30 INT'L LAW 835 (1996).

13 Pharmaceutical patents cover both products and processes. However, this chapter focuses more on pharmaceutical products. Graham Dukes defines pharmaceutical products as "a substance or a complex of substances which is administered to man or to animals in order to prevent, diagnose, alleviate or cure a disease, to relieve a symptom, or to modify bodily function in some way" (DUKES, *supra* note 8, at 3). For the purpose of this chapter, the discussion about pharmaceutical products is limited to a substance which is administered to human beings.

14 Pharmaceutical patents (both process and product patents) were given limited protection in Indonesia for the first time under the Indonesian Patent Act of 1989.

15 The tension is more evident after the Indonesian government complied with the TRIPS Agreement in 1997.

On the other hand, Indonesians' need to reduce the cost of medicines is pressing for four reasons. First, the government budget for medications is limited.[16] Second, the rate of generic drugs sale is low.[17] Third, the burden of chronic diseases and emerging problems, such as HIV/AIDS, is increasing at alarming levels.[18] Fourth the price of drugs has increased

---

[16] Indonesia's public health expenditure on health (0.6% of GDP or US$7.6 per capita annual) is significantly less than other ASEAN countries such as Thailand (1.9 % of GDP or US$35.5 per capita annual) and Philippines (1.6% of GDP or US$16.4 per capita annual) (BPS-Statistic, Bappenas and UNDP Indonesia, The Economics Of Democracy: Financing Human Development in Indonesia, http://www.undp.or.id/pubs/ihdr2004/ihdr2004_full.pdf (last visited Jan. 7, 2014). The estimated data for Indonesia is from 1996–1997 and for Malaysia and Thailand is between 1995 and 1999); Tomi Suryo Utomo, *Pharmaceutical Patent Protection and the Introduction of Generic Drugs in Indonesia in the Post-TRIPS Era – Is Patent Law the Only Factor Affecting the Introduction of Generic Drugs?,* 42 IIC 760 (2011).

[17] Furthermore, Indonesian sale of generic drugs, which would be an effective strategy of providing cheaper drugs to the public, is only 10% of drug sales. This is lower than other countries in Asia, such as Thailand (23%), Singapore (22%) and Taiwan (70%) (in Media Indonesia Online, Tarif RS Tidak Standar, *Askes Sulit Berkembang [Hospital Fees Are Not Standard; Health Insurance Cannot Grow]*, http://mediaindo.i2.co.id/cetak/berita.asp?action=cetak&id=2003042923442560 (last visited Apr. 30, 2003). Compared to developed countries, such as Germany, US and Japan, generic drug sales in Indonesia are lower than those countries where the sales comprise more than 30% of drug sales (Kompas Newspaper, *Dana Masyarakat Dihemat Rp. 1 Trilyun, Jika 30 Persen Dokter Gunakan Obat Generik [Public Funds Can Be Saved Rp. 1 Trillion, If 30% of Indonesian Doctors Use Generic Drugs]*, http://www.kompas.com/kompas-cetak/0105 /23/iptek/ dana10.htm (last visited May 23, 2001); Utomo, *id.*

[18] Relating to HIV prevalence, there is a significant increase in number, particularly in the regions of Kalimantan, Papua and Riau (UNAIDS AND WHO, AIDS EPIDEMIC UPDATE : DECEMBER 2003, SWITZERLAND, UNAIDS, at 5, 20–21 (2003)). Nowadays, it is predicted that 90 000–130 000 Indonesians are infected by HIV (UNDP, Laporan Perkembangan Pencapaian Tujuan Pembangunan Millennium Indonesia [A Progress Report of How to Realize the Indonesian Millennium Development], http://www.undp.or.id/pubs/imdg2004/BI/IndonesiaMDG_BI_Goal6.pdf). In Papua, HIV prevalence reached 17% in 2002 (UNAIDS and WHO, *id.* at 21). Even though this number is not as high as in Africa or other Asian countries, the government should anticipate the steady growth of HIV due to the fast spread of this disease. In the near future, it is not impossible that the growth will be a national epidemic. Similarly, from 1987 to 2002 the number of AIDS sufferers in Indonesia was also significantly increasing. Up to the end of September 2003, there were 1239 reported AIDS cases in Indonesia (UNDP, *id.*).

due to pharmaceutical patent protection.[19] This situation was aggravated in the past by the Indonesian government's failure to maximize a number of safeguards included within the TRIPS Agreement. This is attributable both to the fault of the Indonesian government and the unclear and flexible nature of those safeguards.[20] This chapter will consider the options or alternatives open to the Indonesian government to address the access to essential medicine issues that confront Indonesia as a member of the WTO from the perspective of the implementation of TRIPS safeguards. A number of questions will be considered: Which safeguards are most appropriate for Indonesia? Based on Indonesia's situation and the experience of other countries, what policies or strategies outside of the TRIPS Agreement might be considered?

The answers to those questions can help the Indonesian government to consider several policies derived from the TRIPS Agreement. These should improve drug prices and generic drug availability. To provide a comparative discussion, this chapter also describes the experience and policies of the Indian government in handling the impact of pharmaceutical patents on essential medicines.

---

[19] *See* some studies done by researchers in developing countries (UNITED NATIONS CONFERENCE ON TRADE AND DEVELOPMENT; Bala and Sagoo, *supra* note 11).

[20] Regarding public health issues, the TRIPS agreement did provide the safeguards, such as bolar provision, parallel imports, compulsory license and government use for every member of the WTO to handle the impact of pharmaceutical patent on public health. But, the Indonesian government has not yet used those safeguards effectively in its national patent law. Even though those safeguards were included in patent law, those cannot be applied due to lack of detailed implementing regulations. Besides that, the government tries to act carefully in implementing the safeguard because the TRIPS Agreement consists of minimum standards only but is not a uniform law. Through these minimum standards, the TRIPS Agreement allows its members to "have considerable room to develop their own patent" (CORREA, *supra* note 6, at 3). Consequently, each member of the WTO has a different patent law standard, including how to interpret the safeguards and to what extent those safeguards applications are consistent with the TRIPS Agreement (*see* CORREA, *id.*, at 4). In practice, the different interpretation of the TRIPS safeguards creates a conflict mainly between developed countries and developing countries that needs to be solved at the dispute settlement body of the WTO. If one country is proved to be applying the safeguards inconsistently with the TRIPS Agreement, the country will face sanctions from the WTO for violating the principles of international trade. Not surprisingly, most developing countries hesitate to apply the safeguards on the ground of avoiding sanctions.

I. THE IMPLEMENTATION OF THE TRIPS SAFEGUARDS IN THE INDONESIAN PATENT LAW[21]

The discussion about access to essential medicine issues nowadays cannot be separated from the TRIPS Agreement. Many countries worried about the impact of pharmaceutical patent protection on access to essential medicines before the TRIPS Agreement in 1994. Most countries did not provide protection for pharmaceuticals because it would impact their society's access to affordable drugs.[22] To accommodate these concerns, most countries negotiating the TRIPS agreement inserted some pro-public health articles. These are the safeguard articles, including parallel imports, bolar provision, compulsory license and government use (discussed below) and Article 8 which mandates that the members of the WTO "adopt measures necessary to protect public health."[23]

The TRIPS Agreement contains 12 articles relevant for pharmaceutical patent protection[24] and three articles about policies of managing the impact of pharmaceutical patent protection on public health (the TRIPS safeguards).[25] In adopting those policies, the members are advised that

---

[21] Portions of this subchapter were first published in the article "Pharmaceutical Patent Protection and the Introduction of Generic Drugs in Indonesia in the Post-TRIPS Era – Is Patent Law the Only Factor Affecting the Introduction of Generic Drugs?" 42 IIC 759 (2011).

[22] *See* Kirsten Peterson, *Recent Intellectual Property Trends in Developing Countries*, 33 HARV. INT'L L.J. 277, 1 (1992); DGDFC AND WHO, THE TRIPS AGREEMENT AND PHARMACEUTICALS 11 (2000); Nabila Ansari, *International Patent Rights in a Post-Doha World*, 11 INT'L TRADE L J. 57, 3 (2002).

[23] Article 8 of the TRIPS Agreement.

[24] The relevant 12 articles of the TRIPS Agreement are as follows: Articles 3 and 4 (non-discrimination principles), Article 7 (objectives of TRIPS), Article 8 (protection of public health), Article 27 (process and product patents; and subject matter which may be excluded from patentability), Article 33 (the 20-year minimum term of protection), Article 34 (reversal of burden of proof for process patents), Article 39 (data protection and exclusivity), Articles 65 and 66 (transitional arrangements for developing country WTO members), Articles 66 and 67 (transfer of technology and technical cooperation), Article 70/8 (mailbox filings) and Article 71/1 (review) (WHO ESSENTIAL DRUGS AND MEDICINES POLICY, *supra* note 7, at 17).

[25] Article 6 (parallel importation), Article 30 (Bolar Provision) and Article 31 (compulsory license and government use) (*id.*, at 17); Utomo, *supra* note 17, at 778; *see* also Tomi Suryo Utomo (2), *Access to Essential Medicine Issues in the TRIPS Agreement and the Existence of the TRIPS Safeguards in Managing the*

those measures must be consistent with the provisions of the TRIPS Agreement. The TRIPS Agreement does not provide either uniform international law or legal requirements to implement those safeguards in members' national laws.[26] Consequently, the adoption of those safeguards, including how to interpret them, varies among members, notably between developed and developing countries.[27]

The following discussion will describe four TRIPS safeguards that can be used to manage the impact of pharmaceutical patent protection. Since the TRIPS safeguards are purposed to manage the impact of pharmaceutical patent protection on public health, particularly introduction to generic drugs, the explanation below will discuss this issue by focusing on the implementation of the TRIPS safeguards in Indonesia.[28]

(i) Parallel Imports

Article 6 of the TRIPS Agreement classifies parallel imports as "exhaustion" of intellectual property and "not subject to the WTO dispute settlement process."[29] In the international context, the justification of parallel imports is based on the doctrine of first sale and exhaustion of rights.[30] According to the doctrine of first sale, owners of intellectual property will lose their rights of controlling goods once they sell them in a market. Theoretically, by putting their products in a market, the owners exhaust their intellectual property rights dealing with goods sold.[31]

Parallel imports are covered by article 135(a) of the Indonesian Patent Act of 2001 that defines parallel imports as the importation of a pharmaceutical product that has been patented and marketed in another country. Under this article, importation is exempt from criminal liability.

Impact of Pharmaceutical Patent Protection, 43 JURNAL YUSTISIA 66–73 (2009), January–April, 2009, Faculty of Law, University of Sebelas Maret (UNS), Solo (Surakarta), Indonesia.

[26] CORREA, *supra* note 6, at 3; Utomo, *id*; Utomo (2), *id*.

[27] CORREA, *id,* at 4.

[28] Utomo, *supra* note 26.

[29] WHO Policy Perspectives On Medicines, *Globalization, TRIPS and Access to Pharmaceuticals*, http://apps.who.int/medicinedocs/pdf/s2240e/s2240e.pdf (last visited Jan. 7, 2014).

[30] Tait R. Swanson, *Combating Gray Market Goods in a Global Market: Comparative Analysis of Intellectual Property Laws and Recommended Strategies*, 22 HOUS. J. INT'L L. 327, 3 (2000).

[31] *Id.*

While there is no corresponding provision on civil-law infringement, the courts are likely to take Art. 135 as a guidance in this respect as well, thereby exempting the parallel importation of goods lawfully marketed abroad.[32] The main goal of regulating parallel imports in the Indonesian Patent Act is to gain access to more affordable drug prices. The use of parallel importation depends upon government policy to support the availability and affordability of drugs for general society (article 135 (a)). Parallel importation regulated in the Indonesian Patent Act is aimed at obtaining alternatives to pharmaceutical products that are marketed above international market prices.[33]

(ii) Bolar Provisions

Bolar provisions are regulated in article 135(b) of the Indonesian Patent Act of 2001. This provision allows Indonesian companies to prepare to make a generic drug for a medicine still patented, two years before the patent expires. The Bolar provision allows local generic manufacturers to carry out tests, to prepare for production, and to seek marketing approval before the patent expires. If a generic drug is promptly marketed, it can be offered at lower prices and provide more affordable drugs. Article 135 (b) was part of the 2001 Patent Act to improve the availability and affordability of important pharmaceutical products.[34]

Bolar provisions are a form of limited exception to the exclusive rights of patent holders. Under Article 30 of the TRIPS Agreement, such exceptions are not prohibited as long as the exceptions "do not unreasonably conflict with a normal exploitation of the patent and do not unreasonably prejudice the legitimate interests of the patent owner." The Bolar provision is only for activities prior to actual production and selling. These activities do not damage the patent holder's interests during the patent period and therefore Bolar provisions under the Indonesian patent act are consistent with the TRIPS Agreement. However, the impact of this exception is limited due to the fact that a generic manufacturer would not normally obtain access to the originator's clinical studies supplied to the health authorities in order to get marketing approval. This is understandable because Bolar provisions are used when patents are still in the period of protection and therefore data held by the health authorities are not yet available

---

32 Utomo, *supra* note 28, at 778–79; *see* also Utomo (2), *supra* note 26.

33 Utomo, *supra* note 32, at 779; Utomo (2), *supra* note 32.

34 Utomo, *id*; Utomo (2), *id*.

to public. For this reason, carrying out studies on bioequivalency would not be sufficient for the generic manufacturer, and the requirement of conducting all clinical trials *de novo* certainly reduces any incentive to develop generic drugs.[35]

(iii) Compulsory Licenses

Compulsory licensing is provided in patent laws to allow public authorities to grant licenses to a third party without the consent of the patent holder. They may be issued for specified grounds, including public health. They are used to protect public interest, such as unaffordable patented drugs due to abnormally high prices. Indonesia regulates compulsory licenses in Article 74-87 of the Indonesian Patent Act of 2001. Compulsory licensing is decided by the Directorate General of Intellectual Property Office.[36]

Article 31 of the TRIPS agreement allows a WTO member to use "the subject matter of a patent without the authorization of the right holder, including use by the government or third parties authorized by the government." According to the article, such provisions should be respected.[37]

Even though compulsory licenses fulfill all requirements of the TRIPS Agreement, the Indonesian government has never applied compulsory licenses to manage the impact of pharmaceutical patents on the introduction of generic drugs.[38]

(iv) Government Use

According to Article 99 of the Indonesian Patent Act of 2001, government use is defined as a decision to allow a government to exploit the relevant patent owned by a patent holder "for the conduct of defense and security of the State and for an urgent need for the sake of public interest". Examples are patents for epidemic diseases and pesticides that may avoid harvest failures. Government use does not require prior efforts to obtain license permission from rights holders; an important difference from compulsory licensing.[39]

---

35 Utomo, *id*; Utomo (2), *id.*

36 Utomo, *id*, at 779–80, Utomo (2), *id.*

37 Utomo, *id*, at 780; Utomo (2), *id.*

38 Utomo, *id*; Utomo (2), *id.*

39 Utomo, *id*; Utomo (2), *id.*

III. THE TRIPS SAFEGUARDS AND ACCESS TO ESSENTIAL MEDICINES IN INDONESIA[40]

(i) The TRIPS Safeguards in Indonesia: Which Safeguards Are Most Appropriate for Indonesia?

Indonesian public health policies have dynamically developed from year to year. At the early independence of 1945, this sector was much neglected because the focus of the government policies at the time was to defend its sovereignty against Dutch military aggression.[41] But over time the public health sector's influence has become prominent in social welfare-oriented policy. People demand that the government serve the Indonesians in achieving certain objectives to access affordable and cheaper drugs: to guarantee the availability of drugs; to improve the quality of human resources; and to monitor and reinforce public health facilities and the rational use of drugs.

According to the WHO, the four factors influencing access to essential medicines include: (1) Rational selection and use of medicines; (2) Sustainable and adequate financing; (3) Affordable prices; and

---

[40] Portions of this subchapter were first published in the article "Pharmaceutical Patent Protection and the Introduction of Generic Drugs in Indonesia in the Post-TRIPS Era – Is Patent Law the Only Factor Affecting the Introduction of Generic Drugs?" 42 IIC 759 (2011).

[41] Indonesia gained its independence in 1945 from Japan. At that time, public health facilities, such as hospitals and medicines, were insufficient and the public health sector in Indonesia was neglected. The situation was getting worse when Dutch soldiers landed in Indonesia and attacked Indonesian sovereignty through military aggression in July 1947. Their goal was to re-colonize Indonesia. In this critical situation, the Ministry of Health of the Republic of Indonesia decided to move the office of the Ministry to Central Java. The departments and units of the ministry were split into several offices located in several cities, including Magelang, Yogyakarta, Klaten and Solo. Schools of Medicine also moved to Klaten and Solo. Meanwhile, the Pasteur Institute, which functioned as the center for research in finding vaccines for cholera and measles, was still in Klaten. Basic medicines were made in a simple way during the conflict. The second Dutch aggression in 1948 caused city people to flee to suburbs or villages. Most health workers remained in town to coordinate the distribution of drugs from city to villages. In this situation, the government could not plan policies in public health. The government started to plan and develop the program of public health during the period of 1950–1959 (DEPKES RI [THE DEPARTMENT OF HEALTH OF THE REPUBLIC OF INDONESIA] (I), SEJARAH KESEHATAN NASIONAL INDONESIA [THE HISTORY OF THE INDONESIAN NATIONAL HEALTH] (Jilid 1/volume 1) 16–19 (1978).

(4) Reliable health and supply systems.[42] Attaran notes that only 1.4% of the WHO Essential Medicines List (EML) are patented so that the large majority of essential drugs should be accessible. He draws attention to poverty, lack of donor funding, and health system infrastructure as barriers to access.[43]

The International Federation of Pharmaceutical Manufacturers Association (IFPMA) makes a similar argument. This association states that patent protection affects only a very small proportion of drugs in developing countries because over 95% of the WHO's list of essential drugs, those that are most needed for treatment in developing countries, are non-patented drugs.[44] The protection of pharmaceutical products, therefore, does not impact the drug prices listed in the WHO's essential medicines.[45]

A large majority of articles disagree and argue that patent laws create barriers to access to affordable drugs. These studies show that pharmaceutical patent protection increases the price of drugs in developing countries.[46] Since the literature shows a debate about patents and prices, with the majority indicating patents are associated with higher prices, Attaran's paper and the research pharmaceutical companies' opinion challenges us to ask: What essential drugs are affected by patents?

In Indonesia, only 55% of drugs listed on the National Essential Medicines List or DOEN are generic drugs.[47] Therefore, an analysis

---

[42] WHO ESSENTIAL DRUG AND MEDICINES POLICY (*Network for Monitoring*), *supra* note 24, at 20.

[43] Amir Attaran, *How Do Patents and Economic Policies Affect Access to Essential Medicines in Developing Countries?*, 23 HEALTH AFFAIRS, no. 3, at 155–66, http://content.healthaffairs.org/content/23/3/155.full.pdf+html (last visited Jan. 7, 2014); *see also* Harvey E. Bale Jr., *Patents and Public Health: a Good and Bad Mix?*, at 1, http://www.cnehealth.org/pubs/bale_patents_and_public_health.htm (last visited Mar. 21, 2006); Owen Lippert, *Poverty, Not Patents, is the Problem in Africa*, at 1, http://www.umich.edu/~spp638/news/pfizerdoc.pdf (last visited Jan. 7, 2014); Utomo, *supra* note 39, at 760.

[44] IFPMA, THE QUESTION OF PATENTS: THE KEY TO MEDICAL PROGRESS AND INDUSTRIAL DEVELOPMENT 10 (1998).

[45] *Id.*

[46] For examples: Nogues (1990, 1993), Challu (1991), Chambouleyron (1995), Watal (1996, unpublished) (*see* UNITED NATIONS CONFERENCE ON TRADE AND DEVELOPMENT, *supra* note 11, at 62; and K. Bala and Kiran Sagoo (1999) (in K. Bala and Kiran Sagoo, *supra* note 19, at 1).

[47] Until September 2005 (when the draft of the National Drug Policy was published), 13 000 branded drugs were marketed in Indonesia. Among these, there were 400 types of drugs listed in the National Essential Medicines List

of the relation between pharmaceutical patents and the price of drugs is relevant for Indonesia and other countries where patented drugs constitute a significant market share. There are three factors influencing the impact of patented drugs in Indonesia: (1) The government's limited ability to finance all of the generic drugs listed in DOEN; (2) Low generic drug prescribing pattern; and (3) Weak commitment by local authorities in prescribing generic drugs under health decentralization.[48]

TRIPS safeguards provided under Indonesian law are congruent with the TRIPS Agreement, but they need to be improved, in particular by implementing specific and targeted regulations.[49] The Indonesian government has received conflicting interpretations of safeguard provisions including that proposed safeguards exceed the TRIPS standards. However, since the Doha declaration was launched in 2001, there is no reason for the Indonesian government not to use the safeguards effectively. The Declaration, paragraph 4, states clearly that "the TRIPS Agreement does not and should not prevent members from taking measures to protect public health." This is a strong legal basis for implementing the TRIPS safeguards. Use of the Bolar provision to shorten the period between patent expiration to starting local production and marketing could help access to new generic drugs.

Other safeguards, such as compulsory licenses and government use, are relevant to Indonesia and can be justified for urgent public needs. If the public needs are clearly presented, challenges by a patent owner can be disallowed. These can be used to procure patented drugs with affordable prices. Several HIV/AIDS drugs are listed in the DOEN or EML (Essential Medicine List), such as Lamivudine, Zidovudine and Nevirapine, but lack generic equivalents. Patent protection prevents production of generic versions. The government has obtained several drugs using a government use tactic since 2004 by issuing Presidential Decree No. 83 of 2004. This includes procurement of Nevirapine and Lamivudine, important HIV drugs at affordable market prices.

(DOEN) and only 220 generic drugs (around 55%) are included in the DOEN (Depkes or The Ministry of Health), *Kebijakan Obat Nasional/KONAS [The National Drug Policy – draft – September 23, 2005]*, http://henriprihantono.blogdetik.com/files/2009/01/kebijakan-obat-nasional.pdf, at 9 (last visited Jan. 7, 2014).

[48] These factors are based on my PhD research (library and field research) in 2004–2005 (Tomi Suryo Utomo (3), Indonesian Drug Policy and Patent Regulation after the TRIPS Agreement: Better Access to Essential Medicines? PhD thesis, School of Law, University of Washington, 178–83 (2006).

[49] Utomo, *supra* note 43, at 780.

Three years later, the Indonesian government issued Presidential Decree No. 6 of 2007 to produce three anti-retroviral drugs under government use. Nevirapin, Lamivudin and Efavirenz are on the list of drugs produced until the end of patent protection on October 31, 2011, January 28, 2012, and August 7, 2013, respectively. Due to the urgent need for providing drugs for HIV/AIDS and Hepatitis B patients, the Indonesian government issued Presidential Regulation No. 76 of 2012. It includes Efavirenz, Abacavir, Didanosin, the combination of Lopinavir and Ritonavir, Tenofovir and the combination of Tenofovir and Emtrisitabin, and the combination of Tenofovir, Emtrisitabin and Efavirenz on the list of drugs produced under the government use provision.

In applying compulsory licenses or government use, the government considers the interests of patent holders, including a reasonable remuneration (royalty) based upon explicit remuneration criteria. To reimburse patent holders, the Indonesian government pays a royalty of 0.5% from the net sales value of those drugs. In the future, these safeguards need to be used to cover drugs not only for antiviral and anti-retroviral but also for tropical diseases, such as drug-resistant malaria and tuberculosis.

(ii) Policies or Strategies outside of the TRIPS Agreement Might be Considered to Increase Access to Essential Medicines in Indonesia

Patent law is not the only factor reducing access to essential medicines.[50] Use of TRIPS safeguards alone is, therefore, insufficient to solve access to medicine problems in Indonesia. Additional factors that affect access to essential medicines include: 1) rational selection and use of medicines; 2) sustainable adequate financing; 3) affordable prices; and 4) reliable health and supply systems,[51] which are all issues that must be considered by the Indonesian government.

---

[50] *See* CORREA, *supra* note 27, at 2; Utomo, *supra* note 49, at 773.

[51] WHO ESSENTIAL DRUG AND MEDICINES POLICY, NETWORK FOR MONITORING THE IMPACT OF GLOBALIZATION AND TRIPS ON ACCESS TO MEDICINES, Report of a Meeting, February 2001, Bangkok Thailand, Health Economics and Drugs EDM Series No. 11, at 20; *see* also Tomi Suryo Utomo (4), *Proposals to Address Non-Patent Issues That Affect the Distribution and Availability of Essential Medicines in Indonesia*, 12 JURNAL MANAJEMEN PELAYANAN KESEHATAN [THE INDONESIAN JOURNAL OF HEALTH SERVICE MANAGEMENT] 3 (2009), March edition, Faculty of Medicine, University of Gadjah Mada, Yogyakarta, Indonesia.

Decisions about rational use of drugs in Indonesia involve two problems. First, neither the government nor the Indonesian Medical Association undertake monitoring of prescription patterns or corrective action if doctors prescribe non-generic drugs.[52] Pharmaceutical companies influence doctors by means of various promotions and incentives.[53] Secondly, hospital pharmaceutical and therapeutic committees have failed to promote the rational use of drugs in hospitals.[54]

Drug financing from the public and private sectors is a serious problem in Indonesia. The government cannot increase its budget for drug financing due to other obligations. After health decentralization was instituted, drug financing became the responsibility of local governments.[55] They have concluded that public health is a non-profit

---

52 *See* Republika Online, *Problema di Seputar Obat Generik [The Problems of Generic Drugs]*, 8 March 2005, at 1–2, http://www.republika.co.id/cetak_berita.asp?id=190295 &kat_id=150 &edisi … (last visited Sep. 20, 2006); Utomo (4), *id*, at 3.

53 Kompas, *"Industrio-Medical Complex" Makin Kompleks ["An Industrio-Medical Complex" is more complicated],* 22 November 2000, at 1–7, http://www.Kompas.com/kompas-cetak/0011/22/iptek/indu37.htm (last visited Jan. 11, 2005); Kompas, *Buku Biru Farmasi Disosialisasikan [Introducing the Pharmaceutical Ethics Code]*, 22 April 2002, at 1, http://www.kompas.com/kompas-cetak/0204/22/iptek/buku10.htm (last visited Jan. 11, 2005); *see* Suara Pembaruan Daily, *Jaminan Kesehatan Nasional Menjamin Keterjangkauan Obat [The National Insurance Guarantees the Affordability of Drugs]*, at 1, http://www.suarapembaruan.com/News/2003/02/08/Kesra/kes03.htm (last visited Apr. 11, 2005); Kompas, *Obat Rasional Kuncinya Dokter [The Rational Use of Drugs Is Dependent on Physicians]*, 22 December 2000, at 1–6, http://www.kompas.com/kompas-cetak/0011/22/iptek/obat39.htm (last visited Apr. 11, 2005); Harian Suara Indonesia Baru, *Kolusi antara Produsen Obat Dengan Oknum Dokter dan Rumah Sakit [The Collusion between Drug Producers, Physicians and Hospitals],* 23 August 2006, at 1, http://www.hariansib.com/index2.php?option=com_content&task=view&id=11 … (last visited Sep. 24, 2006); *see* also Kompas, Obat, *Komoditas atau Produk Karitas [Are Medicines a Commodity or a Charity?]*, 22 December 2000, at 1, http://www.kompas.com/kompas-cetak/0011/22/iptek/obat38.htm (last visited Nov. 4, 2005); Iwan Darmansjah, *Obat Esensial Sebagai Strategi Dasar Kebijakan Obat Nasional [Essential Drugs Are a Basic Strategy of National Drug Policy]*, at 3, http://www.iwandarmansjah.web.id/print.php?id=114 (last visited Sep. 20, 2006); Utomo (4), *id.*

54 Depkes RI (KONAS), *supra* note 47, at 11; Utomo (4), *id.*

55 *See* Article 13 of Act No.32 of 2004 on Local Government; Article 2 (10) of Government Regulation No. 25 of 2000 on the Authority of Government and Province as an Autonomous Area; Utomo (4), *id.*

sector and is not a priority in their development agendas.[56] Although social insurance is being promoted by the government, it has not been well received by the private sector, which would bear some of its costs through taxation. Only a small percentage of society purchases private social insurance.[57]

There are four main problems connected with the affordable price of drugs in Indonesia. The first one is because the government controls only essential drugs and certain generic drugs but does not control patented drugs and branded generics.[58] The second one is due to the practice of unreasonable markups by pharmaceutical companies through distribution and dispensing systems.[59] Thirdly, there is an assumption among patients in Indonesia that more expensive drugs must be better drugs and are desirable; many people assume that better drugs are more expensive.[60] Fourthly, Indonesian insurance companies have little bargaining power to influence hospital purchasing or drug producers with regard to the type and price of drugs.[61]

Another consequence of health decentralization is fragmentation of the drug distribution system. Drug storage has been shifted from the

---

[56] Buletin Desentralisasi Kesehatan [Health Decentralization Bulletin], *Desentralisasi Kesehatan dan Perubahan Peran Pemerintah dalam Pembiayaan Kesehatan [Health Decentralization and the Change of the Government Role in Health Financing]*, Volume II/02/2004, at 16, http://www.desentralisasi-kesehatan.net (last visited Jan. 11, 2005); *see* Global Forum Health, *The 10/90 Report on Health Research 2003–2004,* at 9, http://www.isn.ethz.ch/Digital-Library/Publications/Detail/?id=17141 (last visited Jan. 7, 2014); Utomo (4), *id.*

[57] "Between 50–70% of household expenditures in 1995 to 2000 were for foods" (Hasbullah Thabrany et al., *Social Health Insurance in Indonesia: Current Status and the Plan for National Health Insurance (Annex 3)*, presented in Social Health Insurance Workshop, WHO SEARO, New Delhi, March 13–15, 2003, at 146, http://w3.whosea.org/LinkFiles/Social_Health_Insurance_an3.pdf (last visited Mar. 6, 2006) ;Utomo (4), *id.*, at 3–4.

[58] GP Farmasi, Pengantar Pemahaman Komoditi Obat (Acara Pertemuan dengan KPPU), 2006, at 4; Utomo (4), *id., at 4.*

[59] Suara Pembaruan Daily, Perkembangan Obat Generik *Lamban [The Development of Generic Drugs is Slow]*, 06 May 2004, at 1, http://www.suarapembaruan.com/News/2004/05/06/Kesra/kes03.htm (last visited Sep. 20, 2006; Utomo (4), *id.*

[60] *See* Republika Online, *supra* note 52, at 1–2; Utomo, *supra* note 50, at 774: *see* also Pikiran Rakyat, *Sosialisasi Obat Generik Kurang [The Socialization of Generic Drugs Is Insufficient]*, 27 September 2003, at 1, http://www.pikiran-rakyat.com/cetak/0903/27/0506.htm (last visited Sep. 20, 2006); Utomo (4), *id.*

[61] Media Indonesia Online, *supra* note 17; Utomo, *Id*, at 775; Utomo (4), *id.*

district pharmaceutical warehouse or GFK to a section or smaller unit under the local health department. This tends to minimize the role of that warehouse and the officers who work with drug distribution.[62]

Underlying causes are complex and will require review and problem solving by a multi-disciplinary group with the power to make necessary changes. Therefore, other countries' experiences in public health and academic writings offer options worth considering in Indonesia. These include controlling drugs promotion, maximizing the use of generic drugs; improving administrative competence, drug procurement, distribution and storage. Finally, prescribing practices by physicians, pharmacists and drug vendors should be a priority.

These factors are major influences on access to essential medicines, including generic drugs in Indonesia. The burden of drug promotion and control cannot be put exclusively on the government's shoulders, but rather must be a shared responsibility with professional associations, such as the Indonesian Pharmaceutical Company Association and the Indonesian Medical Association.[63]

Moreover, the government can address inappropriate drug use by reemphasizing its 1989 regulation on the use of generic drugs in public health facilities. This should include sanctions for physicians who fail to prescribe appropriate generic drugs to their patients.[64] Another tactic to reinforce the use of generic drugs is to disseminate clinical practice guidelines that include generic drugs and then monitor practitioner compliance rates. Paper guides or exhortations alone are insufficient; training programs, surveillance and feedback need to be incorporated as well.

The Indonesian Medical Association could play a pivotal role by requiring their members to prioritize a patient's needs and finances rather than incentives given by pharmaceutical companies. All these challenges should be addressed to increase the use of generic drugs in Indonesia by involving key shareholders and the government in working out a set of strategies and a timetable. This would allow the government to monitor progress toward specific achievements.[65]

Meanwhile more complex long-term goals, such as establishing an industry to produce raw materials for pharmaceuticals, can be considered.[66] Advocates claim that it can reduce drug production costs.

---

62 Depkes RI (KONAS), *supra* note 54, at 7–8.

63 Utomo, *supra* note 61, at 783.

64 *Id.*

65 *Id.*, at 783–84.

66 *See* Kompas, *Industri Farmasi Indonesia (Masih Tetap) Industri*

Opponents argue that the local market for pharmaceutical raw materials is too uncertain to support an industry.[67]

IV. HOW HAVE OTHER COUNTRIES REDUCED THE EFFECT OF THE TRIPS SAFEGUARDS ON ACCESS TO ESSENTIAL MEDICINES?[68]

(i) India's Approach to Pharmaceutical Patents: Legal and Other Strategies

The success of the Indian government in expanding its domestic pharmaceutical industry can be attributed to the utilization of legal and other strategies. Legal strategies have included the application of compulsory licensing under the Indian Patent Act. Prior to the TRIPS Agreement, India developed its pharmaceutical industry through a strict compulsory license regulation.[69] In the post-TRIPS era, this strategy was modified by the government to comply with the TRIPS Agreement. Under India's Patent Act amendment 2005, the government explicitly states the legal bases for allowing compulsory licensing. Compulsory licensing is allowable for: (1) national emergencies; or (2) extreme urgencies; or (3) in instances of public, non-commercial use. The most important part of this Act is that the government includes public health crises relating to AIDS, TBC, Malaria and other epidemics as sufficient legal bases for granting compulsory licenses.[70]

Tukang Jahit [The Indonesian Pharmaceutical Industry Is Still the Same as a Tailor Industry], 22 November 2000, at 3, http://www.kompas.com/kompas-cetak/0011/22/iptek/indu42.htm (last visited Jan. 11, 2005); *see* also Ilham Kuncahyo, *Potret Industri Farmasi di Indonesia [the Portrait of the Indonesian Pharmaceutical Companies]*, Kompas, 12 April 2004, at 1, http://www.kompas.com/kompas-cetak/0404/12/opini/906297.htm (last visited Jan. 11, 2005); Utomo (4), *supra* note 61, at 7.

67 Utomo (4), *id.*

68 Portions of this subchapter were first published in the article "Pharmaceutical Patent Protection and the Introduction of Generic Drugs in Indonesia in the Post-TRIPS Era – Is Patent Law the Only Factor Affecting the Introduction of Generic Drugs?" 42 IIC 759 (2011).

69 Utomo, *supra* note 63, at 777; *see* also David K. Tomar, *A Look into the WTO Pharmaceutical Patent Dispute between the United States and India*, 17 WIS. INT'L L.J. 579 (1999).

70 *See* Article 92 par. 3, the Indian Patent Act of 2005; Utomo, *id.*

Other strategies that affect drug availability include policies for price control, for maximizing the use and the production of generic drugs, and others that support strong infrastructure, such as a raw material industry for pharmaceutical companies, a well-established computer industry, and technological know-how for the manufacture of bulk drugs and formulations. In addition, the government benefits from India's well-educated scientists as a core element of the modern pharmaceutical industry.[71]

These approaches can be considered as a model for Indonesia. The Indian compulsory license is a good model for Indonesia because it defines specific public health crises. Since infectious diseases such as TB, malaria and HIV are potentially large-scale epidemics, the Indonesian government should amend its compulsory license regulation under the Patent Act and specify certain circumstances which qualify as emergency situations. This would give the Indonesian government a clearer legal basis for granting compulsory licenses.[72] Since compulsory license regulation in developing countries is often challenged by developed countries, the strategy to provide a clear legal basis for granting a compulsory license could minimize the likelihood of future disputes. But the process of amendment is time consuming and requires education and committed leadership.

The Indian success in applying additional strategies may also be beneficial for Indonesia. For example, the establishment of good infrastructures, including qualified human resources, helps to provide a strong foundation for the domestic pharmaceutical industry.[73] India's experience should be considered by the government in establishing an independent local pharmaceutical industry in Indonesia since it complies with the TRIPS Agreement. The Indonesian government should focus on two important components: the establishment of a raw materials industry for pharmaceuticals and the preparation of human resources in the pharmaceutical sector.

---

[71] Utomo, *id*, at 778; *See* Hemant N. Joshi, *Analysis of the Indian Pharmaceutical Industry with Emphasis on Opportunities in 2005*, PHARMACEUTICAL TECHNOLOGY at 74, http://www.pharmtech.com/pharmtech/data/articlestandard/pharmtech/042003/44039/article.pdf (January 2003) (last visited Jan. 7, 2014).

[72] Utomo, *id*, at 782.

[73] Utomo, *id*, at 783.

V. CONCLUSION

The enforcement of pharmaceuticals patent law has created a tension between national needs and domestic developmental policy and international patent standards. Since the introduction of the TRIPS Agreement in 1994, this tension has particularly affected developing countries. The TRIPS Agreement's protection of pharmaceutical patents has had adverse consequences for the health needs of Indonesia since many patients cannot afford expensive patented drugs.

However, this chapter concludes that access to essential medicines is not only caused by pharmaceutical patent protection under the TRIPS Agreement but is also because of additional factors in the public health sector in Indonesia, such as rational selection and use of medicines, sustainable adequate financing, affordable prices and reliable health and supply systems.

In order to increase access to essential medicines, Indonesia should seek a balance between pharmaceutical patent protection and the improvement of public health policy. From the perspective of the TRIPS safeguards implementation, the Indonesian government should optimize the use of compulsory licenses and government use. However, several areas need to be improved so that the safeguards can be effectively used to increase access to essential medicines. Examples of these include specifiying the category or appropriate amount of royalty and remuneration (for compulsory licenses), providing clear procedures for negotiation or appeal, and implementing provisions for appeal and cessation if patent holders lose their cases in commercial court (for government use).

Apart from the implementation of the TRIPS safeguards, the Indonesian government should also focus on public health policy. Since Indonesia applied a policy of health decentralization in 2001, the role of local governments in regulating and monitoring access to essential medicines has been significant. Without comprehensive structural reform, the public health sector, and in particular access to medicines, may become neglected under health decentralization.

Index